Marshall and Schumpeter on Evolution

Marshall and Schumpeter on Evolution

Economic Sociology of Capitalist Development

Edited by

Yuichi Shionoya

Emeritus Professor of Economics and former President, Hitotsubashi University, Japan

Tamotsu Nishizawa

Professor, Institute of Economic Research, Hitotsubashi University, Japan

Edward Elgar

Cheltenham, UK • Northampton, MA, USA

Published by
Edward Elgar Publishing Limited
The Lypiatts
15 Lansdown Road
Cheltenham
Glos GL50 2JA
UK

Edward Elgar Publishing, Inc.
William Pratt House
9 Dewey Court
Northampton
Massachusetts 01060
USA

A catalogue record for this book
is available from the British Library

Library of Congress Control Number: 2008937419

ISBN 978 1 84720 813 2

Printed and bound in Great Britain by MPG Books Ltd, Bodmin, Cornwall

Contents

Figures and tables

FIGURES

TABLES

Contributors

Richard Arena is Professor of Economics, University of Nice/Sophia Antipolis, France.

Roger E. Backhouse is Professor of the History and Philosophy of Economics, University of Birmingham, UK.

Mauro Boianovsky is Professor, Department of Economics, University of Brasilia, Brazil.

Katia Caldari is Professor of International Economics, Department of Economics, University of Padua, Italy.

Kenji Fujii is Professor, Management School, Aoyama-gakuin University, Japan.

Harald Hagemann is Professor, Department of Economics, University of Hohenheim, Germany.

Geoffrey M. Hodgson is Research Professor, Business School, University of Hertfordshire, UK.

Fabio Masini is Professor of Political Economy, Department of Public Institutions, Economics and Society, University of Rome 3, Italy.

J.S. Metcalfe is Emeritus Professor, University of Manchester and Visiting Fellow, Centre for Business Research, Judge Institute, Cambridge, UK.

Tamotsu Nishizawa is Professor, Institute of Economic Research, Hitotsubashi University, Japan.

Tiziano Raffaelli, is Professor, Department of Philosophy, University of Pisa, Italy.

Yuichi Shionoya is Emeritus Professor of Economics, Hitotsubashi University, Japan.

Richard Swedberg is Professor, Department of Sociology, Cornell University, USA.

Hans-Michael Trautwein is Professor, Department of Economics, University of Oldenburg, Germany.

Kiichiro Yagi is Professor, Faculty of Economics, Kyoto University, Japan.

Introduction

Yuichi Shionoya and Tamotsu Nishizawa

Alfred Marshall (1842–1924) and Joseph Schumpeter (1883–1950) have rarely been discussed jointly as serious subject matter in the history of economic thought. The absence of concern in contemporary Marshall and Schumpeter scholarship to link the two giants of economics cannot be wholly attributed to the research practice of specialization in the history of economic thought. Rather, it might be explained by the traditional understanding that while Marshall was the synthesizer of neoclassical economics, Schumpeter challenged the dynamic conception of the economy in place of the static structure of economics. Although the difference between their works appears obvious, it would not become an appealing topic such as the contrast between Schumpeter and Marx, Walras or Keynes, which historians of economics have been much concerned with.

Then, the question may arise whether there is anything similar between Marshall and Schumpeter, the former regarding the capitalist economic process as a cumulative process ('*natura non facit saltum*') and the latter characterizing it as 'creative destruction'. It might be argued that an effort to establish similarities in place of differences would be more effective in stimulating exploration and synthesis of knowledge. As the logic of the dialectics might indicate, the synthesis of antitheses requires a logically higher dimension than that on which antitheses are located. This volume attempts to put Marshall and Schumpeter in the perspective of evolutionary thinking.

The concept of evolution must be loosely defined here because it belongs to a field of economics under incipient exploration and is subject to different approaches and interpretations. Moreover, the contributors to this volume working in different fields of thought are invited to freely explore evolutionary aspects of either Marshall or Schumpeter, or both of them. In these circumstances, the imposition of any stringent definition on their works would suffer from the charge of the Procrustean bed.

Nevertheless, it is incumbent on us to describe our broad vision of evolution which helps shed new light on the economic thought of Marshall and Schumpeter, keeping 'the many in the one' and 'the one in the many' as the ways of interpretation. Our vision of evolution to be applied to both

Marshall and Schumpeter studies will demand a departure from the received view on the nature of their works, that is, the stereotyped view on Marshall as the synthesizer of neoclassical economics and on Schumpeter as the theorist of economic development. Indeed, in each scholarship there are strong recent movements extending beyond the traditional lines of interpretation; these movements are seen as the attempts to peruse what Marshall and Schumpeter really wanted to accomplish even if they failed to develop it fully in practice and their visions remained more or less unfulfilled goals. Such attempts to discover the neglected aspects of their works naturally disclose diverse directions reflecting different theoretical structure and background of Marshall and Schumpeter. It is our intention to gather these views for creating the common ground of evolutionary thinking. We propose to identify their theme of evolution as the economic sociology or the theoretical formulation of history (reasoned history) in the process of capitalist development.

The idea of evolution is familiar to the reader of Schumpeter's *Theory of Economic Development* (1912 [1934]), if evolution is interpreted as synonymous with development. Although he sometimes used the terms 'evolution' and 'development' interchangeably, he definitely distinguished evolution (or development) of the economic sphere from that of the society as a whole. The terms as such do not matter, but the phenomena do. Schumpeter's system of economics consists of three branches: economic statics, economic dynamics and economic sociology. His conception of economic statics is represented by the Walrasian general equilibrium theory, which provides us with the basic logic of an economy and explains the establishment of equilibrium through the adaptive behaviour of economic agents. In contrast, Schumpeter's idea of economic dynamics is uniquely concerned with the revolutionary process of an economy caused by innovation of the entrepreneurs. Underlying the distinction between statics and dynamics is the distinction between the types of man: the hedonistic man and the energetic man. Schumpeter applies this typology of human being not only to the economic sphere but also to all spheres of social activity, and constructs a set of statics–dynamics dichotomies for all aspects of social life including the economy, politics, science, the arts and morality. His conception of economic sociology as the third branch of economics deals with the interactions between the economy and other social areas, under the assumption that each area is equipped with a distinctive type of the statics–dynamics mechanism. For him, the development of society as a whole through the interactions among various areas is better characterized as immanent evolution.

In his famous essay on Gustav von Schmoller, the leader of the younger German historical school, Schumpeter appraised the research programme of Schmoller as a prototype of economic sociology and described its goal as a 'unified sociology or social science as mentally ('theoretically') worked out universal history' (1926: 382). He called the goal also a 'universal social science' (ibid.: 365). Later, when he surveyed the whole areas of economics in the *History of Economic Analysis*, he regarded economic sociology as one of the tools in economics, defining it as 'a sort of generalized or typified or stylized economic history' (1954: 20). As a simplified expression, he liked to use 'a reasoned (=conceptually clarified) history' (1939: vol. 1, 220) or '*histoire raisonnée*' (1954: 690, 818). The economist of top rank to whom Schumpeter (1950: 44) attributed the term '*histoire raisonnée*' was Karl Marx.

In Schumpeter's view there is another slightly different way of explanation: economic sociology deals with the institutional framework of economic life which is exogenously given to static as well as to dynamic economic theory (1954: 21). Combining this explanation with the above definition in terms of a reasoned history, we can say that economic sociology is the attempt to integrate history and theory through the analysis of institutions, because the specification in terms of institutions will make the method of economic sociology incorporating a 'generalized or typified or stylized economic history' more articulate.

In Schumpeter's view, a universal social science is closely connected with study of history. He emphasizes that the subject matter of economics is a unique process in historical time and that the historical materials reflect the development phenomenon and indicate the relationship between economic and non-economic facts, thus suggesting how the disciplines of the social sciences should interact. The recognition of the connection between the unity of social life and historical development was the essence of the German historical school as he understood it, and constituted his central idea of a universal social science (Schumpeter, 1914 [1954]: 176–80). The historicity of an economy and social unity in a development process can be addressed only by the apparatus of economic sociology. In his book *Capitalism, Socialism and Democracy*, the major work of economic sociology, he presented the thesis of falling capitalism due to its economic success based on the interaction between economic and non-economic areas (Schumpeter, 1950).

Schumpeter, the polymathic historian of economic thought, did not fail to critically evaluate a number of past attempts of a universal social science. He favourably appraised Vico, Marx and Schmoller among others, who were more or less related to historicism, while he rejected a 'single hypothesis of the Comte-Buckle-Marx kind' that attributed historical evolution to simple factors (Schumpeter, 1954: 811). Schumpeter's evaluation of Marx and Schmoller was mentioned above with regard to their methods of a reasoned history: here a reference to Giambattista Vico, the precursor of historicism, is still necessary. Schumpeter discussed Vico as follows:

> His New Science (*scienza nuova*) is best described by the phrase 'an evolutionary science of mind and society.' But this must not be interpreted to mean that the evolution of the human mind shapes the evolution of human society; nor, though this would be nearer the truth, that the historical evolution of societies shapes the evolution of the human mind; but that mind and society are two aspects of the same evolutionary process. (Ibid.: 137)

Nothing expresses Schumpeter's view of a universal social science than this passage. He also identified the social sciences in the form of eighteenth-century moral philosophy with 'the sciences of "mind and society"' (ibid.: 141).

The science of mind and society can be interpreted and constructed in various ways. It is an approximation in terms of dichotomy to the development of society as a whole instead of all-embracing treatment of relevant factors such as the general equilibrium approach. It focuses on the division and interaction between human beings and the institutions of society among which they live; between the ideational-cultural field and real-social field, as defined in German cultural sociology; between the superstructure and substructure in Marx's sense; between mind-subject-self and body-object-world in the philosophical sense; and between the system of metatheory of economics and the system of economics, as defined by one of us (Shionoya, 1997: 260–65). In so far as economic sociology, institutional economics and evolutionary economics, as distinct from economic statics and economic dynamics, take into account non-economic factors along with economic factors, they are all concerned about the interactions between economic changes, on the one hand, and non-economic changes in value, culture, and *Zeitgeist*, on the other. For Schumpeter, the analysis of the concurrent evolution of mind and society is the third branch of economics which remains to be explored.

In sum, what might be called the postulates constituting Schumpeter's idea of evolution is summarized as follows:

1. Evolution consists in the development of society as a whole, which is the object of a universal social science. The unity of social phenomena is one of the basic premises of a universal social science.
2. Evolution is scientifically worked out as the reasoned history or *histoire raisonnée*, which is obtained by the integration of theory and history in terms of changing institutional framework. The concern for the historicity of development is another premise of a universal social science.

3. Evolution depends not so much on mechanistic motion as on organic adjustment of a society, which consists of social interactions based on the statics–dynamics typology of human nature and the adaptive–active forces in various social areas.
4. Evolution is addressed in practice by a strategic approach to the mind and society (or the economic and non-economic spheres) rather than by an all-embracing approach to the development of society as a whole.

These headings articulate the form of evolutionary thinking, still allowing for a variety of substantive approaches that can be formulated in practice.

Although both Marshall and Schumpeter admitted the legitimate role of pure economic theory as the economic organ or economic logic, they were not satisfied with it because it was unable to explain the problems of real life, and refused to separate the study of economic from that of social, cultural and institutional factors at a more advanced stage of knowledge. Compared with Schumpeter's utmost concern for history, Marshall was much more motivated by ethics in opening up a broader vista for economics. Marshall's famous definition of economics that it is not only a study of wealth but also a part of the study of man suggests its broader orientation than its well-defined scope (Marshall, 1920: 1). Evaluating Marshall's *Principles of Economics*, Schumpeter found out an economic sociology constructed on historical foundations 'behind, beyond, and all around' the core of the analytical apparatus and characterized it as follows: 'His mastery of historical fact and his analytic habit of mind did not dwell in separate compartments but formed so close a union that the live fact intrudes into the theorem and the theorem into purely historical observations' (Schumpeter, 1951: 94). Marshall himself would emphasize the nature of his own task as a close union between ethical aspirations and the economic theorem. For him, history must be a history of man as the object of philosophy and psychology.

> In economics we deal with the whole of man's nature, though we lay chief stress on certain special aspects of it. From this it follows that, in so far as we base ourselves upon the history of past times at all, it must be history as a whole. We need more than economic history . . . we want a history of man himself, and economic history as contributing to that. (Marshall, 1897 [1925]: 299)

Thus, he coined the term 'the reasoned history of man' as a synonym of social science, implying that 'social science is seeking her unity in the forces of human character' (ibid.: 299–300). For both Marshall and Schumpeter the study of human character was the real foundation for expanding the narrow boundary of economic statics in order to explain the problems of real life. If Schumpeter replaced the model of 'economic man' with that of 'energetic man', Marshall did the same job of restoring real life by the model of 'public spirit' based on the social interaction among agents.

Progress, for Marshall, means not merely an increase in material wealth but also a rise in the quality of life made possible by an increase in the physical, intellectual and moral faculties of human beings. Progress would be available only if an increase in material wealth contributed to a rise in the quality of life. The study of wealth and the study of man are connected by a study of changing human nature in relation to socio-economic circumstances. His theory of organic growth describes the evolutionary process of a national economy as an organism, in which an increase of national income would be accompanied by an improvement in character, quality and ability of human beings, and vice versa. The plasticity of the human mind with respect to environmental conditions is the focal point of industrial organization and economic institutions.

Nothing describes Marshall's conception of economics better than Pigou's memorial remark:

> So economics for him was a handmaid to ethics, not an end in itself, but a means to a further end: an instrument, by the perfecting of which it might be possible to better the conditions of human life. Things, organisation, technique were incidents: what mattered was the quality of man. (1925: 82)

If Marshall's economic inquiry was motivated by ethical aspirations for the improvement of human life, there were two major tasks for him. First, business and industry had to be explored as the organizations for creating those opportunities for human improvement. Problems of organization, knowledge, technique and training, which are reservedly inserted into Book IV (*The Agents of Production*) of *Principles* and extensively discussed in *Industry and Trade* (Marshall, 1919), are not a historical appendix to economic theory but constitute a historical-ethical approach to economic sociology in terms of the evolution of mind and society. Underlying his thought on organizations there was the unique philosophical idea of piecemeal evolution in terms of the interaction between conventional automatism and innovative conscious efforts, as argued by Tiziano Raffaelli in Chapter 2 of this volume.

Second, an ethical theory had to be established to evaluate economic activities and institutions in place of hedonistic utilitarianism. Marshall tried to develop some substantive thoughts on ethical beliefs based on the theory of evolution, most of which remained as fragmentary manuscripts (Whitaker, 1990). Whereas his attitude against utilitarianism is clear, his ethics of economic chivalry addressed to members of the social organism was not accomplished. Virtue ethics or perfectionist ethical theory should be taken into account in the critical consideration of mind and society.

Virtue ethics, which is concerned not only with the improvement of human capabilities, the perfection of character and self-realization but also with the corresponding organizations and institutions for human development, was consciously pursued by the contemporaneous Oxford philosophers and economists, including T.H. Green, A. Toynbee, J.A. Hobson, L.T. Hobhouse, and so on. Marshall's well-known urge for 'cool heads but warm hearts' (1885 [1925]: 174) in his inaugural lecture at Cambridge must have been inspired by a moral atmosphere of Oxford which he had encountered during his short tenure as the successor of Toynbee.

It is illuminating to see how Marshall's work fits our Schumpeterian conception of evolution under the four postulates derived in the above. Despite the differences in their styles of thought, they share formidable challenges to a broader type of social science beyond economics. Marshall's economic sociology is addressed to:

1. the development of society as a whole based on 'the whole of man's nature',
2. the reasoned history of mind and society in terms of changes in industrial organization and economic institution,
3. the organic adjustment between human nature and institutional conditions through piecemeal evolution in the gradual process of 'history as a whole', and
4. a strategic approach to the mind and society in terms of the science of character formation as an intermediary between economics and ethics.

It is not an accident that Marshall and Schumpeter can be viewed from the evolutionary perspective, because they were influenced by the German historical school, Schmoller in particular, along with other sources of ideas. The reference to German historicism has been mentioned only as a biographical episode not as a scientific legacy in both Marshall and Schumpeter studies. The present volume not only demands a departure from the traditional views on the two giants, but also an introduction of historicism into the research perspective. Whether such a reorientation yields results of interest in the future, we leave the reader to judge.

The present volume emanates from an international workshop on the history of economics, 'Marshall, Schumpeter, and Social Science', held at Hitotsubashi University, Tokyo, Japan on 17–19 March 2007. While the workshop started several years ago and has dealt with several aspects of the Cambridge school of economics, the conference as the source of this volume was organized with a focus on Marshall and Schumpeter. The workshop was made possible through the generous support of Hitotsubashi University,

COE/RES project, and JSPS's Grant-in-aid for scientific research. We wish to record our acknowledgement to these for making possible a stimulating and productive meeting. We would also like to thank the authors for developing their papers, and we are also very grateful for participants' thoughts and comments over the three days, particularly to Heinz Kurz, Marco Dardi, Bradley Bateman, Marcello de Cecco and Robert Dimand.

The following chapters take up specific topics about Marshall and Schumpeter under the overarching theme of the book as just outlined. The book is organized into four parts: I) Vision and Method of Evolution; II) Social Science and Evolution; III) Conceptions of Evolution; and IV) Evolution and Capitalism, although these parts are not rigidly differentiated.

Part I is devoted to the detailed observations on the vision and method of evolution in Marshall and Schumpeter based on the brief general explanation in the above.

The first chapter, by Yuichi Shionoya, goes deeply into the ontological foundations of Schumpeter's idea of evolution. It presents the first attempt of ontological reading of Schumpeter. Referring to the distinction between analytical philosophy and continental philosophy, Shionoya characterizes Schumpeter's idea of evolution as reflecting German Romanticism and historicism, and interprets his statics–dynamics dichotomy as a central theme of hermeneutics concerning the volitional projection and social embeddedness of the self. Shionoya's interpretation of evolution in Schumpeter differs in scope and method from that of neo-Schumpeterian economics largely confined to the discussions of technological innovation, entrepreneurship and market competition.

In Chapter 2 on the general pattern of Marshallian evolution, Tiziano Raffaelli highlights the evolutionary interpretation of Marshall based on the recent research in Marshall scholarship. He tries to confirm Marshall's standpoint with regard to the different contemporaneous conceptions of evolution by natural and social scientists and Marshall's metaphorical attempt to extend the knowledge of neurophysiology to a model of human and social evolution. This chapter formulates Marshallian conception of the evolution of mind and society in which tradition and innovation are interacted through the standardization and innovation of component parts of a society.

In Chapter 3, Roger Backhouse traces Schumpeter's attitude to Marshall from his maiden work to posthumous work and argues that his evaluation of Marshall reflects the different battles he was fighting in his career. Schumpeter is seen here from the viewpoint of his economic theory rather than of his history of economics. Backhouse demonstrates Schumpeter's shift of emphasis in his attitude to Marshall, from Marshall the creator of the engine of economic analysis to Marshall the user of these tools. He deals with a subtle question whether Schumpeter's antagonism against Keynesian economics was reflected in his critical view on Marshall's quasi-macroeconomic concept of social value.

Part II of the volume focuses on methodological position of evolutionary thinking in social science with special reference to Marshall and Schumpeter. In Chapter 4, referring to the two authors, Richard Arena contributes an absorbing chapter on, first, the complementary relationship between economics and sociology, and second, the incorporation of organization and institutions in economic analysis. Despite the different approaches of Marshall and Schumpeter, Arena enumerates the main points of their agreement on the scope and function of economic sociology primarily focused on the institutions of market economies.

In Chapter 5, Geoffrey Hodgson points out that although Marshall and Schumpeter were devoted to reorganize economics as an exact science, they also tried to broaden the scope and boundaries of economics to establish economic sociology under the influence of the German historical school. Meanwhile, economists following Lionel Robbins chose the narrow definition of economics as the 'science of choice', while sociology was concerned with the explanation of values and ends. By the 1990s, however, Hodgson maintains, these disciplinary definitions were breaking down, and a major re-examination of their scope and boundaries is required.

Chapter 6 by Stanley Metcalfe explores the foundations of evolutionary approach to economics by considering Marshall, Schumpeter and Hayek in the light of evolutionary theory. In particular, he demonstrates that they are linked by a thread of evolutionary reasoning addressed to the link between wealth creation and the growth of knowledge in the context of economic development. He argues that, although with the elaboration of the cannon of economics the thread was broken and neglected by the mainstream, the evolutionary reasoning depending on the intertwining of dynamic principle, institutional analysis and historical record is necessary to understand the working of capitalism.

Part III is concerned with various conceptions of evolution, which will serve to analyse the evolutionary schemes in terms of more substantive, socio-economic concepts. Chapter 7 by Tamotsu Nishizawa offers a comprehensive account of Marshall's historical-ethical approach against the background of the growing attention to social policy and historicism in the period from the 1870s to 1914. While the main topic of this period in the history of economics is usually taken as the establishment and development of neoclassical economics, Schumpeter defined an aspect of economics during this period as the 'social policy and the historical method'. Following this interpretation, Nishizawa's chapter extensively discusses the relationship between economics, history and ethics in Marshall.

Katia Caldari and Fabio Masini in Chapter 8 deal with the issue of sustainable growth based on Marshall's view of economic development and progress. The conventional approach of economists to the question of the limits to growth has been concentrated on the price mechanism that creates incentives for technological progress and input substitution. In contrast, some British economists of the nineteenth century considered the worsening of quality of life as the consequences of economic growth. Among others, the authors maintain, Marshall offered a pioneering contribution to the modern concepts of limits to growth and sustainable growth by proposing the goal of higher quality of life. They enquire into the cultural heritage and scientific background which preceded and accompanied his work, and demonstrate his continuities and innovations along the line of nineteenth-century economic thought.

Chapter 9 is by Richard Swedberg, who contributes a compelling essay on the theory of entrepreneurship. He argues that Schumpeter's work can serve as the point of departure for the general theory of entrepreneurship that is still missing in modern social science. He calls attention to the original definition of economic dynamics and entrepreneurship in the first German edition of Schumpeter's *Theory of Economic Development*. Schumpeter discussed the typology of human beings as the basis of the statics–dynamics dichotomy: the 'Man of Action' was the model of the entrepreneur compared with the static person. Swedberg suggests a way of sociological conceptualization of the idea of entrepreneurship as a combination, on the one hand, and the idea of resistance to entrepreneurship as tradition, norm and order, on the other.

In Chapter 10, on Schumpeter's distinction between invention and innovation, Kiichiro Yagi discusses Schumpeter's exchange of ideas with Harvard scholars (A.P. Usher, A.H. Cole, and so on) on technological invention and entrepreneurial history. He argues that a peculiar scheme of social evolution lay behind Schumpeter's distinction between invention and innovation. Although Schumpeter distinguished between invention and innovation on a theoretical level, technology and economy are no longer independent in the context of evolutionary historical process, which he finally arrived at in the form of the empirical research of entrepreneurial history.

Analysis of capitalist economy in terms of evolution is the focus of attention in Part IV. In Chapter 11, Harald Hagemann outlines the skeleton of Schumpeter's system of thought and is specifically concerned with his changing attitude towards the use of the term 'evolution'. Schumpeter was against the biological analogy and the implication of progress, both of which the term 'evolution' can invoke. Later, however, Schumpeter accepted the term 'evolution' by defining it as 'the changes in the economic process brought about by innovation, together with all their effects, and the response to them by the economic system' in his book *Business Cycles* (1939: vol. 1, 86).

Mauro Boianovsky and Hans-Michael Trautwein write Chapter 12 on a topic – frictions and unemployment – which is the dark as well as neglected side of economic development in Schumpeter's theory. In his analysis of economic development and business cycles, unemployment is explained as frictional as well as technological unemployment. The authors of the chapter regard this conception as unconventional compared with the contemporaneous view of frictional unemployment and Marxian view of technological unemployment. They try to provide a comprehensive investigation of Schumpeter's view on the relationship between unemployment and technological innovation and its relevance to the modern neo-Schumpeterian search and matching paradigm. The chapter suggests that Schumpeter's view still remains to be exploited in the modern framework.

The final chapter is concerned with Marshall on economic chivalry and business ethics. Kenji Fujii opposes the conventional view of Marshall's advocacy of economic chivalry as trivial digression that has no relation to his economic theory. Starting from Marshall's notion of a firm, he argues that a firm is the basic context in which economic agents (workers and entrepreneurs) create and acquire shared knowledge and values. It is argued that the role of an entrepreneur is to control and lead a firm as a context because both the economic productivity and moral quality of a firm depend on the nature of its underlying contexts. Economic chivalry is nothing but the social ideal of entrepreneurship.

As we have noticed, there has been a growing interest in evolutionary thinking in evolutionary economics, institutional economics and economic sociology independently of Marshall and Schumpeter. We hope that this volume will provide a stimulus not only to Marshall and Schumpeter scholarship in the perspective of the history of economic thought, but also to the recent efforts of economists to explore a research field beyond mainstream equilibrium economics. Evolutionary thinking is the best context in which the co-operation between economists and historians of economics could be obtained because it has been the economist's Mecca.

REFERENCES

Marshall, A. (1885), 'The present position of economics', in A.C. Pigou (ed.) (1925), *Memorials of Alfred Marshall*, London: Macmillan.

Marshall, A. (1897), 'The old generation of economists and the new', in A.C. Pigou (ed.) (1925), *Memorials of Alfred Marshall*, London: Macmillan.
Marshall, A. (1919), *Industry and Trade: A Study of Industrial Technique and Business Organization; and their Influences on the Conditions of Various Classes and Nations*, London: Macmillan.
Marshall, A. (1920), *Principles of Economics*, 8th edn, London: Macmillan.
Pigou, A.C. (1925), 'In memoriam: Alfred Marshall', in A.C. Pigou (ed.) *Memorials of Alfred Marshall*, London: Macmillan.
Schumpeter, J. (1912), *Theorie der wirtschaftlicen Entwicklung*, Leipzig: Duncker & Humblot, trans. R. Opie (1934), *The Theory of Economic Development*, Cambridge, MA: Harvard University Press.
Schumpeter, J. (1914), *Epochen der Dogmen- und Methodengeschichte*, Tübingen: J.C.B. Mohr, trans. R. Aris (1954), *Economic Doctrine and Method: An Historical Sketch*, New York: Oxford University Press.
Schumpeter, J. (1926), 'Gustav v. Schmoller und die Probleme von heute', *Schmollers Jahrbuch*, **50**, 337–88.
Schumpeter, J. (1939), *Business Cycles: A Theoretical, Historical, and Statistical Analysis of the Capitalist Process*, 2 vols, New York: McGraw-Hill.
Schumpeter, J. (1950), *Capitalism, Socialism and Democracy*, 3rd edn, New York: Harper & Brothers.
Schumpeter, J. (1951), *Ten Great Economists: From Marx to Keynes*, London: Allen & Unwin.
Shionoya, Y. (1997), *Schumpeter and the Idea of Social Science: A Metatheoretical Study*, Cambridge: Cambridge University Press.
Whitaker, J.K. (1990), 'What happened to the second volume of the *Principles*? The thorny path to Marshall's last books', in J.K. Whitaker (ed.), *Centenary Essays on Alfred Marshall*, Cambridge: Cambridge University Press.

PART I

Vision and Method of Evolution

1. Schumpeter and evolution: an ontological exploration

Yuichi Shionoya

1.1 INTRODUCTION

Schumpeter introduced the ideas of innovation, development and evolution in his *Theorie der wirtschaftlichen Entwicklung* (1912). In the final chapter (chapter 7) on the 'Overall view of the economy' (*Das Gesamtbild der Volkswirtschaft*), he located the economy in the wider context of social life and attempted to provide a comprehensive vision of the evolution of society as a whole, which was to be addressed by a universal social science, covering such areas as the economy, politics, social relations, the arts, science and morality. His argument in this chapter offers an important viewpoint on a comprehensive grasp of social phenomena, applying the static–dynamic dichotomy of human beings to all these areas and gaining a picture of the overall evolution of society through interactions between them.[1]

Recent works on evolutionary economics, sometimes labelled 'neo-Schumpeterian economics', are largely confined to the studies of economic development and technological change. They seem to start from Schumpeter's English version *The Theory of Economic Development* (1934), which is the abridged translation of the second German edition (1926) and does not include chapter 7 of the first edition. Compared with Schumpeter's original view of sociocultural development, the current conception of evolution is narrow for two reasons: the lack of the sociological perspective and of the philosophical foundations (Shionoya, 2007).

This chapter attempts a return to Schumpeter's original view of the evolution of society as a whole and explores the ontological foundations of his conception of evolution. It is widely acknowledged that the concept of the economic world emerges with a pre-scientific act called 'vision'. The term 'vision' was made familiar to economists by Schumpeter himself. Vision, however, is not an ultimate factor which constitutes the viewpoint and object of scientific inquiry. Ontological premises always

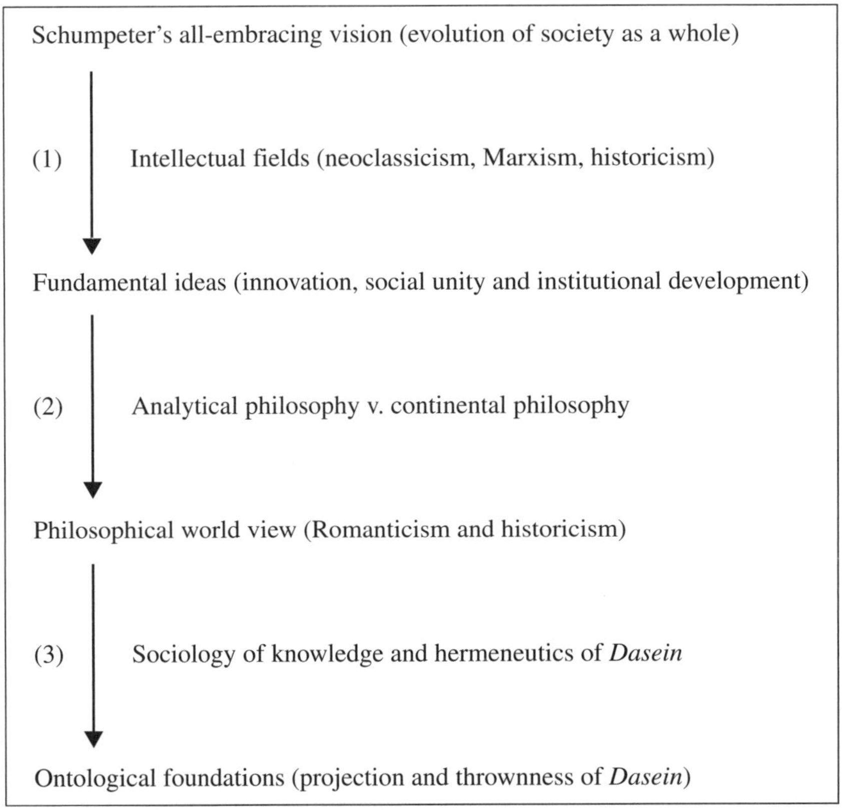

Figure 1.1 The structure of this chapter

underlie a vision. Ontology, a branch of philosophy, is the science of being or existence in general. Economic ontology concerns the foundations of an economic universe, which is explicitly or implicitly posited by economists as a vision concerning the subject matter and basic method of economics. The boundaries and contents of the economic universe are given by the ontological commitments of economists as the *Weltanschauung*.

This chapter is organized into three steps, as indicated in Figure 1.1.

First, I analyse Schumpeter's all-embracing vision of evolution, which is to be addressed by a universal social science, into three fundamental ideas relating to socio-economic concepts (innovation, social unity and institutional development). This analysis is carried out in the context of the intellectual fields in which Schumpeter was involved (neoclassicism, Marxism and historicism) (section 1.2).

Second, I proceed from the socio-economic dimension to the philosophical level in pursuit of an ontological basis of Schumpeter's vision. Referring to the division between analytical philosophy and continental philosophy, I examine the conformity of his ideas with continental philosophy (section 1.3), and identify his commitments to Romanticism and historicism based on his inquiry into the history of economic thought (section 1.4).

Third, since Romanticism and historicism, the two grand systems of *Weltanschauung*, are interpreted as the outcome of ontological investigations, it is necessary to look at an underlying process from which they are derived to depict the object of inquiry. This process shows how the objects of scientific enquiry are constructed as a vision in the pre-scientific stage. I first examine Schumpeter's approach to the sociology of science in terms of vision and ideology (section 1.5), and then extend it by the intermediaries of Karl Mannheim and Max Scheler to the ontological investigations in terms of Martin Heidegger's framework of hermeneutics (section 1.6). The chapter concludes with some remarks on the implications of the present approach (section 1.7).

1.2 THE FUNDAMENTAL IDEAS OF SCHUMPETERIAN EVOLUTION

Schumpeter had a strong interest in the intellectual products of the past in a wide area of the social sciences, and constructed his positions by responding to the totality of challenges posed by the intellectual fields of the time. He chose not to follow any single school of thought. Rather he was keen to examine all points of view and to absorb everything that was good in them. His erudition is well known, yet it was not a matter of taste but of resources for scientific work. For Schumpeter the most relevant intellectual fields were neoclassicism (represented by Léon Walras), Marxism (Karl Marx) and historicism (Gustav von Schmoller). No other authors could ever address such wide intellectual fields. Schumpeter could assimilate plural, even conflicting ideas, since, for him, they were not alternatives to be chosen for professional specialization but materials to be integrated for intellectual innovation.

To understand Schumpeter's framework of a universal social science, I set out the fundamental ideas underlying the framework by referring to the intellectual fields in which he was interested. There are three such ideas in Schumpeter's thought:

1. the pair notion of innovation and routine based on the dynamic–static typology of man,

2. the idea of the unity of social life through interaction between social areas, and
3. the idea of institutional development as the synthesis of theory and history.

Each of these ideas represents his responses to the problematics of neoclassicism, Marxism and historicism.

Although Schumpeter discerned the strength of these intellectual fields, he had a keen awareness of their weakness. He offered alternative conceptions to eliminate their defects, while accepting their merits. Each response is not only offered as a solution to what he perceived as shortcomings in the dominant intellectual fields, but also designed in total as scaffolding to organize the framework of a universal social science. The conjunction of these responses constitutes his tripartite idea of a universal social science: innovation, social unity and institutional development.

Schumpeter's first fundamental idea was to introduce the dynamic type of man into social science. The conception of the agent as the rational utility-maximizer based on fixed preferences has occupied the central place in mainstream economics. Although Walras's general equilibrium theory was essential as the logical foundation of economics, Schumpeter thought it was deficient in a dynamic analysis of a capitalist economy. His problem was to explore a new horizon of dynamic economics vis-à-vis static economics.

For this purpose, he proposed to construct economic dynamics on the basis of the concept of the dynamic man as the carrier of the creative power of life (innovation) as distinct from the traditional economic man who is concerned with the adaptation to given conditions and the restoration of economic orders (routine). The concept of innovations views the economic world as an organism with a living unity and has no parallel in Marx and Schmoller. Schumpeter's division of the static–dynamic typology can only be compared with Nietzsche's distinction of artistic forms between Dionysian creation and destruction and Apollonian equilibrium and order. Life resides only in the animate and organic entities. This is a Romanticist legacy to economics in emphasizing the individual creative spirit, but remains orthodox in keeping methodological individualism in comparison with other competing dynamic approaches attempted by the twentieth-century economists in terms of saving-investment relations, monetary disturbances, period analysis, disequilibrium analysis and expectations.

There is no question about the limitation of economic agents in neoclassical economics. Schumpeter's criticism of the classical school including Marx pointed out the lack of 'the element of personal initiative' and the overemphasis on the importance of mere increase in physical goods in their conception of economic development (1954: 572). In examining the future of capitalism, Schumpeter was absorbed in estimating the source of innovations that was nothing less than a 'particular "human element" of what is after all a human organism' (1950: 388).

Schumpeter described the social process as the interactions between innovations led by the dynamic men and routines followed by the static men. Innovation and adaptation are integral parts of social life: while innovation disrupts existing equilibrium, adaptation absorbs the consequences of innovation as a new order, just as the Apollonian harmonizing form integrates the Dionysian disruptive forces of life. In the economic sphere, this process takes the form of business cycles.

Schumpeter's second fundamental idea was the evolutionary development of society as a whole through interactions between various social areas. This was first and foremost his response to the Marxian economic interpretation of history. Schumpeter appraised that 'Marxist analysis is the only genuinely evolutionary economic theory that the period provided', calling it a 'unitary social science' (1954: 441). However, he was critical of Marx's view of historical processes for unilateral relations from production processes (as the substructure of society) to political, social and cultural processes (as the superstructure of society) through the pivotal position of the class structure of capital and labour. For Schumpeter, social classes occupied an important place in evolutionary development as a whole, but his concept of social classes was not confined to the economic area but consisted of more open social dynamics derived from changing leadership formation in various social areas (1927 [1951]).

The focus of his sociological concern was a theory of social class that would serve as the crucial link between the concept of leadership in various areas of social life, on the one hand, and the overall concept of civilization and the *Zeitgeist*, on the other (1912: 525–35). This sociological link became the key to his thesis of failing capitalism in *Capitalism, Socialism and Democracy* (1950), an immortal analysis of capitalism.

His third fundamental idea observes that the concept of institutional development is intended to achieve the synthesis of theory and history. This was his response to the *Methodenstreit* between theory and history, and opened a new frontier to the theoretical analysis of history, or what he called a 'reasoned history' (1939, vol. 1: 220) or '*histoire raisonnée*' (1950: 44). In accordance with the German historical school, Schumpeter believed that history is much more important than theory because 'the subject matter of economics is essentially a unique process in historic time' (1954: 12). But he was critical of the German historical school for its undue emphasis on historical relativity and individuality. The concept of institution is a means of generalizing historical events, but is generally limited due to its historical relativity. Thus it is a compromise between the generality meant by theorizing and the individuality meant by historicizing. For him, institutional economics or economic sociology was a device of integrating economic theory and economic history. In this respect, Schumpeter admitted that Marx was the first great economist who synthesized theory and history and set the goal for the historical school of economics (1950: 44), while characterizing the goal of Schmoller's programme as a 'unified sociology or social science as the mentally ("theoretically") worked out universal history' (1926: 382).

The set of Schumpeter's fundamental ideas suggests that the broad tenet of Schumpeterian evolutionary economics is a challenge to mainstream economics. Both what he wanted to add to neoclassicism (the concept of leadership) and what he succeeded in taking from Marxism and historicism (the concepts of social unity and institutional development) were heterodox elements to mainstream economics.

1.3 SCHUMPETERIAN EVOLUTION IN THE PHILOSOPHICAL PERSPECTIVE

Starting with Schumpeter's fundamental ideas, I descend gradually to the ontological foundations of his whole structure of thought, instead of ascending the structure of his substantive theory. In this section I describe an overview of philosophical doctrines to understand how his basic ideas differ from mainstream economics in the philosophical perspective.

Classical economics was established by François Quesnay and Adam Smith against the philosophical background of the eighteenth-century Enlightenment. While their works were restricted by existing economic and social conditions, they presented the exemplars of what economics looked like and succeeded in establishing the paradigm of economics. Neoclassical economics also belongs to this line of thought as far as its philosophical world view is concerned. The scientific world view of the Enlightenment, which was expressed by a series of concepts with different nuances, such as rationalism, positivism, empiricism, objectivism and naturalism, has dominated mainstream classical and neoclassical economics. The Enlightenment was a philosophy of social science that was modelled after natural science. Schumpeter's idea of evolution differs from the basic philosophy of the Enlightenment: it cannot be understood within the scope of the scientific world view of the Enlightenment.

Towards the end of the eighteenth century powerful currents of anti-Enlightenment thought, including idealism, subjectivism, historicism and Romanticism, were developed – particularly in Germany – against the natural-scientific world view. Philosophical efforts after Kant's 'Copernican turn' resulted in the developments of German idealism by Fichte, Schelling and Hegel, and gave a philosophical basis for anti-Enlightenment thought. An important consequence was the emergence of an epistemology and ontology for cultural, social and historical science as distinct from those designed to support natural science. In terms of the present configuration of philosophical thought, the conflict between the Enlightenment and anti-Enlightenment is represented by the contrast between analytical philosophy and continental philosophy.[2]

The Enlightenment or analytical philosophy claims:

1. the primacy of reason in knowledge,
2. the analysis of objects into components,
3. the mechanistic view of man and the universe, and
4. the generalization and universality of knowledge by the dismissal of history.

Anti-Enlightenment or continental philosophy, in contrast, maintains:

1. the relevance of feelings and intuition to knowledge,
2. the holistic synthesis of objects,
3. the organic view of man and the universe, and
4. the historicity and plurality of knowledge.

Occasionally – in economics too – several versions of alternative thought, more or less influenced by continental philosophy, have appeared to challenge mainstream economics: for example, socialist economics, Romantic economics, historical economics, institutional economics and economic sociology.

The differences seem to arise out of the differences of the two philosophies with respect to the perspective between the life-world and the science-world and with respect to the target between pre-theoretical and theoretical knowledge. Continental philosophy starts from the life-world and formulates the rules and procedures not for theory but for pre-theory, whereas analytical philosophy addresses the science-world and describes a methodology for theory construction. Thus understood, the two philosophies are not inconsistent but coexistent.

In twentieth-century economics Schumpeter was one of the practitioners of continental philosophy. He was not a philosopher; he pretended to be an anti-philosopher and hated metaphysics. As economist, he behaved as an analytical and empirical economist, even as a patron of mathematical economics and econometrics. In fact, he was an unconscious practitioner of the philosophy of the continental tradition, and played a role in introducing it into the Anglo-Saxon world of economics under the guise of theoretical and empirical economics, especially after he moved to the USA. It is our contention that the background for Schumpeter's conception of evolution should be understood in a wider context of the conflict between analytical philosophy and continental philosophy. Indeed, it is a mistake to view the two philosophies as mutually exclusive (Glendinning, 2006), but the philosophical context of the division can be used to shed light on Schumpeter's deviation from mainstream economics.

According to the criterion of the science-world an overload of continental philosophy in excess of the standard of analytical philosophy must be jettisoned. Occasionally Schumpeter swayed between the two standards and attempted to reduce the apparent overweight of continental philosophy. But he never renounced his claim for a universal social science based on the sociological perspective and the human typology.

1.4 ROMANTICISM AND HISTORICISM IN SCHUMPETER

Against the background of the two major philosophies, it is now necessary to give more specific thought to interpret Schumpeter's research programme. I argue that Schumpeter's acceptance of German Romanticism and historicism represented his departure from analytical philosophy and his excess weight on the standard of analytical philosophy. Although the two overlap and strengthen each other to a certain extent, they are unique and significant components of continental philosophy.

Schumpeter writes about Romanticism: 'Unlike utilitarianism, romanticism was not a philosophy, or a social creed, or a political or economic "system." It was essentially a literary fashion that linked up with a certain attitude toward life and art' (1954: 418–19). This means that the Romanticist world view is so flexible that it can be developed in any direction because it consists of primitive intuitions and feelings directly derived from the life-world. He tries to formulate the Romanticist attitude as follows:

> On the surface, it spelled revolt against classic canons of art, for instance, against Aristotle's three dramatic unities (of time, place, and action). But below this surface, there was something much more important, namely, revolt against convention, particularly against rationalized convention: feeling (possibly genuine) rose against cold reason; spontaneous impulse against utilitarian logic; intuition against analysis; the 'soul' against the intellect; the romance of national history against the artefacts of the Enlightenment. Let us call this attitude anti-intellectualism. (1954: 419)

In his later years Schumpeter talked about his long-standing research programme, which was forged from his early 'idea of a rich and full life' including 'economics, politics, science, art and love' (*Harvard Crimson*, 1944). This idea was the embodiment of the Romanticist world view, and his peculiar conception of economic development was nothing less than a Romanticist antithesis of the conventional circular flow of a static economy, which was arranged on the utilitarian hedonistic calculation of life. His static–dynamic dichotomy based on the human typology was an ingenious device to integrate hedonism and Romanticism into the foundations of economics.

Dynamic man as the key concept of evolution is characterized by energetic behaviour and non-rational motivations. With regard to behaviour, while this type of person encounters uncertainty and resistance, he has enough energy and will, foresight and creativity to overcome difficulties in introducing innovations. Regarding motivations, the dynamic man has different principles from those of the rational economic man: the dream and the will to found a private kingdom, the will to conquer and the joy of creation (1934: 93).

In parallel with his contempt for Benthamite utilitarianism, Schumpeter favourably discussed its cultural antipode Romanticism and evaluated the importance of Romanticism for sociology and economics. With regard to sociology, he described:

> It seems possible to speak of a romanticist sociology or at least of definite contributions of romanticist writers to economic, political, and general sociology. . . . It consists in the insertion, into the analysis of institutions and of behavior within institutions, of the compound of nonrational – not necessarily irrational – human volitions, habits, beliefs, and so on, which largely make a given society what it is and without which a society and its pattern of reaction cannot be understood. (1954: 422)

The Romanticist concern for 'the compound of nonrational . . . human volitions, habits, beliefs, and so on' in the analysis of institutions and behaviour within institutions corresponds with an aspect of the research programme of the German historical school. Thus he argued: 'The [German historical] school professed to study *all* the facets of an economic phenomenon; hence *all* the facets of economic behavior and not merely the economic logic of it; hence the *whole* of human motivations as historically displayed' (1954: 812). The meeting point of Romanticism and historicism is provided by the common recognition of the whole of human motivations and all the facets of social phenomena. While Romanticist ideas seek for the wholeness of life on the level of the life-world, historicist ideas emphasize an understanding of the way in which a society as a whole actually changes. It is just here that Schumpeter found an important relevance of Romanticism with economics:

> The chief importance of the romanticist movement for analytic economics consists in the impulse it gave to all kinds of historical research. It taught us better understanding of civilizations other than our own – the Middle Age, for example, and extra-European cultural worlds as well. This meant new vistas, wider horizons, fresh problems, and, above all, the end of the stupid contempt that Voltairians and utilitarians professed for everything that preceded 'this enlightened age'. (1954: 422–3)

Schumpeter's account of historicism is more comprehensive. In his early work on the history of economic doctrines and methods, he summarized six viewpoints of the German historical school:

1. a belief in the unity of social life and the inseparable relationship among its components,
2. a concern for development,
3. a recognition of the plurality of human motives,
4. an organic and holistic point of view,
5. an interest in individual relationships rather than the general nature of events, and
6. a viewpoint of historical relativity rather than universality (1914 [1954]: 176–80).

This is an excellent analysis of the methodological characteristics of the German historical school in particular and historicism in general.

The greatest significance of historicism for Schumpeter was the recognition that historical materials reflect the development phenomena and indicate the relationship between various areas of social life. It is not possible to explain a historical process of development merely in terms of economics alone, because in history all aspects of society change together with interactions between them. Thus, the concern for development in history necessitates the notion of the unity of social life. This recognition, that is the combination of 1 and 2 above and supported by 3, together with the Romanticist conception of dynamic human type, constitutes Schumpeter's central ideas of a universal social science. Schumpeter accepted viewpoints 1, 2 and 3 as the valuable contributions of the German historical school.

Referring to viewpoint 4, he repudiated the contention that the economy or society has its own aims and interests, except for the influences of the institutional and cultural factors on the behaviour of individuals. For economic sociology incorporates the notion of institutions and social rules as the determinants of individual behaviour. Although the unity of life is a vision of Romanticism, Schumpeter offered an alternative approach of integrating individual or partial elements into the whole, instead of starting from an indivisible metaphysical whole. When all variables are seen as endogenous and interdependent, investigations of these interactions among the social areas will reveal functional relations rather than causal relations, and will substantiate the idea of the unity of social life without presupposing an organic and holistic point of view.

Schumpeter wanted to overcome viewpoints 5 and 6, the most controversial issues of the *Methodenstreit*, by his conception of economic sociology that would integrate theory and history by means of the concept of institutions. According to Ernst Troeltsch, who contrasted naturalism and historicism as 'the two gigantic creations of knowledge in the modern world', historicism means making all our thinking about human beings, their culture and values basically history orientated, in contra-distinction to a rationalist and universalist view of knowledge in the Enlightenment (1922: 104). Without commitment to such an extreme standpoint, economic sociology and institutional economics have contributed to incorporating the contention of historicity into economic analysis.

It becomes clear that although Schumpeter's vision of a universal social science was constructed as responses to neoclassicism, Marxism and historicism, the concept of dynamic human type and the related concepts of leadership and innovation are to be found elsewhere, namely in German Romanticism, the thinking least relevant to economics so far.

Isaiah Berlin characterized Romanticism as follows: 'the importance of romanticism is that it is the largest recent movement to transform the lives and the thought of the Western world. It seems to me to be the greatest single shift in the consciousness of the West that has occurred' (1999: 1–2). Despite Berlin's statement, Romanticism has not left its mark on economic theory. Schumpeter's invaluable dream might mean a renaissance of the neglected modern thought in the field of economics. In the rest of this chapter, I examine the locus of historicism and Romanticism in Schumpeter's fundamental ideas and all-embracing vision of evolution.

1.5 KNOWLEDGE FORMATION BETWEEN VISION AND IDEOLOGY

The question how a vision emerges in the pre-scientific stage is exactly the central problem of ontology concerning the objects of knowledge and can be approached from two standpoints: the sociology of science and the philosophy of ontology. The present section and the next are concerned with these approaches. Since vision is a pre-scientific preconception of the objects of study, it has not been regarded as the proper subject for discussion in the positivist philosophy of science. However, in his article 'Science and ideology' (1949) and his unfinished chapter on 'The sociology of economics' in *History of Economic Analysis* (1954, pt I, ch. 4), Schumpeter discussed this question by focusing on the relationship between vision and ideology in the context of the sociology of science.

By 'vision' Schumpeter means the perception of facts as having some meaning or relevance that justifies our interest in them. On the other hand, there exist in our mind preconceptions about the economic process, which are given to us before we start scientific work; Schumpeter called them 'ideology'. His conception of ideology is different from the ordinary usage orientated to moral and political claims of values.

Schumpeter's concern is that ideology must inevitably intervene in the plotting of vision. Vision of the economic universe does not emerge from nothing but from the historical world into which economists are thrown. Economists are constrained by the historical world in two senses: first, the historical world consists of the structure of the scientific-world that is defined by given research problems and methods, and second, it consists of the changing nature of the real world or life-world that is characterized by time and space. By interpreting Schumpeter's conception of ideology in terms of the historical world, we get one of the pillars of economic ontology, that is, a disciplinary tradition. Although pre-scientific knowledge of the economic universe is largely governed by the disciplinary conventions that have been established by the past scientific activities, Schumpeter holds the view that economic knowledge is not only built up through the accumulation of legacies from the past, but also is developed by a struggle to escape from habitual modes of thought. The latter path crucially depends on a role of creative vision on the economic universe, another pillar of economic ontology.

According to Schumpeter, the combination of vision and ideology, though both are delusive concepts, provides us with dual moments: the creation of the future and constraint by the past. It can be argued that the relationship between creative vision and traditional convention in knowledge formation is patterned after the relationship between the creative destruction by innovations and the preservation of the existing order in economic life. Our next task is to enquire into the basis of the dual forces working in knowledge formation.

In view of the fact that Schumpeter referred to two sociologists of science, Karl Mannheim and Max Scheler, I recognize that two contrasting approaches are implied in his discussion: historicism and phenomenology. Mannheim defined the key theme of the sociology of knowledge as 'knowledge being existentially related' (*Seinsverbundenheit des Wissens*), meaning that social existence is linked with knowledge through the structure of a perspective. Perspective is a *Weltanschauung*, a style of thought, and an intellectual viewpoint, which in turn depends on various social factors (Mannheim, 1964: 377–8). The idea of knowledge correlated with the totality of social existence is based on the thought of historicism, in which knowledge is characterized by social conditions at particular time and space. But the problem with Mannheim is that a perspective is not uniquely socially given.

Scheler took a different approach to the sociology of knowledge. Mannheim called his own approach 'historicist approach' in contrast to Scheler's 'phenomenological approach'. He criticized the latter for the atemporal, static and universal criteria of truth. With respect to the central theme of the sociology of science that knowledge is conditioned by social existence, Scheler's concern was to seek the essential and eternal truth that is not volatile in accordance with historical conditions (Scheler, 1926). This attempt was made possible by his phenomenological approach (Scheler, 1954). Phenomenology focuses on the facts given by intuition, which makes us experience the world directly; the slogan is '*Zu den Sachen*'. Intuition does not presuppose reason or analysis but addresses the facts that exist before logical operation in the life-world. It allows feelings and desires to work in order to grasp all that exists in the mental experience of human beings.

The approaches of Manheim and Scheler are not inconsistent but complementary. It is possible to interpret the relationship between historicism and phenomenology as the philosophical representation of the relationship between ideology and vision in Schumpeter's argument of knowledge formation. While Mannheim's historicist sociology of knowledge regards knowledge as constrained by social existence, Scheler's phenomenological sociology of science identifies knowledge with a reflection of human existence in the community. Both approaches are one-sided. Later Martin Heidegger located human beings (*Dasein*) plunged into a social and historical context at the centre of his ontology. Human beings are historically thrown into the world (*Geworfenheit*), but still project themselves into the future (*Entwurf*). According to Heidegger, the analysis of *Dasein*'s understanding entails the ontological formation of the world. Historicity and subjectivity are intertwined with each other at the precognitive stage of science.

From the preceding discussion of the sociology of knowledge arises the importance of phenomenology as a principle organizing pre-scientific activity together with historicism. Although an orientation towards theory emerges out of the experience of life, theory construction means a departure from the life-world. To fill a gap between theory and the life-world, phenomenology grasps our experience in the life-world by intuition and recurs to the life that prevails before the theoretical work of abstraction and formulation begins; from that perspective, the subjectivity is understood as the whole person having various facets of human existence, as Romantics maintain. Thus, phenomenological approach, on the one hand, tries to break up the historical givenness of theories, which Schumpeter called ideology, and clarify its meanings by tracing back to their origins in the world view. On the other hand, it tries to find the origins of the pre-scientific ideas, which Schumpeter called vision, in the context of the life-world and the life experience.

1.6 *DASEIN* BETWEEN STATICS AND DYNAMICS

To quest for the ontological structure of being as the object of study under the historical constraints and forward-looking projection, it is necessary to proceed from the sociology of science to philosophical hermeneutics developed by Wilhelm Dilthey, Martin Heidegger and Hans-Georg Gadamer, among others. Dilthey (1910 [1927]) called disciplines addressed to historical and social phenomena 'human sciences' (*Geisteswissenschaften*), meaning that activities of human mind create history and society. The *Geist* in this context characterizes whole aspects of human life with plural functions including 'intellect, feeling, and will'. Intellect grasps an object, feeling prescribes a value and will sets an objective. Dilthey attempted to build the human sciences on the structural nexus of the psychological functions and to reconstruct the existence by means of 'lived experience, expression, and understanding' (*Erlebnis*, *Ausdruck* and *Verstehen*). Through this attempt he finally arrived at hermeneutics, that is, a discipline of understanding and interpretation of all human behaviour and products. Hermeneutic is the self-reflection of human beings addressed to the historical and social world; whereas the natural sciences are concerned with the formulation of causal relationship, the human sciences interpret the structural relationship among the objects from a teleological viewpoint and clarify their values, significance and meanings. An interpretation of the historical and social world leads us to various world views or visions, which are constructed in accordance with different weighing of the structural nexus of life. The most comprehensive system was Dilthey's 'theory of world views' (*Weltanschauungslehre*). It is suggested that Schumpeter's vague concept of vision can be interpreted as the self-reflection concerning the economic universe by the use of hermeneutics.

In this connection, Heidegger's framework will be useful. For him, phenomenology of the *Dasein* (human beings) means nothing but hermeneutics because phenomenology is an ontology concerning the existence in general, based on *Dasein*'s own understanding of being. The basic thesis of his ontology is that 'only as long as *Dasein* is, is there being' (Heidegger, 1927 [1962]: 255). He attempted a hermeneutics of human beings and tried to interpret the understanding of existence with which they were implicitly endowed. An interpretation must understand in advance what is interpreted; here is what is called a 'hermeneutical circle', that is, a circle between preceding understanding and present interpretation. Heidegger put forward a notion: 'pre-structure (*Vor-struktur*) of understanding' (ibid.: 191).

According to Heidegger, interpretation in hermeneutics aims to advance understanding which includes pre-knowledge from the life experience of the *Dasein*. *Vor-struktur*, namely the pre-structure of understanding, consists of three concepts: first, *Vorhabe*, which is what we have in advance or fore-having; second, *Vorsicht*, which is what we see in advance or foresight; and third, *Vorgriff*, which is what we grasp in advance or pre-conception. *Vorhabe* indicates an object of interpretation, *Vorsicht* a viewpoint of interpretation, and *Vorgriff* a world view of interpretation. This set of concepts shows the structure of preconception in the pre-scientific process of knowledge formation, in which the duality of existential projection of the *Dasein* orientated to the possibilities of human beings (creation) and of its 'thrownness' (*Geworfenheit*) into, or its constraint by, the historical and social world (tradition) should be developed. In Schumpeter's terminology, *Vor-struktur* is the combined result of vision and ideology.

After Heidegger, hermeneutics has been developed again more in the direction that emphasized the historicity of human existence. Gadamer (1960 [1975]) criticized Dilthey for the split of hermeneutics into psychologism and historicism, and aimed at the construction of hermeneutics rooted in the historical existence of the self. Dilthey had attached much importance to the correspondence between the psychological nexus and the structure of the objective world. For Gadamer, historical reason is not only reason conditioned by our historical condition, but also reason for shaping a new history; he thus stressed a forward-looking viewpoint of history. He advocated the 'fusion of horizons' (*Horizontverschmelzung*) of the past and the present; this idea is parallel to Troeltsch's 'present cultural synthesis' and Heidegger's 'projection under thrownness'. All these ideas are the philosophical efforts to go deeper into Schumpeter's duality of vision and ideology, which was presented in the context of the sociology of knowledge as the prelude to the history of economics.

Depending on hermeneutical ontology, I have tried to show that Schumpeter's insight into the interactions between vision and ideology has been a focus of philosophical discussions in historicism, phenomenology and hermeneutics. The next task is an analysis of the *Dasein* which leads to Schumpeter's static–dynamic dichotomy.

Schumpeter's two types of agency are not Heidegger's *Dasein*, which has a privilege of interpreting the being of entities. Heidegger distinguishes between entity and its being', and calls the difference an 'ontological difference'. According to him, whereas an investigation into entities (*Seiende*) is an 'ontical' (*ontisch*) study – economics is an ontical study of the economy – an investigation into the being (*Sein*) of entities is an 'ontological' (*ontologisch*) study – economic ontology is an ontological study of the economy. Among various entities in the world, the human being is special in that it exists with the understanding of its own being and has a role of understanding the meanings of other entities; hence it is called *Dasein* (being-there), meaning that human being is the place where the meanings of being of all entities are made clear. For Heidegger, being is nothing but a viewpoint or vision which is projected by the *Dasein* as a plot of the universe. In other words, being is the meaning of the entities in question. Thus the Schumpeterian concepts of static and dynamic agencies are not ontological but ontical. To identify the ontological basis of the economy, one must stand on the ontological level of agency (the *Dasein*) and ask the meaning of the economy based on the capacity of the *Dasein* to understand its being.

The *Dasein* or the ontological self is not an abstract rational entity presupposed by modern philosophy after the Enlightenment, but a person living an everyday life with whole aspects of personality including 'intellect, feeling and will', as characterized by Dilthey's psychological investigation. There is a difference of chemistry between Heidegger's *Dasein* and Schumpeterian *Dasein*. Heidegger's *Dasein* tends to project oneself with a general 'concern' (*Sorge*) for the universe and with a basic mental state of 'anxiety' (*Angst*) due to its 'being to death' (*Sein zum Tode*). As a result, it contributed to a rise of existentialism based on a critical mind towards a crisis of the age. The *Dasein* that is assumed to sustain Schumpeter's two kinds of the ontical selves is more optimistic and passionate about the projection of self. Although Schumpeter did not reveal his own ontological self, it is possible for us to construct it so as to be consistent with his definition of the ontical selves. My hypothesis is to interpret the essence of Schumpeterian *Dasein* as a Romanticist constrained by a historicist.

Romanticism depended on emotion and volition as the motive powers of life rather than on the pursuit of reason and uniform knowledge. Instead of seeking the reason as the Enlightenment thinkers did, the Romantic thinkers pursued 'imagination, feelings, tradition, organism and the mystery of the soul' (Porter, 2001: 2). The Romantic agenda sought to heal the wounds of modernity and technology, and to restore unity with the self, with others (communities) and with nature (Beiser, 1998: 349). Defining Romanticism as the counter-Enlightenment, Isaiah Berlin regards Johann Georg Hamann as the first person who began the whole Romantic process of revolt against the Enlightenment; he repeats an assertive judgement that Hamann was the true originator of modern anti-Enlightenment. The following passages from Berlin on Hamann convey the contrasting essence of the Enlightenment thinker, Voltaire, and the anti-Enlightenment thinker, Hamann:

> Voltaire thought that they [men] wanted happiness, contentment, peace, but this was not true. What men wanted was for all their faculties to play in the richest and most violent possible fashion. What men wanted was to create, what men wanted was to make, and if this making led to clashes, if it led to wars, if it led to struggles, then this was part of [the] human lot . . . For Hamann, of course, creation was a most ineffable, indescribable, unanalysable personal act, by which a human being laid his stamp on nature, allowed his will to soar, spoke his word, uttered that which was within him and which would not brook any kind of obstacle. (Berlin, 1993: 42–3)

This contrast is compared to Schumpeter's static–dynamic dichotomy of human beings and economic conditions.

The ideal of Romanticism was not objectively given universal truth but creation of the mind based on emotion, imagination, introspection, desire and aspiration, all of which reflect dynamic life. Creation is everything; it has originality; it is based on the energies of man. Thus, Ricarda Huch (1924: 49) summed up the thesis of Romanticism as '*Das Romantisierung besteht in Lebendigmachen*'. Schumpeter's conception of innovation and dynamic economy retains remarkable traits of the Romanticist view of man and the universe. First, innovation is the only ways and means to make an active economy; second, it is contrasted with the routine of a changeless economy; third, it is based on the maximum realization of human faculties and energies; fourth, it causes destruction and disturbance to the existing order but the outcome is uncertain and unpredictable; fifth, it is unique with respect to a historical context; and sixth, it emphasizes the causal importance of volition rather than reason.

Indeed, for Schumpeter, innovation and its consequences for the economy and society are the subject matter of economic research, which is the concern of an ontical study of the economy. But the causes of innovation reside in the *Dasein*, which is the concern of an ontological study of the economy. Schumpeter did not conceal his ontological root of the dynamic economic vision, despite his pretension to be a positivist economist. The notion of Schumpeterian evolution aims to crystallize and substantiate a vision derived from the life-world. Addressing a wide range of phenomena covering the nature, human beings and society, the Romanticist viewpoint tempts one to integrate arts, science and ethics (Richards, 2002). This was Schumpeter's lifetime dream.

1.7 CONCLUSIONS

Starting with the critical remark about neo-Schumpeterian evolutionary economics, this chapter attempted to identify Schumpeter's notion of evolution in a broader perspective. His notion of evolution is sociologically wider and philosophically deeper than the contemporary view and is ultimately based on the ontological premises of the static–dynamic interrelationship of multifaceted agents.

To illuminate the pre-scientific process which would have led to the notion of evolution, we have discussed Schumpeter's meta-theoretical view from two perspectives: first, his view on vision and ideology in the context of the sociology of knowledge, and second, his view on the static–dynamic dichotomy in the context of the philosophy of ontology. Against the background of a contrast between analytical philosophy and continental philosophy, it was argued that Schumpeter entertained the world view of historicism and Romanticism. In terms of ontological decision, Schumpeter's *Dasein* was confronted with a tension between volitional projection and social embeddedness. In the sociology of knowledge, in the philosophy of ontology, as well as in the economic theory of development, there is a parallel structure of creation versus tradition, which can be called isomorphic duality. It is illuminating to interpret Schumpeter's concepts of innovation and evolution in the context of phenomenological-hermeneutical ontology, because innovation seen in this basic context represents the isomorphic manifestations of human energies, a theme recurring like a refrain in all areas of social activities.

Human creativity alone is not enough as a theme of social science. Some institutional schemes must link creative projection with thrownness into the world. Social science used to describe the existing institutional orders into which the *Dasein* is ordinarily thrown. The process of changing social orders is the concern of volitional projection of the *Dasein*. Schumpeter found that the institutions of markets in capitalism are the most effective means to attract human creativity into an economy and to permit the established orders to be invaded by innovations. Markets and related institutions are more important than innovations in the sense that they enable the creation and destruction of orders at the same time. Schumpeter's *Dasein* depends on the existence of effective institutions in various social areas. He mentioned the greatest contribution of capitalism in attracting the best brains to business:

> by creating the social space for a new class that stood upon individual achievement in the economic field, it [capitalism] in turn attracted to that field the strong wills and the strong intellects . . . So, in this sense, capitalism – and not merely economic activity in general – has after all been the propelling force of the rationalization of human behavior. (Schumpeter, 1950: 124–5)

Despite his thesis of declining capitalism, he did not complain about the future of a modern society because even if the economic world loses the only source of romance and heroism, there would be a transfer of talents and energies from the economic area to the non-economic areas. Schumpeter writes: 'Human energy would turn away from business. Other than economic pursuits would attract the brains and provide the adventure' (1950: 131).

The crucial question raised by Schumpeter's thesis of falling capitalism is whether the present method of recruiting human energy into the economic sphere will continue by force of habit. He thought that after capitalism had accomplished the task of increasing the standard of living through economic development, another system would take its place, one based on a highly rationalized economy that would allocate economic resources and social leadership into broader areas of a society. For him, the true crisis of capitalism is that the whole scheme of innovations in the economy has become an obsolete routine. Routinization of innovations is not innovation any more. It is a paradox that innovations become a routine. This is exactly the case that Heidegger diagnosed as the degradation of the *Dasein* under the pressure of the historical givenness.

From the ontological perspective, the solution to the problem depends on how an existing balance between the projection into the future and the thrownness into the past will be upset. The function of the *Dasein* on the ontological level is to posit a new meaning of the economy in a historical context and in a wide perspective of human nature, and to shift creative energies to non-economic areas. The significance of Schumpeter's vision will be determined by the plasticity of Schumpeterian *Dasein* that would lead to a vision of a post-capitalist society.

NOTES

1. An analysis of chapter 7 of Schumpeter's *Entwicklung* (1912) is given in Shionoya (1990). Also see Shionoya (1997: 31–53).
2. For historical and contemporary issues around continental philosophy, see Critchley and Schroeder (1998).

REFERENCES

Beiser, B. (1998), 'German Romanticism', in E. Craig (ed.), *Routledge Encyclopedia of Philosophy*, vol. 8, London: Routledge.

Berlin, I. (1993), *The Magus of the North: J.G. Hamann and the Origins of Modern Irrationalism*, London: John Murray.

Berlin, I. (1999), *The Roots of Romanticism*, Princeton, NJ: Princeton University Press.
Critchley, S. and Schroeder, W.R. (eds) (1998), *A Companion to Continental Philosophy*, Oxford: Blackwell.
Dilthey, W. (1910 [1927]), *Der Aufbau der geschichtlichen Welt in den Geisteswissenschaften*, in B. Groethysen (ed.), *Gesammelte Schriften*, vol. 7, Leipzig: Teubner.
Gadamer, H.G. (1960), *Wahrheit und Methode*, Tübingen: J.C.B. Mohr, trans. J. Weinsheimer and D.G. Marshall (1975), *Truth and Method*, London: Continuum.
Glendinning, S. (2006), *The Idea of Continental Philosophy*, Edinburgh: Edinburgh University Press.
Harvard Crimson (1944), 'Professor Schumpeter, Austrian Minister, now teaching economics here', 11 April.
Heidegger, M. (1927), *Sein und Zeit*, in *Jahrbuch für Phänomenologie und phänomenologische Forschung*, vol. VIII, trans. J. Macquarrie and E. Robinson, 1962 *Being and Time*, Oxford: Blackwell.
Huch, R. (1924), *Die Romantik*, teil II, 12th edn, Leipzig: H. Haessel.
Mannheim, K. (1964), 'Das Problem einer Soziologie des Wissens' [1925], reprinted in *Wissenssoziologie*, Berlin: Luchterhand.
Porter, R. (2001), *The Enlightenment*, 2nd edn, London: Palgrave Macmillan.
Richards, R.J. (2002), *The Romantic Conception of Life: Science and Philosophy in the Age of Goethe*, Chicago, IL: University of Chicago Press.
Scheler, M. (1926), *Die Wissensformen und die Gesellschaft*, Leipzig: Der Neue-Geist Verlag.
Scheler, M. (1954), 'Phänomenologie und Erkenntnistheorie', *Gesammelte Werke*, bd. X, Schriften aus dem Nachlass, bd. 2.
Schumpeter, J.A. (1912), *Theorie der wirtschaftlichen Entwicklung*, Leipzig: Duncker & Humblot.
Schumpeter, J.A. (1914), *Epochen der Dogmen- und Methodengeschichte*, Tübingen: J.C. Mohr, trans. R. Aris (1954) *Economic Doctrine and Method: An Historical Sketch*, London: George Allen & Unwin.
Schumpeter, J.A. (1926), 'Gustav v. Schmoller und die Probleme von heute', *Schmollers Jahrbuch*, **50**, 337–88.
Schumpeter, J.A. (1927), 'Die sozialen Klassen in ethnisch homogenen Milieu', *Archiv für Sozialwissenschaft und Sozialpolitik*, **57**, 1–67, trans. H. Norden (1951) *Imperialism and Social Classes*, New York: Augustus M. Kelley.
Schumpeter, J.A. (1934), *The Theory of Economic Development*, trans. R. Opie, Cambridge, MA: Harvard University Press.
Schumpeter, J.A. (1939), *Business Cycles: A Theoretical, Historical, and Statistical Analysis of the Capitalist Process*, 2 vols, New York: McGraw-Hill.
Schumpeter, J.A. (1949), 'Science and ideology', *American Economic Review*, **39** (2), 345–59.
Schumpeter, J.A. (1950), *Capitalism, Socialism and Democracy*, 3rd edn, New York: Harper & Brothers.
Schumpeter, J.A. (1954), *History of Economic Analysis*, New York: Oxford University Press.
Shionoya, Y. (1990), 'The origin of the Schumpeterian research program: a chapter omitted from Schumpeter's *Theory of Economic Development*', *Journal of Institutional and Theoretical Economics*, **146** (2), 314–27.

Shionoya, Y. (1997), *Schumpeter and the Idea of Social Science: A Metatheoretical Study*, Cambridge: Cambridge University Press.
Shionoya, Y. (2007), 'Schumpeter and evolution: a philosophical interpretation', *History of Economic Ideas*, **15** (1), 65–80.
Troeltsch, E. (1922), *Der Historismus und seine Probleme: Erstes Buch: Das logische Problem der Geschichtsphilosophie*, Tübingen: Mohr.

2. The general pattern of Marshallian evolution[1]

Tiziano Raffaelli

2.1 PARTIAL EQUILIBRIUM ANALYSIS AS A MODEL FOR PIECEMEAL EVOLUTION

Marshall is usually considered the champion of static equilibrium analysis; so much so that the point of intersection of the Marshallian cross epitomizes the very notion of static equilibrium, the final aim of economic analysis. However, as is widely acknowledged, he was not fully satisfied with static economic analysis per se. In his eyes, statics was 'but a branch of dynamics' (Marshall, 1920: 366 n.) and the latter itself ought to be replaced by economic biology (ibid.: xiv), the economist's Mecca, which required economics to be supplemented with sociological, historical and institutional research. Notwithstanding these reservations on their role, the tools he devised helped economics to develop static analysis and, thanks to them, static value theory became its prominent research field.

This reconstruction relies on the unchallenged and almost obvious static interpretation of partial equilibrium analysis, the theoretical core of Marshall's economics. Even though there is general recognition that he is concerned with time, as when he resorts to time period analysis, he does not appear to be interested in change itself, but in its termination, in the way change can be disposed of through the action of equilibrating forces. The somewhat mechanical operation of the principle of substitution is the leading force that brings the system into equilibrium. Although the principle does not always lead to straightforward, unambiguous solutions, especially when the time horizon widens, its prevailing aim appears to be that of charting the path towards equilibrium.

It is no surprise that from the point of view of a pioneering evolutionary economist (Veblen, 1900), or of the more combative members of the historical school (Cunningham, 1892), Marshall was heavily criticized for failing to realize the intrinsic limits of marginal analysis and its inability to deal with the truly relevant problems of social and economic change. More recently, advances in evolutionary economics, playing havoc with mainstream equilibrium theory, have indirectly shown that the tools of Marshallian analysis were inappropriate to convey the evolutionary aspirations he held in reserve.[2]

That the conclusion inexorably points to the inadequacy of Marshall's analytical apparatus for 'economic biology' is beyond doubt, but in order to gain a more adequate historical perspective, we need to clear the ground from a whole set of commonplaces and misunderstandings that have counterfeited Marshall's research programme. Let us begin with a history of economics perspective: Marshall is usually enlisted in the mainstream as a half-baked general equilibrium theorist, one who did not go all the way through to the natural end point of the research project he had undertaken. Scholars deeply acquainted with Marshall's work (Becattini, 1975; Dardi, 1984; Loasby, 1978; 1989), recently supported by information and material previously unavailable (Groenewegen, 1995; Raffaelli, 1994a; Whitaker, 1996), have shown that this assessment is completely wrong and that his research agenda was incompatible with that of general equilibrium theory (GET). His partial equilibrium models, which never pretend to explain more than a circumscribed subset of economic and social phenomena, cannot be considered as approximations to GET (Dardi, 2006). The relationship between partial and general equilibrium analysis is not analogous to that between a part and the whole to which it belongs; rather, they represent two irreconcilable research strategies. Unlike general equilibrium economists, Marshall looks for localized adjustments of the economic system, a process that strictly mimics the way Darwinian evolution works.

Let us recollect that one of the main objections to the theory that species evolve was George Cuvier's 'principle of the correlation of parts', which stated that each part of any organism is always in a necessary relation to all the other parts (like the economic variables of GET models). According to Cuvier, this interconnection ruled out the possibility of evolutionary change, since, for any organism to remain viable, modifying a single part of it would require a corresponding, simultaneous modification of all the other parts. By contrast, evolutionism rests on the possibility of localized change. Loosening the grip of Cuvier's fundamental principle, it makes room for piecemeal modifications that do not subvert or impair the working of other parts and the whole organism itself. Evolution can be said to rely on a principle similar to Marshall's *ceteris paribus* clause, opposite to that of the correlation of parts. Organisms evolve because in the main they continue working as usual while the modifications they undergo are localized, although in the course of time they become cumulative and affect other features of the original organism. Marshall's conception of social evolution corresponds to the 'empty world hypothesis' (Simon, 1996: 209) according to which the world is only partially connected and is quasi-decomposable into sub-systems 'within which connections are relatively dense, and between which connections are sparse' (Loasby, 2006b: 71). Simon himself indirectly vindicates Marshall's partial equilibrium analysis when, to illustrate the 'nearly decomposable structure of the system', he writes that 'it is empirically true that the price of any given commodity and the rate at which it is exchanged depend to a significant extent only on the prices and quantities of a few other commodities' (Simon, 1996: 200). Marshall's principle of continuity also finds support in the idea of piecemeal evolution, in which it is firmly rooted.

2.2 EVOLUTION BY INNOVATION AND STANDARDIZATION AND THE ROLE OF VARIATION BY DESIGN

So far, we have highlighted the existence of deep, fundamental analogies between the core of Marshall's economic analysis and evolutionary theory. But is this connection supported by historical evidence, or is it a bare coincidence?

To answer this query, it is necessary to go back to Marshall's philosophical training and especially to the model of the human mind embodied in his early paper 'Ye machine' (Loasby, 2006a; Raffaelli, 1994a; 2006a). Stripped of its psychological and physiological specificity, the model of the mind is exactly the same as that of biological evolution and partial equilibrium analysis. The machine adapts to environmental change by readjusting the inner segment(s) that are no longer viable, while all the remaining parts of its structure are left unchanged and proceed as usual. Once successful change has taken place, it is preserved by being incorporated into the system itself (the function performed by genetic reproduction in Darwin's system): the dialectics between repetition and innovation, order and freedom, custom and competition that characterize Marshall's main economic work here finds their genesis and prototype.

Where the (neo-)Darwinian theory is not fully endorsed by Marshall, at least in its applicability to human and social evolution, is in the idea that variations (changes) are due to pure chance. This idea was – and still is – rather unbearable and Darwin himself was loath to bow his head to its inevitability. Whatever Darwin's opinion on the subject, an issue that is beyond the scope of the present chapter, no doubt the neo-Darwinian revolution[3] marked a clear discontinuity with the theories held by Lamarck and Spencer, who maintained that acquired characters are genetically transmitted and who conceived of evolution as a process orientated by the needs and requirements of the organism itself, in response to environmental change.

This Lamarckian–Spencerian conception sharply contrasts with the (neo-) Darwinian theory, based on the pair chance variation – natural selection. Attributing variation to some sort of intelligent design, and thereby admitting that selection is already at work in the generation of change, the former view downplays the role of natural selection, which comes into effect only *ex post*, after change has occurred. Inheritance of acquired characters is a corollary, required if organisms are to be allowed to mould their own evolution, without leaving full play to chance genetic variation.

Marshall confessed he was unconvinced by Weismann's critique of Spencer (Whitaker, 1996, vol. 2: 114) and held the opinion that chance variation does not provide the only – nor even the main – explanation of human and social evolution. The Darwin versus Spencer opposition helps understand Marshall's views on social evolution, although not in the way which is usually assumed. The strong opposition between the two theories throughout the history of scientific ideas, and the fact that empirical evidence dismisses the latter, induce even the few scholars who place Marshall among the pioneers of evolutionary economics to conclude that his Spencerian leanings prevented him from setting the discipline on the right track.[4] Marshall's resistance to neo-Darwinian genetics is held responsible for his lack of attention to population dynamics and the role of chance variation as the generating spring of social evolution. The main agency of evolution, according to Marshall, is purposeful design rather than the Darwinian interplay between chance variation and natural selection. Although paying lip-service to the view that 'physical peculiarities acquired by the parents during their life-time are seldom if ever transmitted to their offspring' (Marshall, 1920: 247),[5] he inclined to retain, at least for social evolution, the Lamarckian–Spencerian theory of the hereditary transmission of acquired characters.[6] In 1916, in the seventh edition of *Principles* (Marshall, 1920: 248 n.), and later in *Industry and Trade* (Marshall, 1919: 163–4), he dismissed Mendel's findings about peas as a clue to the evolution of society, setting a contrast between natural and cultural evolution. Ready to concede that the former is completely driven by chance variation and natural selection (that is, by trial and error), he stuck to the idea that the latter avails itself of conscious efforts to foresee the outcome of any variation and builds on the ability to record any successful result and transmit it to future generations. Here too, trial and error play their role, but are themselves submitted to conscious investigation.

Indeed, in Marshall's view of historical evolution, human and social progress coincides with the growth of opportunities for the conscious modification of life conditions. Deliberation, resolve, freedom are distinguishing features of modern as compared to primitive society (Cook, 2005; 2006). What they amount to can again be guessed by turning our attention to 'Ye machine', in which two mental circuits are at work, one driven by trial and error and the other by conscious anticipation of future outcomes. The latter affords new and better strategies for change when the former fails.

This hierarchy of the two levels, however, is only part of the whole story. As stated above, Marshall is mainly interested in the way successful changes can be preserved and become cumulative. This process requires the accumulation of those very unconscious elements that the growth of freedom seems to have removed from human life. Consciousness prevails only thanks to the fact that it is used sparingly. Marshall's model of human and social evolution relies heavily on unconscious automatisms, the role of which he had learnt from neurophysiology. The main idea can be summarized as follows: successful operations are stored in the mind to be later repeated without any conscious effort. The physiologist William Carpenter, with whose works Marshall was familiar, referred to the outcome of this process as 'secondarily automatic instincts' (Carpenter, 1875). The role of such unconscious automatisms is twofold: on the one hand, they provide the register where successful behaviour can be recorded to be later reproduced without effort; on the other hand, their existence is a prerequisite for change itself. Deprived of all their automatisms, a mind, an organism, a firm or a society would be unable to go beyond the performance of very limited tasks. It is only thanks to accumulated automatisms that new, more complex tasks can be performed. Variation mainly consists in rearranging pre-existing automatisms and thereby inducing them to perform new tasks. In this evolutionary model we find at work Marshall's principles and guidelines for social evolution: (1) the advantages associated with the automatic performance of repeated tasks, (2) the dangers stemming from excessive rigidity of existing automatisms, and (3) the need to make room for innovation and creativity and concentrate attention and energies on this task.

1. The advantages of automatisms are ubiquitous; without them, life would be impossible; every ordinary task would require ages and absorb all the available energy. It is thanks to acquired automatisms that we can perform new tasks. When we are learning to ride a bicycle, all our energy is absorbed by the task; once the learning process is accomplished, we can cycle while devoting our mental energy to other tasks (see Marshall on skating, 1920: 251 n.). What is even more interesting is that acquired automatisms are a prerequisite for carrying out any novel plan. The ability to type without paying too much attention to the keyboard is a prerequisite for writing a paper. What is true of mental individual activities applies to science and industry as well. Science is of great help because it builds up sets of connections which deal with aspects of the world that are often repeated; by this means,

science saves time and energy, allowing us to resort to standard causal connections to deal with various challenging problems (Raffaelli, 1994b). There is no science of the individual and, when it comes to solving individual cases, the work must be finished up 'by hand' (Marshall, 1920: 779). This statement calls to mind another powerful source of automatism, the factory machine. Here again, we have a system in which processes that are repeated are performed automatically and innovation rests on the existence of previous automatisms, tending in its turn, when successful, to add to their number.

2. Looked at from the opposite viewpoint, these accumulated automatisms generate their own problems. They need updating, and much energy is often consumed in acquiring competencies doomed soon to become obsolete. The painful experience of discovering that a large investment in learning a computer programme has lost its value is all too familiar. One of the antidotes is the fragmentation of automatisms, what we would now call 'modular flexibility'. Marshall uses this argument when he discusses gains and losses from standardization. The benefits are enormous; standardization saves energy and allows the performance of tasks that would otherwise be impossible (Fujii, 2006). However, when it embraces whole processes of production, no room is left for evolution by localized change. Overall re-switching is the only available chance for change and this means that the normal action of piecemeal evolution is no longer viable, to the disadvantage of the small producer:

> The standardization of component parts is at once more productive of economy and less hostile to progress than that of complex structures . . . [A]nd this contrast is of special significance in regard to the contest between giant businesses and those of moderate size. (Marshall, 1919: 227)

One of the main dangers of the excessive size and extension of automatic units is that they tend to discourage creativity and innovation. This is seen at work, in a similar way, in both industry and science. The small producer is displaced by the huge size of elementary automatic processes that require large capital endowments, the would-be young scientist is discouraged by the huge amount of preliminary textbook knowledge he has to acquire before being able to exercise any creative faculties.[7] Let us learn this lesson from Marshall's own suggestive words:

> The fact that Aristotle, Newton and Cuvier would have much to learn, if they should meet a mediocre student of modern science on his arrival in Hades, does not tell entirely on the side of the present age. For creative faculties are developed by exercise; and many who might have been fascinated by opportunities of relatively easy creation fifty years ago, now find that very little of the original work, which remains to be done, and yet has the fascination that belongs

> to bright new ideas, is within the scope of their limited power. This depressing influence, which is already felt in some realms of science, may possibly spread in the realm of business. For the widening range of standardized methods tends generally to increase the dependence of the creative mind on large capitalistic aid in obtaining scope for its activities. (Marshall 1919: 242–3)

3. Combining the considerations under 1 and 2, Marshall has mixed feelings on the overall progress of modern society. It is positive in so far as it helps human creativity and freedom, as it often does. Standardization, for instance, allows attention to concentrate on well-defined specific tasks and helps innovation and creativity. Without standardized nuts and bolts, it would be impossible even to build the simplest mechanical device. And whenever automatisms are able to solve a problem, they are more reliable and less expensive than conscious processes. This is exemplified, once again, by 'Ye machine', which resorts to the upper circuit only when the lower is ineffective. But automatisms can too often be hostile to the exercise of creative thought, as shown under 2. Human reason is asked to assist the growth of automatisms that give greater scope to creativity without hindering its exercise. Business policy (the defence of the small producer), education (the promotion of general education, which does not soon become obsolete) and other remedies are devised, often in response to the aforementioned concern.

2.3 SOCIAL EVOLUTIONARY DEVICES

It is important to keep in mind these general remarks when dealing with Marshall's views on economic and social evolution and the role of economics and social science. The evolution of the economy and society follows the above-sketched pattern and faces the same potentialities and problems. The market is a very powerful device to promote economic evolution, because it works automatically, solving problems that would otherwise require enormous conscious energy. By this means, it allows the state to concentrate on a limited range of tasks and perform them with greater accuracy. Moreover, the competitive market promotes innovation, since what is automatic is the direction of the driving force, not the specific way agents react. Prices signal which way to go, but leave room for personal creativity. Marshall's competition is never 'automatic', as his young pupil, John Maynard Keynes, learned when he got a red pencil in one of his 1905 exercise papers for the expression 'automatic competition', which, as Marshall remarked, 'belongs to the mathematical world on the other side of the looking glass' (Raffaelli, 2003: 113). Marshallian competition is precisely the opposite, the driving force that leads to innovation.

The evolution of the supply side of the economy is characterized by two complementary drives. On the one hand, there is the growth of automatized, standardized, mechanized methods of production, whose value shrinks as the process unfolds. This gives rise to a path of economic growth, exemplified, fundamentally, by the USA, where the width of the market fosters mechanization: large amounts of standardized goods are marketed at very low prices. On the other hand, and at the other end of the spectrum, the benefits of innovation and creativity are illustrated by France, where fashion and design foster the production of high price, non-standardized goods. Any real economy is a combination of these two models, which can never be wholly separated.

Competition brings about change along this bi-dimensional pathway: innovation and standardization; the former leading to, and depending on, the latter. The model of 'Ye machine' helps us form an idea of their interconnection. Innovation that is never transformed into a new standard is pure fancy, doomed to disappear without exercising any impact on the evolution of the system. What really matters is innovation that can establish a new standard. This is only possible if custom plays its complementary part. Like mental automatism, if custom were too rigid its effect would be negative, since it would resist any change whatsoever. On the other hand, the absence of custom, like the absence of mental automatisms, would both reduce the breadth of possible innovation and downgrade it to mere fancy, without the possibility of being recorded. Progress is the continuous sequence of innovations which, once they are accepted, become a new standard, and custom is the whole set of standards that we inherit from the past. Again, it is worth reading Marshall's own reflections on the subject, in a passage that well recapitulates how his general pattern of evolution works:

> If custom had been absolutely rigid, it would have been an almost unmixed evil. But the resistance which it offered to the bold reformer resembled that presented by a glacier to anyone who might try to change its shape: custom and the glacier are plastic, but both refuse to be hurried in their adjustments. Custom has discouraged any attempt at improvement which involved a sudden breach with tradition: but, except in some ceremonial matters, it has been tolerant of modifications in substance, form and method which did not obtrude themselves. On the one hand, stagnant social conditions do not crush out of everyone the desire to humour his own fancy, or his love of novelty, or his inclination to save trouble by a rather better adjustment of implements to the work done: and, on the other hand, the solidity of custom has rendered the supreme service of perpetuating any such change as found general approval. Had each put his individual fancies into practice without restraint, few would have followed his erratic movements: there would have been no corpus, or body of general thought, in which they could have been merged; and, in the absence of written record, they

> might probably have perished without leaving direct successors. But custom supplied a permanent body of general design, on which each fresh mind might try to make some variation for the sake of economy of effort, of increased utility, or more pleasing effect. (Marshall, 1919: 197–8)

2.4 THE LIMITS OF ECONOMIC SCIENCE

What specific contribution does economics bring to understanding how this evolutionary pattern unfolds? Partial equilibrium analysis hardly goes very far. Focusing on a tiny part of the real world, its specific aim is to analyse how the system reacts to exogenous change, readjusting the segment that is more directly exposed to the shock. From the wider perspective of social and economic evolution, this bit of knowledge, when taken in isolation, is almost irrelevant. We have already explained the connection between evolution and partial equilibrium analysis. However, the analytical tools at hand resemble those of mechanics and can only point towards a new equilibrium: a new configuration of the economy emerges from a shift in production and consumption patterns consequent, for instance, on a cattle plague (Marshall, 1920: 369).

If Marshall were moving towards general equilibrium, he should go on to follow the successive waves of change that reverberate onto the rest of the economy. Being interested in a different theoretical problem, that of the evolution of the economy and society, he sets out to consider the more profound modifications that the former is likely to bring about. In the direction indicated by general equilibrium, change is slowly brought to rest; in Marshall's system, by contrast, it is amplified, although along lines which defy his analytical tools. Here is where other social sciences are called in, especially the science of character formation. Partial equilibrium analysis captures the reaction to external change, but this in its turn produces a less visible change in the way human beings think and act, and the latter change is an element of the cumulative succession that in due time will greatly influence the future evolutionary path of the whole system itself (Raffaelli, 2006b). Economics, at least as Marshall knew it, was not equipped to deal with these inner changes brought about by other reactions, the only ones that partial equilibrium analysis could investigate.

What we are left with is an incomplete system of social science, but the missing elements are not those supplied by GET. This explains why Marshall showed little interest in Walras's research programme. The historians concentrated their attention on Marshall's disagreement with Walras concerning 'the right place for mathematics in a treatise on Economics', and this led them to conclude that the former represented the past and the latter the future of the discipline, in which mathematics would play a key role. But the dissent was much deeper, as aptly summarized in the final words of Marshall's letter, which show how distant his own research programme was from Walras's: 'it is most desirable that different seekers after truth should take different routes' (Whitaker, 1996, vol. 1: 300–301).

NOTES

1. The background to the present chapter is to be found in Raffaelli (2003), to which readers are referred. I thank Masashi Kondo and Geoffrey Hodgson for useful comments on an earlier version. The usual disclaimer applies.
2. As Finch (2000: 377) rightly notices 'evolutionary principles of variation, heredity and selection are readily found in Marshall's work and in post-Marshallian contributions, but are rarely formally developed'.
3. Triggered at the beginning of the twentieth century by the rediscovery of Mendel's findings, the neo-Darwinian revolution was led by August Weismann. In Cambridge, its main supporter was William Bateson, Professor of Biology and Marshall's friend and correspondent on genetics and heredity (Whitaker, 1996, vol. 3: 201–2). Bateson's assistance is acknowledged in 1895 in the preface to the third edition of *Principles*, in which Marshall suppressed the unfortunate example of the giraffe's neck, lengthened by use and taken as a representative case of how the struggle for survival works (Guillebaud, 1961: 326). Another change concerning evolution was also introduced in the third edition (see note 5).
4. See Hodgson (2006); for a different and more favourable interpretation, see Metcalfe (2006).
5. The sentence was added to the third edition, almost certainly on William Bateson's advice (see note 3).
6. Following Nelson and Winter (1982), Simon (1996: 48) also maintains that social evolution, in contrast to biological evolution, is Lamarckian.
7. Here Marshall fails to consider that the growth of scientific knowledge often takes place not by accumulation, but through the discovery of new connecting principles that make it easier to acquire the basic tools required for creative work (Simon, 1996: 92).

REFERENCES

Becattini, Giacomo (1975), 'Invito a una rilettura di Marshall', introduction to Alfred Marshall and Mary P. Marshall, *Economia della produzione*, Milano: ISEDI.

Carpenter, William B. (1875), *The Doctrine of Human Automatism*, London and Glasgow: W. Collins, Sons & Co.

Cook, Simon (ed.) (2005), 'Marshall's *Essay on the History of Civilisation*', *Marshall Studies Bulletin*, **9**, available at http://www.dse.unifi.it/marshall/ welcome.htm.

Cook, Simon (2006) 'The early historical notes', in Tiziano Raffaelli, Giacomo Becattini and Marco Dardi (eds), *The Elgar Companion to Alfred Marshall*, Cheltenham, UK and Northampton, MA, USA: Edward Elgar, pp. 31–7.

Cunningham, William (1892), 'The relativity of economic doctrine', *Economic Journal*, **2**, 1–16.

Dardi, Marco (1984), *Il giovane Marshall. Accumulazione e mercato*, Bologna: Il Mulino.

Dardi, Marco (2006), 'Partial equilibrium and period analysis', in Tiziano Raffaelli, Giacomo Becattini and Marco Dardi (eds), *The Elgar Companion to Alfred Marshall*, Cheltenham, UK and Northampton, MA, USA: Edward Elgar, pp. 215–25.

Finch, John H. (2000), 'Is post-Marshallian economics an evolutionary research tradition?', *European Journal of the History of Economic Thought*, **7**, 377–406.

Fujii, Kenji (2006), 'Standardization', in Tiziano Raffaelli, Giacomo Becattini and Marco Dardi (eds), *The Elgar Companion to Alfred Marshall*, Cheltenham, UK and Northampton, MA, USA: Edward Elgar, pp. 407–11.

Groenewegen, Peter D. (1995), *A Soaring Eagle: Alfred Marshall 1842–1924*, Aldershot, UK and Brookfield, US: Edward Elgar.

Guillebaud, Claude W. (ed.) (1961), *Marshall's Principles of Economics*, vol. 2, London: Macmillan.

Hodgson, Geoffrey M. (2006), 'Economics and biology', in Tiziano Raffaelli, Giacomo Becattini and Marco Dardi (eds), *The Elgar Companion to Alfred Marshall*, Cheltenham, UK and Northampton, MA, USA: Edward Elgar, pp. 197–202.

Loasby, Brian J. (1978), 'Whatever happened to Marshall's theory of value?', *Scottish Journal of Political Economy*, **25**, 1–12.

Loasby, Brian J. (1989), *The Mind and Method of the Economist*, Aldershot, UK and Brookfield, US: Edward Elgar.

Loasby, Brian J. (2006a), 'The early philosophical papers', in Tiziano Raffaelli, Giacomo Becattini and Marco Dardi (eds), *The Elgar Companion to Alfred Marshall*, Cheltenham, UK and Northampton, MA, USA: Edward Elgar, pp. 16–25.

Loasby, Brian J. (2006b), 'Making connections', *Storia del Pensiero Economico*, **3**, 69–76.

Marshall, Alfred (1919), *Industry and Trade*, 2nd edn, London: Macmillan.

Marshall, Alfred (1920), *Principles of Economics*, 8th edn, London: Macmillan.

Metcalfe, J. Stanley (2006), 'Evolutionary economics', in Tiziano Raffaelli, Giacomo Becattini and Marco Dardi (eds), *The Elgar Companion to Alfred Marshall*, Cheltenham, UK and Northampton, MA, USA: Edward Elgar, pp. 651–7.

Nelson, Richard R. and Sidney G. Winter (1982), *An Evolutionary Theory of Economic Change*, Cambridge, MA: Harvard University Press.

Raffaelli, Tiziano (ed.) (1994a), 'The early philosophical writings of Alfred Marshall', *Research in the History of Economic Thought and Methodology, Archival Supplement*, **4**, 51–158.

Raffaelli, Tiziano (ed.) (1994b), 'Marshall on "Machinery and life"', *Marshall Studies Bulletin*, **4**, 9–22, available at http://www.dse.unifi.it/marshall/welcome.htm.

Raffaelli, Tiziano (2003), *Marshall's Evolutionary Economics*, London and New York: Routledge.

Raffaelli, Tiziano (2006a), 'Ye Machine', in Tiziano Raffaelli, Giacomo Becattini and Marco Dardi (eds), *The Elgar Companion to Alfred Marshall*, Cheltenham, UK and Northampton, MA, USA: Edward Elgar, pp. 26–30.

Raffaelli, Tiziano (2006b), 'Character and capabilities', in Tiziano Raffaelli, Giacomo Becattini and Marco Dardi (eds), *The Elgar Companion to Alfred Marshall*, Cheltenham, UK and Northampton, MA, USA: Edward Elgar, pp. 488–94.

Simon, Herbert A. (1996), *The Sciences of the Artificial*, 3rd edition, Cambridge, MA: MIT Press.
Veblen, Thorstein (1900), 'The preconceptions of economic science', *Quarterly Journal of Economics*, **14**, 240–69.
Whitaker, John K. (ed.) (1996), *The Correspondence of Alfred Marshall. Economist*, 3 vols, Cambridge: Cambridge University Press.

3. Schumpeter on Marshall: a reconsideration*

Roger E. Backhouse

3.1 INTRODUCTION

This chapter examines Schumpeter's attitude to the work of Alfred Marshall, an economist with whose ideas he engaged throughout his career, from his first book, *Das Wesen und der Hauptinhalt der theoretischen Nationalökonomie* (1908) to his posthumously published *History of Economic Analysis* (1954a). Although he was at times critical of Marshall, and did not heap on him the exaggerated praise he reserved for Antoine Cournot and Léon Walras, he nonetheless considered him one of the four greatest economists ever. The details of his attitude towards Marshall are of interest because Marshall's way of doing economics was not Schumpeter's, and because, late in Schumpeter's life, his attitude towards Marshall became entangled, so it will be argued, with his attitude towards other members of the Cambridge school.

Schumpeter's attitude towards Marshall has received comparatively little attention. There are brief remarks made in the context of much broader studies (for example, Shionoya, 1997). Awan (1986) has compared their views of evolution, but this is comparatively narrow and fails to explore Schumpeter's attitude towards the Marshallian system as a whole. Feiwel (1986) briefly explores Schumpeter's view of Marshall alongside his views of Walras and subsequent developments in economic theory. The one general study is Duval (2002). This takes as its starting point the historiographic perspective of the *History of Economic Analysis* and concludes that had Schumpeter adopted a relativist historiography, he might have been able to see more clearly where and how Marshall went beyond Walras (Duval, 2002: 84). This is an interesting argument but it seems worth exploring the problem from another angle.

The approach taken here is to approach Schumpeter's attitude to Marshall as informed not by his historiography but by his attitude to economic theory: after all, Schumpeter considered himself first and foremost an economist (or social scientist), not primarily a historian. Although the

History of Economic Analysis contains important evidence, this chapter seeks to build up a picture of Schumpeter's attitude on the basis of his earlier writings, only then turning to his final book.

3.2 EARLY REACTIONS TO MARSHALL, 1908–31

Schumpeter first discusses Marshall in the context of the evolution of the history of economics, where he focuses on the relationship between classical and neoclassical economics. Marshall was, for him, representative of the school that, unlike that represented by Jevons, Menger and Walras, emphasized continuity with the classical economists (1908: 16–17). Schumpeter saw this extension of the work of the classical school as a significant achievement, although he did not achieve the same purity and uniformity as Walras had achieved (1908: 140). Part of the reason for Marshall's failure to see things with the same clarity as Walras was his belief in continuity: his motto, '*natura non facit saltum*' applied both to his economics and to his view of the past (1908: 8).

Although Marshall's place in the history of economics, and his failure to recognize the similarity of his theory to that of Walras, was a theme to which Schumpeter returned repeatedly, a question that is more important is the economic analysis that resulted from this approach. The answer is that Schumpeter appreciated Marshall's aggregative concepts. In his article on social value (1909), which took up, for an English-speaking audience, the theme of methodological individualism addressed more fully in his book of the previous year, he observed that Marshall's aggregative concepts of social capital and national dividend were useful (1909: 213). So, too, could Marshall's concept of the representative firm be useful (1909: 217). Although his aim in the article was to argue the case for individualism, and against attributing value to society as a whole, these particular aggregative concepts were exempted from the charge of being conceptually flawed.

This attitude towards Marshall persists in *Economic Doctrine and Method* (1954c [first published in 1912]). The concepts of national wealth and production can be useful, something Schumpeter illustrates with the example of Marshall's work (1954c: 53). Furthermore, whereas in *Das Wesen* he had merely pointed to Marshall's achievement in building on the work of the classical school, here he points to the benefits of Marshall's having not adopted a bolder strategy towards the new marginal utility theory, Marshall was the one who 'directed English theory carefully and slowly, but *the more effectively for that*, on to the new course' (1954c: 185, emphasis added), where the new course referred to marginal utility economics. Schumpeter disagreed with Marshall's view that his work owed much to the classics, commenting on his 'coolness' towards Jevons and the Austrians: Marshall had 'the form, not the essence' of the classical approach, for in reality his theory was the same as theirs. 'Yet in fact he had taken over their whole doctrine, particularly that of Walras so that it would be possible to omit those points in which he deviates from them, without an attentive reader noticing the change' (ibid.). However, although Schumpeter clearly believed that Marshall had not correctly portrayed the relationship of his theory to that of his predecessors and contemporaries, he does not criticize Marshall for this: in the circumstances of the time, such a strategy was the most effective one.

This attitude towards Marshall continues through the 1920s and into the 1930s. Although records of what Schumpeter said on the occasion appear not to have survived, he gave some lectures at LSE, around 1925 or 1926, in which he 'incidentally' praised Marshall (Schumpeter, 1954b: 91). He later recounted how a member of the audience wrote to him to ask whether Marshall's message would not pass away, just as John Stuart Mill's had done. Setting aside for the moment his later response to this question,[1] the significant point about this is that his praise of Marshall, in a talk where he presumably did not need to make any such remark, was sufficiently strong for a listener to object that surely Marshall was not among the immortals.

Schumpeter's next discussions of Marshall come in two articles around 1930. The first is interesting because he chooses to use Marshallian analysis, even though he could, so he claimed, have used Walrasian (1928: 363). The two were the same. The only differences concerned exposition, technique, conceptual tools (such as the demand curve) and problems tackled. Thus, when Schumpeter proceeded, over the next few pages, to analyse the problem of instability, he used notions of supply price and increasing or decreasing cost. These were Marshallian concepts, but although they were the most convenient tools for his purpose, he could in principle have used Walrasian tools instead. Schumpeter repeated his earlier claim that various forms of marginal theory were identical. 'For within serious economic theory there are no such things as "schools" or differences of principle, and the only fundamental cleavage in modern economics is between good work and bad' (Schumpeter, 1928: 363).

The second was his appraisal of Wesley Mitchell's book on business cycles where, in order to criticize Mitchell, he praised Marshall. 'It is natural, in trying to answer this question, to think of that mighty structure which, tho battered in places by the impact of newer methods and results, still stands broadly in the background of much, if not most, of the best work of the day – Marshall's great treatise' (1930: 154). He then went on to draw a methodological contrast, unfavourable to Mitchell:

> Marshall's fame and influence rest on his mastership in constructing tools of analysis, on his having built, out of the material of the theoretic ideas of his time, an engine of analysis. It is the fifth book of the Principles (and matter placed elsewhere which really belongs in that book) which is immortal in the sense in which scientific achievement can ever be called immortal. (ibid.)

This is consistent with what Feiwel (1986: 763) considers the 'extraordinary weight' that Schumpeter was prepared to attach to 'the engine of economic analysis'. Mitchell has no such view but regards theory as 'a store of rational hypotheses' or generalizations from facts. Schumpeter then 'scales down' the difference between Mitchell's world view and Marshall's in order to draw a contrast between the 'Principles' Mitchell might have written and Marshall's. The effect of this is to reinforce Schumpeter's view that Marshall's attitude towards theory is the better one. This is entirely consistent with his view, expressed two decades before, that what Marshall had contributed to economics was techniques that were useful for tackling certain types of problem. Mitchell is reluctant to use theory as a tool: theory could, for example, be used to suggest reasons for different behaviour of the cycle in different countries but Mitchell did not do this (1930: 168). The importance of using good theoretical tools is reiterated in Schumpeter's claim that it is important to recognize 'the serious and even glaring defects' in the equipment available to Schmoller and Veblen, for this lack helps explain and even excuse some of the things they said (1930: 158). In looking for such mistakes, he picked on the implications of the existence of money for economic theory. Mitchell was not guilty of the 'provable error' that 'a money economy must be explained on principles differing *toto caelo* from those applicable to a non-monetary life', but of holding the view that calculation in terms of money had implications for economic life (Schumpeter, 1930: 159–60). Schumpeter argued that this fell into the realm of sociology rather than economics, observing that as far as economists were concerned, this was simply one aspect of the division of labour. The use of theoretical tools helped clarify what was involved in Mitchell's claims (and, of course, showed the error of those who made the stronger, erroneous statement about the implications of money).

From 1931 onwards, Schumpeter's comments on Marshall are explicitly informed by his reading of John Maynard Keynes's memorial (Keynes, 1972: 161–231 [first published in 1924]).[2] In a lecture in Japan in 1931 (Schumpeter, 1991), assessing recent developments, he pointed out that Marshall discovered marginal utility analysis independently of Jevons, something claimed by Keynes, though subsequently disproved by Whitaker's (1975) analysis of Marshall's early economic writings. Echoing his previous theme that all marginal analysis was the same, Schumpeter argued that Marshall was 'marginal utility analysis and nothing else'

(1991: 294). Whereas 20 years earlier he had simply focused on desirable strategic benefits from maintaining this, now he described it as a 'blemish' that Marshall tried to pretend that the two blades of his scissors were not both made of utility.

3.3 SCHUMPETER'S SEMI-CENTENNIAL APPRAISAL OF MARSHALL'S *PRINCIPLES*, 1941[3]

The appraisals of Marshall discussed so far were all limited in scope, either in surveys of economics (historical and contemporary) or, perhaps more revealing, as incidental remarks made in the course of articles on other topics. He praised Marshall in general terms, pointing to the usefulness of the theoretical tools he had created, these tools including various aggregative methods. Schumpeter's first systematic appraisal of Marshall did not come until the end of 1940. The significance of that date will be considered later on. Here we find Schumpeter continuing to praise Marshall and his *Principles*, but it is now combined with much more developed criticism, to the extent that it begins to be possible, for the first time, to see clearly the ways in which Schumpeter's views parted from Marshall's.

Drawing on Keynes's biographical essay (Keynes, 1972), Schumpeter discusses Marshall's move into economics through having translated Mill's doctrines into mathematics in the 1860s. Even though Marshall had the assistance of Cournot, von Thünen and Jevons's paper given to the British Association in 1862, this was, Schumpeter writes, 'a very considerable performance. Many a theoretical physicist has gained immortality for less' (1954b: 96). He considered Marshall's treatment of contemporaries and predecessors, concluding that 'no serious objection can be raised to Marshall's acknowledgement to persons' (1954b: 97).[4] One sting in the tail was that this was only 'subjective originality' (1954b: 95), for the ideas were not in fact new. The more substantial one is Marshall's failure to acknowledge the important part played by mathematics in this achievement: 'the actual use of the methods of mathematical analysis *produced* that achievement and . . . the transformation of the Smith-Ricardo-Mill material into a modern engine of research could hardly have been accomplished without it' (1954b: 97; emphasis added). He cannot make sense of Marshall's reservations about mathematics, gently ridiculing his idea that the *Principles* should be readable by businessmen.

Schumpeter also describes Marshall as 'an economic historian of the first rank', citing *Industry and Trade* (Marshall, 1919).[5] He praised him not on account of his technical historical skills, but because, 'his mastery of historical fact and his analytic habit of mind did not dwell in separate compartments but formed so close a union that the live fact intrudes into the theorem and the theorem into purely historical observations' (1954b: 94). When taken in the context of his endorsement of Marshall's view of theory as an engine of economic analysis, and his criticism of Mitchell for not using it this way, this is strong praise, reinforced by the observation that, within certain limits, 'a realism was attained which greatly surpasses that of Adam Smith – the only comparable instance' – thereby which helped prevent the rise of institutionalism in Britain.[6] Not only was this high praise, especially when compared with Schumpeter's hostility to Mitchell and Veblen, who also sought to theorize in a way that was grounded in reality, but it echoed his earlier remarks on the effectiveness of Marshall's strategy for establishing marginalist economics in Britain. However, when the point is developed, a note of criticism enters. Marshall's integration of theory and facts was one of the reasons why Marshallian economics had passed away:

> His vision of the economic process, his methods, his results, are no longer ours. . . . Marshall's historic-philosophical culture tells on almost every page – his analytic schema is embedded in a luxuriant frame that conciliates and comforts the layman . . . Moreover, his idea of the Noble Life, his views about social problems, his general outlook on the public as well as on the private sphere happened to coincide with the ideas, views, and outlook of his country and his time. More precisely, his ideals and convictions were the ideals and convictions not indeed of the average Englishman of 1890, but of the average intellectual Englishman of 1890. (1954b: 92, 102, 103)

Marshall's ideas had passed away not merely because of the normal obsolescence of ideas caused by theoretical progress, but because his theory was infused with historically specific assumptions and values, with the result that economic and social change had dated them.

A third element in Schumpeter's positive appraisal of Marshall is that he recognizes that there is more to Marshall than the skeleton that his work shares with Walras and other marginal utility theorists: 'Full justice cannot be rendered to it [Marshall's performance] by going straight to the core of the analytic apparatus the *Principles* presents' (1954b: 94). One of the reasons for this was Marshall's 'evolution-mindedness' which spread over into his theoretical work (1954b: 93). In a phrase that was later echoed in his *History*, Schumpeter observed that Marshall pointed beyond himself. Marshall's theory of evolution had been influential, underlying even the econometric research of H.L. Moore (Schumpeter, 1954b: 106). But once again, admiration is accompanied by criticism: the malleability of human nature, central to human nature, as Schumpeter's Harvard colleague

Talcott Parsons (1931) had pointed out, was no longer of interest. Having at last recognized the evolutionary dimension to Marshall, Schumpeter concluded that it was not the right direction.[7] This reinforced Marshall's use of economic history in causing his theory to become dated.

The final, and perhaps most interesting, point again concerns the type of theory he claims that Marshall is creating. Picking up on an argument that goes back to his 1909 article, he argues that Marshall offers an aggregative theory. Marshall pushed general equilibrium theory into the background, focusing on partial equilibrium theory, but at the same time 'launch[ed] out into wide generalizations about the economic process as a whole' – 'a third type of theory – in my own workshop it is called "aggregative"' (1954b: 106). However, where he had, 30 years earlier, praised this as a useful tool of analysis, this time he criticizes him for leaving out money.

> His failure to [link his theory with money] . . . is perhaps the only fundamental criticism that I could level against him. But really, if one starts from partial analysis and then wishes to say something about the economic process as a whole, is it not natural that, despairing of the possibilities of the unwieldy idea of general equilibrium, one should turn to aggregative theory? And would not the theory of money automatically come in, to use Mrs. Robinson's phrase, as the theory of total output and employment? (1954b: 106)

It is impossible not to see here echoes of the debates surrounding Keynes's *General Theory* (1973 [first published in 1936]). Schumpeter was interested in developing Marshall's partial analysis to analyse dynamics, but he did not wish to develop it in the direction of Keynesian aggregative models.

3.4 THE *HISTORY OF ECONOMIC ANALYSIS*

Marshall is cited frequently in Schumpeter's *History*, in the context of money, trade, the firm and many other specific branches of economics. However, for the present purpose, the most relevant passages are the coverage of Marshall in his general appraisal of Marshall (1954a: 834–40) and his discussion of partial equilibrium theory (1954a: 990–98). The former opens, after a bibliographic survey,[8] by comparing Marshall with Smith. Not only were they successful and they shared a vision, in particular in respect to evolution, but there were similarities in the structure of the two books, and both were the polished result of decades of work (1954a: 835). In subsequent pages, Schumpeter praised Marshall the economic theorist, but also Marshall the applied economist.

We find the familiar Schumpeterian theme that Marshall's theory was substantially the same as that of Jevons and Walras,[9] but he denies that

Marshall was an eclectic when he found continuity with Ricardo. 'Marshall's powerful engine of analysis – though it may look antiquated by now – was the result of a creative effort and not of a synthetic one (1954a: 837).[10] Marshall the creative theorist is the creator of the analytic engine, a theme dating back to Schumpeter's earliest writings. But here, Schumpeter also pointed to what the reader who 'pierce[d] the highly polished surface' would find:

> the tremendous wealth of analytic and factual detail, drilled into order by a stupendously skilled taskmaster . . . [and] . . . In the second place, that reader will discover a quality that comes near to constituting Marshall's chief claim to immortality: in Marshall he beholds not only a high-powered technician, a profoundly learned historian, a sure-footed framer of explanatory hypotheses, but above all a great economist. Unlike the technicians of today who, so far as the technique of theory is concerned, are as superior to him as he was to A. Smith, he understood the working of the capitalist process. In particular he understood business, business problems, and businessmen better than did most other scientific economists, not excluding those who were businessmen themselves. He sensed the organic necessities of economic life even more intensively than he formulated them . . . I am afraid that this achievement . . . accounts in part for the unpopularity that surrounds his name today. (1954a: 835–6)

Schumpeter is here painting a picture, not so much of Marshall the economic theorist who created an engine of analysis, but more of the skilled technician who also understands – has a vision of – how capitalist economies worked. The comparison made with the 'technicians of today' – highly qualified economic theorists – might even be a comment that Schumpeter could have made about himself.

Schumpeter also makes a significant criticism of Marshall's treatment of evolution, which serves to distance Marshall from his theoretical engine. The theoretical analysis was static, but this did not stop Marshall from using it to deal with 'evolutionary phenomena or indeed any phenomena of economic life that are refractory to the application of the methods of statics' (1954a: 836). However, to analyse such problems required him to 'get off the driver's seat of his analytic engine, the arms of which do not reach these problems' (1954a: 837). This is a subtle argument, for while praising Marshall for analysing evolution and dynamics, Schumpeter is portraying this work almost as applied economics, detached from the theoretical apparatus Marshall may have sought to tackle evolution, but he was not tackling it as an economic theorist.[11] There is thus a sense in which Schumpeter is portraying Marshall as an applied economist, going beyond what can be said using the theoretical engine.

Evidence as to why Schumpeter was changing the emphasis in the way he was presenting Marshall is found later, where he discusses partial equilibrium analysis (1954a: 990–8). He points to specific concepts (the demand curve, elasticity of demand, the law of substitution) that represent important Marshallian analytical tools. This is a further illustration of the generous tribute he had always paid to Marshall as a maker of useful tools. What is of more interest is his perceptive discussion of what is involved in going beyond Marshall's partial equilibrium analysis. Partial analysis deals with very small pieces of economic activity but, Schumpeter argues, they shade gradually into general analysis. 'It follows that partial analysis is not separated from general analysis by any sharp dividing line but rather shades off into general analysis as we extend the scope of the concepts that have been in the first instance conceived for its purposes' (1954a: 994). Thus partial analysis dealt with industries that are small relative to the whole, and the crucial assumption that supply curves in different industries are independent rests on some very strict assumptions. Had these been exposed, the relevance of the analysis would have been thought very limited but, because Marshall 'clothed his schema with . . . a mass of luxuriant detail', it appeared to be of more importance and even to be 'the backbone' of the study of 'all non-aggregative industrial processes' (1954a: 994). Out of this analysis, designed for units that were but a small part of the whole, emerged concepts such as quasi-rent and the principle of substitution that were useful in general analysis – in analysing the economy as a whole. Tools of partial analysis were thus used to analyse problems that were properly part of a general analysis. Such work raises problems, but Marshall was aware of these: he did not postulate production functions applying to the economy as a whole (1954a: 996).[12]

However, although Marshall was prepared to use partial analysis to analyse problems that were wider in scope, there were limits to how far he would go, for beyond a certain point partial analysis became misleading. At this point, it is useful to recall Schumpeter's earlier (1954c [first published in 1914]; 1954b [first published in 1941]) approval of Marshall's moves towards aggregate analysis: he had argued that such methods were useful for certain problems including quantification. Now, in contrast, he takes a different stance.

> [I]t is obvious from his appendix (note XXI) that, had he wished to go further, he would have sought the necessary complements of partial analysis in the methods of general microanalysis of the Walrasian type rather than in a separate body of aggregate analysis (macroanalysis). (1954a: 997)

The following paragraph explains that this solution, spurned by Marshall, is what appeals to 'members of the Keynesian group', who divide economic theory into a theory of the firm and a macroeconomic theory. Schumpeter concludes, 'It is therefore worth our while to point out . . . the historical connection that exists in this respect between Marshall and his apparently so rebellious followers of the 1930's' (1954a: 997). The Cambridge economists were pursuing a strategy pioneered by Marshall. However, they were applying Marshall's methods to problems to which he would never have applied them, and where Marshall himself would have used Walrasian methods.

At this point it is useful to return to the concluding paragraph of his general appraisal of Marshall.

> More than any other economist – with the exception, perhaps, of Pareto – Marshall pointed beyond himself. He had no theory of monopolistic competition. But he pointed toward it by considering a firm's Special Market. It has been stated above that his pure theory was strictly static, but also that he pointed toward economic dynamics. He did no econometric work. But he always reasoned with an eye to the statistical complement of economic theory and did his best to frame concepts that would be statistically operational . . . Naturally his work is out of date. But there is in it a living spring that prevents it from becoming stale. (1954a: 840)

Marshallian economics was now in the past, unlike that of Walras. However, Marshall's work pointed to the future, to monopolistic competition (and here it is important to note that he distinguished this from Robinson's imperfect competition), dynamics and econometrics. In claiming this, he was claiming Marshall for the econometric movement. Those who were, as it were, his natural heirs (Keynes and those other Cambridge economists developing macroeconomics as something completely separate from microeconomics), had misconstrued his work. Although they may have developed new concepts, they were not so much engaging in revolutionary departures from Marshall, as applying Marshallian methods to problems to which Marshall would, with good reason, never have applied them.

3.5 CONCLUSIONS

Schumpeter admired Marshall as the creator of a remarkable engine of analysis that could be used to analyse the dynamic problems with which Schumpeter was concerned. The theoretical core of his work might be the same as that developed by Jevons and Walras, but he developed that theory in important ways. However, in the accounts he gave of Marshall's work, Schumpeter's emphasis changed significantly. In part this was because his later studies of Marshall's work were more detailed, but in part it also reflected the changing intellectual environment in which he was writing. The starting point is nicely illustrated by a story told by one of his biographers about the only occasion on which they met, in 1907:

> Schumpeter went to Cambridge to visit the venerable Marshall. The spark-filled meeting pitted German youth and impatience, tinged with arrogance, against English age, tranquillity and calm assurance. As gentlemen do on such occasions they met for breakfast. In Marshall's home . . . the constant Mary Marshall hovered about while the young man and the elder statesman talked . . .
>
> Being polite and earnestly seeking advice, the young man queried the great one on topics regarding the fundamentals of economic science, the role of pure economic theory, and the prospects for a young man in economics. Schumpeter already knew from reading Marshall's book much of the attitude of his companion, whose interest in economics stemmed from a utilitarian outlook and a desire to improve the lot of mankind. Perceiving that Schumpeter's interests were nonutilitarian, Marshall replied to the effect that *l'art pour l'art* has but a minor role to play in economics, and that the purely scientific content of economics is not large and has no great significance. He told Schumpeter that he who pursued economics as a pure science wasted his time. Marshall believed that economics was an applied science – a subject for businessmen and statesmen, not for theoretical scientists. (Allen 1991, vol. 1: 61)

In the manuscript he was preparing, he was arguing for the type of pure science to which Marshall was objecting.[13]

However, although they had very different conceptions of economic theory and the nature and role of pure science, Schumpeter shared Marshall's belief that economic theory should be seen as an analytical engine. Although they differed about what dynamic theory should look like, and about how it was related to static theory, they both realized that static theory needed to be extended. Schumpeter thus praised Marshall pointing out that Marshall's methods were useful for specific problems. Moreover, because the background to Schumpeter's earliest writings was the German *Methodenstreit*, Marshall, a known admirer of Schmoller but who was also known as an economic theorist, was an important ally in arguing for the importance of theory. The same considerations applied when Schumpeter engaged with Mitchell and, to a lesser extent, other institutionalists after his move to Harvard.[14] Marshall showed how theory needed to be used – as a tool – when analysing the business cycle.

By the end of the 1930s, however, the situation had changed dramatically. Mitchell's eclectic attitude towards theory was no longer a major concern, the econometric movement was becoming established (Schumpeter having played an important role) and he had a group of mathematically inclined colleagues at Harvard, both theorists and empirical workers. The challenge now was posed by Marshall's students at Cambridge, and Keynesian economics. Schumpeter's assessments of Marshall in this period have to be seen against the background of the methodological critiques made offered in Schumpeter's own (1936; 1954a: 472) methodological critique of Keynes and the Ricardian vice, and in his Harvard colleague, Leontief's (1937) critique of the Cambridge school's method of implicit theorizing. Given the obvious close association between Keynes and Marshall, how was he to respond? By treating Marshall as a theorist whose work had been undertaken against an institutional background that was now dated, and whose brilliance lay in the way he used economic analysis, and by arguing that Marshall, although he had pioneered the techniques being used by the younger generation at Cambridge, would never have gone down the same route as they were following. Marshall was an ally against the younger generation at Cambridge. Simultaneously, presenting Marshall as the supreme user of the engine of economic analysis, combining technical skill with vision of the economic system, served to reinforce his own position in relation to his younger, mathematical colleagues.

Schumpeter's view of Marshall's economics may have been limited in that he failed to appreciate the depth of the latter's evolutionary theorizing. Duval (2002) has blamed this on an absolutist historiography and has suggested that had he adopted a more relativist approach, he might have been able to see more. Schumpeter's historiography certainly did affect his view of Marshall, notably in his repeated concern with originality and Marshall's relations with his predecessors and contemporaries. However, it seems implausible that it was the factor behind his seeing Marshall, as it were, through the lens of his heroes Cournot and Walras. For that we must turn to Schumpeter the theorist, not Schumpeter the historian. Here the answer would seem to be that Marshall's evolutionary thinking was well obscured. Given his treatment of demand and consumer behaviour, it was hard not to take his psychology as utilitarian.[15] It took Parsons, a sociologist, to penetrate the Victorian moralizing (objectionable to Schumpeter) and to perceive the evolutionary dynamics (Parsons, 1931). Therefore the answer as to why Schumpeter failed to appreciate Marshall's evolutionary theorizing more fully is, perhaps, that he did not have the benefit of seeing the unpublished psychological manuscripts uncovered by Raffaelli (2003). Whether those would have changed his view is, however, quite beyond the scope of this chapter.

NOTES

* I wish to thank Yuichi Shionoya for his invaluable comments on an earlier draft and for drawing attention to some errors that I hope are now eliminated. This chapter was first written while I was Ludwig Lachmann Fellow in the Department of Philosophy at the London School of Economics. I wish to thank the Charlottenberg Trust for its support.

1. Discussed in section 3.3 below.
2. The last two works cited, published in 1928 and 1930, might have been written after Schumpeter first read Keynes's essay, but there is no indication of it.
3. It should also be noted that though the 1941 paper was based on a talk given in 1940, Schumpeter (1954b: 91) observed that it contained some remarks taken from an earlier, unpublished paper. That paper had clearly been written before he absorbed the message of Keynes's biography of Marshall, but Schumpeter does not make it clear whether that was after the 1924, 1925 or 1933 editions, all of which he cites.
4. It is worth noting that, recent scholarship has shown that, even apart from the treatment of Jevons discussed above, this remark was undeservedly generous (O'Brien, 1990).
5. Although Schumpeter would presumably have been well aware that, for all that he praised it, economic historians would have been more critical of *Industry and Trade*.
6. It is, of course, relevant to point out that Schumpeter did not place Smith in the pantheon alongside Cournot and Walras, but at a lower level, later evaluating the *Wealth of Nations* as containing no original ideas. Comparison with Smith is in itself two-edged.
7. Marshallian and Schumpeterian attitudes to evolution have been discussed elsewhere, and will not be explored here.
8. This draws attention to Shove (1942), an article that seeks to differentiate Marshall's economics from the more formal work being done by Joan Robinson and others in the 1930s.
9. See also 1954a: 952.
10. This leads into a discussion of Marshall's originality, more detailed than earlier assessments, but significantly changing the assessment.
11. This is not to imply that there were not other differences between Marshall's and Schumpeter's concepts of evolution, or that these differences were not very important.
12. Given that Schumpeter is emphasizing substitution and income distribution, and is denying the appropriateness of aggregate production functions, he would appear to have in mind here targets such as Hicks (1933) rather than simply Keynes.
13. Given that Marshall was on poor terms with Schumpeter's teacher, Böhm-Bawerk (O'Brien, 1990: 134; Whitaker, 1996, vol. 3: 99) there was all the more reason for Schumpeter to be critical of him. However, Marshall was notoriously averse to public controversy and according to Stolper (1994: 6) Schumpeter never allowed his scholarly opinions to be affected by personal feelings.
14. For this argument it is not necessary to take a view on the development of Schumpeter's attitude towards Schmoller and the institutionalists, as discussed by Hodgson (2001: 187–9).
15. Where utilitarian is understood in the sense of Bentham, Mill and Sidgwick.

REFERENCES

Allen, R.L. (1991), *Opening Doors: The Life and Work of Joseph Schumpeter*, 2 vols, New Brunswick, NJ: Transaction.

Awan, A.A. (1986), 'Marshallian and Schumpeterian theories of economic evolution: gradualism versus punctualism', *Atlantic Economic Journal*, **14** (4): 37–49.

Duval, N. (2002), 'Schumpeter on Marshall', in R. Arena and C. Dangel-Hagnauer (eds), *The Contribution of Joseph Schumpeter to Economics: Economic Development and Institutional Change*, London: Routledge, pp. 66–85.

Feiwel, G.R. (1986), 'Schumpeter on Walras, Marshall, and beyond', *Rivista Internazionale di Scienze Economiche e Commerciali*, **33** (8): 729–61.

Hicks, J.R. (1933), *The Theory of Wages*, London: Macmillan.

Hodgson, G.M. (2001), *How Economics Forgot History*, London: Routledge.

Keynes, J.M. (1972), *Essays in Biography*, in *The Collected Writings of John Maynard Keynes*, vol. 10, London: Macmillan.

Keynes, J.M. (1973 [1936]), *The General Theory of Employment, Interest and Money*, in *The Collected Writings of John Maynard Keynes*, vol. 7, London: Macmillan.
Leontief, W.A. (1937), 'Implicit theorizing: a methodological criticism of the neo-Cambridge school', *Quarterly Journal of Economics*, **51** (2): 337–51.
Marshall, A. (1919), *Industry and Trade*, London: Macmillan.
O'Brien, D.P. (1990), 'Marshall's work in relation to classical economics', in J. Whitaker (ed.), *Centenary Essays on Alfred Marshall*, Cambridge: Cambridge University Press, pp. 127–63.
Parsons, T. (1931), 'Wants and activities in Marshall', *Quarterly Journal of Economics*, **46** (1): 101–40.
Raffaelli, T. (2003), *Marshall's Evolutionary Economics*, London: Routledge.
Schionoya, Y. (1997), *Schumpeter and the Idea of Social Science*, Cambridge: Cambridge University Press.
Schumpeter, J.A. (1908), *Das Wesen und der Hauptinhalt der theoretischen Nationaloekonomie*, Munich: Duncker & Humblot.
Schumpeter, J.A. (1909), 'On the concept of social value', *Quarterly Journal of Economics*, **23**: 213–32.
Schumpeter, J.A. (1928), 'The instability of capitalism', *Economic Journal*, **38**: 361–86.
Schumpeter, J.A. (1930), 'Mitchell's business cycles', *Quarterly Journal of Economics*, **45**: 150–72.
Schumpeter, J.A. (1936), 'Review of J.M. Keynes's *General Theory of Employment, Interest and Money*', *Journal of the American Statistical Association*, **31**: 791–95.
Schumpeter, J.A. (1954a), *History of Economic Analysis*, New York: Oxford University Press.
Schumpeter, J.A. (1954b), *Ten Great Economists: From Marx to Keynes*, London: Routledge.
Schumpeter, J.A. (1954c), *Economic Doctrine and Method: A Historical Sketch*, trans. R. Aris, London: Allen & Unwin.
Schumpeter, J.A. (1991), *The Economics and Sociology of Capitalism*, ed. R. Swedberg, Princeton, NJ: Princeton University Press.
Shove, G.F. (1942), 'The place of Marshall's Principles in the development of economic theory', *Economic Journal*, **52** (208), 294–329.
Stolper, W.F. (1994), *Joseph Alois Schumpeter: The Public Life of a Private Man*, Princeton, NJ: Princeton University Press.
Whitaker, J.K. (ed.) (1975), *The Early Economic Writings of Alfred Marshall, 1867–1890*, London: Macmillan.
Whitaker, J.K. (1996), *The Correspondence of Alfred Marshall, Economist*, 3 vols, Cambridge: Cambridge University Press.

PART II

Social Science and Evolution

4. On the relation between economics and sociology: Marshall and Schumpeter*

Richard Arena

This contribution is devoted to the relationship between economics and sociology in the respective works of Alfred Marshall and Joseph Schumpeter. Differences are unavoidable between these authors if we consider their different periods of life and their specific ways of connecting both disciplines. Marshall began to write papers and books in the period of birth and early development of sociology, while Schumpeter could attend and even participate in its period of maturity. However, in spite of these differences, we try to show that Marshall and Schumpeter shared a common conception of the role of economic theory within the realm of social science. To put it in a few words, they both considered that economic analysis (in its Schumpeterian sense) could not be reduced to pure economic theory as it is often argued in the post-Walrasian tradition (in contradiction, however, to the works of Léon Walras himself) but had to combine this theory and history with the intermediary help of what Schumpeter called 'economic sociology' and Marshall called a 'reasoned history of man'. Our chapter comprises two sections. The first focuses on the nature of the complementarity that Marshall and Schumpeter pointed out between economic theory and sociology. The second shows how both authors incorporated the investigation of organization forms and economic institutions within economic analysis, and why their approaches may provide some ideas and tools for the modern economist who is not satisfied with axiomatic approaches.

4.1 ECONOMICS AND SOCIOLOGY IN MARSHALL AND SCHUMPETER: AN INTRODUCTION

Marshall's 'Reasoned History of Man'

Alfred Marshall was aware of the first developments of sociology at the end of the nineteenth century but he was also inclined to underestimate its potential developments. One of the main explanations of his scepticism as regards sociology is certainly his critique of the contribution of Auguste Comte (cf. Marshall, 1916: 771, app. C):

> The present movement towards Sociology in America, England and other countries recognizes the need for the intensive study of economics and other branches of social science. But perhaps the use of the term Sociology is premature. For it seems to claim that a unification of social sciences is already in sight: and though some excellent intensive studies have been published under the name of Sociology, it is doubtful whether those efforts at unification which have been made so far have achieved any great success beyond that of preparing the way and erecting danger posts at its pitfalls for the guidance of later generations . . . (Marshall, 1916: 771, n. 1)

These statements, however, do not mean that Marshall was a strict defender of pure economics. Quite the contrary, in 1899, he wrote to his colleague William Hewins:

> It seems strange to me to be asked my views as to the study of pure economic theory; as tho' that were a subject on wh[ich] I were fit to speak. For indeed I was never a partisan of it; & for more than a quarter of a century I have set my face away from it. As early as 1873 (I think that was the year) Walras pressed me to publish something about it; & I declined with emphasis.
>
> The fact is I am the dull mean man, who holds Economics to be an organic whole, & has as little respect for pure theory (otherwise than a branch of mathematics or the science of numbers), as for that crude collection & interpretation of facts without the aid of high analysis which sometimes claims to be a part of economic history. (Marshall, 12th October 1899, letter to William Albert Samuel Hewins, in Marshall, 1996, vol. 2: 256)

The last sentence of this quotation offers a good summary of Marshall's viewpoint. Thus, in his 'Present Position of Economics' (in 1885) (1925 [1966]), he attributes to economic theory as such the role it has to play within social science. He defines the 'economic organon' as the 'analysis of the positive motives of desire for different goods, and of the negative motives of unwillingness to undergo the fatigues and sacrifices involved in producing them' (Marshall, 1925 [1966]: 161). He then rejects two opposite approaches.

The first consists in 'separating' the 'study of economic from that of other social phenomena' (ibid.: 161) and using a pure 'formal analysis' (ibid.: 164). This approach appears to be wrong if it is 'exaggerated' and this is the reason why Marshall was so sceptical about pure economic theory. However, the fact that 'complex social phenomena are . . . intricately interwoven with one another' (ibid.: 161) does not plead in favour of a new synthetic social science that will replace both sociology and economics. The adequate methodology consists 'to break the problem up into its several parts' (ibid.: 164), to utilize the different sciences which are needed one after the other and then to draw conclusions. From this standpoint, the 'economic organon' must be used in its proper place, that is, the analysis of the part of a given social phenomenon which is related to 'those actions and sacrifices which commonly have a money price' (ibid.: 164).

The second approach which Marshall rejects is the one which 'urges . . . to reason direct from facts to facts, without the intervention of any formal theory' (ibid.: 163). Observation does not allow actually to discover the 'causes' of actions and 'gives no guidance except for . . . cases in which exactly the same set of facts occurs over again, grouped in just the same way. [Now] . . . history does not repeat itself' (ibid.: 163).

Marshall appears therefore to be in favour of a combination of economic theory (that is, the 'economic organon'), of common sense ('the final arbiter' according to Marshall in 1885; 1925 [1966]: 164) and of economic history (Marshall, 1916: 774–5). The methodological reference to common sense should not be neglected. It is nothing more than the means to deal with complexity in breaking problems into their component parts and discussing 'one set of considerations after another' (Marshall, 1925 [1966]: 164). For instance, economic history helps to understand 'what has been the institutional framework of society at the several periods, what has been the constitution of the various social classes and their relation to one another' (Ashley, *On the study of economic history*, quoted by Marshall, 1916: 775). It concerns the organization of labour, the various forms of production and distribution, the institutional set-up of the economic system, and so on. Therefore, what is called by Marshall 'economic history' is closer to an analytical view of social organization, institutions and institutional change rather than to an accumulation of facts. This definition of economic history explains Marshall's 1897 characterization of 'social science' as '*the reasoned history of man*' (our emphasis) since according to the author, 'the two things are the same' (Marshall, 1925 [1966]: 299). This historical feature of social science explains why Marshall's combination of economic history and theory is useful when he is considering economic dynamics.

To understand this statement, it is first necessary to remind ourselves of Marshall's conception of economic agents. This conception is different from an axiomatic one according to which it is possible 'to construct an abstract science with regard to the actions of an "economic man", who is under no ethical influences and who pursues pecuniary gain warily and energetically, but mechanically and selfishly' (Marshall, 1916: XIV). According to Marshall, the main topic of economists is to study the behaviours of 'ordinary people' (Marshall, 1916: XIV) and this is why he defined 'political economy or economics' as 'a study of mankind in the ordinary business of life' (Marshall, 1916: 1). 'Ordinary people' certainly imply normality. Now, if economies are considered to be in a 'normal' state, social interaction among agents corresponds to Marshall's 'normal economic action', namely 'which may be expected in the long run under certain conditions (provided those conditions are persistent) from the members of an industrial group' (Marshall, 1916: 34). This standpoint explains why Marshall abandoned what he considered to be a too extreme form of individualism and developed an original view of the relation between individuals and society:

> Perhaps the earlier English economists confined their attention too much to the motives of individual action. But in fact economists, like all other students of social science, are concerned with individuals chiefly as members of the social organism. As a cathedral is something more than the stones of which it is made, as a person is something more than a series of thoughts and feelings, so the life of society is something more than the sum of the lives of its individual members. It is true that the action of the whole is made up of that of its constituent parts; and that in most economic problems the best starting-point is to be found in the motives that affect the individual, regarded not indeed as an isolated atom, but as a member of some particular trade or industrial group. (Marshall, 1916: 25)

This view means that agents had to be considered as embedded agents, belonging to a specific historical and social context and to a particular group or trade. Within statics, this remark is not crucial since the logic of 'economic man' is prevailing: The predominant motive is pecuniary self-interest and the economist can easily neglect other social motives. On the contrary, within dynamics, the 'economic man' is replaced by the 'man of flesh and blood' or the 'man as he is' (Marshall, 1916: 27). New motives have to be considered and, therefore, pure economic theory is no longer sufficient; it must be completed by other social sciences as history or sociology.

A good illustration is provided by Marshall's 1907 characterization of the motives of 'economic chevalry' (Marshall, 1925 [1966]: 323–46). Before Schumpeter but perhaps not independently from Wieser, Marshall actually developed the idea that, in market economies, a 'chivalry in business' replaced the 'chivalry in war' of the Middle Ages (Marshall, 1925 [1966]: 329). Now, as in Schumpeter later, even if Marshall did not really see innovation as the predominant function of entrepreneurship, one of the main characteristics of entrepreneurs is that their rationality cannot be reduced to pecuniary self-interest. On the one hand, 'chivalry in business' includes public spirit. Entrepreneurs earn profits but 'they may be' – and often are – 'proud of the elevation of life which have been achieved by training the finer elements of human nature to full account in the production of wealth and in its use' (Marshall, 1925 [1966]: 330). Therefore, it is clear that self-interest strictly speaking is not the only motive of entrepreneurs even if they do not disdain to gain profits. On the other hand, Marshall also foreruns Schumpeter's developments on 'energetic' rationality. He notes that among the main motives, it is also necessary to include 'a delight in doing noble and difficult things because they are noble and difficult' (Marshall, 1925 [1966]: 330). This motive is therefore subjective and it is impossible to measure it, but it can be evaluated indirectly by the degrees of success and of leadership obtained by a given businessman.

Another example of the difficulties related to the use of the concepts of 'economic man', and of the self-interest assumption, comes from Marshall's conception of society. It is clear that his rejection of atomism, subjectivism or selfish individualism excludes a view which characterizes society as a set of competitive and isolated individuals. Marshall indeed accepts the idea that society presupposes social interaction between individuals. Even if he never built a complete theory of social interaction in an economy, his writings reveal a very rich vision of inter-individual relations. Marshall was indeed perfectly aware that 'in human conduct one condition does not control another, but altogether they mutually determine one another' and that 'to grasp at one view this manifold mutual action is a very difficult task' (Marshall, 1925 [1966]: 161). However, he offered a typology of social interaction which we can reconstruct. First, Marshall stressed *innovative behaviour*. A good illustration is provided by behaviour based on 'trial and error':

> When we speak of the measurement of desire by the action to which it forms the incentive, it is not to be supposed that we assume every action to be deliberate, and the outcome of calculation. For in this, as in every other respect, economics takes man just as he is in ordinary life: and in ordinary life people do not weight beforehand the results of every action, whether the impulses to it come from their higher nature or their lower.
>
> Now the side of life with which economies is specially concerned is that in which man's conduct is most deliberate, and in which he most often reckons up the advantages and disadvantages of any particular action before he enters on it. And further it is that side of his life in which, when he does follow habit and customs, and proceeds for the moment without calculation, the habits and customs themselves are most nearly sure to have risen from a close and careful watching of the advantages and disadvantages of different courses of conduct.

> There will not in general have been any formal reckoning up of two sides of a balance-sheet: but men going home from their day's work, or in their social meetings, will have said to one another, 'It did not answer to do this, it would have been better to do that', and so on. (Marshall, 1916: 20–21)

Therefore, according to this view, agents are involved in a learning more than an optimizing process. They are confronted with various types of uncertainty and they react by experimenting solutions according to their current expectations, which clearly requires a procedural rationality. The process of trial and error described by Marshall also implies a confrontation with other agents. Thus, *learning processes* are also *teaching processes* for other agents:

> Again, each man profits by the ideas of his neighbours: he is stimulated by contact with those who are interested in his own pursuit to make new experiments; and each successful invention, whether it be a new machine, a new process, or a new way of organizing the business, is likely when once started to spread and to be improved upon. (Marshall and Marshall, 1881: 53)

Therefore, the trial and error behaviour reveals a double aspect. On the one hand, it is a procedural device which allows the agent to face uncertainty and try to find in historical time a satisfactory solution to the problems faced. On the other hand, it also provides a process of dissemination of private knowledge. In other words, while performing his experiments, the agent teaches his neighbours a part of his own knowledge. However, the reverse might also happen if the other agents try to help our first agent to solve the problem. This means that a generalization of Marshall's 'social meetings' at the level of the whole society could be interpreted as a massive process of codification of private or tacit knowledge into a social one. Learning and knowledge diffusion are here conceived as simultaneous processes. They provoke the kind of *concentration of capabilities* which occur in industrial districts through reciprocal education (Marshall and Marshall, 1881: 53). They include the different forms of learning, whether by using or by doing. Individual motivations are not hedonistic here. Moreover, they are incompatible with a scheme in which pure 'economic men' are only related by a unique centralized price mechanism (as in post-Walrasian price theory) and not through a set of various decentralized social interactions.

The analysis of the impact of social interaction on the economic system provides a second example of the reasons which led Marshall to combine economic theory and economic sociology and/or social interaction models. As in the case of chivalry behaviour, the 'economic organon' is insufficient to analyse the complexity of some economic phenomena which are founded on usual economic rationality but also on other 'good reasons', beliefs or motives.

Schumpeter's Techniques of Economic Analysis

It is now time to recall Schumpeter's own characterization of the role of economic sociology as a complementary technique, alongside the three techniques of economic analysis he lists at the beginning of his *History of Economic Analysis*, namely, history, statistics and 'theory':

> The schemata of economic theory derive the institutional frameworks within which they are supposed to function from economic history, which alone can tell us what sort of society it was, or is, to which the theoretical schemata are to apply. Yet, it is not only economic history that renders this service to economic theory. It is easy to see that when we introduce the institution of private poverty or of free contracting or else a greater or smaller amount of government regulation, we are introducing social facts that are not simply economic history but are a sort of generalized or typified or stylized economic history. And this applies still more to the general forms of human behavior which we assume either in general or for certain social situations but not for others . . . To use a felicitous phrase: economic analysis deals with the questions how people behave at any time and what the economic effects are they produce by so behaving; economic sociology deals with the questions [of] how they came to behave as they do. If we define human behavior widely enough so that it includes not only actions and motives and propensities but also *the social institutions* that are relevant to economic behavior such as government, property inheritance, contract, and so on, that phrase really tells us what we need. (Schumpeter, 1954: 20–21; emphasis added)

In this passage, Schumpeter explains the relationship between economic analysis and economic sociology. To get the full picture, it is, however, necessary to complement this statement with Schumpeter's remarks on this question in *Das Wesen und der Hauptinhalt der theoretischen Nationalökonomie* as well as in his sociological writings. These texts do, in effect, add considerable substance to Schumpeter's statement in the above passage. Careful reading reveals that Schumpeter regarded the 'science of organisation' as part of economic sociology (Schumpeter, 1908: 133). Thus, economic sociology includes

> the science of State forms but also the science of the forms of law and of the remaining social relations and structures and, thirdly, the science of economic organisation as such: on the one hand, the division of labour and on the other hand, the formation of cartels, of labour associations, etc. (Schumpeter, 1908: 133)

What Schumpeter argues in his *History of Economic Analysis* is that, for the economist, history provides the raw material that consists of empirical sets of diverse institutions and forms of organization. However, this raw material requires further work in order to produce the assumptions that are made when the economist sets out to build an economic theory. First, economic sociology must 'generalize', 'typify' and 'stylize' the empirical forms of institutions and organizations in order to transform the historical set from which they are drawn into a more abstract set of ideal types on which the economist can then build his analytical assumptions. Second, referring to the example of fiscal sociology, Schumpeter (1918 [1953]: 177, n. 18) emphasizes that the historical order according to which institutions and organizational forms emerge, develop and decline *must not* be confused with the analytical process by which sociology provides a logical explanation of these changes. Seen thus, historical chronology is partially arbitrary, whereas economic sociology must respect the necessary requirements of consistent analysis. Third, economic sociology must extract from history what is strictly economic, and this obviously presupposes a relative autonomy or 'self-containment' of the economic sphere (Schumpeter, 1908: 135). Schumpeter provides an illuminating example of this when he argues that the legal aspects of the institution of credit (namely, the strict requirement for the borrower to repay the lender) must be distinguished from – but also determine – its economic aspects (namely, the implications of this requirement for the expectations and economic behaviour of agents) (Schumpeter, 1917–18 [1956]: 155–7). Finally, if we consider economic activity from the point of view of dynamics, it can also create feedback effects on institutions, organization or law. A case in point is Schumpeter's analysis of taxation and, more specifically, his emphasis on the limitations of fiscal impositions arising from the need not to squeeze profits beyond a certain point (Schumpeter, 1918 [1953]: 149). Economic sociology, according to Schumpeter, can thus be defined as the science of the emergence, maintenance and decline of societal institutions and forms of organization that influence economic behaviour.

From this standpoint, according to Schumpeter, human motives are never strictly individual. Rather, as in Marshall, they are always embedded in a social context and related to the historical circumstances under which they have emerged. From this point of view, two main concepts are essential.

On the one hand, following Wieser's conception of economic sociology, Schumpeter argues that, whatever the social environment, men are always divided into two categories: leaders and followers. It should, however, be noted that Schumpeter does not regard leaders as superior or 'great men' (Schumpeter, 1927 [1951]: 216). They are not in possession of special intellectual qualities that would lead them to play a pre-eminent social role. Nor do they have a conscious concept of social optimality that they would strive to put into practice (ibid.). Rather, '[w]e are content to say that social leadership means to decide, to command, to prevail, to advance. As such it is a special function, always clearly discernible in the actions of the individual and within the social whole' (ibid.: 217).

Leaders' motives are related to their 'instinctive urge to domination' (Schumpeter, 1919 [1951]: 15), an 'excess of energy' (ibid.: 34) or 'activity urges springing from capacities and inclinations that had once been crucial to survival, though they had now outlived their usefulness' (ibid.: 44). These 'urges' (or this *Trieb*, ibid.: 83) are defined by Schumpeter as human inclinations that have more to do with 'instinct' than with reason (ibid.: 83–4). They involve creativity and entail permanent changes to the sphere in which they appear (be this the arts, science, economic activity, and so on). Always following Wieser, Schumpeter regards followers as playing a more passive role in that they are the mere recipients of leaders' decisions, acting to diffuse them. They can reinforce these decisions and contribute to their social generalization through the adoption of imitative behaviour or the manifestation of trust. But they can also resist them, slowing down the process of diffusion or sometimes even preventing the mechanisms of social diffusion from working.

On the other hand, however, leadership is not independent from the social context in which it appears. Schumpeter strongly stresses this aspect of social behaviour. First, the *Trieb* or 'urge' provides only part of the social explanation of leaders' motives. Referring to warlike societies, Schumpeter argues that

> [t]he explanation lies, instead, in the vital needs of situations that molded peoples and classes into warriors – if they wanted to avoid extinction – and in the fact that psychological dispositions and social structures acquired in the dim past in such situations, once firmly established, tend to maintain themselves and to continue in effect long after they have lost their meaning and their life-preserving function. (Schumpeter, 1919 [1951]: 83–4)

Second, the social scientist must also integrate the 'subsidiary factors that facilitate the survival of such dispositions and structures' (ibid.). Put differently, he must pay attention to the interests of social classes and of those individuals whose interests are being served by maintaining a state of war. In other words, the second concept that needs to be introduced at this stage of our discussion is the concept of 'social class'. For Schumpeter, a social class is defined as a set of individuals who, in a specific social context, are able to perform a given and specific social function:

> The ultimate foundation on which the class phenomenon rests consists of individual differences in aptitude. What is meant is not differences in an absolute

> sense, but differences in aptitude with respect to those functions which the environment makes 'socially necessary' – in our sense – at any given time; and with respect to leadership, along lines that are in keeping with those functions. (Schumpeter, 1927 [1951]: 210)

Schumpeter, therefore, does not seem to think that it is possible to define social classes from either a purely individualistic or holistic methodological point of view: 'We cannot help those who are unable to see that the individual is a *social* fact, the psychological an *objective* fact, who cannot give up toying with the empty contrasts of the individual *vs.* the social, the subjective *vs.* the objective' (Schumpeter, 1927 [1951]: 211, original emphasis). This characterization of social classes explains why class interest exists as such, and why the fact that an individual belongs to a given social class influences this individual in a way that does not solely depend on his or her own free will but also on what Wieser called social 'compulsory forces'.

What then is the relationship between leadership and social classes? It is clear that, for Schumpeter, these two ideal typical concepts must be carefully distinguished. In a market economy for instance, leaders – that is, entrepreneurs – do *not* form a social class (Schumpeter, 1912; 1934 [1978]; 1939: 104). Although they exert a strong influence on social order through their innovative role, thus contributing to the evolution of the social structure, this does not imply that 'the entrepreneurial function will *lead* to certain class positions for the successful entrepreneur and his family' (Schumpeter, 1912 [1934]: 78). Moreover, the entrepreneurial function cannot be inherited (ibid.: 79). Finally, leaders use the social structure to achieve their ends. For instance, in ancient Egypt, kings used the military aristocracy to organize society according to their own objectives (Schumpeter, 1919 [1951]: 165).

Entrepreneurs are the economic leaders of the market economy. This represents 'a fundamental truth of the sociology of industrial society' (Schumpeter, 1939: 96) since entrepreneurs create the 'institutional patterns' of economic development. The excess energy that characterized the leaders of ancient societies based on aristocratic hierarchies and military objectives now turns into what Schumpeter calls 'energetic'– as opposed to 'hedonistic' – rationality or egoism in *Das Wesen des Geldes* as well as in the first German edition of the *Theory of Economic Development* in modern societies,

> [t]here is much less excess energy to be vented in war and conquest than in any pre-capitalist society. What excess energy there is, flows largely into industry itself, accounts for its shining figures – the type of the captain of industry – . . . In a purely capitalist world, what was once energy for war becomes simply energy for labor of every kind. (Schumpeter, 1919 [1951]: 90)

In market economies, excess energy is channelled into the introduction of innovations, such as new products or new productive techniques. These innovations do not result from exogenous shocks or endogenous mechanisms of technology creation generated by firm managers or owners. Rather, they are introduced by what Schumpeter called 'New Men' (Schumpeter, 1939: 96). In other words, they presuppose the emergence of leaders who use their excess energy to promote the transition from the circular flow to economic development. Therefore, innovations and economic development appear to be the natural consequences of the particular new form of leadership that prevails in a market economy.

However, innovations do not last for ever. Gradually, they are diffused throughout the economic system and transformed into routines or 'habitual economic methods' (Schumpeter, 1912; 1934: 8). As they come to prevail, these individual routines and the resulting network of social rules or norms eventually produce the 'institutional patterns' that pervade the markets and influence the internal organization of the firm.

4.2 FORMS OF ORGANIZATION AND INSTITUTIONS

Marshall, Social Organization and Economic Institutions

As soon as 1879, Alfred Marshall and Mary Paley gave their definition of *organization*:

> A body is said to be highly *organized* when each part has its own work to perform, when by performing this work, it contributes to the well-being of the whole; while, on the other hand, each part depends for its own well-being on the efficient working of the other parts. (Marshall and Marshall, 1881: 45–6; original emphasis)

Since, for Marshall, firms, 'industrial towns', districts, nations and so on are all organized, this view of organization implies that individual agents cannot be conceived as homogeneous atoms playing the same role in the economy. Agents have specific 'works' to 'perform'; these 'works' are complementary and their combination is the condition of an 'efficient working' of the system. Therefore, to a certain extent, agents are always heterogeneous and the key which permits us to understand how this heterogeneity is compatible with the existence of a coherent system lies in the understanding of the principle of organization, namely, of a rule which is exogenous to individual agents and assigns to them specific functions to perform. This is the significance of Marshall's well-known metaphor of the cathedral, which we referred to earlier.

This metaphor also stresses the importance given by Marshall to the problem of individual interaction. However, individual interaction is not only behavioural. It is also organizational. To explain this circumstance, Marshall refers to a biological analogy, pointing out the

> fundamental unity of action between the laws of nature in the physical and in the moral world. This central unity is set forth in the general rule, to which there are not very many exceptions, that the development of the organism, whether social or physical, involves an increasing subdivision of functions between its separate parts on the one hand, and on the other a more intimate connection between them. (Marshall, 1916: 241)

Then, Marshall makes more precise this coexistence of differentiation and unification, stressing that

> this increased subdivision of functions, or 'differentiation', as it is called, manifests itself with regard to industry in such forms as the division of labor, and the development of socialized skill, knowledge and machinery: while 'integration', that is, a growing intimacy and firmness of the connections between the separate parts of the industrial organism, shows itself in such forms as the increase of security of commercial credit, and of the means and habits of communication by sea and road, by railway and telegraph, by post and printing press. (Marshall, 1916: 241)

At the level of the nation, this 'differentiation' entails the emergence of what Marshall calls 'sections', 'strata' or 'compartments' in *Industry and Trade* (Marshall, 1923: 8) and corresponds to social division of labour. At the level of the firm, it corresponds to technical division of labour and specialization. This is why Marshall notes that organization 'has many forms, e.g., that of a single business, that of various businesses in the same trade, that of various trades relatively to one another, and that of the State providing security for all and help for many' (Marshall, 1916: 138).

The reference to 'integration' reminds us that differentiation must be compatible with inter-individual co-ordination and the examples of railways, telephones, telegraphs and so on given by Marshall show how travel facilities, geographical mobility and the development of communication means make co-ordination easier.

Marshall's concept of organization seems to imply that the adaptation of the 'social organism' obeys natural laws comparable to the laws of mechanics and independent from individual behaviour. This is, however, a first impression which must be dissipated. On the one hand, individual agents are not naturally and necessarily adapted to the organizational constraints they have to face. In the context of economic change, they must learn how to adapt and that takes time and requires 'trial and error' behaviour. On the other hand, the concrete organizational forms are shaped by innovative individual decisions, which means that the *accumulation of the different* behaviour exert feedback effects on organization. The analysis of the interaction between organization and human behaviour, however, implies the investigation of the role played by technology.

The characterization of organization proposed by Marshall in relation with the notions of differentiation and integration is sufficiently general to be applied to any type of social 'body': the biological analogy still confirms this interpretation. However, in his contributions, Marshall essentially applied the concept of organization to the activity of production. This choice appears clearly in one of the most famous passages of the beginning of Book 4 of Marshall's *Principles* dedicated to 'the agents of production'. More specifically, organization is initially related to one of these agents, namely, capital:

> Capital consists in a great part of knowledge and organization: and of this some part is private property and other part is not. Knowledge is our most powerful engine of production; it enables us to subdue Nature and force her to satisfy our wants. Organization aids knowledge . . .
>
> In a sense there are only two agents of production, nature and man. Capital and organization are the result of the work of man aided by nature, and directed by his power of forecasting the future and his willingness to make provision for it. If the character and powers of nature and of man be given, the growth of wealth and knowledge and organization follow from them as effect from cause. But on the other hand man is himself largely formed by his surroundings, in which nature plays a great part: and thus from every point of view man is the centre of the problem of production as well as that of consumption; and also of that further problem of the relations between the two, which goes by the twofold name of Distribution and Exchange.
>
> The growth of mankind in numbers, in health and strength, in knowledge, ability, and in richness is an aim to which economics can do no more than contribute some important elements. (Marshall, 1916: 138–9)

This quotation implies that the change of the character of man and mankind is the ultimate end of the theory of economic evolution. However, in the economic framework, the activities of production, consumption and distribution of wealth which it carries have not the same role in the explanation. For Marshall, production (and related to it, productive organization and knowledge) is the main 'engine'. This view is developed in chapter 2 of Book 3 of the *Principles* dedicated to 'wants in relation to activities'. In this chapter, Marshall indeed stresses the importance of the variety of wants we will consider later but he subordinates this increase of the number of wants to the evolution of the activities which permits it:

> Speaking broadly therefore, although it is man's wants in the earliest stages of his development that give rise to his activities, yet afterwards each new step

> upwards is to be regarded as the development of new activities giving rise to new wants, rather than of new wants giving rise to new activities. (Marshall, 1916: 89)

Marshall also gave a fundamental role to economic *institutions* in his conception of economics. We, however, favour here a specific example, namely, the case of *national institutions* since it is both central and meaningful in the Marshallian framework (for a more detailed approach, see Arena, 1999). A first example is given by the institutional set-up of the magnitudes which modern economists assimilate to *fundamentals*, namely, consumers preferences, productive techniques and natural or human endowments.

The first case to consider is *consumer preferences*. These preferences cannot be analysed independently of their social and institutional environment, according to Marshall. Thus, he first refers to public or collective goods consisting 'of the benefits which (an individual) derives from living in a certain place at a certain time, and being a member of a certain State or community' (Marshall, 1916: 158). In other words, these goods usually correspond to a *national* structure of preferences. According to the country or the industrial district in which they live, consumers follow some *specific habits* or *customs* which lead them to some specific types of consumption. Here again, the social stratification of tastes can become rather complex according to the general tendency of economies towards complexity:

> Many commodities with regard to which the tendency to increasing returns acts strongly are, more or less, specialities; some of them aim at creating a new want, or at meeting an old want in a new way. Some of them are adapted to special tastes and can never have a large market; and some have merits that are not easily tested, and must win their way to general favour slowly. (Marshall, 1916: 287)

Collective goods include 'civil and military security and the right and opportunity to make use of public property and institutions of all kinds, such as roads, gaslights, etc. and rights to justice or to a free education' (Marshall, 1916: 59).

Marshall also considers *free goods*, that is, 'free gifts of nature'. He does not forget *immaterial goods* ('non material elements of national wealth', ibid.: 59) such as 'the organization of society or the State', a part of 'scientific knowledge' (the other part being 'cosmopolitan') or national literature.

Finally, Marshall also exhibits the influence of national elements such as the climate on the *necessaries of life*, among which food or other familial categories of expenditures (Marshall, 1916: 195–6).

The social or institutional framework also exerts its influence on private tastes as such. The reference to art according to the kind of spatial environment of the individual (countryside, small towns, large towns, and so on) is a good instance of this type of action (Marshall, 1916: 108): music is not listened to in the same way in a town or in a country in which people are supposed to have very different musical tastes.

Another important element of what economists today call 'fundamentals' is the state of *productive techniques*. Marshall distinguished, in this context, three different themes.

On one side, he afforded a large room in *Industry and Trade* to the causes of the technological supremacy of the UK after the Industrial Revolution. Books 1 and 2 of *Industry and Trade* are predominantly concerned with this type of issue. The last editions of the *Principles* showed how England little by little lost its comparative advantages, especially within the technological competition process implemented by Americans and Germans at the end of the nineteenth and the beginning of the twentieth centuries (for instance Marshall, 1916: 210–11).

On the other side, Marshall also developed substantial considerations on the problem of technical education. He invoked the old institutional system of technical education based on apprenticeship, which he did not consider to be 'exactly suited to modern conditions' (Marshall, 1916: 210) but which had, however, interesting advantages. He compared it with a more school-orientated system, also stressing its qualities and drawbacks (ibid.: 208–10). He, finally, investigated the advances realized by the respective national institutions and systems of technical education in England, Germany and North America.

One of the most stimulating analyses provided by Marshall dealt with the problem of the diffusion of technical and scientific knowledge. Our author was indeed convinced that if, at his epoch, this type of knowledge still permitted some countries to gain comparative advantages, it would, however, be less and less the case since knowledge was diffused more and more internationally. Therefore, it could tend to become, in future, a cosmopolitan collective good rather than a national one (Marshall, 1916: 210–11).

As we know, *initial endowments* are the last element of the triad of 'fundamentals'; Marshall did not neglect it, mainly focusing however on its *human dimension*. This choice is significant since Marshall did not pay too much attention to natural resources as such. This meant that, for our author, the lack or abundance of natural resources was far less important than the way and the extent according to which a given national population would be able to use them efficiently. On the contrary, Marshall strongly emphasized the part played by human factors, investigating them in great detail. Four main themes were successively considered.

The first theme was the influence of nature on the inner qualities of a national population. He began with physiological qualities, referring to 'man's strength and energy' (for instance, Marshall and Marshall, 1881: 10). He attributed a major importance to those factors, showing how they contributed to 'industrial efficiency, on which the production of material wealth depends' (Marshall, 1916: 193). He related those factors to the influence of climate and race, emphasizing the first of these two elements (ibid.: 195). He mentioned the role of the national health system, showing its main effects on demography.

Marshall also coped with what he called 'mental and moral' qualities, such as integrity, self-confidence, patience, temperance, honesty, loyalty, and so on (Marshall and Marshall, 1881; Marshall, 1916: 16). He attributed most of these qualities to Englishmen and was convinced they strongly helped the emergence of the Industrial Revolution. Demographic qualities are not only natural, however. Intellectual and technical capabilities also strongly depend on the system and the institutions of national education. In this framework, Marshall distinguished between general and technical educations:

> General education should . . . aim at causing a man to form an intelligent opinion with regards to the ordinary matters of life and to be full of resources for meeting new emergencies.
>
> Technical education should aim at enabling him to understand the processes and the machinery of the special work in which he is engaged. It should help him to understand the reason of everything that goes on in his trade, and thus enable him to accommodate himself to new machinery or new modes of production. (Marshall and Marshall, 1881: 11)

Finally, Marshall tried to illustrate how all these physiological, moral and educational qualities combined to contribute to the emergence of what he called 'a national spirit in industry and trade' (Marshall, 1922: 1). This emergence was favoured by three main convergent factors. On the one hand, the consciousness of national qualities reached through education was able to convince citizens that they belonged to a great nation:

> Industrial leadership comes for much among national ideas. And if an individual, devoted merely to material ends, is but a poor creature, still more ignoble is a nation that is devoided of national ideas: that is of ideals which recognize a national life as something more than the aggregate of individual lives. (Marshall, 1923: 3)

Moreover, education contributed to the reduction of social differences.

> The spread of education is rapidly effacing those distinctions of mind and character between different social strata, which have prevailed in nearly all the very peopled countries during several thousand years . . . We are indeed approaching

> rapidly to conditions . . . under which the relations between the various industrial strata of a civilized nation are being based on reason, rather than tradition. (Marshall, 1923: 5)

On the other hand, institutions which favour free industry and enterprise were spreading and their multiplication contributed to reduce sectional rigidities and the weight of tradition and custom (Marshall, 1916: 270). Finally,

> universal education, cheap and popular newspapers combined with the commodious and relatively cheap facilities of railway travel have at least removed almost every trace of the difficulties, which formerly prevented the attainment by a whole country of that full economic unity, which used to be regarded as belonging only to compact trading and industrial cities. (Marshall, 1923: 6)

Apart from the institutional set-up of education, Marshall also refers to a nation in relation with its *monetary and financial institutions*. According to his view, a given national monetary and financial system combines four main ingredients. The first and basic one lies in the existence of a specific national currency. The national currency is indeed the expression of the social acceptance of a *common* instrument of economic measurement defined within the institutional framework of the monetary powers of the national state: 'Causes deep set in human nature underlie the facts that national currency has been a chief symbol of national unity' (Marshall, 1922: 9). The existence of a national currency then allows the set-up of a central bank and of a national money market. The central bank is a crucial institutional ingredient of the system according to Marshall. It is absolutely necessary since a free banking system would allow the predominance of particular or 'sectional' interests on the national interest. It would therefore weaken national unity:

> The Bank of England has become not only the Bank of bankers, but also their leader in matters that directly affect the security of general credit in the business of the country. Its Directors include many leading business men: and it has been stated publicly that, as a general rule, their stakes in the Bank itself are so much less than their stakes in the general commercial prosperity of the country, that they cannot be tempted to sacrifice public interests to those of the shareholders of the Bank. (Marshall, 1922: 8)

The presence of common national financial and money markets within the country also contributes to the internal monetary and financial unification of the nation considered. It provides a space for firms eager to finance their investments. The contents of the working of these markets may vary according to the institutional devices defined for each different country. In

Industry and Trade, Marshall dedicated substantial developments to what he considered to be *national* 'banking systems' (Marshall, 1923: 858). He especially dedicated the whole chapter 9 of Book 2 to what he called the 'financial basis' of 'business organization', providing the reader with a comparative study of the performances of British, German and North American banks. He attributed to the banking systems and institutions of the various countries considered the role of adapting industry and trade 'to the enlarged financial requirements of the modern age' (Marshall, 1923: 347–9).

Finally, we should also refer to the existence of national statistics institutes. The existence of monetary and financial statistics is one of the most important requirements for rational policy-making and individual decision-taking. This is why national independent institutes are necessary and help the state or its finance minister to define economic and monetary policies.

When we consider institutions from a dynamic standpoint, several schemes devoted to the explanation of the interaction between their change and economic evolution can be retraced in Marshall's works, often implying the notions of self-organization and cumulative causation (see Arena, 2002). We only consider these in more detail in the notion of *institutional inertia*. Institutional inertia is reflected by the role played by conventions, customs or institutions in the determination of individual behaviour:

> the present never reproduces the past: even stagnant people gradually modify their habits and their industrial techniques. But the past lives on for ages after it has been lost for memory; and the most progressive peoples retain much of the substance of earlier habits of associated action, industry or trade; even when the forms of those habits have been so changed under new conditions, that they are no longer represented by their old names. (Marshall, 1923: 6)

The role of custom is ambivalent according to Marshall. On the one hand, custom might undoubtedly be a brake for economic progress. Yet, as Reisman (1986) stressed, economic change might be slower because of tradition but customs are not rigid. They change according to the evolution of economic constraints. We could invoke here a quotation of A. and M. Marshall taken from Reisman (1986: 344): 'Human nature is never absolutely rigid; and custom never holds its own opposition to a strong active economic force working for many generations persistently in the same direction' (Marshall and Marshall, 1881: vii). On the other hand, as Marshall also wrote,

> the greater part of custom is doubtless but a crystallized form of oppression and suppression. But a body of custom which did nothing but grind down the weak

> could not long survive. For the strong rest on the support of the weak, their own strength cannot sustain item without that support; and if they organize social arrangements which burden the weak wantonly and beyond measure, they thereby destroy themselves. Consequently every body of custom that endures, contains provisions that protect the weak from the most reckless forms of injury. (Marshall, 1916: 725–6)

Paradoxically however, the slowness of cultural evolution and the protective aspect of customs combine to generate *institutional inertia*. Inertia, however, cannot prevent gradual but irreversible change towards more knowledge and more modern economic rationality:

> Violence is required for keeping broad forces in the pound of Ceteris Paribus, say, a whole generation, on the ground that they have only an indirect hearing on the question in hand. For even indirect influences may produce great effects in the course of a generation, if they happen to act cumulatively; and it is not safe to ignore them even provisionally in a practical problem without special study. (Marshall, 1925 [1966]: 379)

This view entails a subsequent remark. If we interpret normality in the Marshallian way, namely, in relation to a specific context, it is clear that a normal state of affairs must include the prevailing social conventions, norms, customs or institutions. Economic evolution therefore appears as a succession of different economic regimes to which normal situations are associated. There are therefore *at least* as many normal situations as there are different regimes. The change of regime is never brutal in accordance with Marshall's principles of continuity but continuity is compatible with evolution and irreversibility. This interpretation is reinforced by the forms of communication, dissemination and interpretation of information: 'One of the most important of the unwritten chapters in Economics is that of the time that elapses between economic causes and their effects in consequences of the slowness with which knowledge diffuses itself' (Marshall and Marshall, 1881: vii).

It is clear indeed that there is a strong connection between the resistance of custom and the penetration of modern knowledge and rationality. In societies characterized by limited means of communication, custom is easily maintained and appears to be more protective. Dissemination is also a problem as the example of industrial districts positively confirms it. In the absence of an 'industrial atmosphere', positive externalities are scarcer and social interaction more limited. Pockets of relative ignorance and archaic common sense remain during a longer period. At last, information is not knowledge. Knowledge presupposes the interpretation of information and its incorporation in the structure of men's minds. Now, if minds are not prepared for an open and progressive interpretation of information, informative inputs can be completely useless and exert no influence on the existence of customs, even if these appear to be a brake to social and economic evolution.

Schumpeter, Forms of Organization and Institutions

Schumpeter and Marshall share a common conception of the relations between economics, sociology and history. Therefore, it is not surprising to find similarities in their respective investigations of forms of organization and institutions. Schumpeter, however, did not give economic nations the importance that Marshall devoted to them. He preferred to focus on capitalist institutions and forms of organization as such. We could check, however, that this was also a major preoccupation of Alfred Marshall.

For Schumpeter, one of the main institutions of capitalism is certainly *entrepreneurship*. Its investigation gives an excellent example of the relation that Schumpeter established between history, economic sociology and economic theory in shaping his approach to institutional change (Arena and Romani, 2002). In this context, the existence of both a specific social structure and the social phenomenon of leadership play a fundamental role.

In accordance with Marshall's view, the existence of a social structure can best be described as the subdivision of society in social groups to which individuals belong or aspire to belong. This, in turn, influences, for example, the way in which they make their choices:

> [I]t is society that shapes the particular desires we observe; . . . wants must be taken with reference to the group which the individual thinks of when deciding his course of action – the family or any other group, smaller or larger than the family; . . . the field of individual choice is always, though in very different ways and to very different degrees, fenced in by social habits or conventions and the like . . . (Schumpeter, 1912 [1934]: 91)

This social structure also provides the social framework within which institutional changes are embedded. A good example of the way in which Schumpeter employs this framework is provided by his analysis of what happens when the 'New Men' become entrepreneurs. On the one hand, certain institutions must already exist as a matter of 'logical priority' (Schumpeter, 1939: 114) to render the emergence of the entrepreneur feasible. Thus, the existence of a banking system based on credit allows entrepreneurs to employ new means of production without these having to be transferred a priori from existing industries to innovative ones (ibid.: 114). On the other hand, these institutions are not simply forms of social organization. They also take the form of new behavioural rules, that Schumpeter called 'the attitudes of the public mind' (Schumpeter, 1950: 135).

The social phenomenon of leadership, too, is instrumental in providing an explanation of institutional change. Social leadership based on 'energetic' effort is, in fact, the main source of such change:

> Certain other things, such as, for example, the element of 'effort', could perhaps be even more useful for an 'energetic' theory of economics that would have something to say about economic development. Moreover, changes in human nature, social organisation, etc., often have economic causes. Finally, even a development that cannot be explained in economic terms often has economic consequences so that we might well have *something* to contribute to its clarification. (Schumpeter, 1908: 621)

Here, Schumpeter highlights a major characteristic of leaders' behaviour. Leaders do not follow the logic of prevailing rules, namely, minimizing their efforts in order to reach a given objective. Quite the contrary, they invent new rules to reach new objectives. This invention – or, more precisely, this 'innovation' – requires efforts. Leaders are able to produce these efforts because they possess an excess of energy that is obviously useless when individual behaviour relies on routines and is purely 'hedonistic'. The success of an innovation does not, however, depend on its intrinsic characteristics but on it being accepted by the community of followers or imitators. This process is based on self-organization and self-reinforcement, and can be found already in Menger as well as in Wieser. It is based on the phenomenon of social imitation, which is why Schumpeter considers that its analysis falls within the realm of economic sociology. As already noted, economic sociology plays here the role of a conceptual 'bridge' between history and economic theory. For instance, when defining the function of the entrepreneur in *Business Cycles*, Schumpeter writes:

> For actions which consist in carrying out innovations we reserve the term Enterprise; the individuals who carry them out we call Entrepreneurs. This terminological decision is based on a historical fact and a theoretical proposition, namely, that carrying out innovations is the only function which is fundamental in history and essential in theory to the type usually designated by that term. (Schumpeter, 1939: 102)

And later, to explain that entrepreneurs' 'genealogies display most varied origins', he asserts that 'economic theory and sociology should combine to account for their institutional patterns' (ibid.: 104). At a given point of historical time, leaders introduce new institutions that are more adequate to new objectives and followers accept them (or not), thereby turning them (or not) into innovations. This self-organizing process is of great general importance to Schumpeter's explanation of institutional change. Hence, the emergence of entrepreneurs as well as of large firms is essentially described as the result of leadership. Moreover, the explanation extends to banks that are simply a 'new kind of firm': 'They are nothing but establishments for the manufacture of means of payment' (ibid.: 112). Thus, for Schumpeter, banks, like firms, appear to be, at least partially, the result of a process of self-organization.

Banks, however, are not only firms. They also support the second fundamental institution to be found in market economies, namely, *money and credit*. To carry out new technical combinations firms must indeed invest, and this investment must, in turn, be financed:

> Another [problem] exists for us: the problem of detaching productive means (already employed somewhere) from the circular flow and allotting them to new combinations. This is done by credit, by means of which one who wishes to carry out new combinations outbids the producers in the circular flow in the market for the required means of production. And although the meaning and object of this process lies in a movement of goods from their old towards new employments, it cannot be described entirely in terms of goods without overlooking something essential, which happens in the sphere of money and credit and upon which depends the explanation of important phenomena in the capitalist form of economic organisation, in contrast to other types. (Schumpeter, 1912 [1934]: 71)

According to Schumpeter, money is an institutional device and a logical prerequisite of the market economy. This is why Schumpeter was so insistent on the idea that money could not be seen as a particular good or commodity. Instead, 'the monetary circulation is, in its nature and main function in the market economy . . . nothing but a [social] clearing system' (Schumpeter, 1917–18 [1956]: 155). This does not mean, however, that money is a creation of the state or of law as, for instance, Knapp had argued:

> [M]oney is as little and in no other sense a creature of the law than is any other social institution such as marriage or private property. The comparison is instructive. . . . [T]he essential nature of marriage relations explains the legal provisions which regulate them, but the legal provisions do not explain the essential nature and causes of marriage relations. Similarly, money transactions are regulated or shaped by the legal system, but as an object of regulation they retain a separate existence apart from the legal system itself and can be explained only by their own nature or by the inner necessities of the market economy. (Schumpeter, 1917–18 [1956]: 160–61)

Money is thus analysed by Schumpeter as a 'claim ticket' and 'receipt voucher' recognized by every agent in the economy as socially valuable. In this sense, Schumpeter's analysis of the existence of money provides us with another example of how he builds a 'bridge' between economic sociology and economy theory, or between money as an institution and money as the basis of income circulation.

Financial markets are another important institution of capitalist economies. As we know, Schumpeter did not consider financial markets as fundamentally speculative. For him, they participated, together with banks, in the process of transforming the financing of innovation into more permanent funding. Thus, Schumpeter did not ascribe to financial markets the role that Keynes assigned to them. According to Schumpeter, financial markets are neither as autonomous nor as predominant as they are in Keynes's approach. However, they play a key role in the transformation of saving into investment. This is why Schumpeter characterizes them as the 'heart, although . . . not . . . the brain' of capitalist economies (Schumpeter, 1939: 127).

Another aspect of Schumpeter's approach to institutional change derives from the fact that such change takes time. As in Marshall, this is mainly a consequence of individual agents' resistance and propensity to routine: 'Everyone knows, of course, that to do something new is very much more difficult than to do something that belongs to the realm of routine, and that the two tasks differ qualitatively and not only in degree' (ibid.: 99). Schumpeter highlights three 'classes' of reasons to explain such *institutional inertia*. First, innovations often face an environment characterized by resistance. This can come in very different forms, from 'disapproval' to 'aggression' (ibid.: 100). Second, this environment can be well adapted to routine and is, therefore, a priori not prepared to welcome innovation. The third 'class' of reasons is related to the attitude of individual agents towards uncertainty. As Schumpeter notes, 'most people feel an inhibition when the possibility of treading a new path offers itself' (ibid.).

The notion of resistance to institutional change is particularly important for Schumpeter's approach to capitalist market economies. On the one hand, it explains why innovations may spread only slowly among entrepreneurs. On the other hand, it also explains the rise of large firms. According to Schumpeter, 'trustified capitalism' is characterized by a tendency for entrepreneurial leadership to disappear.

> This social function is already losing importance and is bound to lose it at an accelerating rate in the future even if the economic process itself of which entrepreneurship was the prime mover went on unabated. For . . . it is much easier now than it has been in the past to do things that lie outside familiar routine – innovation itself being reduced to routine. (Schumpeter, 1950: 132)

Once innovation itself is routinized, resistance to it lessens or even disappears.

Institutional inertia, however, is not specific to market economies. It is present in any type of society. An example is Schumpeter's analysis of the militarization of the ancient Egyptian society under the 'New Empire'. It pointed out how an external event – the war of liberation from the Hyksos – led to the emergence of a class of professional soldiers. However, having come into existence, this class contributed to the emergence and maintenance of a new social and political organization based on the centralization of power under a military aristocracy. As Schumpeter noted, 'created by wars that required it, the machine now created the wars it required' (Schumpeter, 1919 [1951]: 33). Taken together, these characteristics of Schumpeter's conception of institutional change find substantial analogies with the approach of Marshall.

The purpose of economic sociology is not only to define the main institutional patterns of capitalism but also to analyse its prevailing *forms of organization*. A very good example is provided by the Schumpeterian approach to firms and competition. For Schumpeter, the analysis of market forms is an objective not only of economic theory but also of the 'science of organization' and, therefore, of economic sociology. This, of course, explains why the analysis of the evolution of forms of productive organization received such considerable attention in his writings, be it in the context of his discussion of entrepreneurship, of capitalism's tendency to 'trustification' or of their respective impact on innovations. From this point of view, a significant example of Schumpeter's approach is contained in *Business Cycles*. Chapter 3 of the first volume (Schumpeter, 1939: 72–123) is devoted to the analysis of 'how the economic system generates evolution'. In this chapter, Schumpeter formulates his 'theory of innovation' (ibid.: 87–102). Apart from defining the notion of innovation, this theory of innovation – containing the essence of what Schumpeter calls 'the sociology of industrial society' – explains the emergence of innovations (ibid.: 96). Far from explaining innovations in terms of some kind of stochastic process or as the result of a purely economic transition from old to new production functions, Schumpeter locates them in economic sociology. This is precisely what he means when he notes that 'innovations are always associated with the rise to leadership of New Men' (ibid.). He justifies this view by invoking a methodological argument that directly reflects his interpretation of the relation between economic theory and economic sociology: 'The main reason for introducing this assumption [the assumption of the relation between "innovations" and "New Men"] into a purely economic argument not primarily concerned with the structure of society is that it provides the rationale for the preceding assumption' (Schumpeter, 1939: 96).

More precisely, the emergence of entrepreneurs or the transition from 'competitive' to 'trustified capitalism' is described as a change in the forms of organization. This change is the result of the emergence of new men or new leaders who, through their innovative activity, generate 'a process subject to institutional change'. Changes in the forms of organization are therefore primarily sociological rather than economic in nature. Entrepreneurs are the new leaders who replace the owners in the circular and, in particular, old leaders. At some point in historical time and as the result of organizational change, the managers of giant firms become the 'new' leaders, replacing individual entrepreneurs who have become 'old' leader-types. Here again, the sociological distinction between leaders and followers appears to be the key to organizational transformations.

Marshall's and Schumpeter's approaches to institutions and forms of organization sensibly differ. For instance, Marshall analyses the economic consequences of institutional change focusing on the factors which directly affect 'fundamentals': variation of consumers' tastes and motives, variation of particular social strata, variation of 'mankind', organizational and technological change, impact of education, diffusion of technical progress, and so on. Schumpeter prefers to stress the role of social leadership and its main impact on technical, cultural and social innovations. However, both authors give a fundamental role to institutions (entrepreneurship and monetary and financial institutions especially) and to organizational forms (particularly in relation to firms and markets) in the explanation of economic change. Moreover, they share the idea that reasoned history especially matters when dynamics is introduced and pure economic theory becomes insufficient.

4.3 CONCLUSIVE REMARKS

Our contribution never pretended that Alfred Marshall and Joseph Schumpeter shared an identical conception of the relations between economics and sociology, defined institutions and forms of organization according to identical concepts and criteria, and developed a common dynamic theory. What we pretended is that both authors offered developments which converge on several main analytical points of agreement and permit to draw the foundations of a research programme which clearly contrasts with the axiomatic tendencies of many modern contributions. Let us now sum up the main points of this agreement.

1. Marshall and Schumpeter never denied the importance and utility of formal economic theory. However, they argued that its scope was much more limited than it was pretended since the Marginal Revolution. To put it briefly, economic theory is sufficient within statics but entirely insufficient within dynamics.

2. Marshall and Schumpeter argued that, within dynamics, it was impossible to understand the real world with the help of the sole economic theory or of the sole economic history. Economic theory and history must necessarily be complementary. Co-operation between both disciplines has to be helped by a third discipline. This discipline is called 'reasoned history' by Marshall and 'economic sociology' by Schumpeter.
3. Marshall and Schumpeter shared common ideas concerning institutions and forms of organization. They both limited their investigation of social organization to firms and markets. They agreed to consider that the prominent institutions of market economies were entrepreneurship, monetary and financial institutions and market institutions.
4. Marshall and Schumpeter assimilated long-run economic dynamics to structural change. This is consistent with the view that 'fundamentals' are permanently affected and exert permanent economic effects.
5. Marshall and Schumpeter considered that the usual selfishness assumption of economic theory is not always valid. They admitted that, within dynamics, other types of rationality might emerge and require the help of history and sociology.

These points of agreement allow the definition of the foundations of a research programme which seriously contrasts with the usual assumptions of modern axiomatic approaches. This is why Marshall's and Schumpeter's ideas are still alive and useful for modern economists interested by the revival of an economic analysis clearly embedded in social science.

NOTE

* This contribution was written when the author was a visiting fellow of Wolfson College, Cambridge (UK) and presented to the International Workshop 'Marshall, Schumpeter, and Social Science' (17–19 March 2007) in Hitotsubashi University, Tokyo. The author wants to express his deep gratitude to Wolfson College for its material help and its intellectual atmosphere and stimulation. He would also like to thank R. Backhouse, M. de Cecco, H. Hagemann, G. Hodgson, T. Hirai, H. Kurz, C. Marcuzzo, T. Nishizawa, Y Shionoya, R. Swedberg, K. Yagi and all the participants of the Hitotsubashi workshop for their valuable criticisms and comments.

REFERENCES

Arena, R. (1998), 'The nation as an organized system of production: Smith, Marshall and the Classics', in M. Bellet and C. L'Harmet (eds), *Industry, Space and Competition*, Cheltenham, UK and Lyme, USA: Edward Elgar, pp. 51–103.

Arena, R. (1999), 'Austrians and marshallians on markets: historical origins and compatible views', in S. Dow and P. Earl (eds), *Economic Organization and Economic Knowledge: Essays in Honour of Brian J. Loasby*, vol. 1, Cheltenham, UK and Northampton, MA, USA: Edward Elgar.

Arena, R. (2002), 'Organisation and knowledge in Alfred Marshall's economics', in R. Arena and M. Quéré (eds), *The Economics of Alfred Marshall: Evolution and the Organisation of Industry*, London: Palgrave Macmillan.

Arena, R. and P. Romani (2002), 'Schumpeter on entrepreneurship', in R. Arena and C. Dangel-Hagnauer (eds), *The Contribution of Joseph Schumpeter to Economics, Economic Development and Institutional Change*, London: Routledge.

Boland, L. (1990), 'The methodology of Marshall's "principle of continuity"', *Economie Appliquée*, **43** (1), republished in J. Cunningham-Wood (ed.) (1996), *Alfred Marshall, Critical Assessments*, vol. 7, London: Routledge.

Glassburner, B. (1955), 'Alfred Marshall on economic history and historical development', *Quarterly Journal of Economics*, **69** (November), reprinted in J. Cunningham-Wood (ed.) (1993), *Alfred Marshall, Critical Assessments*, vol. 1, London: Routledge.

Gonce, R.A. (1982), 'Alfred Marshall on industrial organization: from *Principles of Economics* to *Industry and Trade*', in J. Cunningham-Wood (ed.), *Alfred Marshall, Critical Assessments*, vol. 4, London: Routledge.

Marshall, A. (1916), *Principles of Economics – an Introductory Volume*, 7th edn, London: Macmillan.

Marshall, A. (1922), *Money, credit and commerce*, London: Macmillan.

Marshall, A. (1923), *Industry and Trade*, 3rd edn, London: Macmillan.

Marshall, A. (1925), *Memorials of Alfred Marshall*, C. Pigou (ed.), London: Macmillan, reprinted in 1966 by M.A. Kelley, New York.

Marshall, A. (1996), *The Correspondence of Alfred Marshall, Economist*, 3 vols, J. Whitaker (ed.), Cambridge: Cambridge University Press.

Marshall, A. and M. Marshall (1881), *Economics of Industry*, 2nd edn, London: Macmillan.

Reisman, D. (1986), *The Economics of Alfred Marshall*, London: Macmillan.

Shionoya, Y. (1997), *Schumpeter and the Idea of Social Science – a Metatheoretical Study*, Cambridge: Cambridge University Press.

Schumpeter, J.A. (1908), *Das Wesen und der Hauptinhalt der theoretischen Nationalökonomie*, Munich and Leipzig: Dunker & Humblot.

Schumpeter, J.A. (1912), *Theorie der wirtschaftlichen Entwicklung*, Leipzig: Dunker & Humblot. Preface dated July 1911, Vienna, English translation of the 2nd edn in 1934 as *The Theory of Economic Development: An Inquiry into Profits, Capital, Credit, Interest, and the Business Cycle*, Cambridge, MA: Harvard University Press.

Schumpeter, J.A. (1917–18), 'Das Sozialproduct und die Rechenpfennige. Glossen und Beiträge zur Geldtheorie von heute', *Archiv für Sozialwissenschaft und Sozialpolitik*, vol. 44, trans. into English by A.W. Marget (1956), 'Money and the social product', *International Economic Papers*, pp. 627–715.

Schumpeter, J.A. (1918), *Die Krise des Steuerstaates*, Graz and Leipzig: Leuschner & Lubensky, reprinted in *Aufsätze zur Soziologie*, ed. by E. Schneider and A. Spiethoff (1953), Tübingen: J.C.B. Mohr.

Schumpeter, J.A. (1919), 'Zur Soziologie der Imperialismen, *Archiv für Sozialwissenschaft und Sozialpolitik*, **46**, 1–39, 275–310, trans. into English as 'The sociology of imperialisms', in J.A. Schumpeter (1951), *Imperialism and Social Classes*, ed. P. Sweezy, New York: Augustus M. Kelley.

Schumpeter, J.A. (1927), 'Die sozialen Klassen im ethnisch homogenen Milieu', *Archiv für Sozialwissenschaft und Sozialpolitik*, **57**, 1–67, trans. into English as 'Social classes in an ethnically homogenous environment', in J.A. Schumpeter (1951), *Imperialism and Social Classes*, ed. P. Sweezy, New York: Augustus M. Kelley.
Schumpeter, J.A. (1934), *Théorie de l'évolution économique*, Paris: Dalloz, reprinted 1958.
Schumpeter, J.A. (1939), *Business Cycles. A Theoretical, Historical, and Statistical Analysis of the Capitalist Process*, 2 vols, New York: McGraw-Hill Book Company.
Schumpeter, J.A. (1950), *Capitalism, Socialism and Democracy*, 3rd edn, New York: Harper & Brothers.
Schumpeter, J.A. (1951), *Imperialism and Social Classes*, ed. P. Sweezy, New York: Augustus M. Kelley.
Schumpeter, J.A. (1954), *History of Economic Analysis*, London: Allen & Unwin, reprinted 1994, London: Routledge.

5. Marshall, Schumpeter and the shifting boundaries of economics and sociology

Geoffrey M. Hodgson

Alfred Marshall and Joseph Schumpeter rank as two of the most important economists of all time.[1] They both had a major impact on the development of the discipline. Their writings have several common characteristics, including minimal explicit reliance on mathematics, a rich knowledge of the social and behavioural sciences, a methodological and philosophical awareness, fluently engaging styles of writing, and a primary aim to explain the world rather than to exhibit knowledge or technique for their own sake.

Marshall played a crucial role by synthesizing the paradigm that Thorstein Veblen (1900: 261) was later to describe as 'neoclassical' (Ekelund and Hébert, 2002). Marshall was the main systematizer of the partial equilibrium variant of neoclassical theory, which held sway in Britain, the USA and elsewhere, until it began to be displaced by the Walrasian general equilibrium approach at around the time of the Second World War.

Both Schumpeter and John Maynard Keynes were born in 1883. Marshall died in 1924, leaving his former pupil and the Austrian economist to tackle the catastrophic global events of the Great Depression in the 1930s. Schumpeter and Keynes took very different views on this topic. Schumpeter (1931) initially proposed that the downturn was the unfortunate but unavoidable outcome of the coincidence of the three troughs of the 50-year Kondratieff cycle, with the shorter Juglar and Kitchin cycles. By contrast Keynes (1936) saw the fall in 'effective demand' as the key explanatory factor, and promoted government expenditure to increase aggregate demand for goods and services.

In the 1930s and 1940s Schumpeter (1934; 1942) offered other major insights, including analyses of the relationship between technological development, political institutions and economic activity. Despite these major contributions, overall Keynes was more influential than Schumpeter, at least from the 1940s to the 1970s.

However, since the 1980s Schumpeter's overall contribution has enjoyed a renaissance, with an explosion of secondary literature devoted to his life and work. Nevertheless, some important and related aspects of his thought are less widely discussed. Among these are his views on the boundaries of economics as a science and his related appraisal of the contribution of the German historical school. Here in several respects there are contrasts with Marshall. Indeed, it is argued here that Schumpeter played a catalytic role alongside others in the redefinition of the boundaries and scope of both economics and sociology. A narrower definition of economics emerged in the anglophone world in the 1930s, and it eventually displaced the previous and wider definitions of the subject held by Marshall and the German historical school.

This chapter assesses this legacy and points out that the boundaries are now being transgressed from both sides. This means that a reassessment of the relationship between economics and sociology is in order. Some knowledge of the history of these changing boundaries and its relationship to various doctrines is relevant to this project.

MARSHALL AND THE GERMAN HISTORICAL SCHOOL

The historical school prospered in the German-speaking world from the 1840s to the 1930s and went through several phases of development (Hodgson, 2001). Throughout its existence, and despite many internal differences, its members argued that national economic systems differed substantially in time and place, and emphasized the importance of historically sensitive theory. However, in its early years this school was marked by a naive empiricism – a faith in the explanatory role of facts alone. Carl Menger's (1883 [1985]) opening salvo in the *Methodenstreit* included a powerful methodological attack on these empiricist views. He brought the individual to the centre of the methodological discussion, and argued that some a priori theoretical principles were essential in order to understand economic phenomena.

Menger (1883 [1985]: 49) identified 'that error which confuses theoretical economics with the history of economy' and tried instead to establish a central place in economics for deductive and abstract theory. Menger (1883 [1985]: 87) argued that economics should be concerned with the aspect of human life concerned with economizing action by individuals, that is 'the manifestations of human self-interest in the efforts of economic humans aimed at the provision of their human needs'. Consequently, the *Methodenstreit* was not simply about methodology, it was also about the legitimate boundaries of economics as a discipline.

While members of the historical school generally retained a broad view of the subject, the *Methodenstreit* prompted their leaders to refine their methodological views and to abandon any exclusive reliance on empirical evidence alone. Gustav Schmoller (1900: 109) proposed a combination of inductive evidence with deductive theory as a means of revealing and understanding causal relations. His pupil Werner Sombart became the *de facto* leader of the historical school after his teacher's death in 1917. Sombart (1929: 1) criticized 'the mistaken idea that history can be approached without theory' and attempts 'to banish all theory from the investigation of historical reality'. For Sombart (1929: 3): 'Theory is the pre-requisite to any scientific writing of history.' The Austrian and later historical schools differed not in terms of being one against the other for theory, but on the type of theory they proposed.

Although Marshall was educated largely in England, and Schumpeter in Austria and Germany, they both were highly influenced by the German historical school.[2] Marshall was fluent in German. Like many aspiring young economists in the nineteenth century, he went to Germany to study under the tutelage of members of the historical school. Contrary to some accounts, he was not an opponent of this school of thought (Hodgson, 2001; 2005).

Marshall's long-standing opposition to the views of William Cunningham in Cambridge focused largely on Cunningham's (1892) claim that valid general theoretical principles were unobtainable and, consequently, that economics had to be largely descriptive and taxonomic. Marshall's stance did not signal any opposition to the historical school as a whole. Instead, Cunningham represented the more naive empiricist views of some German economists in the years before the *Methodenstreit.* Significantly, even in his critiques of Cunningham, and repeatedly elsewhere, Marshall (1885; 1890; 1892; 1897) endorsed key historical school arguments (Hodgson, 2001).

By contrast, Robert Skidelsky (1983: 43) stated that Marshall 'rejected the main contentions of the German historical school'. There is no evidence for this. On the contrary, in his works, Marshall heaped praise on Schmoller and other German writers, including in the later editions of his *Principles*. For Marshall, Schmoller was a foremost methodological inspiration. In the opening pages of his definitive text, Marshall (1920: 29) quoted and endorsed Schmoller's methodological statement that: 'Induction and deduction are both needed for scientific thought as the left foot and the right foot are both needed for walking.' In his letters, Marshall repeated this endorsement of Schmoller's attempt to steer a midway course between empiricism and deductivism. Marshall wrote on 30 January 1897:

'Most of the suggestions which I made on the proofs of [John Neville] Keynes's *Scope and Method* were aimed at bringing it more into harmony with the views of Schmoller' (Whitaker, 1996, vol. 2: 179). Ten years later, at his address at a dinner of the Royal Economic Society, Marshall (1907: 7) optimistically declared: 'Disputes as to method have nearly ceased; Schmoller's dictum that analysis and the search for facts are, like the right and left foot in walking, each nearly useless alone, but that the two are strong in combination, is accepted on all sides.' Contrary to a modern myth that Marshall was an opponent of the German historical school, Marshall (1920: 768) retained a highly laudatory view of their work, seeing it as 'one of the great achievements of our age'.

Accordingly, Gerard Shove (1942: 309) later remarked: 'If any school of thought outside the Ricardian tradition set its mark on the *Principles* it was the Historical School, rather than the marginal utility school, that did so.' Similarly, Terence Hutchison (1988: 529) wrote: 'Alfred Marshall, under German influence, made a strenuous attempt to re-graft a historical-institutional approach on to the neo-classical abstraction.'

Overall, instead of taking sides with Menger in the *Methodenstreit*, Marshall proposed that historically grounded insights should enrich and to some extent qualify the apparatus of neoclassical theory.

MARSHALL'S DEFINITION OF ECONOMICS

There is no space here to review earlier conceptions of the scope and boundaries of economics, other than to quote two prominent contemporaries of Marshall. William Stanley Jevons (1888: vi), for instance, saw economics as the 'science of the development of economic forms and relations'. Jevons saw 'economic' behaviour as dominated by self-interest. Hence 'economics' was focused on the arena where self-interest prevailed. Similarly, Francis Edgeworth's (1881: 16) 'first principle of economics is that every agent is actuated only by self-interest'. Rather than universal claims that individuals were always self-interested, these were statements that economics as a discipline was concerned with self-interested behaviour.

Marshall's definition of economics was broader and sufficiently capacious to accommodate historical and other insights within the discipline. For Marshall (1920: 1):

> Political Economy or Economics is the study of mankind in the ordinary business of life; it examines that part of individual and social action which is most closely connected with the attainment and with the use of the material requisites of wellbeing. Thus it is on the one side a study of wealth; and on the other, and more important side, a part of the study of man.

Although Marshall preferred the term 'economics' to the earlier one of 'political economy', this did not for him signal a narrowing of the legitimate subject matter of the discipline. On the contrary, Marshall (1920: 43) saw political economy as 'the narrower term' because it often referred merely to politically desirable economic policies, rather than the analysis of 'the best methods' of reaching proposed ends. However, in adopting a broad definition of the subject, Marshall implicitly leaves space for other social sciences, as the scope of economics was not universal. For Marshall (1920: 22) economics had a core preoccupation:

> 'money' or 'general purchasing power' or 'command over material wealth,' is the centre around which economic science clusters; this is so, not because money or material wealth is regarded as the main aim of human effort, nor even as affording the main subject-matter for the study of the economist, but because in this world of ours it is the one convenient means of measuring human motives on a large scale.

Hence for Marshall, economics is not exclusively concerned with pecuniary values but they are the most convenient data available to examine human motives and behaviour 'in the ordinary business of life'. Within his broad and inclusive conception of the subject, prices and other monetary values play central roles. This conceded potential territory to other social sciences such as anthropology and sociology, but left the boundaries rather vague.

He focused on individual motives but did not always take them as given. For Marshall (1920: 89) tastes were malleable, as 'the development of new activities giving rise to new wants'. Furthermore, for him, the incorporation of changing wants or preferences was entirely within the scope of economic theory. As noted below, this inclusive view was later to be overturned by mainstream economists.

Marshall did not react to the *Methodenstreit* by drawing from Menger a narrower conception of economics, based on the universal logic of choice and individual self-interest. While Marshall defended the role of core theoretical principles, his conception of economics remained broad and inclusive. Marshall wrote to Francis Edgeworth on 28 August 1902: 'In my view "Theory" is essential . . . But I conceive no more calamitous notion than that abstract, or general, or "theoretical" economics was economics "proper"' (Whitaker, 1996, vol. 2: 393).

Marshall's definition of economics in terms of 'the study of mankind in the ordinary business of life' did not define the discipline in terms of assumptions or methods, but in terms of a real zone of analysis. However, this zone was not sharply defined. Instead, economics was a locus of concern within the broader social sciences as a whole. This picture was consistent with the then influential conception of Auguste Comte who, in defining and coining the term 'sociology', saw it broadly as the study of society, with economics as a specialist and subordinate discipline within.[3]

Marshall's spacious interpretation of the boundaries of economics endured for several decades in Britain and the USA, at least until the 1940s. This sustained not only capacious disciplinary boundaries but also the tolerance of different theoretical approaches and schools of thought. Such a pluralistic spirit was evident when Edgeworth (1891: 1), a leading neoclassical economist and first editor of the *Economic Journal*, opened the first volume: 'The *Economic Journal* . . . will be open to writers of different schools. The most opposite doctrines may meet here as on a fair field . . . Nor will it be attempted to prescribe the method, any more than the result, of scientific investigation.'

The American institutionalists, who were dominant in the USA in the inter-war period, inherited a broad conception of the discipline from both Marshall and the historical school. The highly influential Wesley Mitchell (1916: 157) was echoing Marshall when he wrote: 'Money may not be the root of *all* evil, but it is the root of economic science' (original emphasis). Like many other institutionalists, Mitchell incorporated key elements of Marshallian theory within his work, regarding the two as generally compatible. Veblen is often depicted as taking a contrasting, more iconoclastic and anti-neoclassical position. However, in lectures delivered during 1926–27, Mitchell (1969, vol. 2: 685) gave some evidence to support the view that 'Veblen himself at times makes casual, implicit use of orthodox economic theory'.

In sum, Marshall followed the German historical school and others in adopting a relatively broad conception of the scope of economics as a discipline. Concerned with 'the study of mankind in the ordinary business of life', economics focused especially on individual incentives and (potentially malleable) human motives, expressed in pecuniary outcomes. From Adam Smith to Marshall, a broad and inclusive definition of economics prevailed, in both Germany and the anglophone world. Economics was widely conceived as the study of pecuniary or business phenomena. However, within a few years of Marshall's death, this situation was to change radically.

SCHUMPETER'S REACTION TO THE *METHODENSTREIT* AND HIS CONCEPTION OF ECONOMICS

Schumpeter (1941: 239) long admired the general equilibrium approach of Léon Walras, regarding him as 'the greatest of all theorists' while rejecting Marshall's 'vision of the economic process, his methods, his results'. One of Schumpeter's enduring but unfulfilled ambitions was to dynamize the Walrasian theoretical system. While he became increasingly preoccupied with developmental and 'sociological' areas of research, for Schumpeter the Walrasian system remained the centrepiece of all economic analysis.

Influenced by both the Austrian and German historical schools in the *Methodenstreit*, Schumpeter (1908: 6–7) came to the conclusion that 'both sides are mostly right . . . their sole difference lies in their interests in different problems'. He argued that their differences were largely due to different disciplinary preoccupations: compared with Menger and his followers, the historical school were less concerned with 'pure theory' or 'pure economics'.

For Schumpeter (1908), 'pure economics' was at one apex of a disciplinary triangle, with 'economic history' and 'economic sociology' as the others. In the *Methodenstreit* the historical and Austrian schools had emphasized different zones of enquiry, but for Schumpeter investigations in all areas of the triangle were legitimate. Nevertheless economics was dominated and partly defined by the abstract theoretical system at one apex.

Schumpeter (1908) defined the overall subject matter of 'economics' in terms of the formal analysis of 'exchange relations' or catallactics. Influenced in this respect by Walras, Schumpeter saw the basic unit of analysis as the reciprocal transfer of goods or services. Also like Walras, Schumpeter retained the concepts of utility and utility maximization. As Shionoya (1997: 134) puts it, 'the quantity of goods and utility functions were assumed as given, but this assumption was made to treat the phenomenon of exchange as the first step in the analysis'.

Schumpeter (1908) regarded 'exchange' as a highly general concept, occurring in production and consumption as well as trade. Schumpeter's aim was to demarcate and develop an ahistorical and highly abstract system of 'pure economics', applicable to all past and possible forms of human activity. Any study of historical specific institutions was thus outside 'pure economics' (Graça Moura, 2003; Shionoya, 1997).

Adopting the ideals of this abstract and general project, he maintained a view that other theoretical approaches were not 'economic theory' proper. Schumpeter (1928: 363) wrote: 'within serious economic theory there are no such things as "schools" or differences of principles, and the only fundamental cleavage in modern economics is between good work and bad'. However, in a Japanese journal in 1931 Schumpeter modified this doctrinal view to the empirical claim that there exist 'no differences as to fundamental standpoints among serious economists' but he was unclear as to whether institutionalists or members of the historical school were included in this 'serious' group (quoted in Shionoya, 1997: 63). Schumpeter allowed no more than a highly limited set of approaches within the core of theoretical economics.

Schumpeter (1908) upheld in some passages that 'economic analysis' or 'pure economics' started from the assumption of universal regularities in human behaviour such as an inverse relation between price and quantity consumed. For example, Schumpeter (1908: 64) wrote: 'The fact we see is only that the individual offers a decreasing price. *Why* he does so is not interesting from the standpoint of economics' (original emphasis).[4]

On this passage Shionoya (1997: 116) comments: 'It is clear that when Schumpeter said this he had Menger in mind.' In addition, Schumpeter went further than Menger, to declare that the causes of wants and how they are satisfied were outside the realm of economic theory. Psychology as a whole was regarded as separate from economics. This exclusion of psychological ideas from economics was too radical even for some Austrians, and it drew criticism from Schumpeter's teacher, Friedrich von Wieser (Shionoya, 1997: 117–18). Instead, Schumpeter built foundationally on the presumably universal regularities of exchange behaviour. This was consistent with the view of Menger and others that in economics wants or preference function are taken as given (although Schumpeter did not use these terms).[5] Like other economists who take this view, Schumpeter accepted that wants may change, but saw the investigations of these causes as outside economic analysis.

Accordingly, Schumpeter (1909: 216) wrote in an article published in English: 'For theory it is irrelevant why people demand certain goods: the only important point is that all things are demanded, produced, and paid for because individuals want them.' For him, the task of theory is to consider the outcomes of individual decisions, individual interactions and their consequences, but not on the causes of their wants or preferences.[6]

The contrast with Marshall's contrasting depiction of economic theory as a mere tool in the service of empirical enquiry was dramatized in the account of their only personal meeting in 1907. Against Schumpeter's youthful veneration of 'pure economics', Marshall claimed that 'the purely scientific content of economics [is] not large and has no great significance' and he 'told Schumpeter that he who pursued economics as a pure science wasted his time' (Allen, 1991, vol. 1: 61).

After 1908 Schumpeter rarely revisited his definition of economics in terms of the formal analysis of 'exchange relations' or catallactics. While he gave more and more attention to dynamic analysis and economic development, some but not all later statements suggest the retention of a narrow definition of 'pure economics'. In some passages he broke his 1908 stipulations of the boundaries of economics; in other mature statements he seemed to reaffirm them.[7]

In a posthumously published book, written in English, Schumpeter (1954: 21) wrote: 'economic analysis deals with the questions of how people behave at any one time and what the economic effects are that they produce by so behaving; economic sociology deals with the question of how they came to behave as they do'. Although Schumpeter had made other statements with different connotations, this statement is consistent with the postwar consensus established by Lionel Robbins, Paul Samuelson and Talcott Parsons. Note that 'economic' in this passage is the adjective rather than the noun in both 'economic sociology' and 'economic history'. Schumpeter promoted neither 'sociological economics' nor 'historical economics' as descriptive terms. Whatever Schumpeter actually meant, this logically would suggest that economic sociology is a branch of sociology and economic history is a branch of history, neither being in economics proper. However, Schumpeter did not consistently pursue this line of argument.

In another passage, Schumpeter (1954: 819) opined that the study of institutions, including 'economic institutions', was the subject matter of 'economic sociology' rather than economics. One awkward logical consequence is that if markets are institutions, as several economists and sociologists uphold (Fligstein, 2001; Hodgson, 1988; Lie, 1997; Solow, 1990), then the study of markets is not the subject of economic analysis. Another uncomfortable corollary is that the work of 'new institutional economists' – including Oliver Williamson and Nobel Laureates in economics such Ronald Coase and Douglass North – do not qualify as economics by Schumpeter's (1954: 819) suggestion. However, as noted below, Schumpeter elsewhere recoiled from such restrictions. He did not follow the logic of this remark to its conclusion. Generally his statements on these issues are patchy, incomplete and partially inconsistent.

In a more inclusive mode, Schumpeter sometimes endorsed the inclusion of 'history' and 'statistics' within economics. For example, in another passage in this last book, Schumpeter (1954: 12) elliptically and briefly put 'history' as part of 'economic analysis'.

Ironically, much of Schumpeter's work, largely upon which his currently high reputation is built, was in the sphere of 'economic sociology' by some of his definitions. This is true of especially influential works such as his *Capitalism, Socialism and Democracy* (1942). Schumpeter frequently narrowed the definition of 'economic analysis' but always he saw it as extremely important to broaden the mind by travel across its boundaries. He also argued that the social science disciplines should learn from one another.

As Shionoya (1990; 1997) highlights, a key piece of evidence here is the seventh chapter in the *Theory of Economic Development*, omitted from the second German edition and from the English translation (Schumpeter, 1912; 2002). Here Schumpeter (2002: 94) argues that after the study of the 'static system . . . economic development poses the second most important problem faced by economists'. This chapter has a particularly interesting passage, involving some equivocation. Schumpeter (2002: 97) writes:

> Pure economic laws are similar to the laws of mechanics which tell us how bodies with mass behave under the influence of any external 'forces', but which do not describe the nature of those 'forces' . . . In the same way pure economics provides us with formal laws as to how the economy is shaped under the influence of conditions coming from the outside . . . Therefore, in such a conception, pure economics almost by definition excludes the phenomenon of a 'development of the economy from within'.

Yet in the next paragraph Schumpeter (ibid.) immediately qualifies the last striking statement above:

> Only rarely will such a conception be formulated explicitly. Frequently, it is the very reason for the silence of the theoreticians on the phenomenon of development itself; this corresponds to the standpoint of many of the best theorists. We do not completely deny that such a conception might be justified. It is true that this way of thinking corresponds to the fundamental principles of static economics . . . Those static laws are the basis of a scientific understanding of the economy. And to explain those effects is an important task of theoretical economics. As an abstraction, this conception is justified, even indispensable.

After noting with regret that traditional 'pure economics almost by definition' excludes the critical phenomenon of economic development, Schumpeter cannot quite bring himself to overturn this definition. Hence the equivocal phraseology when he does 'not completely deny that such a conception might be justified'. But he does not partially deny it either.

Shionoya (1990; 1997) suggests on the basis of this chapter that Schumpeter was moving towards the idea of a unified social science. There is much stronger evidence that Schumpeter retained from 1908 to his death in 1950 a supreme place for economic theory within the terrain of social science, alongside a clear recognition of the importance of historical and sociological perspectives.

The very removal of this chapter, especially for Schumpeter's (1926b: xi) declared reason that its historical and sociological leanings diverted attention from 'dry economic theory' in the volume, suggests a priority and narrower theoretical focus for economics as a discipline. On the other hand, this declaration itself suggests that Schumpeter regarded the chapters remaining in the later (1926b; 1934) editions as constituting 'economic theory' together with all the dynamic elements they contained. This position contrasts with the 1908 book, where static conceptions of economic theory are more prominent.

SCHUMPETER'S JOURNEY TO HARVARD

We have discussed Schumpeter's declared views on the boundaries of economics. To understand his catalytic role in the shift from Marshallian to Robbinsian conceptions of the subject, we have to consider the period of his life when his ambitions shifted from Europe to America. As a result of his move to Harvard University, Schumpeter became involved with authors who played a major part in redrawing the boundary between economics and sociology, and who helped to establish the consensus on these disciplinary boundaries after the Second World War.

In a related development, Schumpeter's explicit attitude to the German historical school altered remarkably in a short period of time. As late as 1926 Schumpeter published a sympathetic account of the work of Schmoller and other historical school theorists. In this article Schumpeter (1926a: 3, 18, 22, 24 n., 46) wrote of Schmoller's 'great achievements', of his 'greatness', of his work being 'the programme for the future', of 'his overall achievements' and of his 'success'. In the same article, Schumpeter saw much merit in the work of the leading American institutionalist Wesley Mitchell. Although he also raised thoughtful criticisms, the disposition was largely positive. Within four years, however, Schumpeter was to shift the balance of his assessment of historicism and institutionalism, towards severe criticism.

At this time, in producing the second (1926b) German edition of his *Theory of Economic Development*, Schumpeter decided to drop its rich and important seventh chapter, discussed above. This chapter was also omitted from the later English edition (Schumpeter, 1912; 1926b; 1934). On this issue, John Mathews (2002: 2) asks:

> Why then, did Schumpeter drop this innovative chapter from the second edition, and never refer to it again in his own published work? There is no clear or easy answer to this question. Perhaps he saw it as too precocious, too bold, and not appropriate for a mature man who by now aspired to a professorship at Harvard . . .

There is no evidence that Schumpeter wanted a job at Harvard as early as 1926, and he continued for a while to retain professional aspirations in Germany. However, Harvard was definitely an attraction, as he was a visiting professor at that university during 1927–28. At a time when many leading US departments of economics were dominated by institutionalists, Harvard inclined more to neoclassical ideas. One hypothesis is that the broader conception of economics suggested in this chapter of the 1912 work was perceived as too inclusive for Harvard economists. His 1926 book was of course published in German, but at that time the majority of US economists could read that language, given the global importance of the German literature in economics. Also after 1926, Schumpeter became more openly critical of the historical school and highly dismissive of the institutionalist tradition.[8]

In the Harvard-based *Quarterly Journal of Economics*, Schumpeter (1930: 158) referred scathingly to the intellectual capacities of both Schmoller and Veblen, and to 'the serious and even glaring defects in their equipment, both natural and acquired'. Schumpeter (1930: 159) also pronounced on the 'unsatisfactory state of economic science in Germany' and dismissed Veblen's work without adequately detailed criticism. In a talk in Japan in 1931, Schumpeter (1991: 292) referred to the 'methodological errors of German historians'. He also described institutionalism as 'the one dark spot in the American atmosphere'. Overall, there was a remarkable transformation from Schumpeter's sympathetic 1926 article on Schmoller, to the largely hostile statements of 1930–31, in which Schumpeter was keen to dismiss, and to detach himself from, the entire German historical school and American institutionalism. These negative statements may have aided his application for a professorship at Harvard.

Schumpeter attained a permanent post at Harvard in 1932. He had wanted to get Sombart's former chair in Berlin when it became vacant in 1931 but he was unsuccessful. Schumpeter's move to Harvard coincided with an increasing criticism of both the institutionalist and historical school traditions. Yet the irony is that Schumpeter continued throughout his life to draw on the work of the German historical school, and many of Schumpeter's ideas are traceable to their leading scholars.[9] Although there were oscillations in Schumpeter's views in this area, he remained devoted to broader research with historical and 'sociological' features.

At the same time, Schumpeter's residence in Harvard provided him with the opportunity to participate in discussions concerning the redrawing of the boundaries of economics itself, and particularly between economics and sociology. In this and other respects, his personal contacts with both Parsons and Samuelson in Harvard were of indubitable importance.

THE RECASTING OF ECONOMICS AND SOCIOLOGY

Previously educated in the American institutionalist tradition, in 1927 Parsons was appointed as an instructor in economics at Harvard University. He attended Schumpeter's economics classes and discussed a number of issues with him (Brick, 1993). At this time, Parsons was shifting away from institutionalism and was becoming more sympathetic to the neoclassical economists at Harvard (Camic, 1992). Schumpeter encouraged Parsons to study the work of Vilfredo Pareto, which had attracted the interest of a number of Harvard economists. Importantly for Parsons's line of research, Pareto had attempted a general theory in both economics and sociology, and tried to establish a boundary between the two disciplines.

Parsons had previously studied in Germany and was a translator of some of Max Weber's works into English. As David Zaret (1980: 1193) has argued, 'Parsons saw in Weber's writings a non-Marxian foundation for general theory.' The general theory for which Parsons aspired was to be even more general than the Paretian and Walrasian approaches admired by Schumpeter. As Hans Joas (1995: 275) pointed out: 'by dint of the approach he was taking, Parsons realized that he was being forced out of the prestigious discipline he had started his career in'. In 1931 Parsons transferred to a new department at Harvard, which was eventually named the department of sociology. 'Sociology offered Parsons a way out of this personal and theoretical crisis as well as a solution to the problem of the definition of the proper field of economics' (ibid.).

Consequently, Parsons became deeply engaged with the problem of demarcation between economics and sociology. To accommodate culture and institutions while rejecting the role of biology or instinct, sociology itself had to be transformed. Furthermore, it had to reach a new modus vivendi with the rising new wave of neoclassical economics and preserve its own intellectual territory. As Parsons (1970: 827) himself remarked: 'It gradually became clear to me that economic theory should be conceived as standing within some sort of theoretical matrix in which sociological theory also was included.'

Parsons and Schumpeter were both influenced by Pareto, who made a distinction between 'logical' and 'non-logical' actions. With 'logical' actions, the means were consistent with, and appropriate for, the given ends. For Pareto (1971), the study of such 'logical' actions was the domain of economics. On the other hand, Pareto (1935) upheld that the other class of 'non-logical' actions governed much of human behaviour, and these were the subject matter of sociology. Accordingly, economics was a limiting case of the broader theory of social action, which it was the task of sociology to build.

Pareto's limitation of economics to the 'logical' domain of means–ends relations meant that the discipline could sever its former links with psychology (Bruni and Sugden, 2007). Within economics, ends or preferences could be taken as given, and no longer required explanation. Here Pareto's stance paralleled Schumpeter's (1908: 64) claim that psychology was 'unrelated to economics'. A number of other authors returned to the writings of Pareto for inspiration at the time, including the British economists John

R. Hicks and R.G.D. Allen (1934) who attempted to recast utility theory in terms of the logic of choice rather than the psychology of behaviour.

While Schumpeter and Parsons discussed Pareto at Harvard, Robbins at the London School of Economics was working on a radical redefinition of the scope and boundaries of the dismal science. Particularly influenced by economists of the Austrian school, and echoing Pareto's exclusion of psychology from the discipline, Robbins redefined economics as the universal 'science of choice'. For him, economics was about the rational choice of means to serve given ends. The 'economic problem' was then to determine the best means available to meet those given ends. It applied to all economic systems, as long as there were choices to be made and a scarcity of resources. Economics was no longer defined in terms of a real object or zone of analysis, but in terms of specific assumptions and methods.

Parsons (1934) appraised Robbins's (1932) influential book in an important essay in the *Quarterly Journal of Economics.* For Parsons, in contrast to Robbins, ends and means could not entirely be separated. Furthermore, ends could not always be taken as 'given' because they were likely to be affected by the processes involved in their attainment. Second, Parsons stressed that social action was always framed and driven by social and institutional norms.

Crucially, however, Parsons did not reject Robbins's redefinition of economics. In fact, it served his purposes. By defining economics narrowly, as the science of rational choice, Robbins conceded a substantial territory to the sociologist. For Parsons, sociology was about the social and normative origin of the ends that Robbins had taken as given.

Parsons's tactic was to show that Robbinsian economics had to be grounded upon a general sociological theory. Economics would focus merely on the examination of the logical relationships between means and given ends. Sociology would then assume its place as the study of the social origin of the ends. Hence, Parsons (1937: 768) defined sociology as 'the science which attempts to develop an analytical theory of social action systems in so far as these systems can be understood in terms of the property of common-value integration'. This definition of the subject was not in terms of the analysis of 'social action systems' as a whole, but in terms of the impact and integration of common values. Sociology was thus defined as the study of an *aspect* of the social system. It had a delineated domain of enquiry. The study of other features was conceded to economists and others.

An implicit contract emerged between both economists and sociologists. Economics was henceforth to concern itself with the rational choice of means to serve given ends; sociology was to be concerned with the explanation of those values and ends. With Robbins (1932), economics became the 'science of choice' without much consideration of what 'choice' actually meant in philosophical terms. Under Parsons (1937: 768) sociology was reconstructed as 'the science . . . of social action' without much discussion of the materialist causes behind intention or action itself.

Crucially, both Parsons and Robbins avoided any direct and integrated analysis of socio-economic structures and institutions as a whole. Each of them focused on a selected analytical aspect. Each science was defined in terms of concepts and assumptions, rather than real objects of enquiry. Neither addressed the structured reality in its totality. By contrast, Schumpeter retained a strong integrating ambition in his work.

Both economics and sociology became redefined in terms of the study of types of analytical problem rather than in terms of the explanation of a distinct reality. They became compartmentalized, self-reflective discourses. After Parsons and Robbins, no social science addressed the study of socio-economic systems as a whole. The Comtean vision of a unified social science was finally abandoned.

Samuelson was a student of Schumpeter at Harvard in the 1930s. When Samuelson (1947; 1948) re-laid the foundations of post-war neoclassical economics and published his best-selling textbook, he adopted Robbins's definition of economics. Samuelson synthesized the approaches of Walras and Pareto in microeconomics with a version of Keynesian macroeconomics. Following Robbins, he took individual preference functions as given.

It is inconceivable that Schumpeter failed to discuss the boundaries between economics and sociology with Parsons. He is also very likely to have discussed the nature and scope of economics with Samuelson. Nevertheless, neither Parsons nor Samuelson adopted Schumpeter's exact position on these matters. Across the Atlantic, Robbins (1932) made several references to Schumpeter (1908), including criticism of Schumpeter's definition of economics as the science of 'exchange relations'.

Although Schumpeter's extensive involvement in discussions with Parsons is well documented, there is no clear evidence that he approved of the emerging Robbins–Parsons consensus on the boundaries of economics and sociology. However, it is also remarkable that he seemed reluctant to declare openly and forcefully his views on the legitimate and more inclusive boundaries of economics, at a critical time. A mystery concerning Schumpeter's role in this major redefinition of disciplinary boundaries was that he did not intervene more strongly, especially given his strong emphasis on economic evolution and dynamic transformation. Statements to this effect in the crucial period of the 1930s are extremely rare, despite his close connections at Harvard with two of the three most important people involved.

For example, in his 1937 preface to the Japanese edition of the *Theory of Economic Development*, he criticized Walras for conceiving of economic theory exclusively in static terms. Schumpeter also rejected the view that 'as economic theorists we cannot say much about the factors that account for historical changes'. He called instead for 'a purely economic theory of economic change' and upheld that he was trying to build such a theory (Clemence, 1951: 159–60).

On the other hand, we have to take into account the later statement, quoted above, where Schumpeter (1954: 21) describes 'economic analysis' and 'economic sociology' in terms that are consistent with the post-war Robbins–Parsons consensus on the boundaries between economics and sociology. Furthermore, during the 1930s and 1940s Schumpeter witnessed the much-delayed rise in popularity of the Walrasian general equilibrium approach, which he had championed many years earlier. He played a role in the shift of mainstream economics from a Marshallian to a Walrasian paradigm. It is possible that he became more flexible about the precise boundaries between economics and other disciplines, but retained a conception of economics where the Walrasian system was a defining pole of attraction within a broad field.

However, in his final essay, there is a hint that he was worried about some of the consequences of the Robbins–Parsons consensus and the dominance of general equilibrium theory over economics. His concern was that the study of historical and institutional factors would be diminished, as the discipline became more focused on formal models. Schumpeter (1951: 308) thus wrote: 'there is an argument for historical or institutional study in almost any department of economics'.

But it was too little and too late. The Robbins–Parsons redefinitions had already taken hold and were spreading in their influence. Economics recast as the narrower 'science of choice', underwent a 'formalistic revolution' (Blaug, 1999, 2003; Ward, 1972) and excluded many Marshallian concerns from the very scope of 'economics' itself. At least until the 1970s, Parsons's ideas dominated sociology, along with his conception of the scope and boundaries of the subject. Despite the huge influence of Marshall, especially in the first half of the twentieth century, economics in the second half generally defined itself in narrower and Robbinsian terms, as the 'science of choice' taking purposes or preferences as given.

Overall, rather than being leading or decisive, it seems that Schumpeter played an equivocal but catalytic role in the recasting of the boundaries of economics from the 1930s. Significantly, in the crucial debates of the time, he mounted no strong defence of broader boundaries in any work intended for an English-speaking audience. In the critical 1930–50 period he failed to challenge openly and directly the emerging Robbins–Parsons consensus. But some evidence in the final years of his life suggests that he was concerned about the emerging outcome.

CONCLUSION: THE END OF THE PARSONS–ROBBINS CONSENSUS AND THE NEED FOR REDEFINITION

Schumpeter was involved in intellectual circles that not only changed the prevailing definition of economics from the Marshallian study of the 'ordinary business of life' to the narrower Robbinsian 'science of choice' but also shifted the definition of sociology from the Comtean science of society to the Parsonian emphasis on the origin and integration of values. Schumpeter at least played the role of a catalyst in these shifts, although the outcome was different from his own views on the boundaries of 'economics' or 'economic theory'.

The Robbins–Parsons conceptions of the nature and boundaries of both economics and sociology endured from the 1930s to the 1980s. The result of the Robbins–Parsons settlement was that economics and sociology were each concerned with an *aspect* of the social system as a whole. 'Sociology' existed, but no science was devoted to the study of the whole society. 'Economics' endured, but no science was principally devoted to the study of the economy as such. Ironically, despite his role in this schism, Schumpeter's own work retained a strong integrative and interdisciplinary character.

However, by the end of the twentieth century, the Robbins–Parsons settlement had crumbled. The core concepts in each discipline came under attack. Furthermore, researchers calling themselves 'economists' or 'sociologists' enthusiastically trespassed on the traditional domain of the other discipline. There have been consequent challenges to core ideas, and open trespassing on territories claimed by other disciplines.

Within sociology, the Parsonian hegemony eventually crumbled after sustained criticism from all sides. Owing to James Coleman (1990) and others, rational actor models – formerly the exclusive preserve of economists – invaded sociology as well as political science.

On the other side, 'economists' such as Gary Becker (1981) ventured into the 'sociological' territory of marriage and the family. More dramatically, within economics game theory showed that the concept of rationality was itself insufficiently well-specified, and experimental economists became increasingly persuaded by evidence that seemed to undermine the rationality assumption (Kagel and Roth, 1995; Kahneman, 1994; Sugden, 1991). Against the tenet of given preferences, several leading economists now admit endogenous and situation-dependent preference formation in economics (Akerlof and Kranton, 2005; Bowles, 1998; 2004).[10] Based in part on evidence from interviews of graduate students at the most prestigious departments of economics, David Colander (2005b: 930) has studied how the upcoming generation of mainstream economists are abandoning the ' "holy trinity" assumptions of rationality, greed and equilibrium'.[11]

Consequently, with the erosion of core concepts on both sides, the very meaning and identity of 'economics' and 'sociology' are open to question. Furthermore, previously established frontiers between the disciplines are being transgressed from both sides. Despite claims to the contrary, there are no adequately specified accounts that 'economics' or 'sociology' can be defined in terms of their core methods or results (Hodgson, 2008; Kalleberg, 1995; Rojas, 2006; Velthuis, 1999; Zafirovski, 1999). Particular methodological claims and related definitions are contested by multiple dissenting voices from within each discipline.

These circumstances call for a concerted re-examination of the boundaries between economics and sociology, the nature of each subject, their subject matter and the subdivisions within the social sciences as a whole. This is one of the most important – but hitherto neglected – tasks for economists and sociologists at the beginning of the twenty-first century. I hazard to suggest that in such circumstances both Marshall and Schumpeter would have fully appreciated its urgency.

NOTES

1. This chapter makes use of some material from Hodgson (2001). I am extremely grateful to Markus Becker, Mário da Graça Moura, and Thorbjørn Knudsen for extensive critical comments on previous drafts, including the correction of several significant errors. Others including Mark Blaug, Yanis Varoufalis and participants at the Hitotsubashi conference are also warmly thanked for their helpful suggestions.
2. The influence of the German historical school on Schumpeter has been more widely discussed. See Machlup (1951), Swedberg (1989), Streissler (1994), Chaloupek (1995), Shionoya (1997), Ebner (2000) and Hodgson (2001).
3. Sociology was then in its infancy as a discipline. Marshall (1920: 771 n.) argued that sociology was not yet ready to play a unificatory role for the social sciences as a whole. This suggests that Marshall adopted a Comtean understanding of the relationship between economics and sociology, where the latter provided an overarching framework for the social sciences.
4. See Schumpeter (1908: 64–8, 77–9, 85–91, 154–5, 261, 541–7).
5. As Shionoya (1997) explains, Schumpeter was strongly influenced by Ernst Mach's positivism and its stress on observable behaviour. Accordingly, Schumpeter (1908: 47, 93–4, 454) argued that the investigation of the causes of phenomena are irrelevant for 'pure theory' (Graça Moura, 2003: 288–90). Hence in his 1908 book Schumpeter focuses on behavioural regularities rather than explicit underlying assumptions about wants or preferences. Nevertheless, in its demarcating effects, his 1908 position is equivalent to the idea of taking wants as given, or assuming given preferences, as a basis for the definition of the boundaries of economic theory.
6. Schumpeter (1909: 216) also admits the study of 'social wants' as within economic theory, but only on condition that they can be accounted for by 'individuals acting as a community consciously and jointly'. Again, for him, the appropriate focus for theory is on explanations in terms of individuals, but not on explanations of the origins of individual wants themselves.
7. Schumpeter later expressed some dissatisfaction with his 1908 position. Ludwig Lachmann recollected that in in London 1936 Robbins asked Schumpeter why *Das*

Wesen had not been published in English. Schumpeter replied: 'Because I don't like it . . . There are things in it I no longer believe' (Mittermaier, 1992: 11).

8. Strikingly, some of the positive appraisals of German historicists in Schumpeter (1926b) were removed from the first English edition of that work. Compare, for instance, the positive footnote on Sombart in Schumpeter (1926b: 90 n.) with Schumpeter (1934: 61).
9. For example, Schumpeter's famous phrase 'creative destruction' has a precedent in a work by Sombart (1913: 207). See also Appel (1992: 260–62).
10. An earlier admission, in a prominent mainstream journal, is found in Hammond (1976).
11. See also Colander (2005a), Colander et al. (2004a; 2004b), Davis (2006).

REFERENCES

Akerlof, George A. and Rachel E. Kranton (2005), 'Identity and the economics of organizations', *Journal of Economic Perspectives*, **19** (1), 9–32.

Allen, Robert L. (1991), *Opening Doors: The Life and Work of Joseph Schumpeter*, 2 vols, New Brunswick, NJ: Transaction.

Appel, Michael (1992), *Werner Sombart: Historiker und Theoretiker des modernen Kapitalismus*, Marburg: Metropolis.

Becker, Gary S. (1981), *A Treatise on the Family*, Cambridge, MA: Harvard University Press.

Blaug, Mark (1999), 'The formalist revolution or what happened to orthodox economics after World War II?', in Roger E. Backhouse and John Creedy (eds), *From Classical Economics to the Theory of the Firm: Essays in Honour of D.P. O'Brien*, Cheltenham, UK and Northampton, MA, USA: Edward Elgar, pp. 257–80.

Blaug, Mark (2003), 'The formalist revolution of the 1950s', in Warren J. Samuels, Jeff E. Biddle and John B. Davis (eds), *A Companion to the History of Economic Thought*, Malden, MA and Oxford: Blackwell, pp. 395–410.

Bowles, Samuel (1998), 'Endogenous preferences: the cultural consequences of markets and other economic institutions', *Journal of Economic Literature*, **36** (1), 75–111.

Bowles, Samuel (2004), *Microeconomics: Behavior, Institutions, and Evolution*, Princeton, NJ and New York: Princeton University Press and Russell Sage Foundation.

Brick, Howard (1993), 'The reformist dimension of Talcott Parsons's early social theory', in Thomas L. Haskell and Richard F. Teichgraeber (eds), *The Culture of the Market: Historical Essays*, Cambridge: Cambridge University Press, pp. 357–96.

Bruni, Luigino and Robert Sugden (2007), 'The road not taken: how psychology was removed from economics and how it might be brought back', *Economic Journal*, **117** (1), 146–73.

Camic, Charles (1992), 'Reputation and predecessor selection: Parsons and the institutionalists', *American Sociological Review*, **57** (4), 421–45.

Chaloupek, Günther K. (1995), 'Long-term economic perspectives compared: Joseph Schumpeter and Werner Sombart', *European Journal of the History of Economic Thought*, **2** (1), 127–49.

Clemence, Richard V. (ed.) (1951), *Essays on Economic Topics of J.A. Schumpeter*, Cambridge, and Port Washington, NY: Cambridge University Press and Kennikat.

Colander, David C. (2005a), 'The making of an economist redux', *Journal of Economic Perspectives*, **19** (1), 175–98.

Colander, David C. (2005b), 'The future of economics: the appropriately educated in pursuit of the knowable', *Cambridge Journal of Economics*, **29** (6), 927–41.

Colander, David C., Richard P.F. Holt and J. Barkley Rosser Jr (2004a), *The Changing Face of Economics: Interviews with Cutting Edge Economists*, Ann Arbor, MI: University of Michigan Press.

Colander, David C., Richard P.F. Holt and J. Barkley Rosser Jr (2004b), 'The changing face of economics', *Review of Political Economy*, **16** (4), 485–99.

Coleman, James S. (1990), *Foundations of Social Theory*, Cambridge, MA: Harvard University Press.

Cunningham, William (1892), 'The relativity of economic doctrines', *Economic Journal*, **2** (1), 1–16.

Davis, John B. (2006), 'The turn in economics: neoclassical dominance to mainstream pluralism?', *Journal of Institutional Economics*, **2** (1), 1–20.

Ebner, Alexander (2000), 'Schumpeter and the "Schmollerprogramm": integrating theory and history in the analysis of economic development', *Journal of Evolutionary Economics*, **10** (3), 355–72.

Edgeworth, Francis Y. (1881), *Mathematical Psychics: An Essay on the Application of Mathematics to the Moral Sciences*, London: Kegan Paul.

Edgeworth, Francis Y. (1891), 'The British Economic Association', *Economic Journal*, **1** (1), 1–2.

Ekelund, Robert B. Jr and Robert F. Hébert (2002), 'The origins of neoclassical economics', *Journal of Economic Perspectives*, **16** (3), 197–215.

Fligstein, Neil (2001), *The Architecture of Markets: An Economic Sociology of Twenty-First Century Capitalist Societies*, Princeton, NJ: Princeton University Press.

Graça Moura, Mário da (2003), 'Schumpeter on the integration of theory and history', *European Journal of the History of Economic Thought*, **10** (2), 279–301.

Hammond, Peter J. (1976), 'Changing tastes and coherent dynamic choice', *Review of Economic Studies*, **43** (1), 159–173.

Hicks, John R. and R.G.D. Allen (1934), 'A reconsideration of the theory of value', Parts 1 and 2, *Economica*, **1** (1), 52–76, and **1** (2), 176–219.

Hodgson, Geoffrey M. (1988), *Economics and Institutions: A Manifesto for a Modern Institutional Economics*, Cambridge and Philadelphia, PA: Polity Press and University of Pennsylvania Press.

Hodgson, Geoffrey M. (2001), *How Economics Forgot History: The Problem of Historical Specificity in Social Science*, London and New York: Routledge.

Hodgson, Geoffrey M. (2005), 'Alfred Marshall versus the historical school?' *Journal of Economic Studies*, **32** (4), 331–48.

Hodgson, Geoffrey M. (2008), 'Prospects for economic sociology' (review article), *Philosophy of the Social Sciences*, **38** (1), March, 133–49..

Hutchison, Terence W. (1988), 'Gustav Schmoller and the problems of today', *Journal of Institutional and Theoretical Economics*, **144** (3), 527–531.

Jevons, William Stanley (1888), *The Theory of Political Economy*, 3rd edn, London: Macmillan.

Joas, Hans (1995), 'Communitarianism, pragmatism, historicism', in Peter Koslowski (ed.), *The Theory of Ethical Economy in the Historical School: Wilhelm Roscher, Lorenz von Stein, Gustav Schmoller, Wilhelm Dilthey and Contemporary Theory*, Berlin: Springer, pp. 267–85.

Kagel, John H. and Alvin E. Roth (eds) (1995), *The Handbook of Experimental Economics*, Princeton, NJ: Princeton University Press.

Kahneman, Daniel (1994), 'New challenges to the rationality assumption', *Journal of Institutional and Theoretical Economics*, **150** (1), 18–36.
Kalleberg, Arne L. (1995), 'Sociology and economics: crossing the boundaries', *Social Forces*, **73** (4), 1207–18.
Keynes, John Maynard (1936), *The General Theory of Employment, Interest and Money*, London: Macmillan.
Lie, John (1997), 'Sociology of markets', *Annual Review of Sociology*, **23**, 341–60.
Machlup, Fritz (1951), 'Schumpeter's economic methodology', *Review of Economics and Statistics*, **33** (2), 145–51.
Marshall, Alfred (1885), 'The present position of economics', in Arthur C. Pigou (ed.) (1925) *Memorials of Alfred Marshall*, London: Macmillan, pp. 152–74.
Marshall, Alfred (1890), *Principles of Economics: An Introductory Volume*, London: Macmillan.
Marshall, Alfred (1892), 'A reply to "The perversion of economic history" by Dr. Cunningham', *Economic Journal*, **2**, 507–19.
Marshall, Alfred (1897), 'The old generation of economists and the new', *Quarterly Journal of Economics*, **11**, 115–35.
Marshall, Alfred (1907), 'The social possibilities of economic chivalry', *Economic Journal*, **17** (1), 7–29.
Marshall, Alfred (1920), *Principles of Economics: An Introductory Volume*, 8th edn, London: Macmillan.
Mathews, John A. (2002), 'Introduction: Schumpeter's "lost" seventh chapter', *Industry and Innovation*, **9** (1–2), 1–5.
Menger, Carl (1883), *Untersuchungen über die Methode der Sozialwissenschaften und der politischen Ökonomie insbesondere*, Tübingen: J.C.B. Mohr, published in English as Menger, Carl (1985), *Investigations into the Method of the Social Sciences with Special Reference to Economics*, New York: New York University Press.
Mitchell, Wesley C. (1916), 'The role of money in economic theory', *American Economic Review (Papers and Proceedings)*, **6** (1), 140–61.
Mitchell, Wesley C. (1969), *Types of Economic Theory: From Mercantilism to Institutionalism*, 2 vols, ed. J. Dorfman, New York: Augustus Kelley.
Mittermaier, K.H.M. (1992), 'Ludwig Lachmann (1906–1990): a biographical sketch', *South African Journal of Economics* ', **60** (1), 7–23.
Pareto, Vilfredo (1935), *The Mind and Society*, 4 vols, trans. from the Italian edition of 1923 by A. Bongiorno and A. Livingston, and ed. by A. Livingston, London: Jonathan Cape.
Pareto, Vilfredo (1971), *Manual of Political Economy*, trans. from the French edition of 1927 by A.S. Schwier, and ed. by A.S. Schwier and A.N. Page, New York: Augustus Kelley.
Parsons, Talcott (1934), 'Some reflections on "The nature and significance of economics" ', *Quarterly Journal of Economics*, **48** (3), 511–45.
Parsons, Talcott (1937), *The Structure of Social Action*, 2 vols, New York: McGraw-Hill.
Parsons, Talcott (1970), 'On building social systems theory: a personal history', *Daedalus*, Winter, 826–81.
Robbins, Lionel (1932), *An Essay on the Nature and Significance of Economic Science*, London: Macmillan.
Rojas, Fabio (2006), 'Sociological imperialism in three theories of the market', *Journal of Institutional Economics*, **2** (3), 339–63.

Samuelson, Paul A. (1947), *Foundations of Economic Analysis*, Cambridge, MA: Harvard University Press.
Samuelson, Paul A. (1948), *Economics*, New York: McGraw-Hill.
Schmoller, Gustav (1900), *Grundriss der allgemeinen Volkswirtschaftslehre, Erster Teil*, München und Leipzig: Duncker & Humblot.
Schumpeter, Joseph A. (1908), *Das Wesen und der Hauptinhalt der theoretischen Nationalökonomie*, München und Leipzig: Duncker & Humblot.
Schumpeter, Joseph A. (1909), 'On the concept of social value', *Quarterly Journal of Economics*, **23** (2), 213–32.
Schumpeter, Joseph A. (1912), *Theorie der wirtschaftlichen Entwicklung: Eine Untersuchung über Unternehmergewinn, Kapital, Kredit, Zins und den Konjunkturzylkus*, München und Leipzig: Duncker & Humblot.
Schumpeter, Joseph A. (1926a), 'Gustav v. Schmoller und die Probleme von heute', *Schmollers Jahrbuch für Gesetzgebung, Verwaltung und Volkwirtschaft im Deutschen Reiche*, **50**, 1–52.
Schumpeter, Joseph A. (1926b), *Theorie der wirtschaftlichen Entwicklung: Eine Untersuchung über Unternehmergewinn, Kapital, Kredit, Zins und den Konjunkturzylkus*, 2nd edn, München und Leipzig: Duncker & Humblot.
Schumpeter, Joseph A. (1928), 'The instability of capitalism', *Economic Journal*, **38**, 361–86. Reprinted in R.V. Clemence (1951), *Essays on Economic Topics of J.A, Schumpeter*, Cambridge and Port Washington, NY: Cambridge University Press and Kennikat.
Schumpeter, Joseph A. (1930), 'Mitchell's business cycles', *Quarterly Journal of Economics*, **45** (1), 150–72.
Schumpeter, Joseph A. (1931), 'The present world depression: a tentative diagnosis', *American Economic Review (Papers and Proceedings)*, **21** (1), Supplement, 179–82.
Schumpeter, Joseph A. (1934), *The Theory of Economic Development: An Inquiry into Profits, Capital, Credit, Interest, and the Business Cycle*, trans. by Redvers Opie from the second German edition of 1926, first edition 1911, Cambridge, MA: Harvard University Press.
Schumpeter, Joseph A. (1941), 'Alfred Marshall's principles: a semi-centennial appraisal', *American Economic Review*, **31** (2), 236–48.
Schumpeter, Joseph A. (1942), *Capitalism, Socialism and Democracy*, London: George Allen & Unwin.
Schumpeter, Joseph A. (1951), 'The historical approach to the analysis of business cycles' in Richard V. Clemence (ed.), *Essays on Economic Topics of J.A. Schumpeter*, Port Washington, NY: Kennikat, pp. 308–15.
Schumpeter, Joseph A. (1954), *History of Economic Analysis*, Oxford and New York: Oxford University Press.
Schumpeter, Joseph A. (1991), *The Economics and Sociology of Capitalism*, ed. Richard Swedberg, Princeton, NJ: Princeton University Press.
Schumpeter, Joseph A. (2002), 'The economy as a whole: seventh chapter of the theory of economic development', trans. Ursula Backhaus from J.A. Schumpeter (1912), *Industry and Innovation*, **9** (1–2), 93–145.
Shionoya, Yuichi (1990), 'The origin of the Schumpeterian research program: a chapter omitted from Schumpeter's *Theory of Economic Development* ', *Journal of Institutional and Theoretical Economics*, **146** (2), 314–27.
Shionoya, Yuichi (1997), *Schumpeter and the Idea of Social Science: A Metatheoretical Study*, Cambridge and New York: Cambridge University Press.

Shove, Gerald F. (1942), 'The place of Marshall's *Principles* in the development of economic theory', *Economic Journal*, **52** (4), 294–329.

Skidelsky, Robert (1983), *John Maynard Keynes: Volume One: Hopes Betrayed, 1883–1920*, London: Macmillan.

Solow, Robert M. (1990), *The Labor Market as a Social Institution*, Oxford: Basil Blackwell.

Sombart, Werner (1913), *Krieg und Kapitalismus*, München und Leipzig: Duncker & Humblot.

Sombart, Werner (1929), 'Economic theory and economic history', *European History Review*, **2** (1), 1–19.

Streissler, Erich W. (1994), 'The influence of German and Austrian economics on Joseph A. Schumpeter', in Yuichi Shionoya and Mark Perlman (eds), *Schumpeter in the History of Ideas*, Ann Arbor, MI: University of Michigan Press.

Sugden, Robert (1991), 'Rational choice: a survey of contributions from economics and philosophy', *Economic Journal*, **101** (4), 751–85.

Swedberg, Richard (1989), 'Joseph A. Schumpeter and the tradition of economic sociology', *Journal of Institutional and Theoretical Economics*, **145**, 508–24.

Veblen, Thorstein B. (1900), 'The preconceptions of economic science: III', *Quarterly Journal of Economics*, **14** (2), 240–69.

Velthuis, Olav (1999), 'The changing relationship between economic sociology and institutional economics: from Talcott Parsons to Mark Granovetter', *American Journal of Economics and Sociology*, **58** (4), 629–49.

Ward, Benjamin (1972), *What's Wrong With Economics?*, London: Macmillan.

Whitaker, John K. (ed.) (1996), *The Correspondence of Alfred Marshall*, 3 vols, Cambridge: Cambridge University Press.

Zafirovski, Milan (1999), 'Economic sociology in retrospect and prospect: in search of its identity within economics and sociology', *American Journal of Economics and Sociology*, **58** (4), 583–627.

Zaret, David (1980), 'From Weber to Parsons and Schultz: the eclipse of history in modern social theory', *American Journal of Sociology*, **85** (5), 1180–201.

6. The broken thread: Marshall, Schumpeter and Hayek on the evolution of capitalism

J.S. Metcalfe*

INTRODUCTION

In this chapter I explore some of the foundations for an evolutionary approach to economics by considering the writing of three important economists, Marshall, Schumpeter and Hayek, in the light of evolutionary theory. In particular, I suggest that these diverse writers are linked by a thread of evolutionary reasoning made evident in their treatment of the dynamics of economic development, its connection to innovation and economic adaptation to emergent novelty and, more deeply, to the link between wealth creation and the growth of knowledge. Within the canon of modern economic thought that thread is broken. It turned out that while Marshall explicitly invoked evolutionary reasoning in his *Principles*, published in 1890 with revised editions through to 1920, his followers systematically eliminated all traces of this dynamic perspective from the body of economic theory. Schumpeter and Hayek, too, wrote in evolutionary terms but remained out of the mainstream. Yet the writings of this triumvirate provide the basis for a general theory of evolutionary economics. Of course, modern evolutionary economists enthusiastically acknowledge a debt to Schumpeter; my claim is that they should also acknowledge the contributions of Marshall and Hayek in providing the foundations for evolutionary economic dynamics.

What is at stake is no mere quibble over terms with mainstream, neoclassical economics but a thoroughgoing difference of view into the nature of modern capitalism and its development. Ideas in relation to equilibrium states, competition, development, institutions and the role of knowledge are deeply contested. The fundamental change in view is that knowledge-based economies of a capitalist kind are necessarily open, non-equilibrium systems for which there is no obvious long-term limit to the kinds of and composition of the economic activities that they contain.[1] They must of course be organized in order to evolve but order should not be equated with equilibrium. I try to show why these differences matter, and they matter in particular in relation to our understanding of the connection between economic organization and development. The undeniable claim that capitalism has never been stationary and that its unfolding is spatially and temporally very uneven is the central historical fact of economic life (Landes, 1968; 2002; Mokyr, 1990; 2002; Nelson, 2005). The argument we pursue here is that the development of economic activity in all its different forms is inseparable from the growth of knowledge, boosted by the emergence of organized science and technology and witness to immense economic transformation. What is it about capitalism as a system that has made this possible? The answer is that these features arise because it is an evolutionary system, with instituted rules of conduct that promote economic mutation through the search for and application of new knowledge, to challenge and transform the prevailing disposition of activities and resources. How to represent this complex skein of possibilities in our economic thinking is the question that Marshall, Schumpeter and Hayek addressed in very different but complementary ways. I should perhaps add that in the following I take a semantic view of theories in economics. To theorize is to abstract and the abstractions are not one-to-one maps of the real phenomena; they are designed to explain, yet the design is false if no correspondence principles can be found to connect the abstraction with reality. It is in the specification of what constitutes the relevant isomorphism that controversy usually arises. A relevant example will be discussed below in terms of the concept of a stationary state, certainly an abstract model but one that has no connecting links to the world of capitalism, or so Marshall, Schumpeter and Hayek would have us believe.

SCHUMPETER

It is appropriate to begin with Schumpeter, the acknowledged father of modern evolutionary economics. His central vision of the dynamics of capitalism was set out in the *Theory of Economic Development* (1912 [1934]) and remained substantially, but not entirely unaltered through *Business Cycles* (1939) and the post-war articles that provide such a convenient summary of his position (1947a; 1947b). It is in all its essentials a variation cum selection model of economic change although Schumpeter never expresses the fact in this way. Like Marshall, though with a different intent, he separates the model of a stationary or even a regularly expanding economy, which in his case comes from Walras, from the reality of capitalist development.[2] Schumpeter's capitalism is not a system in equilibrium but one which through entrepreneurial action and adaptation to that action is continually transformed, and the manner of its transformation is evolutionary. Evolution is not change *simpliciter* but rather change that involves either or both of two separate causal logics, one based on the idea of an unfolding of interconnected possibilities and the other based on a population dynamics of differential growth. In Schumpeter's scheme the content of individual economic activities evolves through time as does their relative importance so that the detailed structures of how economic activity is conducted at different dates may share little in common. This is the high theme of creative destruction; a term which, it is significant to note, has deeper origins in German nineteenth-century economic thought (Renart and Renart, 2005, Santarelli and Pesciarelli, 1990; Streissler, 1994).

To summarize what is already well known, Schumpeter's source of variation is entrepreneurial activity defined as the introduction of novel ways of conducting economic activity, a process which we might term the formulation of business experiments for short. Innovations are the novelties, the impossibilities rendered actual, and the sources of economic variety on which the competitive process operates to evaluate the new and adapt according to the relative advantages that the new ways possess over the old ways. This is a theoretical scheme that makes a distinction between creative action or response and adaptive action or response contingent on whether or not 'the doing of new things or the doing of things that are already being done in a new way' is entailed (Schumpeter, 1947a: 151). Part of the story is about the conditions generating innovations and the kinds of innovation in play. The other part is about the way in which patterns of co-ordinated economic activity, whether in organizations or markets, respond to the potential changes latent in any innovation. Evolutionists would recognize this as a classic variation cum selection process in which the relative fitness of different economic methods, old and new, are jointly determined and jointly adapted, too, for the prevailing economic arrangements always provide the external environment in which the new can be tried and tested. Not all innovations need succeed, but those that do have passed a test of profitability and, whether they are new forms of textile machinery or a new caviar product, the dynamics of adaptation is the same; it is a process of transformation of a population. The differential profit advantage of the new attracts investment in the form of imitation by less adventurous business minds, thus increasing the supply of the relevant class of commodity or service. In so doing, the system of output and input quantities and prices is transformed until the entrepreneurial profit is eliminated. As Schumpeter famously expressed the matter, profit 'is at the same time the child and the victim of development' (1912 [1934]: 154). This perspective, evolution as variation cum selection, shades into the alternative perspective, evolution as unfolding. Innovations are rarely fully developed when they first appear but, rather, offer up an economic design space for exploration through further innovation to define a sequence or trajectory of related developments, a theme which is by now standard fare in the innovation literature (Dosi, 1982; Murmann and Frenken, 2006; Utterback, 1994). How this sequence is realized is not independent of the context in which the innovations are commercialized and spread, so the two perspectives of a development trajectory of related innovations and of a process of competitive selection of rival innovations become intertwined.

From another perspective this is a model of knowledge-based economic transformation. Innovation as business experimentation always engages with a conjecture about a hypothetical, alternative economic structure. The carrying into effect of that conjecture depends on scarce leadership qualities, within the new enterprise and in relation to the mobilization of resources, to give effect to novelty and overcome the manifold liabilities of newness (Metcalfe, 2006; Witt, 1998). In the process, new economic information and knowledge is generated and it is the awareness of that new information that stimulates others to follow as imitators. So Schumpeter's capitalistic dynamic is a knowledge- and information-based dynamic, a point of considerable significance when we turn, below, to Hayek. However, the new knowledge in question is not only, perhaps not even, a matter of high science and technology. Invention is not innovation, technology experiments are not business experiments, and in a telling phrase, the innovation 'need not be of spectacular or of historic importance', the humble innovation is quite essential to the business process (1947a: 151). With the passage of time, Schumpeter's sense of the agency that performs the entrepreneurial function extended from the creative individual to the corporate team but in all cases it required the possibility of imagination to conceive of possible alternate economic worlds, as well as leadership and the sure evaluation of possibilities. Corporate innovation, whatever its merits in terms of access to superior resources to innovate, may be fatally compromised by the conflict between leadership and bureaucratic action that can be characteristic of large organizations. Of course, the large firm need not dominate the innovation process completely, as the modern world of innovation in Internet and biomedicine so powerfully illustrate. No matter what may be the precise form of entrepreneurial agency, the crucial Schumpeterian insight is that capitalism is not a system to preserve the status quo but rather a self-transforming system in which transformation of economic knowing and transformation of economic activity go hand in hand.

One of the great strengths of Schumpeter's approach is that his scheme of innovation is grounded in wider sociological considerations. Any innovation may meet hostility from established incumbents because the gains to novelty are necessarily losses to tradition, and so it is essential that the system is guided by institutions that are sufficiently open to accept the challenge from novelty. Capitalism cannot be conservative in its actions even though it must be conservative in its framing rules. The rules of the decentralized market process certainly facilitate openness and adaptation to innovation, but even they may need supplementing by regulatory action to prevent the suppression of enterprise. It is here that Schumpeter alighted on a matter of the greatest importance, that business experimentation is an investment that requires resources to be committed in anticipation of results. This is not a matter of the finance of routine working capital but rather project finance that must accommodate the incalculable uncertainties carried by emergent novelty, and for which no offsetting collateral assets can be offered directly by the entrepreneur – such assets are yet to be created. Schumpeter's identification of the role of capital and credit in funding and filtering emergent novelty is one of his major contributions to the understanding of innovation: no matter that he may have misunderstood the facts of innovation finance in Austria, the innovation finance connection is at the centre of the capitalist dynamic (Streissler, 1994). Unwillingness on the part of banks and the capital market to fund innovation constrains enterprise within established businesses, those able to deploy internal finance or offer collateral assets not immediately connected with the innovation in view, and so biases the process against the 'new man'. We may suggest that the recently instituted innovations associated with the growth of venture capital and corporate venturing, in the USA in particular, is an instituted Schumpeterian response to the highly uncertain nature of business experimentation in the context of radically new technologies and markets (Freeman, 2005).

The social and instituted framing of capitalism matters in another dimension too, in relation to the cultural acceptance or not of the large rewards that can be associated with successful innovation. Inequality of outcomes is integral to the evolutionary process, success and failure are inevitably conjoined and there is no requirement, *pace* the standards of Paretian welfare theory, for those who gain to compensate those who lose. Creative capitalism is uncomfortable capitalism and competition 'red in tooth and claw' could rightly be dismissed as unacceptable by many.[3] The intrinsic instability of economic arrangements in innovation-driven systems, when combined with a relatively slower rate of social adaptation compared to economic adaptation, is the source of much of the disruption that is imposed on particular individuals in terms of loss of employment, enforced change of locality or obsolescence of human capital. Here there is a paradox that Schumpeter forces us to confront: the stability of the price system, so important to the possibility of a coherent market order, must be set in the context of the instability posed by innovation.[4] Capitalism is a system in which all positions are potentially open to the challenge of creative destruction and will remain so under the present rules of the game. We are straying here into the ethical foundations of capitalism and of how a balance is to be struck between the beneficial effects of creation and the detrimental effects of destruction. It is not that Schumpeter offered solutions to such problems but, rather, that he knew that an evolving cultural, social component would determine the continuing possibilities for innovation-led competition.[5] On average the system is progressive, but progress comes at a cost in terms of the unevenness of rewards generated by a restless capitalism.

Why is Schumpeter's capitalism restless? It is because it has metaphorically struck a Faustian bargain with knowledge and it is the identification of this connection between enterprise and new knowledge which is Schumpeter's enduring contribution to economics. Like Marshall and Hayek, he was well ahead of his time, and economic theory has yet to fully absorb the implications of this conjunction of ideas. Indeed if progress, that is to say development and growth, involve 'putting productive resources to uses *hitherto untried in practice*, and withdrawing them from the uses they have served so far' (Schumpeter, 1928: 378, emphasis in original), this would present three major challenges to economic theory, namely the impossibility of predicting economic evolution *ex ante* even when the general rules of innovation and adaptation are understood; the irreversible effects of the growth of knowledge and the impossibility of placing an economy in equilibrium if knowledge is not in equilibrium; and the inevitable link between individuality and personal knowledge such that socially situated, developing individuals matter vitally to the evolution of the system. Economic agents are not homogeneous, fixed automata and, if they were, no progress would be possible and no history would await their discovery. It will not be lost on the reader that individual heterogeneity is a founding concept in evolutionary theory too. It is these three challenges that surprisingly connect Schumpeter with Marshall and Hayek. As we shall claim in the conclusion, they also connect his thought with modern complexity thinking, but that claim must be held in check for the moment.

MARSHALL[6]

Although Marshall's great work preceded Schumpeter's 1912 opus by fully two decades, it is quite remarkable how much they have in common when describing a dynamics of capitalism based on evolutionary principles. Unfortunately, Marshall's evolutionism was not taken seriously by his followers, who systematically replaced his dynamics of capitalism by a static jigsaw puzzle in which the economic problem is reduced to the explanation of the most appropriate place for each resource in the economic structure (Shove, 1930). All the talk of biology as economic Mecca was soon forgotten and, worse, commentators such as Samuelson (1967) were able to berate poor Marshall for his prattle about the biological method and the deleterious affects this had had on the development of economic theory. With the benefit of a resurgent evolutionary economics, post Nelson and Winter (1982), this dismissal of Marshall's evolutionism is no longer tenable. His evolutionary credentials should not be in doubt. As Schumpeter (1941: 93) argued, in his semi-centennial celebration of the *Principles*, Marshall's is 'one of the first economists to realise that economics is an evolutionary science', his thought 'ran in terms of evolutionary change – in terms of an organic, irreversible process'. That Marshall's evolutionary credentials are no longer recognized is no doubt in part due to Marshall himself (Loasby, 1990) but it does not require much effort to draw them out and place them in perspective.

What is the evolutionary content of Marshall's thought? In a remarkable way it runs parallel to Schumpeter, although it is more formal in terms of its use of the demand and supply apparatus. Just as Schumpeter used the stationary circular flow to describe what capitalism could not be, so Marshall rejects the stationary state as a starting point for economic reasoning. It is a chimera, and it is so because it abstracts from the particular processual nature of a knowledge based economic system. Thus competition in Marshall is not a state of affairs but a process, and what matters is the instituted frame that keeps the process open.[7] It is not perfect competition at all but a matter of rivalry (racing is his alternative description), a contest between competitors of different and changing abilities, grounded in the fundamental characteristics of modern industrial life – self-reliance, deliberation and an awareness of the possible future consequences of actions. Competition is not a dull, equilibrium state but, rather, a creative force promoting spontaneity of action, it is a matter, as he put it, of *Economic Freedom* (1920, Book I, 1: 10), that is, the freedom to use knowledge and capability for economic advantage.[8] Nor is the idea of competition to be confused with the perfection of the market, which is greatly influenced by the prevailing transport and communications technologies, improvements in which have sharpened the forces that establish common prices for common goods and services. Marshall realized that evolution is not random change but rather a process that presupposes an economic structure that can evolve. This is why the demand and supply economics of partial equilibrium play such a central role in his analysis; they describe the economic order and form the substrate on which evolutionary forces can operate. The fact that different forces work with different velocities, is not then the basis for a description of different kinds of equilibria but, rather, a device to account for the connection between structural change and historical time. This is one of Marshall's great contributions to economics, for when different components of the system change at different velocities this necessarily revises and restructures the prevailing order, and the prevailing order is all we ever have.

The focus of the *Principles* is upon the long period when time allows the forces of investment and of innovation in established channels, drawing on established principles, to work their affects. Only in the secular period does Marshall allow radically new, substantive inventions to enter the order.[9] Let us focus first on the investment side, the process by which firms expand and contract their capacity to supply, for this is at the core of Marshall's evolutionary dynamic. In a famous passage Marshall claims that the tendency to variation is the chief source of progress (1920, Book V, 4: 355). This pregnant phrase captures in a single step the deep evolutionary content of Marshall's thought but 'What is meant by this?' The rest of the *Principles* make clear that transformation and progress are connected by a variation cum selection dynamic, Marshall's principle of substitution in which more profitable firms prosper at the expense of weaker brethren. Outcomes are tested in the market so that 'society substitutes one undertaker for another who is less efficient in proportion to his charges' (1920, Book V, 3: 341). Indeed, in introducing a discussion of profit in relation to business ability, Marshall is quite explicit that this principle of substitution is a 'special and limited application of the law of "the survival of the fittest"' (1920, Book VI, 7: 597). Furthermore, innovation is inseparable from the competitive process. For the advantages of economic freedom 'are never more strikingly manifest than when a business man endowed with genius is trying experiments, at his own risk, to see whether some new method or combination of old methods, will be more efficient than the old' (1920, Book V, 8: 406). The relation runs two ways and mutually reinforces the links between free competition and business experimentation.

This is Marshall's theory of the competitive process in which differentiated business traits, including those in relation to innovation, are connected to differential profitability and thus access to resources from the capital market. Yet Marshall's evolutionary credentials are sophisticated; there is no necessary implication that the most profitable activity in terms of time and place is necessarily the best activity when considered from a wider perspective. This is the dynamic significance of external effects, selection is via the price mechanism and the price mechanism does not extend to everything that is of value, especially innovations as yet unborn. The further development of this broad idea is carried out in terms of two devices, the prevailing market order as governed by a demand curve and a particular expenses curve, and the concept of the representative firm – Marshall's Achilles' heel.

The prevailing competitive order in a perfect market, Marshall's base case as it were, is expressed in terms of a market clearing price, but at this price firms with different technical, organizational and managerial traits coexist. The marginal firm just breaks even, any higher-cost firms are non-viable and any lower-cost firms make superior profits (composite rents) which they can deploy to invest in capacity or innovation.[10] That the market order generates a distribution of profitability in any competitive trade, and a correlation between profits and business traits, is the foundation for the system's evolutionary performance. Marshall's theory of industry is of course a dynamic theory, it entails entry and exit and the rise and fall of individual firms both relatively and absolutely: it is a theory of the restructuring of order not only of the establishment of order. The representative firm infamously plays a central role in this framework, for it is the fulcrum around which other firms rise and fall and in relation to which entry decisions are made. It has been much maligned and much misunderstood. On the question of misunderstanding, modern evolutionary theory comes to the rescue. Variation cum selection processes are expressible in terms of the so-called replicator dynamic, in which the changing relative importance of entities (firms in Marshall's case) is governed by how their traits are distributed around the population average vector of traits. This distance from mean basis for evolution is one in which variation and correlation of firm's traits combine to drive the differential growth of the firms in a way that is conditioned by the prices set in an environment of product and factor markets. The theoretical significance of the representative firm is not that it corresponds to some real entity but rather that it is a statistical construct, an analytical device around which evolution occurs. Moreover, it too must evolve as the structure of the industry evolves, even when the traits of the population of firms are frozen; no wonder it gave rise to such misunderstanding for it is an emergent consequence of the evolutionary process not a property to be determined a priori.[11] All of the above is rigorously demonstrable, although Marshall's intuition lacked the inclination if not the means to reason mathematically about the significance of economic variety and the dynamic purpose of the representative firm. On the question of its acceptance in economics more generally, Marshall enjoyed a bad press, and not only from his critics outside Cambridge. Thus when Shove (1930) re-states Marshall's economics as a resource allocation 'jigsaw puzzle' organized by arbitrage principles at the margin, it is not surprising that average behaviours embodied in the representative firm have no place. It was left to Robbins (1928) to apply the *coup de grâce* and from there no recovery was possible. In their own terms Marshall's critics were right, the average firm is of no more significance than the average machine or the average degree of morality. Unfortunately they had lost sight of the fact that their theory was not Marshall's theory: Marshall talked evolution; they talked equilibrium. This is perhaps why Marshall, together with Schumpeter and Hayek, finds no place in mainstream economics; it is not their economics.

Let us turn now to Marshall and the growth of knowledge, for inventions play a significant role in the *Principles* and so do inventors: although the former may take extended periods of time to develop to their full (Marshall's gradualism at work) while the latter may be recompensed in far smaller degree than the true worth of their inventions would merit.[12] Thus Marshall has more to say on invention than Schumpeter and correspondingly less to say about the entrepreneur (the focus of Schumpeter's saltationism). But this does not lead to a conclusion that Marshall ignores the entrepreneurial function; quite the contrary, it is subsumed into his theory of management on which he has a great deal to say. Indeed, Marshall's business leaders are divided into those who open up new and improved business methods and, as in Schumpeter, those who follow beaten tracks (1920, Book VI, 7: 597) but, in contrast to Schumpeter, innovation is part and parcel of the normal routine of business activity, enterprise and innovations are ever present but *sotto voce*. Managerial services in Marshall relate to two broad categories of action: first, the ability to appoint and lead a team of subordinates and to make the most of their abilities while preserving order and unity in the plan of the business; and, secondly, to 'know the trade'. By this short phrase, Marshall means activities that are closely tied to enterprise and innovation, and included in this category are the ability to forecast market demand, (expectations, as always, play an important role in Marshall's assessment of how people act, and different individuals hold substantively different expectations[13]), the facility to judge risks boldly but with care and, finally, the capacity to innovate through the perception of opportunities to supply new commodities or improve methods of production. It is important here to recognize the fact that Marshall, like Schumpeter, benefited from a keen understanding of the German economic tradition which from the nineteenth century onward had given due attention to innovation and enterprise (Streissler, 1990; 1994). Thus it is to Roscher that Marshall is referring when he claims that a characteristic task of the modern manufacturer is to create new wants where none previously existed[14] (1920, Book IV, 11: 280).[15] It cannot be said that Marshall did not have innovation and enterprise very firmly in his grasp when he wrote about the distinctive contribution of management to economic organization. Indeed, Marshall sums up his position in the following terms that serve to intertwine innovation and investment:

> On whichever side we look, we find that the progress and diffusion of knowledge are constantly leading to the adoption of new processes and new machinery which economises human effort on condition that some of the effort is spent a good while before the attainment of the ultimate ends to which it is directed. (1920: 286)

It is not at all surprising, therefore, that Marshall should have devoted a great deal of attention to the instituted context in which the internal knowledge-generating processes of the firm are aided and abetted by externally organized process for generating and disseminating new knowledge. The education system is of vital importance in this regard, but it is Marshall's exposition of an innovation systems perspective which marks him out as an economist who understood the interplay between the evolution of knowledge and the evolution of economic activity. In order to benefit from external economies, the firm needs an external organization; external economies do not come for free and access to them has to be organized and co-ordinated. The firm's internal knowledge-generating processes are embedded in Marshall's thought within a broader matrix of national and sectoral arrangements of two broad kinds: the industrial district and the national system of research. The first is well known, the co-location of firms facilitates the communication of information; thus it correlates knowledge so that 'the mysteries of the trade become no mysteries' and ideas are readily interchanged and, crucially, become 'the source of further new ideas', a perfect Marshallian combination of restless knowledge and restless activity (1920, Book V, 10: 271). The second knowledge-generating structure is not so well known, perhaps because it is only found in *Industry and Trade* (1919). It is articulated in terms of a tripartite ecology of research laboratories in which distinctively different kinds of knowledge are generated. Universities produce fundamental knowledge, technical laboratories in companies develop knowledge of the particular techniques of the trade, and a plethora of specialist laboratories provide knowledge of standards and testing procedures. This ecology reflects a sophisticated division of labour but its economic significance depends on how the different components interact. The technical research laboratory of an industry benefits from keeping in touch with the chief scientific laboratories, and 'the later may gain much and lose nothing' by keeping in touch with the industries whose methods may be improved by the fruits of fundamental research (Marshall, 1919: 136). Thus Marshall's account of the innovation processes is one in which advances in knowledge are made by different individuals, of different capabilities and specialisms, working with different motives and different methods in different organizational contexts.

Having given this attention to knowledge generation, some brief space must be devoted to his discussion of education in so far as it underpins the expression of the individuality of knowing, which is the mainspring of progress in Marshall. Education serves an important social purpose, to enhance vertical mobility and prevent that 'wasteful negligence which allows genius that happens to be born of lowly parentage to expend itself in lowly work' (1920, Book IV, 6: 212). It also serves to supply the skills needed for an industrial society in which machinery displaces lowly skilled activities. While a liberal education adapts the mind to use its best faculties in business, a technical education develops the skills to master the details of particular trades. National differences are evident to Marshall. The German system is better fitted for developing middle ranks of industry and better fitted to imparting scientific training. But, in a passage that is manifestly Schumpeterian in spirit, he claims that the English system is better for developing daring energy and restless enterprise (1920, Book IV, 6: 209). That innovation may rest in education is Marshall's point, and the economic value of one genius, Bessemer, Pasteur, Jenner or Darwin, Shakespeare or Beethoven, can repay the cost of their education many times over.

Before leaving Marshall, we may note that it is somewhat of a surprise to find that Schumpeter never fully accepted the Marshallian vision or rather as he put it the Smith–Mill–Marshall theory of growth (Schumpeter, 1947b: 7), a conclusion that he had reached much earlier (1928). The 1928 article gives a perfectly fair account of Marshall's theory, the interdependence there contained between investment in capacity and the development of new wants, an endogenous expansion of the system in which the interplay between saving and investment is shaped by the distribution of increasing returns and co-ordination of activities. Schumpeter's objection is clear, expansion cannot explain expansion, a self-exciting system needs a stimulus and that stimulus comes from the new combinations. This is surely correct but it is not accurate as a criticism of Marshall, enterprise, innovation and invention are part of Marshall's scheme too.

HAYEK

Let us turn now, albeit more briefly, to Hayek, who provides us with a very different perspective on the evolutionary nature of economic action. His thought is far more abstract, none of the detailed historical understanding of economic arrangements that mark the writings of Schumpeter and Marshall is allowed to surface. Neither are there specific tools of analysis, Schumpeter's instrumental test of good economic work. Yet Hayek also deals uncompromisingly with the very foundations of economic evolution in relation to the distributed nature of social knowledge and the consequent restless nature of capitalism. His thought is complex but it is also profound and the best starting point is contained in the essays of 1945 and 1946, for they are the bridge between his previous work on 'narrow' economic issues and the broad concern with the instituted foundations of an open society that were to follow. It is not the stationary state which is the focus of his objections to prevailing economic thought but, rather, the closely related description of competition as a state of affairs shaped by given and uniformly distributed data. The 1946 essay opens with a challenge: to compete is a verb and verbs are action words yet in competitive equilibrium there is no action, 'How can this be so?' The answer is that competition is a process, more than that it is a discovery process in which different consumers discover which of several possible suppliers will best provide for their needs and conversely. The totality of relevant economic knowledge required to allocate resources in the round is not only known to no one, it does not even exist independently of the economic process. Knowledge of how needs might be best met and then improved upon is not a given datum but an output of the competitive process.[16] This is Hayek's key insight, that knowledge is individual, distributed and restless. The 1945 essay completes this picture by explaining the role of the price mechanism in distributing the information required to co-ordinate individual action, when those actions relate to individuals whose personal beliefs and knowing are entirely different. When individual knowledge changes, a change that may be unbeknown to any other person, the prices adapt to the new pattern of knowing and change the distribution of incentives or future action. But there is more to the price mechanism than this suggests. Individual, differentiated action underpins individual, differentiated rewards, just as it does in the evolutionary schemes of Schumpeter and Marshall, as the following passage makes clear:

> how easy it is for an inefficient manager to dissipate the differentials on which profitability rests, and that it is possible, with the same technical facilities, to produce with a great variety of costs, are among the commonplaces of business experience which do not seem to be equally familiar in the study of the economist. (1945 [1948]: 82)

Hayek's economy evolves because its individual members know different things and hold different beliefs about the economic world, and it is because knowledge is specialized and individual that an economy is an adaptive system that is a marvel of but not an intended product of human design.[17] However, it is not only an adaptive system, it is a creative system, and this is the point, its instituted frame generates economic rewards for further differentiation of knowledge. This is the thread that links our three giants of economic thought; it is why stationary capitalism is a contradiction in terms. Although Hayek never expresses it in these terms, the capitalist system operates by variation and selection for actions and variation and selection of knowledge. It is clear that scientific knowledge is only a part of the relevant totality of knowledge required for economic action. It is the individual knowledge concerning specifics of time and place, not general knowledge alone, which permits the allocation of resources to improve – Schumpeter's humble knowledge (but not humble entrepreneurs). As he puts it, much of this is transient knowledge, knowledge of 'the fleeting moment' not destined to ever reside in any textbook or echo in any university classroom.

If individual action reflects a division of labour, then it necessarily reflects a division of knowledge and this is the most significant form of evolutionary variation with which the economist has to contend. Hayek devoted most of his subsequent efforts to elaborating this theme and its evolutionary credentials rest on three themes that recur in *The Constitution of Liberty* (1960) and the three volumes of *Law Legislation and Liberty* (1973; 1976; 1979). The first theme is the incompleteness of personal knowledge and the impossibility of a global economic rationality, the foundation of the argument against constructivist rationality and central planning. Hayek's individuals are not fools, they calculate advantages as best they can but their calculations are local not Olympian.[18] Since mistakes are common, since the expectations of different individuals cannot be satisfied simultaneously and, since many (most?) intended innovations fail, the economic system is not only a trial and error process but a learning process for revising knowledge. Incompleteness of knowledge leads to transience, to creative destruction in the epistemic realm as well as the real economic realm.

Hayek's second theme relates to the importance of order. Economic action requires organization and the purpose of organization is to coordinate individual efforts to a larger purpose. An evolutionary system presupposes a structure to evolve and, in Hayek's scheme, this is based upon a distinction between purposefully made and spontaneously arising or emergent order. Not all the features of the economic world arise through conscious design; indeed, many are the result of competition between alternative, incompatible designs. Order is not only structure it is also stability in the large. Just as Schumpeter saw the importance of an enduring frame of institutions, so Hayek points to the importance of tradition. Only conservative systems can change in an orderly way, and this is one of the central paradoxes of the capitalist system. It can only change from within because its structure generates conjectures of how it might be changed;

instability in the small must reside within stability in the large. All progress presupposes tradition, but tradition is not immutable; it too evolves through variation and selection with the potential value of new rules and practices only ascertainable in relation to existing rules and practices. This is the nature of spontaneous evolution and its consequences are unevenly distributed over time and place. It is the necessarily uneven pattern of knowledge-driven progress that unites Hayek with Marshall and Schumpeter, and demarcates their account of economic development from anything connected to the idea of a regularly expanding, proportionally growing economy.

The third and final theme relates to the ethical evaluation of the system. Since the progress of knowledge is necessarily uneven it follows that the distribution of economic rewards is also uneven. Property rights are not rights to a certain income flow, returns are as much a matter of chance as they are of skill, and they reflect the very diversity of individual purpose in the economy. There is no common objective around which a concept of distributive justice could be formulated; indeed, injustice will be felt even when no one acts unjustly because the gains for some are necessarily losses for others. To say that restless capitalism is progressive capitalism is not to give a normative judgement because, in Marshallian fashion, the development of knowledge means development of the human material, beliefs and values also change. There is no fixed point to judge history in its normative implications. Rather, progress means that fewer errors are made and more valuable problems are solved. Thus Hayek's spontaneous order is like an ever replenished stream, channelled by the institutional rules of the game which themselves meander more slowly across the cultural landscape: neither economy nor cultural frame can meaningfully be described in equilibrium terms because their foundations in human knowing cannot be so described.

CONSEQUENCES: KNOWLEDGE AND EVOLUTION

Schumpeter, Marshall and Hayek are very different economists, it is not usual to speak of them in the same context, yet it is clear from the above that they are united by a concern to understand the evolution of the economic system. This is the binding thread that has been broken, and its breaking has served to separate them from the canon of mainstream economics. With very few exceptions, their works now rest among the apocrypha of economic thought. In seeking out what they have in common it is not the evolutionary structure of their thought alone that matters, but their understanding of the very foundations of economic dynamics. What is it that, in their thinking, makes the economic process evolutionary? What is it that separates their thought from the mainstream canon? Three answers can be given as a preliminary response, each identifying a strand of that broken thread. We express these in terms of the nature of knowledge-based activity, in terms of the institutions of an open, creative economic system and in terms of the non-equilibrium nature of economic order. Let us take each strand in turn.

The Centrality of Knowledge

The first strand, perhaps the most compelling, which binds our three authors is the idea that the economy evolves because knowledge evolves, the co-evolutionary hypothesis that intertwines variation and development in the epistemic realm with variation and development in the realm of human action. On this view capitalism is a very particular kind of epistemic system. It is a system that has evolved an instituted structure of abstract and more concrete rules that generates a logical order to economic affairs but, at the same time, it is a set of rules that has a remarkable if unintended consequence: it has proven to create a system for the self-transformation of the prevailing order. This is their most penetrating insight, order is necessary for distributed economic activity to be possible but every capitalist order contains within itself the forces of spontaneous development. Randomly ordered systems do not develop; they drift. It is only structured orders flowing from a logic of organization that can develop in a coherent, directed fashion. This duality between self-organization and the spontaneous ordering of events, on the one hand, and the self-transformation of that order through innovation in multiple realms, not all of them narrowly economic, on the other hand, is the principle insight that leads us to capitalism as an evolving system governed by rules of variation, selection and ongoing development. Most fundamentally, our three authors all recognized that capitalism cannot in its very nature be a stationary system, for to be so would be to deny the nature of the human material on which economy and society are based. To say that capitalism is knowledge based is mere wordplay, for it could not be otherwise, but it is a very particular kind of knowledge-based system based upon the articulation of distributed knowledge and so designed to facilitate the growth of knowledge. This is the Faustian bargain struck by our ancestors. Wealth is generated without apparent limit but at the price of a consequential radical uncertainty and indeterminacy in human affairs, in that the future of the system is entirely unpredictable. Is this, as Popper suggests, the price we pay for being curious humans? Pre-capitalism lacked this connection because the order on which evolution might work was too fragmentary and a stationary state was then a logical possibility, something capitalism could never be without ceasing to be capitalism. Berlin captures the essential point: when writing of Vico and his understanding of history we are told, 'man is a self transforming creature, the satisfaction of each set of needs alters his character and breeds new needs and forms of life', he cannot therefore live his life 'according to unvarying, timeless principles, for then there would be no growth, no historical change, only eternal repetition as in the lives of animals' (Berlin, 2000: 65). Is this what Marshall had in mind when he warned his readers of the limits of the stationary state?

> But nothing of this is true in the world in which we live. Here every economic force is continually changing its action under the influence of other forces which are acting around it . . . Further, all these mutual influences take time to work themselves out, and, as a rule, no two influences move at equal pace. (1920, Book V, 5: 366)

It would take far too long to explore all the ramifications of this position in relation to our triumvirate, so only some limited remarks are possible. Economic action is purposeful and belief dependent, whether organized and carried out by individuals or by teams, and for beliefs to be reliable they must be grounded in the knowledge of the circumstances of economic action, knowledge of many different kinds not just that related to science, technology and productive opportunity. The multiple kinds of knowledge are reflected in a complex division of labour within and between organized activities of which individuals possess specialized but limited knowledge. To render compatible the actions of idiosyncratically knowing humans is the primary purpose of instituted co-ordinating rules of action: of which those in relation to purposefully designed, locally bounded organizations such as firms lie at one end, and the spontaneous, emergent, unplanned order of market relations lie at the other end of a broad spectrum. This is standard fare from a Hayekian perspective. Designed and evolved orders provide the local and the general rules of conduct to enable each type of order to benefit from the specialized knowledge contained in and organized through the others. As a knowledge system, capitalism has always reflected a balance between two broad ordering principles: those that lead to the correlation of understanding necessary if social action is to be feasible, and those resulting in the de-correlation of understanding and the development of the system. The successive making and re-making of patterns in the minds of individuals carries over to the creation and destruction of economic order more generally. These are the basic principles that underpin order and transformation and make them inseparable. Order is a solution to a set of problems but the solution of problems necessarily adds to knowledge somewhere in the system, so changing the data on which any general or specific order is based. The system is auto catalytic, 'self-exciting' in Frank Knight's felicitous phrase, the solution of any problem serves only to change the nature of the problem and those problems connected to it in logic or action.[19] While scarcity is rightly identified as a central, perhaps the central, economic problem, it is not only just a problem of order it is necessarily also a problem of transformation. That problems of scarcity promote mental effort and invoke solutions ad infinitum is the lesson of history: yet it is because scarcity is an insoluble problem that it is the basis of dynamics not the basis of statics. Here a little disquisition on the relation between knowledge and information will help.

What we know as individuals arises and develops partly in the context of our innate curiosity as human beings, and partly via the stimuli provided by everyday experience of interaction with others. When Adam Smith drew attention to the individually idiosyncratic, specialized nature of personal knowledge, the corollary is that not only the use of knowledge but also the development of knowledge is embedded in a social process, one that is co-ordinated through appropriate patterns of rule-bound social interaction. The problem here entails a distinction between private knowledge and shared understanding. For social action to be possible, for actions to be mutually supporting and collaborative, even when motivated by very different intentions, it is necessary that there is shared understanding to the requisite degree. This correlation might happen by chance (mark the famous conundrum that with probability 1 a troupe of monkeys could exactly replicate Shakespeare's works, given enough time) but, in fact, it is social structures that vastly accelerate this correlating process by communicating representations of knowledge in the form of information. The transmission of private knowledge into shared understanding is a socially distributed process and this process depends on institutions for the sharing and common interpretation of flows of information.[20] The multiple innovations in information technologies are of vital importance, yet any exclusively technological view – from Gutenberg to Gates – leaves the account incomplete. Equally crucial has been the invention and adoption of standards or norms to distinguish reliable from less reliable knowledge. The process of establishing error, of identifying mistakes, is absolutely essential to the growth of understanding. Instituted criteria for the falsification and rejection of knowledge claims have provided the critical edge to combat the problem of superfecundity, the problem of being unable to distinguish which of the too numerous rival sets of information is reliable and fit for purpose.[21] In regard to science, we enquire of the truth of the relation between conjecture and natural phenomenon. In regard to technology, we enquire whether the device works in the environment in which it is intended such as to achieve the desired effect. In regard to business, we enquire if the plan achieves the profitability required to justify its continuation. In regard to social practices we enquire if they are acceptable to the relevant community. Without these instituted and thus shared winnowing processes it is not at all clear how knowledge and understanding can grow. Thus the development of private knowledge and shared understanding reflect multiple, instituted processes of trial and error of variation and selection. In this regard we would agree with Campbell (1960) when he argues that all growth of knowledge is predicated upon a process of blind variation and subsequent selection. It should be noted that blind does not mean random nor unintended; rather, it means that the validity of new conjectures can never be known in advance since those tests of validity always lie in the future when the relevant knowledge has emerged and been tested.

What of the de-correlation of knowledge? Note first that modern societies devote significant resources to the process of correlating understanding through education and of reinforcing these correlations through ideas of law, justice and acceptable rules of behaviour. Out of this process comes understanding in common, correlated knowledge, of which the processes that generate science are typical examples. However, a world in which every individual knows the same as any other individual would be a world of stationary knowledge, in which individuality could not be given any substantive meaning. Knowledge grows because it is individually grounded and because individuals react differently to common information, that is, a representation of the knowledge of others, transmitted in a continuous process of communication and challenge. What the paradigm-breaking scientist and the radical entrepreneur have in common is that they participate in a common information flux with others but reach quite different conjectures about the nature of the respective worlds. Information flux leads to change of knowledge and thus to further change of information flux perhaps the most powerful example of a positive feedback, irreversible process that we can identify in the course of modern history. Thus the connection between knowledge and evolution is not only a matter of co-ordination and agreement but of disagreement and dissent, the themes of Schumpeter, Hayek and Marshall. The instituted rules of modern capitalism are not simply devices for generating order but, inseparably and crucially, devices for provoking dissent from the established order and for channelling that dissent for productive purposes. It is not simply variation of existing knowledge that is the striking feature but variation in the origination of new knowledge, and this is the theme of enterprise, novelty and innovation not only in the economy but in all fields, science included.

In this regard, the characteristic aspect of the Schumpeter's entrepreneur and Marshall's manager is to de-correlate private knowledge, to sow doubt where previously there was understanding in common. Hence, the emphasis on novelty, on challenging existing practices and understandings that is also typical of the Kuhnian notion of the paradigm-breaking scientist. Thus, entrepreneurs have a dual role. They claim to know differently from others and they challenge the correlated understanding that others possess. It is on this distinction that an understanding of the entrepreneur rests, as the individual who dares to act on the basis thoughts not held by others, who challenges, through imagination not calculation alone, the basis of economic and social co-operation.

That the entrepreneur, whether individual or organized team, is the locus of experimentation in the generation of new knowledge also helps explain the restless nature of modern capitalism. An ever present strand in our broken thread is the claim that economies can never be at rest because knowledge is never at rest, that the prevailing pattern of understanding is always being subjected to challenge. By acting entrepreneurially, an individual generates new information that may lead others to see the world differently in a distributed process of knowledge growth. What is distinctive about modern society is its institutionalization of this process of repeated challenge to existing patterns of knowledge correlation (Gibbons et al., 1994). The successful entrepreneurs generate new patterns of understanding in the use of resources, and those new patterns of activity and understanding become the parent of further entrepreneurial acts, acts that continue the process of economic development. This incessant disruption of the existing economic order is instituted into modern capitalism in a fundamental way. The relevant knowledge-generating ecologies are increasingly rich. Not only do markets serve as the context in which knowledge and conjecture lead to new opportunities for enterprise, the gradual establishment of procedures for generating new knowledge independently of the market context has also proved to be a fertile development in the institutions of modern capitalism. That this creates a problem of connecting the two spheres of knowledge generation should not disguise the remarkable nature of this division of labour. The growth of science and technology in university-style organizations or the research laboratories of corporations (the two playing by different rules of the game, the one open the other proprietorial) further enshrines the restless nature of capitalism by devoting a portion of its resources to finding reasons why the world is not as it seems. Adam Smith recognized this at the outset when he claimed that the principles of the division of labour apply not only to the content of knowledge but to the form of the production of knowledge. No wonder the system is restless or that enterprise is the distinguishing feature of modern capitalism.

Thus the evolutionary properties of modern capitalism rest on the particular dynamics of knowledge generation across distributed individuals, many of whom accept and work within the current order but sufficient of whom challenge that order and stimulate the further growth of knowledge. The instituted frame that makes this possible is capitalism's most important attribute; and it involves a subtle interplay between mutual adjustment to what is known and the disruptive development of that knowledge.

Institutional Design

Economists and other social thinkers have for long understood the link between institutions and the working of the economic system. However, it is remarkable that far less attention is devoted to the idea that the institutions which promote order and co-ordination also facilitate the transformation of the system through innovation and the development of knowledge. Self-organization seems ineluctably to produce self-transformation. A balance is thereby struck between the existing and the emergent, so that the system is an open system for generating economic progress, although no normative connotation should be attached to that word without careful qualification. Property rights and their enforcement through law are a familiar example of the link between abstract rules and a regular ordering of economic and social action. That property might be vested in corporate forms of ownership, that ideas might acquire the status of property are commonplace examples of this theme. Strong property rights defined over the ownership and disposal of assets of any kind are essential to exchange-based economic systems but these provide no guarantee at all of the economic value of the assets in question. As Hayek insisted, what is protected is the expectation of command not the expectation of economic value (1976: 123–5.). Indeed protection of the latter would only be possible in a world of stationary beliefs yet the market process renders that impossible, for it is not the permanence of property rights that matters but their transient market valuations.[22]

What, then, are the instituted features of modern capitalism that create such a strong symbiosis between knowledge and activity? Property rights apart, they are three in number. The first is the open market in which every established business position is liable to face a competitive challenge from somewhere in the prevailing order, unless temporally protected via a patent, copyright or other legal limitation. Entrepreneurship is pervasive because the idea of an open, competitive market process is pervasive. Under the rules of restless capitalism a firm never quite knows where the threats to its existence will come from; and frequently they come from such unanticipated directions that their significance is often discounted until it is too late.[23]

Secondly, markets play fundamental roles in relation to the identification of opportunities for enterprise. Enterprise does not occur in a vacuum, it is shaped and channelled by the existing order. This is wrongly put if stated in terms of the 'price mechanism' for prices alone are insufficient metrics, the structure of quantities and qualities are needed as well if the prospective entrepreneur is to gauge the potential profitability of a new venture. Hence, market signals matter not only in the sense of encouraging the efficient use of existing business knowledge, the traditional argument in favour of the competitive organization of industry, but also in the deeper sense of guiding the competitive process of entrepreneurial change. Efficient markets, those that establish uniform prices for goods and services with identical characteristics, are consequently of great importance to the conduct of enterprise for they indicate the real opportunity costs of innovation. Without them enterprise risks misdirection, which is why getting the prices right is a necessary but not sufficient condition for maximizing the developmental opportunities in any economy. All entrepreneurial conjectures compete with and are designed to compete with some existing activity even if the true margins of competition are initially misconceived and revealed in surprising ways *ex post*. Notice that this remains true even for those radical entrepreneurial conjectures that, for example, introduce products previously unheard of. Even these products must be conjectured to displace existing products in consumers expenditure and to utilise resources employable elsewhere in the economy. We might also add that markets are also instituted devices for generating low-cost access to consumers and productive services; markets are not only structures for indicating the terms on which resources and customers are available, they are the channel to gain access.

This takes us to the final aspect of the institutions of a market economy, the incentives they provide to challenge the prevailing order. Whether or not profits are the *primum mobile* of enterprise, there can be no doubt that profit is a necessary feature of such activity and that the prospect is essential in the process of attracting risk capital to support conjectures for which there cannot be any basis in fact. Novelty of thought may be its own reward but novelty is also the signal that what the entrepreneur does is potentially superior to already established competing activities. Abnormal profits, far from being an index of the absence of competition, are the very proof that competition is actively pursued, that resources are being reallocated. This is the crucial role that profits and losses play in the mobilization of new economic structures, and by focusing on a static competitive equilibrium state we hide this from view. Moreover, one of the key institutions of capitalism, the distinction between contractual returns and residual returns, could have no purpose if the system always and everywhere stood in competitive equilibrium. It is because the system is never in equilibrium that the distinction has real force and points to profit not as the consequence of monopoly power but profit as the consequence of differential, enterprising behaviour. This brings us to the final strand, the troublesome notion of equilibrium.

Order versus Equilibrium

This is the most challenging of issues, even Marshall and Schumpeter make frequent use of equilibrium language, despite their constructing systems of thought to emphasize the non-equilibrium nature of economic activity. Equilibrium is, of course, among the most frequently deployed concepts in modern economics but it is a misnomer. What is called equilibrium is rather a solution to a puzzle created in the mind of the investigator; it is a set of consistency conditions – no more no less. Unfortunately, real economic actors do not solve puzzles; they deal with problems that in their solution create new information and stimulate new thoughts to reveal new opportunities. It is this imperfect mapping between puzzles and problems that is at the root of the difficulty.

If some system is in equilibrium it has reached a balancing state from which no escape is possible without the intervention of external forces, forces that of necessity cannot be part of the specification of the system. Yet capitalism is continuously changing from within, the theme that is our triumvirate's most enduring insight, and it changes from within because problem-solving stimulates the growth of knowledge. As pointed out above, the solution of one problem simply reveals new problems somewhere in the system in a continuous process of stimulus and adaptive response.[24] I doubt if any business person thinks of their field of influence in terms of equilibrium without risking the very future of their business. However, equilibrium is not the same as order. All evolutionary change presupposes a substrate of order, of organization on which the processes of variation, adaptation and development can operate, the system is restless but it is not chaotic. This might be thought a small point if it were not for the fact that it is precisely the equilibrium perspective that the triumvirate react against. Consider three implications of this for the way economic puzzles are constructed. When a modern economist invokes the representative agent what is meant is not some statistic forced on the investigator by a need to accommodate to variety but, rather, a uniform, homogeneous agent, conceived of a priori, as if the concept of individuality was a non-essentialist diversion. No evolutionary economist could make such a step without rendering the basis for his theory incoherent and Marshall, Schumpeter and Hayek do not make this false step, they reason in the presence of human individuality, human difference and it is the differences that lead to change. In a world of uniform agents how quite, we may ask, are we to introduce innovation?

Secondly, consider the dichotomy between a state of equilibrium and the dynamics of adjustment to that equilibrium, a standard piece of puzzle-solving. Apart from the fact that the logic defining the state of rest is separate from the logic of out of equilibrium adjustment, and could not be otherwise without destroying the description of the state of rest, this device can only be considered viable if the process of adjustment fails to generate information to change the beliefs of the agents on both sides of the market. In real-world problem-solving one can conjecture that this is never the case, transformations are not movements between states that are invariant to the movement. Rather the very process of movement gives rise to new information, new thoughts, new conjectures that irreversibly change the point from which the movement emerged and the point to which it is directed. This is the essence of an irreversible, historical process. Indeed, Isaiah Berlin puts his finger on the inconsistency with typical and complete accuracy, an equilibrium is a Utopia, a fiction, a solution to a puzzle, a state of perfection in which 'all is still and immutable and eternal' (Berlin, 1991: 22). Not quite an accurate rendering of the capitalist process.

CONCLUDING REMARKS

Human beings are not mere calculators, adjusting rationally to circumstances beyond their control but sentient and imaginative designers of alternative worlds, in art and music no less than in science, technology and the economy. Schumpeter, Marshall and Hayek understood this: and how could they not having lived through immense, internally generated transformations of Western society and economy. To accommodate this perspective certainly does not mean abandoning economics, the principles on which order is established are the first task of the investigator and the differences between flexible and fixed prices, perfect and imperfect markets, product versus process-led competition remain as germane as ever. No evolutionist can start other than from an understanding of the rules of order and their consequences. But that is the beginning not the end of the investigator's task. The focus shifts to how the order is self-transforming not only self-organizing, how the instituted frame stimulates and responds to the possibilities latent in new knowledge. This is the necessary step, the intertwining of dynamic principle, institutional analysis and the historical record, if we are to understand the working of capitalism, how it differs from other instituted economic forms and why it produces such uneven development. It is perhaps telling that the growth of complexity science, of which Hayek was deeply aware, may yet provide the tools and puzzle-solving practices to link emergent innovation with economic growth and development.[25] We should not forget that there is no perfect way of knowing. Perhaps, it is not too late to spin afresh the broken thread, perhaps even rescue our triumvirate from the company of the apocrypha.

NOTES

* I thank Dick Nelson, Ronnie Ramlogan, Davide Consoli and Andrea Mina for much discussion and stimulus in relation to the topic of this chapter. The comments of Geoff Hodgson, Richard Swedberg, Tiziano Rafaelli and Marco Dardi at and after the Hitotsubashi meeting in March 2008 are also acknowledged with pleasure. Special thanks are due to Tamotsu Nisizawa and colleagues for organization, hospitality and discussion during the meeting.

1. There is an obvious link here to the notion of progress, that is, directed development, and to the idea that the outcomes of an open-ended evolutionary process demonstrate increasing complexity – a point that Marshall certainly understood in relation to his discussion of the division of labour. On this theme of open-ended evolution see the paper by Ruiz-Mirazo et al. (2008).
2. See Jolink, for an interesting account of evolutionary ideas in Walras, ideas essentially focused on the concept of evolution as a cumulative unfolding of phenomena.
3. From a modern viewpoint two instituted responses have been invoked. One is the resort to high rates of progressive taxation to equalize more fully *ex post* outcomes, although this threatens the very link between enterprise and profitability. The alternative is a welfare state safety net that buffers the vicissitudes of innovation-driven competition on individuals and localities without undermining the *primum mobile* of the system. This tension between progress and the distribution of its effects is a central theme in Hayek (1944).
4. It is no accident that the famous paper (Schumpeter, 1928) which must have brought his ideas to the attention of most English-speaking audiences is called 'The instability of capitalism' and that it plays on the distinction between institutional durability in the round and the transience of particular arrangements in the small.
5. Schumpeter (1943) is the place where his fears that the internal questioning of the system would destroy it from within are expressed.
6. The following is something of a footnote to the comprehensive treatment by Raffaelli (2003). See also the magisterial encyclopedia of Marshallian thought edited by Rafaelli et al. (2006) which covers much of my material.
7. Here Marshall is demonstrating that his roots lie in Adam Smith. See Richardson (1975) for a compelling account of Smith's dynamic theory of competition.
8. For further discussion the reader is referred to Groenewegan (2003).
9. Although this distinction is central to the modern theory of innovation (radical versus incremental, capability enhancing versus capability destroying, and so on). Schumpeter took a dim view of the attempt to cut up what he saw as a homogeneous phenomenon (see 1928: 378n).
10. On the notion of composite rent, see Kondo (2006).
11. The central theorems of modern evolutionary economics relate this theme to the work of eminent biologists particularly R.A. Fisher and George Price. See Andersen (1994) and Metcalfe (1998; 2008) for relevant discussion. Replicator dynamics is standard fare in evolutionary game theory too; Gintis (2002) is an excellent starting point.
12. 'Those that pioneer new paths may confer on society benefits that are disproportionate to their personal gains even if they "have died millionaires" ' (1920, Book VI, 7: 598).
13. See Loasby (1990) for further elaboration. We note in passing that a business does not expect to make profits, or losses for that matter, by having the same expectations as rivals. At a minimum, rational expectations in relation to business prospects must mean variform expectations.

14. Roscher's maxim to 'create new wants by showing people something which they have never thought of having before; but which they want as soon as the notion is suggested to them' (1920, Book IV, 11: 280).
15. Compare Gideon (1948: 457), when writing of Pullman and Ford 'stirring the dormant fancies of the public until they grew into demands'.
16. This leads to some very Schumpeterian conclusions, as when Hayek suggests that a sequence of temporary monopolies, each displaced through a superior innovation, may be economically superior to a state of perfect competition (1948: 102).
17. Hayek never puts it thus but he means that 'the tape is never played twice' a theme that links the history of economies with the history of the natural world.
18. It is an argument that anticipates the Carnegie school and the case for bounded rationality or, better put, bounded cognition and bounded mental capacity. That Hayek could write a major work in psychology, *The Sensory Order* (1952) is not irrelevant here.
19. See Knight (1935 [1997]: 170).
20. The intriguing point here is that the same economic problem-solving incentives that supported revolutions in energy use and machinery also stimulated developments in the technology of communicating, storing and manipulating information. This record of innovation reflects the fact that information is valuable and the development of information technology from the book to the Internet has created a profound shift in the knowledge-based nature of modern capitalism. The spread of information separately from face to face, verbal communication is one consequence, the copying of information without error is a second, and the non-cultural transmission of information between generations is a third. The many ramifications of this theme lie beyond my present purpose but are fundamental to the nature of restless capitalism (Eisenberg, 1979). That printing involved multiple innovations, far more than the press – inks, paper, the dependence on phonetics, script – is one theme, that the printed book had a profound effect on the nature of individualism is another. On the latter see McLuhan (1962: 158ff).
21. Cf. Mokyr (2002).
22. No better example of this can be found than the rights attached to a patent for invention. These are rights to exploit in a monopoly fashion but in no way do they prescribe the flow of returns that ensues. Indeed, the fact that the principles of the patent (its information content) must be placed in the public domain as a condition of its granting is precisely an invitation for other inventors to find alternative routes to the same effect and thus an incentive to destroy the value of the original patent. Patents are an extremely clever institution, their protection is important but it is not unlimited, and deliberately so, and it is helpless in the face of other genuinely novel entrepreneurial actions.
23. The managerial literature is full of examples of incumbent firms that failed to spot the competitive of innovation by unanticipated rivals. See Utterback (1994) for recent discussion of this disruptive aspect of competition.
24. As this chapter was being finalized I came across the paper by Kauffman et al., (2008) who make a nice distinction involving a process connecting the 'actual' with the 'adjacent possible', a very apt reflection of the process of economic evolution and the growth of knowledge.
25. For important developments on this theme see Foster (1993) and Dopfer et al. (2004).

REFERENCES

Andersen, E.S. (1994), *Evolutionary Economics: Post Schumpeterian Contributions*, London: Pinter.

Berlin, I. (1991), *The Crooked Timber of Humanity: Chapters in the History of Ideas*, ed. Henry Hardy, London: Fontana Press.

Berlin, I. (2000), *The Power of Ideas*, ed. Henry Hardy, Princeton, NJ: Princeton University Press.

Campbell, D.T. (1960), 'Blind variation and selective retention in creative thought as in other knowledge processes', *Psychological Review*, **67**: 380–400.
Dopfer, K., J. Potts and J. Foster (2004), 'Micro-meso-macro', *Journal of Evolutionary Economics*, **14**, 263–280.
Dosi, G. (1982), 'Technological paradigms and technological trajectories', *Research Policy*, **11**, 147–62.
Eisenberg, E.L. (1979), *The Printing Press as an Agent of Economic Change*, Cambridge: Cambridge University Press.
Foster, J. (1993), 'Economics and the self organisation approach: Alfred Marshall revisited', *Economic Journal*, **103**, 975–91.
Freeman, J. (2005), 'Venture capital and modern capitalism', in V. Nee and R. Swedberg (eds), *The Economic Sociology of Capitalism*, Princeton, NJ: Princeton University Press.
Gibbons, M., C. Limoges, H. Nowotny, S. Schwartzman, P. Scott and M. Trow (1994), *The New Production of Knowledge*, London: Sage.
Gideon, S. (1948), *Mechanisation Takes Command*, Oxford: Oxford University Press.
Gintis, H. (2002), *Game Theory Evolving*, Princeton, NJ: Princeton University Press.
Groenewagan, P. (2003), 'Competition and evolution: the Marshallian conciliation enterprise', in R. Arena and M. Quere (eds), *The Economics of Alfred Marshall*, London: Palgrave.
Hayek, F.A. (1944), *The Road to Serfdom*, Chicago, IL: Chicago University Press.
Hayek, F.A. (1945), 'The use of knowledge in society', *American Economic Review*, **35**, 519–30, reprinted in F.A. Hayek (1948), *Individualism and Economic Order*, Chicago, IL: Chicago University Press.
Hayek, F.A. (1946), 'The meaning of competition in economic theory', reprinted in F.A. Hayek (1948), *Individualism and Economic Order*, Chicago, IL: Chicago University Press.
Hayek, F.A. (1948), *Individualism and Economic Order*, Chicago, IL: Chicago University Press.
Hayek, F.A. (1952), *The Sensory Order*, Chicago, IL: Chicago University Press.
Hayek, F.A. (1960), *The Constitution of Liberty*, London: Routledge & Kegan Paul.
Hayek, F.A. (1973), *Law, Legislation and Liberty Volume 1*, Chicago, IL: Chicago University Press.
Hayek, F.A. (1976), *Law, Legislation and Liberty Volume 2*, Chicago, IL: Chicago University Press.
Hayek, F.A. (1979), *Law, Legislation and Liberty Volume 3*, Chicago, IL: Chicago University Press.
Kauffman, S., R.K. Logan, R. Este, R. Goebel, D. Hobill and I. Shmulevich (2008), 'Propagating organisation: an enquiry', *Biology and Philosophy*, **23**, 27–45.
Knight, F.H. (1935 [1997]), *The Ethics of Competition*, London: Transactions Publishers.
Kondo, M. (2006), 'Quasi-rent and composite quasi-rent', in T. Raffaelli, G. Becattini and M. Dardi (eds), *The Elgar Companion to Alfred Marshall*, Cheltenham, UK and Northampton, MA, USA: Edward Elgar.
Landes, D. (1968), *The Unbound Prometheus*, Cambridge: Cambridge University Press.
Landes, D. (2002), *The Wealth and Poverty of Nations*, London: Little Brown & Co.
Loasby, B.J. (1990), 'Firms, markets and the principle of continuity', in J. Whitaker (ed.), *Centenary Essays on Alfred Marshall*, Cambridge: Cambridge University Press.

Marshall, A. (1919), *Industry and Trade*, London: Macmillan.
Marshall, A. (1920), *Principles of Economics*, London: Macmillan.
McLuhan, M. (1962), *The Gutenberg Galaxy: The Making of Typographic Man*, London: Routledge & Kegan Paul.
Metcalfe, J.S. (1998), *Evolutionary Economics and Creative Destruction*, London: Routledge.
Metcalfe, J.S. (2006), 'Entrepreneurship: an evolutionary perspective', in M. Casson, B. Yeung, A. Basu and N. Wadeson (eds), *The Oxford Handbook of Entrepreneurship*, Oxford: Oxford University Press.
Metcalfe, J.S. (2008), 'Accounting for evolution: fitness and the population method', *Journal of BioEconomics*, **10**, 23–49.
Mokyr, J. (1990), *The Lever of Riches*, Oxford: Oxford University Press.
Mokyr, J. (2002), *The Gifts of Athena*, Oxford: Oxford University Press.
Murmann, P. and K. Frenken (2006), 'Towards a systematic framework for research on dominant designs, technological innovations and industrial change', *Research Policy*, **35**, 929–52.
Nelson, R. and S. Winter (1982), *An Evolutionary Theory of Economic Change*, Boston, MA: Belknap Press.
Nelson, R.R. (2005), *Technology, Institutions and Economic Growth*, Boston, MA: Harvard University Press.
Raffaelli, T. (2003), *Marshall's Evolutionary Economics*, London: Routledge.
Raffaelli, T., G. Becattini and M. Dardi (eds) (2006), *The Elgar Companion to Alfred Marshall*, Cheltenham, UK and Northampton, MA, USA: Edward Elgar.
Renart, H. and E.S. Renart (2005), 'Creative destruction in economics: Nietzsche, Sombart, Schumpeter', mimeo, Cambridge University.
Richardson, G.G. (1975), 'Adam Smith on competition and increasing returns', in A.S. Skinner and T. Wilson (eds), *Essays on Adam Smith*, Oxford: Oxford University Press.
Robbins, L. (1928), 'The representative firm', *Economic Journal*, **38**, 387–404.
Ruiz-Mirazo, K., J. Umerez and A. Moreno (2008), 'Enabling conditions for "Open-Ended Evolution"', *Biology and Philosophy*, **23**, 67–85.
Samuelson, P.A. (1967), 'The monopolistic competition revolution', in R.E. Kuenne (ed.), *Monopolistic Competition Theory Studies in Impact. Essays in Honor of E.H. Chamberlin*, New York: John Wiley.
Santarelli, E. and E. Pesciarelli (1990), 'The emergence of a vision: the development of Schumpeter's theory of entrepreneurship', *History of Political Economy*, **22** (4), 667–96.
Schumpeter, J.A. (1912 [1934]), *The Theory of Economic Development*, Oxford: Galaxy Books.
Schumpeter, J.A. (1928), 'The instability of capitalism', *Economic Journal*, **38**, 361–86.
Schumpeter, J.A. (1939), *Business Cycles Volumes I & II*, New York: McGraw Hill.
Schumpeter, J.A. (1941), 'Alfred Marshall's *Principles*: a semi-centennial appraisal', *American Economic Review*, **31**, 236–48.
Schumpeter, J.A. (1943), *Capitalism, Socialism and Democracy*, London: George Allen & Unwin.
Schumpeter, J.A. (1947a), 'The creative response in economic history', *Journal of Economic History*, **7** (2), 149–59.
Schumpeter, J.A. (1947b), 'Theoretical problems of economic growth', *Journal of Economic History*, **7**, 1–9.

Shove, G.F. (1930), 'The representative firm and increasing returns', in 'Increasing returns and the representative firm: a symposium', *Economic Journal*, **40**, 79–116.
Streissler, E.W. (1990), 'The influence of German economists on the work of Menger and Marshall', *History of Political Economy*, **22**, 97–116.
Streissler, E.W. (1994), 'The influence of German and Austrian economists on Joseph A. Schumpeter', in Y. Shionoya and M. Perlman (eds), *Schumpeter in the History of Ideas*, Ann Arbor, MI: University of Michigan Press.
Utterback, J.M. (1994), *Mastering the Dynamics of Innovation: How Companies Can Seize Opportunities in the Face of Technological Change*, Cambridge, MA: Harvard University Press.
Witt, U. (1998), 'Imagination and leadership – the neglected dimension of an evolutionary theory of the firm', *Journal of Economic Behaviour and Organisation*, **35**, 161–77.

PART III

Conceptions of Evolution

7. Alfred Marshall and the historico-ethical approach

Tamotsu Nishizawa

7.1 THE AGE OF ETHICO-HISTORICISM, OR THE AGE OF SOCIAL REFORM

From 1870 to 1914 (and Later)

Around 1870, a new interest in social reform, a new spirit of 'historicism' and new activity in the field of economic 'theory' began to assert themselves (Schumpeter, 1954: 753). During this period, through 'revolutions' and heated discussions, the neoclassical economics based on marginal utility theory and, later, general equilibrium theory were formed and developed, and the field of economics as such was professionalized and institutionalized. At the same time, the ideas of the German historical school, or the historico-ethical school, and the social policy school were also formed, developed and disseminated internationally, in the course of which economic sociology and institutionalism were conceived and elaborated. This development of the historico-ethical and social policy schools was much stronger in backward countries (latecomers) such as Germany, America and Japan. It seems that Marshall and the Cambridge school have been largely discussed in context of the neoclassical economics, but not in context of the historico-ethical and social policy schools. I aim to discuss Marshall against the background of the historico-ethical age or the age of social reform. Indeed it was historicism, not marginal theory, that was more in accordance with the general trend of thought from J.S. Mill's death in 1873 to the appearance of Marshall's *Principles* in 1890, and it was the historical school rather than marginal utility theory that set its mark on the *Principles* (Maloney, 1987: 147–9; Shove, 1942: 309).

Schumpeter characterized an aspect of the discipline of economics prevalent from 1870 to 1914 as 'Sozialpolitik and the historical method' (ch. 4 of Part 4, *History of Economic Analysis*, 1954). The relationship between the Sozialpolitik and historicism was clearly a German doctrine; the crucial factor connecting the two was not so much history as ethics. The ethical claim that led the historical research of the school, served as the basis of the Sozialpolitik. Schumpeter discussed the English historical school as an offshoot of the German historical school and compared the British new-liberal social reform, the British version of the Sozialpolitik, with the better-developed German social policy (Shionoya, 2006a). Britain was rather backward in this aspect and in some other institutional aspects.[1]

A major turning-point in both economic policy and theory in Britain occurred nearly at the same time as the foundation of the Verein für Sozialpolitik (in 1872) (Hutchison, 1978: ch. 4). Mill's recantation of wages fund theory, Ludlow's study of the progress of the working classes and Brentano's study of the English trade unions all occurred at around this time. It was also around this time that Marshall became convinced of the increasing urgency of economic studies as a means for human well-being, as revealed in his *Lectures to Women* (1873b: 85) focusing on 'Some economic questions directly connected to the welfare of the labourer' and *The Future of the Working Classes* (1873a). These works accelerated the fall of the English classical school and the rise of the English historical school, then the Oxford economists influenced by T.H. Green and Arnold Toynbee, such as W.J. Ashley and W.A.S. Hewins, came to prominence, as did the English social policy school led by the Webbs, R.H. Tawney and J.A. Hobson, a group which might be called the 'LSE institutionalists', or the 'English school of welfare economics' as Walton Hamilton called them in 1919.[2]

The German historical (historico-ethical) school, the English historical school, the Oxford economists who relied largely on the Oxford approach of idealism, the American institutionalists and the Japanese Society of Social Policy, were not isolated phenomena but were part of a much larger worldwide intellectual movement of dissent (Boulding, 1957: 3).[3]

Historico-Ethical Approach

The new departure, the distinctive research programme, and the emergence of a genuine school, Schumpeter says, must be associated with the name of Gustav von Schmoller. The research programme of the German historical school was explicitly formulated by Schmoller as an 'historico-ethical' approach to economics. He always protested against an 'isolating' analysis of economic phenomena and held that 'we lose their essence as soon as we isolate them'. This view was the consequence of his resolve to develop economics through historical monographs. For the materials that such monographs were based on, as well as their results, were 'refractory to any attempt at isolating – in most cases, in fact, they become meaningless if isolated'. In principle, the Schmollerian economist was 'a historically minded sociologist'. The historico-ethical school associated with Schmoller intended to express 'protest against the wholly imaginary advocacy of the hunt for private profit of which the English "classics" were supposed to have been guilty'. The school professed to study '*all* the facets of an economic phenomenon'; hence '*all* the facets of economic behavior and not merely the economic logic of it'; hence 'the *whole* of human motivations as historically displayed, the specifically economic ones not more than the rest for which the term "ethical" was made to serve, presumably because it seems to stress hyperindividual components' (Schumpeter, 1954: 812).

The basic and distinctive article of the historical school's methodological faith was that the organon of scientific economics should mainly consist in the results of, and in generalizations from, historical monographs. As far as the scientific part of his vocation is concerned, the economist should first of all master historical technique. By means of this technique, which was all the scientific equipment he needed, he should dive into the ocean of economic history in order to investigate particular patterns or processes in all their detail, local and temporal, the flavour of which he should learn to relish. The only kind of general knowledge that is attainable in the social sciences would then slowly grow out of this work. This was the original core of what became known as the historical method in economics (Schumpeter, 1954: 807). 'Schmoller's historical and ethical economics remained neither a description of history nor a prescription of morality, but became an applied science addressing a practical solution for social reform in Germany' (Shionoya, 2006b: 179).

7.2 MARSHALL AND THE HISTORICAL SCHOOL: 'THE MANY IN THE ONE, THE ONE IN THE MANY'

Schumpeter on Marshall

It was Marshall who changed all that and 'led out of the valley on to a sunlit height' (Schumpeter, 1954: 830). In England, the period was 'emphatically the Marshallian Age'. His success was as great as Adam Smith's. Marshall commanded the scene much more than Ricardo had ever done. The great master made almost the whole of the rising generation of English economists his pupils and followers (Foxwell, 1887: 93; Schumpeter, 1954: 830, 833). Here again I would like to stress the existence of the Marshallian school of industrial and applied economics and the economic historians, who were the product of Marshall's effort to make economics realistic, that is, to produce the blend of analysis and facts encouraged by the motto 'The many in the one, the one in the many'.

'Marshall's *Principles*: a semi-centennial appraisal' by Schumpeter was read to the American Economic Association in 1940. The book was widely respected:

> Full justice cannot be rendered to it by going straight to the core of analytic apparatus the *Principles* presents. For behind, beyond, and all around that kernel there is an economic sociology of 19th century English capitalism which rests on historical bases of impressive extent and solidity. Marshall was, in fact, an economic historian of the first rank, though he may not have been much of a historical technician. And his mastery of historical fact and his analytic habit of mind did not dwell in separate compartments but formed so close a union that the live fact intrudes into the theorem and the theorem into purely historical observations. This shows, of course, very much more obviously in *Industry and Trade* than it does in the *Principles*, in which, even in the historical introduction, historical fact has been so severely scaled down as to be almost lost to follower and critic alike . . . But within those limits a realism was attained which greatly surpasses that of Adam Smith – the only comparable instance. This may be one of the reasons why no institutionalist opposition rose against him in England. (Schumpeter, 1951: 94)[4]

Under the influence of the historical school, Marshall made 'a strenuous attempt to re-graft a historical-institutional approach onto the neoclassical abstraction' (Hutchison, 1988: 529). Stressing that Marshall and Adam Smith had more in common, Schumpeter found 'strong similarity in the visions or general conceptions of the process and, in particular, with respect to economic evolution'. Also he found 'an approximately equal distribution of weights as between "theory" and "facts" '. In Marshall he notes 'not only a high-powered technician, a profoundly learned historian, a sure-footed framer of explanatory hypotheses, but above all a great economist'. Unlike the technicians, Marshall understood the working of the capitalist process. In particular, Marshall

> understood business, business problems, and businessmen better than did most other scientific economists, not excluding those who were businessmen themselves. He sensed the intimate organic necessities of economic life even more intensively than he formulated them, and he spoke as one who has power and not like the scribes – or like the theorists who are nothing but theorists. (Schumpeter, 1954: 836)

Schumpeter appraised Schmoller's research programme as the model for economic sociology, and characterized its aims as 'a unified sociology or social science as intellectually ("theoretically") worked up universal history' (Schumpeter, 1926 [1954]: 382). He defined economic sociology as 'a sort of generalized or typified or stylized economic history' and called it 'reasoned history' (Shionoya, 1995: 233). Schumpeter, in 'Gustav v. Schmoller und die Probleme von heute' (1926 [1954]), based upon his methodological evaluation of Schmoller's historico-ethical economics, characterized its approach as an economic sociology that enabled the integration of theory and history (ibid.: 236).

In the final two paragraphs of the long essay 'Gustav v. Schmoller und die Probleme von heute', Schumpeter asserts that Schmoller could write on his book (*Grundriss der allgemeinen Volkswirtschaftslehre*, 1900, 1904) Marshall's motto '*natura non facit saltum*'. Schumpeter frequently noted the similarity between Schmoller's and Marshall's work. Though Schmoller and Marshall approached different subjects because of their different training and circumstances, they came out of the same world. Marshall's approach was also reliant on 'facts and inferences'. Marshall and Schmoller eventually wrote the same thing, although their stresses were different. They both overcame the economics of simple postulates and striking results, and showed what the economics of the future would look like. Marshall's *Principles* and Schmoller's *Grundriss* contain in embryo a large majority of what could be done in the present and in the future and what had been done. They continue to be seemingly inexhaustible sources of micro- and macro- social-scientific insights (Hodgson, Chapter 5 in this volume: 94; Schumpeter, 1926 [1954]: 387–8).

The Marshallian School of Industrial and Applied Economics

Sydney Chapman, one of Marshall's most distinguished pupils who came under his influence 'in his prime', described Marshall's method, stressing 'realism': while the *Principles* might be described as 'theory fully clothed with realism', *Industry and Trade* could be characterized 'as realism adequately infused with theory'.

> He had a passion for knowing all about the things he was dealing with, . . . He had come to believe more and more that generalizing from facts can yield fruitful results if the facts are exhaustive enough and representative enough; and was never really satisfied that he had got enough. He had grown into a convinced realist, without however ceasing to be a theorist. In his view, the two lines of investigation were not parallel but converging so that they would more or less meet short of infinity. And at the same time his mistrust of the bare results of pure deduction grew on him. Perhaps he began to underrate the value of abstract reasoning because it came too easy to him . . . Marshall stressed the importance of taking evolution into account in Economics. This he had partly in mind in dwelling on 'the many in the one, and the one in the many.' And for an evolutionary study much realism is essential. (Chapman, n.d.: 24–6)

Industry and Trade, which illustrated the value of the motto, 'The many in the one, the one in the many', was a research programme of continuing value to economists interested in the 'realistic' side of the 'science of business'. It initiated a discussion of the foundation of a Chair of 'Applied Economics' or 'Industrial & Commercial Economics' at Cambridge among the people around Walter Layton in the early 1920s. Stressing the prominent 'characteristic of the Cambridge School of Economics', Layton, another of Marshall's eminent pupils, wrote to Colonel Strang that 'Professor Alfred Marshall's desire that economics should not be a mere affair of the study but should be a real analysis and exposition of the laws governing the workshop and the market place will be evident to anyone who dips into his recent book *Industry and Trade*' (19 February 1920, Layton, unpublished: 2/46 (1–4)).

Layton drew up the 'Draft Scheme for a Professorship of Industrial & Commercial Economics at Cambridge University' (Layton, unpublished: 2/46(6)). The professorship would be concerned primarily with that branch of the field of political economy which deals with the organization of industry, trade and commerce, the question of relations between employers and employed and the general economic problems that present themselves either to managers or to trade union organizers. The 'Memo on necessity for formation of school for studying applied economics' was also drafted, in which 'the foundation of a Professorship, or Chair of Applied Economics' or 'a man who will do for applied economics what Darwin did for natural history' was requested. In other words, an individual was sought to collect and collate the masses of facts which can be obtained by studying industry in every part of the world, and, to use these facts, to elucidate economic laws, instead of theorizing on economic laws and trying to fit the facts to the theories (Layton, unpublished: 2/40(1)).

W.J. Ashley, 'the most promising and brilliant English historical economist' (Koot, 1987: 102), was also attracted and praised highly *Industry and Trade*. He was very close to Schmoller and in closest sympathy with the German historical school (Koot, 1987: 103; Schumpeter, 1954: 82). While he was professor at Birmingham, he wrote of Chapman at Manchester and of Clapham at Leeds, suggesting that establishing a professorship of economics in a great industrial centre was likely to lead to valuable publications on the economic problems of the particular district, as illustrated by Chapman's writings on the economics of the cotton industry and Clapham's book on the woollen trades (Ashley, 1908: 187–8).

Ashley noted what he considered a very encouraging growth in the number of books on industrial economics resulting from the creation of commercial faculties or of economics departments serving more or less the same ends. It would have been invidious to single out particular examples, yet he

> cannot refrain from pointing to Dr. Alfred Marshall's *Industry and Trade* as a masterly and informing survey of a large part of the field. Matters as to which some of us had been trying for years to dig out some scrappy material, and which we had been presenting to our classes with a feeling that we were cultivating quite untilled tracts, were there brought together for the first time in a general view. The motto of the book, 'The many in the one, the one in the many', presents our common ideal: the reconciliation of the abstract and the concrete; a reconciliation, let me add, of which each side is equally in need. (Ashley, *c*. 1921: 5)

In a long letter to W.A.S. Hewins, another leading historical economist at LSE, Marshall wrote about his motto, stressing that

> the Many is the ground of study . . . Having discovered the One in the Many, they might set forth afresh the Many in the One. I repeat, I regard the use of mathematics on the way as a gain when convenient, but not as of the essence of the work. In my view the Many is the ground of study; the One is the Holy Grail to be thought by the pious & laborious pilgrim; & the One when so found is to help as a guide through life over the broken ground of the Many'. (12 October 1899, in Whitaker, 1996, vol. 2: 257)

Also, Marshall wrote to A.L. Bowley, a former student and well-known economic statistician at LSE:

> Will you then be so very generous as to forgive me if I ask you to ask yourself whether . . . it is not time to make some further study of the broader relations between economic facts: to leave mathematics for a little on one side; and join more heartily in the quest for 'the One in the Many, the Many in the One'? (21 February 1901, in Whitaker, 1996, vol. 2: 300–302)

7.3 THE SCOPE OF ECONOMICS AND ETHICAL JUDGEMENT

Social Science as 'Reasoned History of Man'

Marshall was the first great economist who devoted his life to building up the subject as a separate science that could stand on its own foundations with standards of scientific accuracy as high as those of the physical or biological sciences (Keynes, 1924 [1972]; 222). Yet, unlike Jevons, Marshall did not entertain a 'narrower' or 'purer' conception of the subject. On the contrary, he harboured a vision of economics that was 'positively imperialist' in its potential scope, and which promised to give economics unique standing as the source of expertise relevant to the resolution of a very wide range of public issues (Collini et al., 1983: 312).

In fact Marshall's well-known statement at the beginning of the *Principles* that economics 'is a study of mankind in the ordinary business of life' has a built-in imperialistic tendency to expand into general sociology. Marshall employed the distinction between 'wants' (the subject matter of a 'science of wealth') and 'activities' (where economics became 'part of the social science of man's action in society') to depart from the mainstream of utilitarian thought and embark on the construction of an ambitious form of economic sociology along evolutionary lines. By confining itself to the study of the satisfaction of given wants, the utilitarian conception of economics cut the subject off from 'the high theme of economic progress'. In contrast, making activities and their dominant influence on the formation of character-type and ideals the central concern of economics could lead to economics becoming the guiding discipline in any 'study of man', past, present and future (Collini et al., 1983: 320–21; Parsons, 1931: 106–13; 1932: 346).

In 'The old generation of economists and the new' (1897) Marshall discussed his vision of social science as 'reasoned history of man': 'Social science or the reasoned history of man', for 'the two things are the same', was working its way towards a fundamental unity; just as had occurred in 'physical science, or, which is the same thing, the reasoned history of natural phenomena' (Marshall, 1897 [1925]: 300). In economics we deal with the whole of man's nature, though we lay chief stress on certain special aspects of it. In so far as we base our study upon history at all, the history that we use must be 'history as a whole. We need more than economic history, more than a history of economic institutions and customs, wages and prices, of trade and finance: we want a history of man himself, and economic history as contributing to that' (Marshall, 1897 [1925]: 299).

For Marshall 'the Many is the ground of study'; he well recognized the historical method and probably believed as Schumpeter did that economists 'should dive into the ocean of economic history in order to investigate particular patterns or processes in all their live details' (Schumpeter, 1954: 807). And like Schmoller, Marshall also always protested against an 'isolating' analysis of economic phenomena and held that such phenomena lose their essence as soon as they are isolated (ibid.: 812). Marshall wrote: 'We have to study mankind as they are. We must not picture to ourselves an unreal world as it might, or ought to be, and make schemes for it . . . Our first duty as economists is to make a reasoned catalogue of the world as it is' (Marshall, 1897 [1925]: 302–3).

Marshall's arguments regarding 'the reasoned history of man' and his vision of social science share common ground with the historical method in economics, as Schumpeter said, and with the Schmollerian economic sociology.

Economic Reasoning (Measurability) and Ethical Judgement

How would Marshall's arguments like these or his vision of social science reconcile with his rejection of Comtist pretensions of creating a science of sociology which would subsume the subject matter hitherto assigned to the economists. In 'The scope and method of economics' (Appendix C to the *Principles*; Marshall, 1890 [1961]), Marshall criticized Comte's 'unified (and all embracing) social science': there were some who held, with Comte, that the scope of any profitable study of man's action in society must be coextensive with the whole of social science. They argued that all the aspects of social life were so closely connected, that a special study of any one of them must be futile; and 'they urged on economists to abandon their distinctive role and to devote themselves to the general advancement of a unified and all embracing social science'. But the whole range of man's actions in society was too wide and too various to be analysed and explained by a single intellectual effort (Marshall, 1890 [1961], vol. 1: 770). In his inaugural lecture Marshall used the same tone: it was vain to speak of the higher authority of a unified social science. No doubt if that existed economics would gladly find shelter under its wing. 'But it does not exist; it shows no signs of coming into existence. There is no use in waiting idly for it; we must do what we can with our present resources' (Marshall, 1885 [1925]: 163–4).

Then how did Marshall think of the role of economic theory or organon? For him, the *raison d'être* of economics as a separate science was that 'it deals chiefly with that part of man's action which is most under the control of measurable motives', and which 'lends itself better than any other to systematic reasoning and analysis' (Marshall, 1890 [1961]: 38–9). The chief motives of business life could be measured indirectly in money, and it was this 'definite and exact money measurement' of the steadiest motives in business life which enabled economics to far outrun every other branch of the study of man. This 'economist's balance', rough and imperfect as it was, made economics more exact than any other branch of social science. But of course economics could not be compared with the exact physical sciences, for it dealt with the ever-changing and subtle forces of human nature (ibid.: 14).

Money was never a perfect measure, but it afforded a fairly good measure of the moving force of a great part of motives. Then Marshall contended for the economic reasoning or organon, leaving to common sense the responsibility of the final decision:

> The economic organon brings to bear the accumulated strength of much of the best genius of many generations of men. It shows how to analyse the motives at

> work, how to group them, how to trace their mutual relations. And thus by introducing systematic and organized methods of reasoning, it enables us to deal with this one side of the problem with greater force and certainty than almost any other side . . . Having done its work it retires and leaves to common sense the responsibility of the ultimate decision; . . . not hampering common sense in the use to which it is able to put any other available knowledge, nor in any way hindering; helping where it could help, and for the rest keeping silence. (Marshall, 1885 [1925]: 164–5)

Criticizing the classical economists' conception of 'economic man', Marshall argues that although he is unselfish, his motives are measurable; but he goes on to say that the idea of measurability should not be prominent. He says first: whenever we glimpse economic man he is not selfish. The desire to provide for one's family acts in a very regular way and can be reduced to law; it is prominent in all economic reasoning, because, though unselfish, it is measurable. If, with Cliffe Leslie, we analyse all the infinite variety of motives under the term 'love of money', we see that they are of all kinds. They include many of the highest, the most refined and the most unselfish elements of our nature. Their common link is that they can be more or less measured by money. However, Marshall also wrote that 'though in wording our economic organon this idea of measurability should be always present, it should not be prominent' (Marshall, 1885 [1925]: 160–61).

Thus Marshall thought of the roles and relations of the judgement of common sense or ethical judgement and the economic theory or organon:

> The only resources we have for dealing with social problems as a whole lie in the judgment of common sense. For the present, and for a long time to come, that must be the final arbiter. Economic theory does not claim to displace it from its supreme authority, nor to interfere with the manner nor even the order of its work, but only to assist it in one part of its work (Marshall, 1885 [1925]: 164).[5]

Common sense certainly does not deal with a complex problem as a whole. Its first step is to break up the problem into its several parts, then to discuss one set of considerations after another, and finally to sum up and give conclusions. Comte seems to have ignored that the human mind has no other method of inquiry than this; that a complex problem is broken up into its component parts, less methodically but no less completely by common sense than by formal analysis. When it is thus broken up each separate part offers a foothold for treatment by a special scientific organon (Marshall, 1885 [1925]: 164).

Later Dennis Robertson in *Lectures on Economic Principles* (1957), going beyond his predecessor in the chair, paid heed to a piece of advice given by his grandparent in the chair. Marshall concluded his arguments on 'The substance of economics' in the *Principles* as follows:

> The less we trouble ourselves with scholastic inquiries as to whether a certain consideration comes within the scope of economics, the better. If the matter is important, let us take account of it as far as we can . . . If it is one on which the general machinery of economic analysis and reasoning cannot get any grip, then let us leave it aside in our purely economic studies; . . . and remembering always that some sort of account of it must be taken by our ethical instincts and our common sense, when they as ultimate arbiters come to apply to practical issues the knowledge obtained and arranged by economics and other sciences. (Marshall, 1890 [1961], vol. 1. 27–8; Robertson, 1957: 18–19)

This statement comes after Robertson noted his predecessor Pigou's hypothesis that material welfare is not the same as total welfare, and the pursuit of the one may sometimes conflict with the pursuit of the other. Nevertheless we can reasonably plan our studies on the working hypothesis laid down by his predecessor in the chair, Pigou: 'When we have ascertained the effect of any cause on economic welfare, we may, unless of course there is special evidence to the contrary, regard this effect as *probably* equivalent in direction, though not in magnitude, to the effect on total welfare' (Pigou, 1920: 20; Robertson, 1957: 18–19).

7.4 MARSHALL AND WELFARE ECONOMICS BEFORE ROBBINS

From Ethics to Economics

The study of economic, social, and human progress with the prospect of eliminating human poverty was always part and parcel of the system of economics Marshall wanted to construct. The solution of economic problems was a prior condition of the exercise of man's own possibilities and higher faculties, but not an application of the hedonistic and utility calculus. He started from mental science, whose fascinating inquiries into the possibilities of the higher and more rapid development of human faculties brought him to the question: to what extent do the conditions of life of the working classes generally suffice to make for fulfilling life? These sentiments were very clear in his *Lectures to Women: Some Economic Questions Directly Connected to the Welfare of the Labourer*, (1873b), and in *The Future of the Working Classes* (1873a); in the former Marshall often referred to the works of Brentano, and the works of Ludlow, about whom he 'was enthusiastic, and evidently valued his work highly' (Marshall, 1947: 44).

In 1868, when he was still in his metaphysical stage, a desire to read Kant in the original led him to Germany. 'Kant my guide,' he once said, 'the only man I ever worshipped.' Hegel's *Philosophy of History* greatly influenced him. Marshall's reading Kant and Hegel in the late 1860s and the early 1870s paralleled the development of T.H. Green in Oxford. As Pigou noted in his 'Memoriam', Marshall used to wander about Switzerland, carrying on his back Kant's *Critique of Pure Reason*. He turned more and more to ethics, and it was through ethics that he came to economics. For him 'economics was a handmaid to ethics, not an end in itself, but a means to a further end: an instrument, by the perfecting of which it might be possible to better the conditions of human life. Things, organization, technique were incidents: what mattered was the quality of man' (Pigou, 1924: 82). It was Pigou's manifest in *The Economics of Welfare* that the complicated analyses which economists endeavour to carry out were not mere gymnastics but, rather, were 'instruments for bettering of human life' (Pigou, 1920: vii).

Marshall insisted until about 1871 that his home was in mental science. Gradually, however, the increasing urgency of economic studies as a means towards human well-being became clear to him. Around 1871–72, he found that he needed to decide whether to give his life to psychology or economics. He spent a year in doubt, 'always preferring psychology for the pleasures of the chase', but 'economics grew and grew in practical urgency, not so much in relation to the growth of wealth as to the quality of life', and he settled down to it (Marshall to James Ward, 23 September 1900, in Whitaker, 1996, vol. 2, 285).

According to Marshall, progress meant improvement of the quality of life; this is pointed out in one of the many notes written for 'A book that never was', Marshall's final volume on progress and ideals. The note dated 23 July 1920 is entitled 'Some influences of economic progress on the quality of life' (Marshall, unpublished: 5/3/2), in which he asserts that progress occurs only when the 'increase of material wealth is turned to account in developing the higher life of mankind'. In 'Progress. Ideals' (Marshall, unpublished: 5/9), he writes: 'The true aim was the elevation of human life, the making it full and strong; the elevation of human life all round, individual and social, moral and religious, physical and intellectual, emotional and artistic.' 'Wealth exists only for the benefit of mankind. It cannot be measured adequately in yards or in tons, nor even as equivalent to so many ounces of gold; its true measure lies only in the contribution it makes to human well-being' ('Fragments', in Pigou, 1925: 366). *Industry and Trade*, appeared as 'a continuation' of the *Principles*, 'with special reference to the technical evolution of industry, and its influences on the conditions of man's life and work'. Another volume, *Money, Credit &*

Commerce was also to be concerned with the 'influences on those conditions' exerted by money, credit and international trade, and by social endeavour. The main purpose of all three volumes was to search for 'possibilities of improvements . . . which may increase the command of the peoples of the world over their resources; and enable them to develop their higher faculties' (Marshall, 1919 [1923]: v; 1923: v). 'It is becoming clear that this and every other Western country can now afford to make increased sacrifices of material wealth for the purpose of raising the quality of life throughout their whole population. A time may come when such matters will be treated as of cosmopolitan rather than national obligation' (Marshall, 1919 [1923]: 5).

Marshall's views on material wealth and human life, work and faculties, economic progress and quality of life, and progress and the 'standards of life', seem close to John Ruskin's idea that 'there is no wealth but life'. Criticizing the dominant value theory of classical economics, Ruskin argued that 'Political economy, being a science of wealth, must be a science respecting human capacities and dispositions'. The economic usefulness of a thing depends not merely on its own nature, but on the number of people who can and will use it. Every material utility depends on its relative human capacity (Ruskin, 1860: 114, 112).

> Usefulness is value in the hands of the valiant; so that this science of wealth being, when regarded as the science of Accumulation, accumulative of capacity as well as of material, – when regarded as the Science of Distribution, is distribution not absolute, but discriminate; not of every thing to every man, but of the right thing to the right man. (ibid.: 125)

The relationship of the Oxford idealism of T.H. Green and Arnold Toynbee to Marshall has been pointed out on occasion. 'What was common to both Marshall and Green was the stress upon a moralized capitalism through which the highest potentialities of mankind were to be developed'. 'Both Marshall and Green saw history not only as a transition from status to contract, but also as a transition from self-interest to self-sacrifice and altruism' (Jones, 1971: 7). In this aspect Marshall separated himself from those contemporaries, chiefly Jevons, Sidgwick and Edgeworth, who preserved a closer relationship between economics and utilitarianism (Collini et al., 1983: 318).[6]

Pigou: Professionalization of Welfare Economics

Pigou was the first British economist to use the general optimum as a framework for policy recommendations. *Wealth and Welfare* (Pigou, 1912) set the state the aim of equalizing the marginal social products of factors in all their alternative uses, by means of a system of taxes and bounties, thus achieving optimality. This was sharply different from Marshall (Maloney, 1985: 176). Pigou's analytical framework is valid on the assumption that economic welfare is a broadly reliable guide to total welfare. For Marshall it is a substantive assumption; Marshall makes it because he believes it to be true and spends considerable time justifying it empirically. For Pigou it is a methodological assumption explicitly made so as to make the subject matter tractable. This is the attitude of a specialist, and it was Marshall's drive to professionalize economics which gave his successors specialist attitudes which he either no longer could acquire, no longer needed to acquire or had never wanted to acquire for himself. Marshall's *Principles* begins by trying to *show* that what is good for economic man is normally good for 'total man'; Pigou's *Wealth and Welfare* begins by *postulating* this (ibid.: 183–4).

Pigou was a very different kind of economist from Marshall. He began to specialize in economics at a very early age. It is likely that this more professional background was at the root of his much more 'professional' treatment of the relationship between economic and other activities. *Wealth and Welfare*, with its initial methodological postulate that changes in economic welfare indicate equivalent changes in total welfare, was a major landmark in the professionalization of economics. The battle to professionalize economics was primarily a battle between those who saw it as a discipline comparable to the natural sciences and those who saw it as an adjunct to immediate social reform: the absolutist 'trait' method and the historical-relativist method, respectively. The absolute approach shows why, other things being equal, an occupation like economics is dominated by advanced theorists who tend to determine the direction of future research; the historical-relativist approach focuses on the fact that other things seldom are equal (Maloney, 1985: 226, 232).

Hobson: Economics of Human Welfare

Work and Wealth: A Human Valuation (Hobson, 1914 [1992]) has been seen as a response to Pigou's *Wealth and Welfare*. Hobson took the view of the 'human standard' of value, adopted Ruskin's axiom that 'There is no wealth but life', and later wrote *Wealth and Life: A Study in Values* (1929). The general assumption was that every growth of wealth enhances welfare cannot be admitted without qualification. To find a standard of human welfare as stable and generally acceptable as the monetary standard is manifestly impossible. The organic nature of man and of human society must also be considered. Economic operations must be treated as organic processes, and the economic values are to be translated into human values by reference to such a standard of organic welfare (Hobson, 1914 [1992]: v–vi).

The distinction between the value of 'a piece of wealth' to an individual and to society was an important component of Hobson's welfare economics. There was no guarantee that maximizing the objective surplus would maximize the subjective surplus, the surplus of subjective utilities over subjective costs. In other words, society was organized so as to maximize production, not to maximize human happiness. Hobson recognized the problems involved in using money income as a measure of welfare. If we turn to Marshall, we find greater similarities. Like Hobson, Marshall refused to accept that individuals were the best judges of their own welfare; some types of consumption yielded gratification, but did nothing to improve character. Marshall, although he recognized these defects in wealth as a measure of welfare, was prepared to set them aside in order to create a workable welfare economics. Hobson, in contrast, preferred to stay close to Ruskin, arguing that social welfare was something organic and qualitative, not amenable to measurement, and denounced the notion that wealth could be used to measure welfare (Backhouse, 1992: xiv).

7.5 EPILOGUE: PLURALISM IN WELFARE ECONOMICS AND MARSHALL

In the period from around the 1880s to the 1920s, ideas regarding welfare economics were being developed by academic economists, by other academics pursuing the subject as part of a political or historico-ethical analysis that could provide a framework for transforming British society, and by new-liberal social reformists seeking solutions to social problems. Their arguments were based on utilitarianism, idealist philosophy, ethico-historicism, and the moralism of Ruskin. Clearly, much of the resulting literature did not meet the academic standards laid down by Marshall and Pigou and, because it made judgements foreign to those of modern economics, did not look like welfare economics as it is understood today. However, it would be rather anachronistic to use modern standards to demarcate part of this literature as welfare economics and the rest as something else (such as political or ethico-historical tracts).

Evidence for this view comes from outside observers. When Walton Hamilton (1919) wrote of the 'English welfare school', he listed 'Webb, Hobson, Cannan, Tawney and Clay' (Hamilton, 1919: 318). Whatever the reasons for his exclusion of Pigou, Hamilton was associating the idea of welfare economics with a group of investigators comprising both academics and political activists involved in advocating a welfare state. Hamilton had appraised Hobson in 'Economic theory and "social reform"' (1915). This was a group with whom he and his institutionalist colleagues in the USA had extensive links (see Rutherford, 2007). Similarly, Wesley Mitchell, in his lectures of 1919, also associated welfare economics not with Pigou but with Hobson (Mitchell, 1969). Paul Homan (1928) singles out Hobson as representing welfare economics. Outside Europe and the USA, the Japanese economist Fukuda (1930) and the Chinese economist Liu (1934) also found more inspiration and far more sympathy for their welfare economics in Hobson and the Oxford approach, or ethico-historicism, rather than in Pigou. This was especially true in Fukuda's case. It was perhaps no accident that Fukuda shared with Hamilton and Mitchell an institutional and ethical focus in his thinking that harked back to the German historical school.

Almost paradoxically, further evidence is provided in Robbins's *Essay* (1932 [1935]) over a decade later, where it is clear that the main target is not Pigou (who receives only brief criticism, on what might be seen as a technical point) but Stamp, Hobson, Hawtrey and Cannan. Hobson, significantly, appears in both this list and in those of Hamilton and Fukuda. The significant point here is that both Hamilton and Fukuda are associated with welfare economics thinkers who, today, would not be taken seriously as welfare economists. The conclusion that should be drawn is that, in this period, welfare economics, in so far as it is appropriate to use the term to describe a body of literature that was not a precisely defined discipline, was pluralistic: it was approached in a wide variety of ways. The significance of Robbins's *Essay* lies in the effect it had on this diverse, pluralistic field, not in any dispute with the Cambridge school.

NOTES

1. Schumpeter attended a course of lectures by Sidney Webb around 1906–07, who presented 'just about what a German Kathedersozialist would have done' (Schumpeter, 1954: 833). W.J. Ashley, the leading English historical economist who wrote of 'Toynbee's resemblance . . . to the Kathedor-Socialisten' (Ashley, 1900: 430), was himself called a 'Socialist of the Chair' (Semmel, 1960: 203).
2. The American Economic Association, strongly influenced by the German historical school in its initial stages, was founded in 1885. The Japanese Society of Social Policy was started in 1896, and the Japanese economist Fukuda co-authored *Labour Economics* with Brentano in 1899, which was an inauguration of Fukuda's welfare economic studies (Brentano and Fukuda, 1899).
3. There seemed to be 'a steady and rising stream of dissent' in Britain, which rose to a crescendo around the turn of the century in the Webbs and the Fabians, in a group which might be called the 'London School Institutionalists', and in a few gifted amateurs such as Hobson (who might almost be placed in the London School group), and finally in a group of quite sober academic institutionalists such as H.A. Marquand and Sargant Florence. The Oxford anti-marginalists such as P.S. Andrews might be included in the list (Boulding, 1957: 3).

4. After its publication in the *American Economic Review*, Mary Marshall wrote to Schumpeter (dated 19 July 1941): Schumpeter's essay indicates how much he thought of the work of Marshall. 'I have been reading your semi-centennial appraisal of Marshall's *Principles* with great interest. I have always known how much you appreciated his work and I am so glad that you have taken this opportunity of expressing this appreciation so warmly and well. Its last paragraph especially delights me' (Schumpeter, 1951: xi).
5. Cf. also Marshall (1890 [1961], vol. 1: 38). 'In all economic questions, considerations of the higher ethics will always assert themselves, however much we try to limit our inquiry for an immediate practical purpose' (Marshall, 1887 [1925]: xxv). Hobson stressed the ethical considerations of Marshall and his followers. Marshall recognized that 'the operations of the economic system, as expounded by its science, do not conform adequately to the dictates of reason, justice, and humanity in the apportionment of labour and the fruits of labour'. The hardships and injustices of current industrialism were not incorporated in the structure of the economic theory, but were of 'the nature of *obiter dicta* or qualifying reflections' (Hobson, 1929: xiv).
6. 'There were two Marshalls; Marshall the theorist of genius and Marshall the economic watcher and social meliorist. As a lecturer at Balliol, he had acquired the Arnold Toynbee attitude' (Chapman, n.d.: 24). Cf. also Marshall (1887).

REFERENCES

Ashley, W.J. (1900), *Surveys, Historic and Economic*, London: Longmans, Green.

Ashley, W.J. (1908), 'The enlargement of economics', *Economic Journal*, **18** (70), 181–204.

Ashley, W.J. (*c*. 1921), 'The universities and training for commerce', University Collection, Birmingham University Library.

Backhouse, R. (1992), 'Introduction', to J.A. Hobson's, *Writings on Distribution and Welfare*, London: Routledge/Thoemmes Press.

Backhouse, R. and T. Nishizawa (2006), 'Reinterpreting the history of welfare economics', paper presented at the Workshop on the Cambridge School of Economics, Hitotsubashi University, December.

Boulding, K. (1957), 'A new look at institutionalism', *American Economic Review*, **47** (2), 1–12.

Brentano, L. and T. Fukuda (1899), *Labour Economics* (in Japanese), Tokyo: Dobunkan.

Chapman, S.J. (n.d.), 'Unpublished autobiography of Sir Sydney John Chapman', Coll Misc. 664, LSE Archives.

Collini, S., D. Winch and J. Burrow (1983), *That Noble Science of Politics. A Study in Nineteenth-Century Intellectual History*, Cambridge: Cambridge University Press.

Foxwell, H.S. (1887), 'The economic movement in England', *Quarterly Journal of Economics*, **2** (1), 84–103.

Fukuda, T. (1930), *Studies in Welfare Economics* (in Japanese), Tokyo: Toko-shoin.

Groenewegen, P. (2005), 'A book that never was: Marshall's final volume on progress and his system of ethical and political beliefs', *History of Economics Review*, **42** (Summer), 29–44.

Hamilton, W.H. (1915), 'Economic theory and "social reform"', *Journal of Political Economy*, **23** (6).

Hamilton, W.H. (1919), 'The Institutional Approach to Economic Theory', *American Economic Review*, **9** (1), Supplement.

Hobson, J.A. (1914), *Work and Wealth: A Human Valuation*, with a new introduction by P. Cain, 1992, London: Routledge/Thoemmes Press.
Hobson, J.A. (1929), *Wealth and Life. A Study in Values*, London: Macmillan.
Homan, P.T. (1928), *Contemporary Economic Thought*, New York: Harper.
Hutchison, T.W. (1978), *On Revolutions and Progress in Economic Knowledge*, Cambridge: Cambridge University Press.
Hutchison, T.W. (1988), 'Gustav Schmoller and the problems of today', *Journal of Institutional and Theoretical Economics*, **144** (3), 527–31.
Jones, G.S. (1971), *Outcast London. A Study in the Relationship between Classes in Victorian Society*, Oxford: Clarendon Press.
Keynes, J.M. (1924), 'Alfred Marshall, 1842–1924', in A.C. Pigou (ed.), (1925), *The Collected Writings of J.M. Keynes*, vol. 10, London: Macmillan, 1972.
Koot, G.M. (1987), *English Historical Economics, 1870–1926. The Rise of Economic History and Neomercantilism*, New York: Cambridge University Press.
Layton, W.T. (unpublished), Layton Papers, Cambridge: Trinity College Library.
Liu, W.T.-C. (1934), *A Study of Hobson's Welfare Economics*, Peiping: Kwang Yuen Press.
Maloney, J. (1985), *Marshall, Orthodoxy & the Professionalization of Economics*, Cambridge: Cambridge University Press.
Maloney, J. (1987), 'English historical school', *The New Palgrave*, vol. 2, London: Macmillan.
Marshall, A. (1873a), 'The future of the working classes', in A.C. Pigou (ed.) (1925), *Memorials of Alfred Marshall*, London: Macmillan.
Marshall, A. (1873b), *Lectures to Women*, in T. Raffaelli, E. Biagini and R.M. Tullberg (eds) (1995), *Alfred Marshall's Lectures to Women. Some Economic Questions Directly Connected to the Welfare of the Labourer*, Aldershot, UK and Brookfield, USA: Edward Elgar.
Marshall, A. (1885), *The Present Position of Economics*, in A.C. Pigou (ed.) (1925), *Memorials of Alfred Marshall*, London: Macmillan.
Marshall, A. (1887), 'Preface', to L.L. Price, *Industrial Peace. Its Advantages, Methods and Difficulties*, A report of an inquiry made for the Toynbee Trustees, London: Macmillan.
Marshall, A. (1890), *Principles of Economics*, 2 vols, ed. by C.W. Guillebaud, 9th (variorum) edn, 1961, London: Macmillan.
Marshall, A. (1897), 'The old generation of economists and the new', in A.C. Pigou (ed.) (1925), *Memorials of Alfred Marshall*, London: Macmillan.
Marshall, A. (1919), *Industry and Trade. A Study of Industrial Technique and Business Organization; and of Their Influences on the Conditions of Various Classes and Nations*, 4th edn, 1923, London: Macmillan.
Marshall, A. (1923), *Money, Credit & Commerce*, London: Macmillan.
Marshall, M. (1947), *What I Remember*, Cambridge: Cambridge University Press.
Mitchell, W.C. (1969), *Types of Economic Theory: From Mercantilism to Institutionalism*, New York: Augustus Kelley.
Nishizawa, T. (2004), 'The economics tripos and the Marshallian school in the making – with special reference to his industrial economics', *Economic Review*, **55** (4), 358–78.
Nishizawa, T. (2007), *Economic Thought of Marshall and the Historical School* (in Japanese), Tokyo: Iwanami-shoten.
Parsons, T. (1931), 'Wants and activities in Marshall', *Quarterly Journal of Economics*, **46** (1), 101–40.

Parsons, T. (1932), 'Economics and sociology: Marshall in relation to the thought of his time', *Quarterly Journal of Economics*, **46** (2), 316–47.
Pigou, A.C. (1912), *Wealth and Welfare*, London: Macmillan.
Pigou, A.C. (1920), *The Economics of Welfare*, London: Macmillan.
Pigou, A.C. (1924), 'In memoriam: Alfred Marshall', a lecture delivered in Cambridge on 24 October, in A.C. Pigou (ed.) (1925), *Memorials of Alfred Marshall*, London: Macmillan.
Pigou, A.C. (ed.) (1925), *Memorials of Alfred Marshall*, London: Macmillan.
Raffaelli, T. (2004), 'Whatever happened to Marshall's industrial economics', *European Journal of the History of Economic Thought*, **11** (2), 209–29.
Raffaelli, T., E. Biagini and R.M. Tullberg (eds) (1995), *Alfred Marshall's Lectures to Women. Some Economic Questions Directly Connected to the Welfare of the Labourer*, Aldershot, UK and Brookfield, USA: Edward Elgar.
Robbins, L. (1932), *An Essay on the Nature and Significance of Economic Science*, 2nd edn, revised and extended, 1935, London: Macmillan.
Robertson, D.H. (1957), *Lectures on Economic Principles*, vol. 1. London: Staples Press.
Ruskin, J. (1860), *Unto this Last: Four Essays on the First Principles of Political Economy*, London: Routledge/Thoemmes Press.
Rutherford, M.R. (2007), 'Institutionalism and its English connections', *European Journal of the History of Economic Thought*, **14** (2), 291–323.
Schmoller, Gustav von (1990, 1904), *Grundriss der allgemainen Volkswirtschaftslehre*, 2 vols, Leipzig: Duncker & Humblot.
Schumpeter, J. (1926), 'Gustav v. Schmoller und die Probleme von heute', *Schmollers Jahrbuch*, 50, reprinted 1954 in Schumpeter, J., *Dogmenhistorische und biographische Aufsätze*, Tübingen: J.C.B. Mohr, pp. 337–88.
Schumpeter, J. (1951), *Ten Great Economists from Marx to Keynes*, London: Allen & Unwin.
Schumpeter, J. (1954), *History of Economic Analysis*, New York: Oxford University Press.
Semmel, B. (1960), *Imperialism and Social Reform: English Social-Imperial Thought 1895–1914*, London: George Allen & Unwin.
Shionoya, Y. (1995), *Schumpeter and the Idea of Social Science* (in Japanese), Tokyo: Toyokeizai-shinposha.
Shionoya, Y. (2006a), 'The Oxford approach to the philosophical foundations of the welfare state', paper presented at the Workshop on the Cambridge School of Economics, Hitotsubashi University, March.
Shionoya, Y. (2006b), 'Schmoller and modern economic sociology', *Schmoller's Jahrbuch*, **126** (2), 177–95.
Shove, G.F. (1942), 'The place of Marshall's *Principles* in the development of economic theory', *Economic Journal*, **52** (4): 294–329.
Whitaker, J.K. (ed.) (1996), *The Correspondence of Alfred Marshall, Economist*, 3 vols, Cambridge: Cambridge University Press.

8. The limits to growth: Alfred Marshall and the British economic tradition

Katia Caldari and Fabio Masini*

8.1 ECONOMIC THEORY AND THE LIMITS TO GROWTH

In an authoritative study on *Valuations for Sustainable Development*, Sylvie Faucheux and Martin O'Connor (1998: 1) stated that the 'classical economists in the eighteenth and nineteenth centuries tended to regard the primary environmental supports for economic production activity as either non-scarce (such as air) or non-depletable (such as arable land)'. As Perelman (2002: 1) has underlined, the biggest paradox of economics seems to be that it is a science based on the scarcity of means but built on the hypothesis of non-scarcity of production factors.

Nevertheless, this paradox does not seem to apply to 'eighteenth- and nineteenth-century' economists. They were perfectly aware of inputs scarcity. They could not escape considering air as a free good but they soon started to consider fresh, healthy air as a scarce input for human activities. And land, water and minerals very soon appeared to be 'scarce'.

It is only with Hotelling (1931) that economic theory starts to consider absolute scarcity, even for non-renewable resources, as a mere transitory problem which does not harm production perspectives, thanks to input substitutions brought about by changes in relative prices.[1]

Faucheaux and O'Connor insist on the fact that Malthus and Mill were the only exceptions among the economists of those centuries, but *only for ethical reasons*. Opocher (2007) extended this ethical preoccupation also to Marshall but this idea may be (and indeed has been; Caldari, 2004) challenged. We can concede that he tried to reconcile ethical pressures with economic theory, as Grey (1913) is usually recognized[2] to have done. But Marshall's main contribution to the idea of progress and to what now might be called an 'economic theory of sustainable development' was to expound ethical arguments from the question, showing that in strict economic terms the problem of the limits to growth, in its many facets, was an economic (in scientific terms) and not (only) an ethical concern. And we have some doubts also on the merely 'ethical' nature of the reflections on the limits to growth in British classical economists before Marshall.

The whole of classical economics, if we exclude (but only partly) Adam Smith, is founded on the awareness of decreasing returns in agriculture owing to a decreasing quality of land. Hence, through the theory of differential rent and Ricardian distributional theories, the feeling of an inevitably declining accumulation process. They were therefore well aware, although to different degrees (Spengler, 1955), of some limits to growth, which during the nineteenth-century spread from land to other production factors and from purely quantitative scarcity to qualitative features, such as indicators concerning the 'quality' of life (degree of water and air pollution, urbanization, and so on).

The question of the *limits to growth* acquired a qualitative dimension which was lost in economic literature until recently, when the topics related to the concept of sustainable development came to the fore.[3] In the twentieth century, economists have mainly enquired into the limits to growth assuming an optimistic perspective of technological progress through inputs substitution: the rise of prices of natural resources signals an increasing economic incentive to turn to alternative inputs.[4] And technical progress allows higher productivity of all factors and of the standards of living.

This chapter is only a part of a wider project aiming at underlining the reasons, places and times in the evolution of the relationship between growth and its limits in economic theory. What we present here is a piece of the story: whether and in what ways the British classical tradition in economic studies influenced the thought and work of Alfred Marshall, who represents a turning point in the economic literature on such a topic.

Marshall's contributions to the idea of sustainable development were already the subject matter of a previous paper (Caldari, 2004), where an important part of Marshall's idea on the limits to growth – namely, the question of absolute, not merely relative, resources scarcity[5] – is considered to be shared with the classical economists, thus assuming an hypothesis of *continuity*.

Collard (1996) had already hinted at this idea when speaking of a 'Cambridge tradition' on the limits to growth, which would go from Mill to Sidgwick, Marshall, later Pigou and on. But this tradition seems to be not only from Cambridge if Garrison (1998: 51) underlies the importance of Smith's reflections on inter-temporal questions, implying the need to slow down growth rates today in order to preserve future perspectives, and Groenewegen (1999a; 1999b) maintains that Marshall derives from Smith an idea of 'wealth' in qualitative terms and of 'capital' in terms of knowledge, two of the main elements of the message of Marshall on sustainable development.

We therefore thought it would be worth enquiring further on this and check whether there really are continuities or breaking innovations in Marshall's ideas on the limits to growth as compared with those scattered in the economic literature by the previous and contemporary British classical authors.

The British culture and economic thought had in fact faced and partially considered several hindrances to growth in terms of resources scarcity/depletion and distributional injustice. Several economists had very clearly in mind the distinction between development and growth, between quantitative and qualitative characters of the economic activity, between relative and absolute scarcity. But this does not imply the same perception of these questions as Marshall had.

Indeed, we found little support to the thesis of continuity. Many of the aspects Marshall mixed in the basket of the idea of progress were there already, but his contribution was precisely to mix them in a very peculiar way. His contribution to the literature of the limits to growth must be considered in many respects as a revolution, posing the question with economic (not only ethical) arguments, abandoning the fiction of a stationary state to look for the elements that could help growth in a difficult context.

In order to illustrate this, we will briefly outline the evolution of the classics' ideas on growth and have a look at the debate in Britain on its limits. In the third section we will show by contrast Marshall's attitude towards progress, growth and their critical elements. We will then conclude in order to underline his specific contribution.

8.2 CLASSICAL ECONOMISTS AND THE MISSING IDEA OF (CUMULATIVE) GROWTH

Growth and progress are critical concepts to classical economists. According to Checkland (1959), while they stressed the importance and the possibility of short-run growth, they agreed on the impossibility of growth and development after a certain limit in the long run. Two main obstacles are underlined: the first is the incapability of man to force nature beyond a certain point; the second is the nature of mankind to proliferate too much. The problem with cumulative growth in classical economists seems therefore to depend on an incoherent dynamics of population and resources. Let us briefly recall their reflections on both sides of the problem.

8.2.1 A Divergent Dynamic between Population and Resources

The question of how much economists feared or favoured population growth is in fact still debated: both attitudes may be sustained through economic theory. Population can be a resource of production inputs (on the supply side), a source of consumption (on the demand side), but also a threat to natural and physical resources.

Malthus himself may be considered to have stressed the importance of increasing growth rates of population only in the first issues of the *Essay on Population* (1798 [1926]): as he was worried about the 'absorption' problem, some think[6] he could not really believe that growing population could be a negative macroeconomic factor, as he in fact stated in the *Principles of Political Economy* (1820). It should also be remembered that the first version of the *Essay* was written as a response to Godwin's and Condorcet's optimism on progress, and the principle of population only played a subsidiary role.

It is quite likely that Malthus, when he realized through the dispute with Ricardo that the ultimate result of population growth was a distributional advantage for rents (thus assuring the effective demand necessary to sustain the reproduction of the economic system), had weakened his aversion towards that phenomenon. But it is also true that as late as 1829, in a letter to Nassau Senior, he was still worried about the fact that the stimulus to better one's own living conditions could be checked by a faster growth rate of population.[7]

From a general point of view, although probably overestimated, the attitude of British classical economists towards a widening gap between decreasing subsistence means, owing to diminishing returns in agriculture, and increasing population pressures was that of an increasing *worry*, although in different degrees.

For Adam Smith the increasing efficiency from the division of labour (with the only limit of the extent of the market) prevails over scarcity (Lowe, 1954: 135) of which he had little consciousness (for example, he considered the *disposal* of trees, not their *conservation*,[8] as a cost). He notes that 'useful fossils and minerals of the earth, etc naturally grow dearer as the society advances in wealth and improvement' (1776, Book I, Chapter xi, Part I: 3) but, as Kurz and Salvadori (2003: 6) observe, 'it cannot be claimed that he paid a lot of attention to the scarcity of natural resources and its impact on economic growth'.

Burke (1795 [1893]) had written about the perspective scarcity of corn. But it was Ricardo that, replacing the Smithian assumption of constant returns with diminishing returns in agriculture (Lowe 1954: 141), incorporated the growth of population within his model as a limit to economic growth. When population rises, the diminishing returns in agriculture start to operate and squeeze profits, the engine of accumulation. Technological progress is possible but not sufficient to contrast diminishing returns in agriculture, hence ultimately envisaging a halt in accumulation and growth (in other words, there can be no backstop technology[9]).

Ricardo and Malthus were living in a period of decreasing growth rates compared to Smith's times. During the century, growth perspectives in agriculture started to enjoy technological progress and higher productivity of production factors. But industrial production was often stagnant, with recurrent crises.

As it is known (Opocher, 2007: 4 ff), John Stuart Mill reversed the attitude towards economics away from the 'dismal science', although Spengler (1955) observes how Senior had already contributed to overcome the Ricardian pessimism over growth perspectives.

According to Mill, progress is unpredictable (Lowe, 1954: 155) but the main features of industrial growth are an increase of capital, an increase of population and improvements in production (Mill, 1848 [1900]: 471). We should add another factor which Mill does not cite with the others, although equally important: the extent of the (international) market (Mill, 1848 [1900]: 464).

Agriculture shows decreasing returns to scale due to the (Ricardian) assumption of different land fertility but this trend might be reversed by growing 'agricultural skill' (Mill, 1848 [1900]: 466). Manufacture, on the contrary, shows increasing returns to scale: higher demand induced by increasing population does not raise the price of industrial output.

This does not mean Mill shows no apprehension towards population growth but the quantitative, Malthusian question harming the economic and social system is changed into a qualitative problem. Avoiding overcrowding has an important economic influence, as it increases creativity and improves the provision of some public goods:

> A population may be too crowded, though all be amply supplied with food and raiment. . . . Solitude, in the sense of being often alone, is essential to any depth of meditation or of character; and solitude in the presence of natural beauty and grandeur, is the cradle of thoughts and aspirations which are not only good for the individual, but which society could ill do without. (Mill, 1848 [1900]: 497)

For both these contrasting attitudes, Spengler (1955) noted that Mill has in mind an idea of 'optimal size of the population'. Below that optimal size there is still room for increasing wealth through a rise in production capacity; beyond that optimal size, negative effects on wealth and on the general standards of living take the lead.

The well-known conclusion is that Mill came to theorize the positive effects of a stationary state, where people are free from need and can aim at a better quality of life. The 'stationary state', which is the constant rate of growth corresponding to the optimal size of population, is no longer the detrimental end of human development[10] but a desirable state attainable in the very long run because, if progress goes on, the disadvantages might turn to be more important than the advantages.

> If the earth must lose that great portion of its pleasantness which it owes to things that the unlimited increase of wealth and population would extirpate from it, for the mere purpose of enabling it to support a larger but not a better or a happier population, I sincerely hope, for the sake of prosperity, that will be content to be stationary, long before necessity compels them to it. (Mill, 1848 [1900], Book 4: 497–8)

But Mill's idea of a stationary state, beyond its apparent positive aspects, should be considered as the product of a defensive attitude. Mill was well aware of several checks to growth. Before the famous contribution by Jevons was published on *The Coal Question* in 1865, Mill had already warned the British government against possible shortages of fuel.[11] But he knew that the main challenge to British growth was at the level of international competition. Britain was losing its supremacy over the world. New 'aggressive' states (Germany, the USA) were progressing at higher rates, challenging the advantageous position earned by Britain through colonies and the origination of industrialization.

The stationary state was therefore a philosophical, more than an economic, response to this state of annoying uneasiness. The awareness of decadence could not be accepted by the 'snobbish' Mill: growth was bound to decline but the threat turned into a blessing. It will be necessary to wait until 1859, when Darwin's *Origin of Species* will be published, to see the concept of a mechanistic harmony crumble again.

8.2.2 Economic Growth and Moral Constraints in the British Debate

From the early nineteenth-century until the 1860s, Great Britain was the leader of the world economy, 'the only thoroughly developed industrial State' (Court, 1967: 302) of the time, although in the meantime she experienced two decades (1830s and 1840s) of a very deep crisis.

As we have seen, in the first part of the century economists were not so optimistic with regard to the growth possibilities of the economy (Malthus, Ricardo); even the most desirable status was not a developing economy but a stationary state (J.S. Mill). In the second half of the century, some limits to economic growth continued to be taken into consideration although with a less dramatic attitude.

Observing the faster industrialization process of Britain compared with other countries in the past century, some economists developed a consciousness about the risks to economic growth owing to a shrinkage of natural resources. One of the main problems was still represented by agriculture and land, under the pressure of a growing population (Court, 1967): 'the idea of diminishing returns to effort on the land lay very deep in human experience, and the doctrine of the division of labour, whatever it might do for industry, promised little for agriculture' (Checkland, 1959: 52). Nonetheless, in time, economists and politicians thought they had found the way out. Foreign trade – and the colonies – became more and more the fundamental condition for escaping the otherwise unavoidable limit imposed by land on production. Britain became an imperial power.

Another problem was connected with the main 'fuel' to feed the industrial engine, that is, 'coal'. They did not conceive an energy saving technological progress; quite the contrary.[12] If the accumulation process sustaining economic growth is supported by technological progress, energy starts to be understood as a finite good, especially under the pressure of a growing production and a (consequent) growing demand for it.

Jevons's (1865) contribution on *The Coal Question* became very much influential. In 1871 a Royal Commission was appointed in order to inquire into the actual state of supply and consumption of coal, as suggested by Jevons himself.[13] The genesis of the famous book[14] is known: British productivity and output growth in the past century had been accompanied by a greater, enormous deployment of natural resources, with a rising risk of running out of energy: 'Coal . . . is the material energy of the country – the universal aid – the factor in everything we do. With coal almost any feat is possible or easy; without it we are thrown back into the laborious poverty of early times' (1865: viii).

Coal is the productive factor upon which Britain's commercial superiority is based: 'we owe almost all arts from Continental nations, except those great arts which have been called into use here by the cheapness and excellence of our coal. . . . there is no probability that when our coal is used up any more powerful substitute will be forthcoming' (Jevons, 1865: xiii). As population keeps on increasing, 'it is thence simply inferred that we cannot long continue our present rate of progress' (ibid.: xiv).

The exhaustibility of coal seemed statistically proved by its rising costs (Forster Brown, 1891). These and other concerns on the possible limits to economic growth became more dramatic in the following years, when Britain started to show signs of economic slowdown. The period between 1873 and 1896 is known as 'the Great Depression'. Even though the 1830s and 1840s were years of a deeper crisis, it is during the Great Depression that Britain ceased to be the 'workshop of the world' (Hobsbawm, 1968: 104).

Great Britain, in late Victorian days, had to face the competition by such countries of rapid and new industrialization as Germany, France and the USA. The awareness and concern for this new international competition were officially recognized in the *Report of the Royal Commission on the Depression of Industry and Trade* in 1886 (Royal Commission, 1886).

The Commission was appointed 'in response to a general feeling of anxiety', in order to take 'into consideration the depression of trade and industry in Great Britain, and to report by what means, if any, the depression could be remedied' (Anonymous, 1887: 197). Among the possible causes of the depression, foreign competition and superior technical education of foreign workers were underlined (ibid.).

Indeed, a pervasive concern for the condition of the British economy was 'in the air' long before the appointment of the Commission, as one can see from the articles published on the subject from the 1860s onwards. Statistical data were called in support either to the optimists, who aimed at proving that the British economy was still in good health (for instance, Bourne, 1875; Brassey, 1879; Farr, 1876; Jeans, 1884; Mundella, 1878) or at proving its decline (as in the articles by anonymous authors; Anonymous, 1879a; 1879b).

Although most articles and essays ended with a moderately optimistic tone, it was clear that, during those years, Britain was really losing its supremacy, as confirmed by the historian E.J. Hobsbawm: 'the immediate benefits of the first phase of industrialization wore off. The possibilities of the technological innovations of the original (British) industrial era tended to exhaust themselves' (1968: 105); 'Britain fell behind her rivals' (1968: 149).

The problem of international competition and the feared slowdown of the British economy were not the only sources for concerns and public debates. At that time, in fact, Great Britain was experimenting with the soft form of socialism through the Fabians, unions, friendly societies and co-operatives (Clapham, 1952) with a high sensitiveness towards the most actual and grievous problems of the time: poverty, health, housing, life in towns, labour conditions, and so on. A large number of articles were published on these topics.[15]

The question of poverty, towns overcrowding and the quality of life in towns became, for instance, widely discussed by commentators, politicians, intellectuals and economists.[16] The British productive system had become mature, expanding intensively and extensively. It had changed the very urban and geographical morphology of territory and society. The growth of population had initially proved favourable to the production process, supplying it with low-cost labour, but had generated great distress in larger proportions of (urban) society. The reference was made to London and to what was then called the 'wear and tear of London life' (Roose, 1886a; 1886b), due moreover 'to a lack of fresh air, recreations of all kinds, and change of scene' (Roose, 1886b: 506). Life in towns was charged by evil effects 'upon the human body' (Fothergill, 1887) and human strength (Brabazon, 1887). The Society for Promoting Industrial Villages and the Garden City Movement were born in order to face these kind of problems.

Also the conditions of labour were very much debated at that time: not only the questions of the eight (working) hours, minimum wage, profit sharing, co-operation, and so on, but also and moreover the urgent problem of the degeneration of people belonging to the working (lower) classes and its effects on their children.[17]

In particular, the more urgent problem to be solved in this connection seemed to be education (Chadwick, 1865). In order to persuade workers not to spend all their spare time getting drunk in the pubs but aim at better conditions for themselves and their families, they should receive a certain degree of education. Quite often the problem of lack of education was discussed on an ethical and moral ground: it was a means through which it was possible to ameliorate the condition of the lower classes and of the society as a whole (Hamilton, 1883; Mouat, 1880). This is also true in the case of Henry Fawcett when he writes:

> if the people were educated they would not become less self-reliant; their dependence upon extraneous help, instead of being increased, would gradually so much diminish that after the lapse of a generation or two the compulsory law, though it might be continued, would virtually cease to operate. . . . when education of parents has been secured, the education of their children is also guaranteed. Education begets education, because people who have enjoyed its advantages will strive hard to let their children enjoy them also. Ignorance, on the other hand, too often begets ignorance . . . Ignorance is an evil which will not cure itself. (1871: 124)

In fact, Fawcett goes a little further suggesting a link between education and the efficiency of work:

> Ignorance therefore takes away a considerable part of the power which an individual possesses to acquire the means of living. This will be more clearly shown as we proceed to explain how greatly the efficiency of labour is promoted by education. Sufficient, however, has here been stated to prove that the injury inflicted by ignorance is so great as to justify the State in carrying out a scheme of general compulsory education. (1871: 126)

But it would be left to Alfred Marshall to clarify the sequence: education means more skilled work, higher (labour) productivity and, therefore, more national competitiveness.

8.3 MARSHALL'S IDEA OF PROGRESS AND THE REQUISITES FOR GROWTH

Not only education, but all the other questions of public debate were discussed at that time mainly on a moral-ethical ground, as for instance in the articles published in the *Fabian Tracts* on the problem of housing and the effects of urban overcrowding, or on sociological grounds (as the contributions cited in the last paragraph). But, again, only with Marshall we find an interpretation that goes beyond a strictly ethical ground. According to him, all those problems (poverty, overcrowded towns, lack of education) – albeit important from a moral point of view – were indeed the true limits to *economic* growth for Britain under the pressure of international competition. This 'economic' point of view and the awareness of the complexity of the various possible limits to growth are synthesized in his concept of progress.

8.3.1 The Marshallian Recipe for Progress

The question Marshall is most interested in is 'progress' and in particular the elements that promote progress *in a nation*. As it is well known (Groenewegen, 1995) 'progress' should have been the topic and the title of his last unfinished book but a huge number of suggestions and observations are scattered in all his writings and public statements.

Marshall very rarely uses the term 'growth', since it suggests just a quantitative meaning, whereas for him true progress and development imply, besides of course the increment of 'wealth', the improvement of some aspects of society. The mere *growth* of *material wealth* does not mean *progress* of a nation. Progress is a very complex term[18] and cannot be identified with a mere increase of material wealth since it involves other and more important factors (Marshall, 1920: 173). On the other hand, human well-being cannot be measured simply in terms of 'quantity of goods' for consumption but also in terms of living standards related to qualitative indicators.

Through his *Blue Books* and *Red Books* (Groenewegen, 1995), with plenty of data and historical notes, Marshall focuses on the actual economic condition of Britain, trying to understand the elements of weakness and the origin of its economic decline. He recognizes, but only privately, that 'England is going to the bad because we English economists have not time and strength enough to deal with the real problems of our age' (letter to Wicksell, 19 December 1904, in Whitaker, 1996, vol. 3: 99). In his (public) writings, where he appears much more optimistic, he insistently underlines the fundamental elements of progress and suggests the necessary changes Britain has to take in order to recover. Let us recall them briefly (Caldari, 2004; 2006).

The first and most important factor of progress is 'man', what we now call 'human capital'. Man is the engine of progress thanks to his work, creative faculties and innumerable potentialities. Man therefore must be the first necessary factor on which to build the 'wealth' of a nation. With regards to this aspect education assumes a paramount importance. Here Marshall is very clear: 'the best investment of the present capital of the country is to educate the next generation' (1873: 106). Education ameliorates the character of people, transforms unskilled in skilled work and increases the efficiency labour.

A particular attention is then dedicated to innovative and creative faculties from which the industrial leadership of a nation depends. Industrial efficiency is deeply enquired into, especially in the comparative study made in *Industry and Trade*. Here, Marshall explores what characterizes the industrial efficiency of Germany, the USA, France, Japan and Britain. Each country has its own peculiarities and shows different paths to economic development and growth. Marshall tries to identify those factors that, according to him, can revitalize the British economy (an example is given by industrial districts) (Becattini, 2006; Martin, 2006). The key elements for efficiency are definitely the innovative, creative and flexible capabilities.

Finally, Marshall pays much attention to the quality of life, which progress should eventually aim at improving for human beings. According to Marshall, a good quality of life requires not only a certain level of income but also other elements as for instance fresh air, green spaces, and so on. This opinion has moved Marshall close to the Society for Promoting Industrial Villages and the Garden City Movement. An increase in wealth does not necessarily imply an amelioration in the quality of life: on the contrary, a blind increase of wealth could have many negative effects on it.

8.3.2 Marshall and the Limits to Growth of the Classics

Although Marshall is widely recognized as 'neoclassical' according to the well-known definition given by Veblen (1900), he can indeed be considered anti-classical[19] for (at least) three aspects of his reasoning, which are in close connection with the very question of the limits to economic growth: (1) the theory of population; (2) the theory of diminishing returns in agriculture; and (3) the idea of stationary state.

8.3.2.1 The theory of population

According to the first point, while classical economists, as we have seen above, refer to the increase of population as a chief limit to growth,

Marshall considers population mainly as an important source of economic growth. In fact, if the production of wealth 'is but a means to the sustenance of man', it is also true that man is 'the chief means of the production of that wealth' (1920: 173). Man must be considered therefore as an important source of economic growth. The increase of population is among the factors of progress; as he puts it in *Principles*: 'the growth of *mankind in numbers*, in health and strength, in knowledge, ability and richness of character is the end of all our studies' (1920: 139; emphasis added).

As regards Adam Smith, even though he has 'said but a little on the question of population, for indeed he wrote at one of the culminating points of the prosperity of English working classes', Marshall recognized that what he had written on the topic 'is wise and well balanced and modern in tone'. Moreover, Smith was correct 'by insisting that the necessaries of life are not fixed and determined in quantity' but unfortunately, he 'did not work out this hint fully' (Marshall, 1920: 177).

Several circumstances occurred at the end of the eighteenth century that had concurred to change this 'optimistic' vision: Malthus and Ricardo were an example of this new trend of thought. On the one hand, Marshall justifies their arguments as the inevitable outcome of the events as, for instance, 'an astonishing series of bad harvests, a most exhausting war, and a change in the methods of industry that dislocated old ties, combined with an injudicious poor law to bring the working classes into the greatest misery . . .' (Marshall, 1920: 177). But, on the other hand, he keeps himself aloof from them.

With regard to Malthus, Marshall recognizes that his book on population must be considered the 'starting point of all modern speculations on the subject' (1920: 178). Nonetheless, only a part of Malthus's reasoning can be considered utterly valid and acceptable: that connected with the supply of labour, in which Malthus proves that the population trend is truly towards an increase in numbers. But the other parts of his reasoning are antiquated, especially because he did not consider (but only because 'he could not foresee') the 'great developments of steam transport by land and by sea which have enabled Englishmen of the present generation to obtain the products of the richest lands of the earth at comparatively small cost' (Marshall, 1920: 180).

According to Marshall, the increase of population is not anymore a menace for national wealth because of the developments of the means of transport and communication and the opening of foreign markets, as it is clarified also in the following passage, that we think worthy to quote at full length:

> The accumulated wealth of civilized countries is at present growing faster than the population: and though it may be true that the wealth per head would

> increase somewhat faster if the population did not increase quite so fast; yet as a matter of fact an increase of population is likely to continue to be accompanied by a more than proportionate increase of the material aids to production: and in England at the present time, with easy access to abundant foreign supplies of raw material, an increase of population is accompanied by a more than proportionate increase of the means of satisfying human wants other than the need for light, fresh air, etc. Much of this increase is however attributable not to the increase of industrial efficiency but to the increase of wealth by which it is accompanied: and therefore it does not necessarily benefit those who have no share in that wealth. And further, England's foreign supplies of raw produce may at any time be checked by changes in the trade regulations of other countries, and may be almost cut off by a great war while the naval and military expenditure which would be necessary to make the country fairly secure against this last risk, would appreciably diminish the benefits that she derives from the action of the law of increasing return. (1920: 321)

Therefore, according to Marshall:

> the growth of population, if not checked by other causes, must ultimately be checked by the difficulty of obtaining raw produce; but in spite of the law of diminishing return, the pressure of population on the means of subsistence may be restrained for a long time to come by the opening up of new fields of supply, by the cheapening of railway and steamship communication, and by the growth of organization and knowledge. (1920: 166)

Technological progress and the widening of markets help reduce the demographic pressures. Nonetheless, according to Marshall, the influence of population has a mischievous and dangerous effect, too often ignored. It is the effect on the quality of those factors impacting on the productivity of labour. An example of this is the question of 'urban sustainability', which – as we have seen – was starting to arise at the end of the nineteenth century.

In analysing contemporary society, Marshall paid much attention to the effects that living in grey and polluted towns, without green open spaces, had on the character and the productive efficiency of people. This interest is manifest in almost all Marshall's writings and in his public activity. Furthermore, throughout his life, Marshall was in close touch with the Society for Promoting Industrial Villages and the Garden City Movement, two associations that aimed at improving the quality of life of the urban population, especially the poor (for further details, see Caldari, 2004).

In modern towns – Marshall observes – people are packed together with some negative consequences, first of all the lack of fresh air, 'the most important side of the pressure of population growth' (1885, in Whitaker, 1975, vol. 2: 391). The same concern is present also in 'Where to house the London poor', a paper published in the *Contemporary Review* one year earlier, where Marshall deals with the housing problem in London (1884:

142) or in the paper presented at the Industrial Remuneration Conference in 1885.

Beyond a social aspect of the problem, an economic one also emerges. The tendency towards urban crowding can have negative effects not only on sanitation, hygiene and the environment, but also on economic efficiency itself. In large towns

> there are large numbers of people with poor physique and a feeble will, with no enterprise, no courage, no hope, and scarcely any self-respect, whom misery drives to work for lower wages than the same work gets in the country. The employer pays his high rent out of his savings in wages; and they have to pay their high rents out of their diminished wages. This is the fundamental evil. (Marshall, 1884: 144–5)

The idea is that high population density on urban land means higher rents paid by enterprises; this, in turn, implies less money left for wages and workers with lower incomes facing the higher rents in towns. Moreover, 'the want of air and light, of peaceful repose out-of-doors for all ages and of healthy play for children, exhausts the energies of the best blood of England which is constantly flowing towards our large towns. By allowing vacant spaces to be built on recklessly we are committing a great blunder from a business point of view' (Marshall, 1920: 659).

8.3.2.2 The theory of diminishing returns in agriculture

According to Ricardo, an increasing population resulted in a limit to economic growth because of the diminishing returns of soil. Marshall, in dealing with the topic of fertility of land, firmly maintains that

> Ricardo's wording of the law of diminishing return was inexact; . . . of course he could not anticipate the great series of inventions which were about to open up new sources of supply, and, with the aid of free trade, to revolutionize English agriculture; but the agricultural history of England and other countries might have led him to lay greater stress on the probability of a change. (1920: 163)

Moreover, Ricardo was wrong in underrating the advantages which a dense population offers to agriculture, generating economies of agglomeration:

> an increase of population tends to develop the organization of trade and industry [so that] the law of diminishing return does not apply to the total capital and labour spent in a district as sharply as to that on a single farm. Even when cultivation has reached a stage after which each successive dose applied to a field would get a less return than the preceding dose, it may be possible for an increase in the population to cause a more than proportional increase in the means of subsistence. (Marshall, 1920: 165)

According to Marshall, the development of the means of communication, together with the gains from international trade could escape the (alleged iron) law of diminishing returns. As pointed out in the Preface to the sixth edition of *Principles*: 'In the present age the opening out of new countries aided by low transport charges on land and sea, has almost suspended the tendency of diminishing return in that sense in which the term was used by Malthus and Ricardo . . .' (Guillebaud, 1961: 59).

Furthermore, Malthus and Ricardo did not pay attention to what, according to Marshall, was the essence of progress: the development of knowledge and its possible applications. In *Industry and Trade*, Marshall underlines: 'In agriculture, improved knowledge and methods are always contending against Nature's resistance to the demands made on her by an increasing population' (1919: 189). Knowledge, the most important outcome of human activities, is the recipe to avoid the law of diminishing returns stated by the classical economists and the main ingredient of progress and growth.

8.3.2.3 Progress and the idea of a stationary state

As we have seen, according to the classical economists a stationary state was the inevitable point towards which the economic system tended. The 'classical' stationary state could be either a dismal and gloomy state, where people were miserable (Ricardo), or a privileged state where people could enjoy all the pleasures of life (Mill). This dichotomy is the aspect of classical reasoning from which Marshall seems to depart more clearly.

According to Marshall, the stationary state is simply 'a fiction' (1920: 366), part of the economist's toyshop, that has nothing to do with the real world.[20] Marshall was not interested in finding an ideal abstract state compatible with the economic forces under consideration; on the contrary, his aim was, as we have seen, to find out the sources of progress.

Marshall considers two kinds of (relative) limits to growth (and progress) which we might call (a) social and (b) natural. National limits have been previously considered. Social limits to growth depend on the fact that men are social animals, living in a particular cultural and institutional setting which is evolving in time. For this reason, progress should be slow and gradual, as explained by the well-known motto on the forefront of *Principles* (1890), 'Natura non facit saltum'.[21] Economic progress must go together with the progress of political, social and cultural institutions that are the 'milieu' in which economic activities take place. Marshall explained this concept in his speech at the Industrial Remuneration Conference' (1885): 'economic institutions – Marshall maintains – are the products of human nature and cannot change much faster than human nature changes' (1885: 173–4).

So, on the one side, progress produces an increase of man's command over Nature but, on the other, it requires the development of higher human faculties, that allow him to use that command correctly. And the acquisition of such human faculties takes time.

8.4 CONCLUDING REMARKS

In classical economics two main attitudes on growth emerge. Smith's optimism is based on the fact that he recognizes the existence of limits and problems concerning accumulation but, in the first phase of industrialization, technological progress and the expansion of markets through trade can overcome the difficulties. Some years later, Malthus influences the debate in Britain pointing at the widening gap between natural resources and population. Ricardo shares Malthus's pessimism, even though from a different perspective: population growth, combined with decreasing returns in agriculture, determines a slowdown in accumulation, the engine of growth, that technological progress can only postpone.

Some decades afterwards, Mill would undertake the burden of reassuring British people. He recognizes the existence of problems and a tendency of productive and economic growth to come to a halt. Britain was still experiencing the deep crisis of the 1830s and 1840s but he speaks of the stationary state as the most desirable result. Mill reads the situation as though the economic crisis could lead (in the best case) to the realization of a stationary state where needs are satisfied without worrying too much about production and consumption.

The debates on the limits to growth would become, at least apparently, quite sharper in the next decades, due to the increasing decline of British economy in international competition. Nonetheless a clear economic analysis of the problem is missing, as we have seen, untill Alfred Marshall's contribution.

Marshall casts new light on the causes of slowdown and on the way to overcome the limits to growth. The latter depend on a decreasing productivity of labour and capital compared to Britain's international competitors. Productivity is what economists should point at – and policy-makers should act upon – to avoid decadence.

It is in this respect that Marshall's 'modern' attention towards the negative effects of industrialization and urbanization can be explained: they are not (only or even mainly) moral questions but economic problems endangering human productivity and therefore national competitiveness.

The existence of many of the elements of Marshall's contribution in the contemporary debate might induce one to think that a coherent line of continuity in British economic thought could be traced. But in fact he combined those elements in a very peculiar way, changing the attitude from a mere observation to a policy prescription. Above all there is a complete refusal of the classical lines of thought.

There is no continuity between Marshall's thought on the limits to growth and the British classical tradition in economics. As regards demographic growth, Marshall considers it a positive factor; it can be negative when concentrated in urban contexts that generate negative externalities upon living conditions because they affect labour productivity. And production is not under decreasing returns to scale, because technological progress and, mainly, creativity and organization can reverse the trend.

The stationary state is an illusion: either a country grows or it goes backward in the international competition and the role of the economist is to find the elements of progress. Marshall, therefore, did not share with his predecessors either a pessimistic approach to the possibility of growth, or an enthusiastic feeling towards a possible tendency to a stationary equilibrium. He simply studied the problem with the instruments of economic thinking he possessed and tried to explain which conditions should be fulfilled in order not to have economic progress come to a halt. Definitely a very modern approach.

NOTES

* Although the chapter was commonly agreed upon, K. Caldari (Department of Economic Sciences, University of Padova, katia.caldari@unipd.it) wrote the paragraphs 8.2.2 and the whole of 8.3, F. Masini (Department of Public Institutions, Economics and Society, University of Roma 3, famasini@uniroma3.it) wrote the paragraphs 8.1, 8.2.1 and 8.4. Part of the work was delivered at an international workshop on 'Marshall, Schumpeter and Social Science' at the Hitotsubashi University in Tokyo, whose participants and organizers the authors wish to warmly thank for their kind hospitality and fruitful discussions.

1. For a brilliant synthesis of the neoclassical approach see Solow (1974).
2. Smith (1982: 486).
3. S*ustainable development* (that is, how to reconcile the legitimate expectations of the living generations to increase the satisfaction of increasing needs without jeopardizing the same opportunities for the future ones) has cyclically surfaced the public debate, at least since the demographic pressure upon resources started to clash with some physical exploitation limits. This happened when the first industrial revolution endangered the very existence of woods in Britain in the eighteenth century, when the coal substituted timber for producing energy and pollution – together with mass urbanization – challenged the quality of life in the nineteenth century, when oil producers raised its price overnight by 400 per cent in 1973. But the most impressive reaction in public opinion and scientific works to the possible threats of a steady growth emerged 20 years ago, when the United Nations published the renowned Brundtland Report, universally considered the first authoritative document stating the question of development sustainability in terms of horizontal (social justice) and vertical (intergenerational) terms. In the same years, the economic literature found a new and promising field of study in the

theory of growth, when knowledge and progress ceased to be exogenous and became endogenous (Romer, 1986) in the production function, thus allowing new optimism for an increasing growth rate even with constraints on physical resources (Nordhaus et al., 1973).

4. Solow (1974).
5. Caldari (2004: 526) states that 'most natural resources are scarce in the absolute sense: this was well known to classical economists'.
6. Perelman (2002: 27), states: 'Malthus dropped any pretence of concern about overpopulation [and] proposed that the ultimate threat to the economy was a deficiency in demand'. On similar theses see also Berdel (1999: 30–1).
7. Malthus (1829 [1953]: 116).
8. Smith (1776, Book IV, Chapter vii: 577), states: 'the expense of clearing the ground is the principle obstacle to improvement'.
9. Inferring from Kurz and Salvadori (2003: 16) a 'backstop technology' might be defined as a productive process with no use of a not-renewable resource through input substitution with renewable ones.
10. Perelman (2002: 25) reminds how Smith's example of China's stationary state (1776, Book I, Chapter viii: 14) means something completely different from Mill, that is, 'an economy with so many people that the effort to provide them with sufficient food exhausted its entire productive potential, leaving no surplus to provide for future economic growth'.
11. We could not find a primary source for this information, which we took from Checkland (1959: 57): according to him, Mill had 'exhorted the House of Commons that the National Debt should be paid before the nation's fuel supplies were exhausted'.
12. An interesting exception is represented by Mundella (1878: 90): he observed that new methods of production and technological improvements could eventually increase the economisation of coal, especially 'in the manufacture of pig iron'.
13. In the second edition published in 1866, at page 26, Jevons writes: 'this subject, I hope, will now receive proper attention from the Royal Commission which is about to be appointed to inquire into the subject of our coal supply'.
14. Jevons is also the first to pose a specific epistemological question: why should economists say something about a problem usually discussed by geologists, namely, the scarcity of a mineral and the possibility of its technological substitution? The answers are that scarcity implies economic choices regarding alternative resources and inter-temporal consumption and energy is the engine of production. Technological progress raises the productivity of coal; this does not imply less but greater demand for increasing the supply of goods and further pressure on the natural resources.
15. See for instance the bound volumes collected by Marshall (Caldari, 2000; 2003), where you can find a great many writings on poverty, housing, towns, conditions of labour and similar topics.
16. For instance, Charles Booth, Thomas Brassey, Edwin Chadwick, Henry Fawcett, Beatrice Potter, George Bernard Shaw, Sydney Webb and many others.
17. See for instance the Industrial Remuneration Conference *The Report of the Proceedings and Papers* published in 1885.
18. 'Progress has many sides. It includes development of mental and moral faculties, even when their exercise yields no material gain. The term progress is narrow and it is sometimes taken to imply merely an increase in man's command over the material requisites of physical mental and moral well-being, no special reference being made to the extent to which this command is turned to account in developing the higher life of mankind. When increase of material wealth is united with the solidity of character sufficient to turn it to good account. . . . True human progress is in the main an advance in capacity for feeling and for thought, yet it cannot be sustained without vigorous enterprise and energy' (Marshall Library Archive, Red Box 1 (3), Identity Code: Marshall 5/3/1).
19. To say that he was anti-classical does not however mean that he was not very close to Adam Smith's reasoning, as Groenewegen (1999a; 1999b) very well shows.
20. See for instance the letter to Clark written in 1902 (Whitaker, 1996, vol. 2: 419).

21. 'In fact our new command over nature, while opening the door to much larger schemes for industrial organization than were physically possible even a short time ago, places greater responsibilities on those who would advocate new developments of social and industrial structure. For though institutions may be changed rapidly; yet if they are to endure they must be appropriate to man: they cannot retain their stability if they change very much faster than he does. Thus progress itself increases the urgency of the warning that in the economic world, Natura non facit saltum. Progress must be slow; but even from the merely material point of view it is to be remembered that changes, which add only a little to the immediate efficiency of production, may be worth having if they make mankind ready and fit for an organization, which will be more effective in the production of wealth and more equal in its distribution; and that every system, which allows the higher faculties of the lower grades of industry to go to waste, is open to grave suspicion' (1920: 249).

REFERENCES

Anonymous (1879a), 'Financial and commercial history of 1878', *Journal of the Statistical Society of London*, **42** (1), 276–305.

Anonymous (1879b), 'General results of the commercial and financial history of 1878', *Journal of the Statistical Society of London*, **42** (2), 480–504.

Anonymous (1887), 'The British Commission on the Depression of Trade', *Science*, **9** (212), 197–200.

Becattini, G. (2006), 'The industrial district and development economics', in T. Raffaelli, G. Becattini and M. Dardi (eds), *The Elgar Companion to Alfred Marshall*, Cheltenham, UK and Northampton, MA, USA: Edward Elgar, pp. 664–71.

Berdel, J.F. (1999), 'The Ricardo-Malthus debate. Effective demand, technical change and the limits to growth', in C. Sardoni and P. Kriesler (eds), *Keynes, Post-Keynesianism and Political Economy. Essays in Honour of Geoff Harcourt*, vol. 3, London: Routledge, pp. 23–41.

Bourne, S. (1875), 'The progress of our foreign trade, imports and exports, during the past twenty years', *Journal of Statistical Society of London*, **38** (2), 215–48.

Brabazon (1887), 'Decay of bodily strength in towns', *Nineteenth Century*, 673–6.

Brassey, T. (1879), 'Agriculture in England and the United States. The Inaugural Address of Thomas Brassey, Esq., M.P., President of the Statistical Society, Delivered on Tuesday, the 18th November, 1879', *Journal of the Statistical Society of London*, **42** (4), 751–64.

Burke, E. (1795), *Thoughts and Details on Scarcity, originally presented to the Right Honourable William Pitt in the Month of November*, reprinted by Charity Organization Society, July 1893.

Caldari, K. (2000), 'Marshall's bound collection of essays (Part 1)', *Marshall Studies Bulletin*, **7**, http://www.cce.unifi.it/dse/marshall/welcome.htm.

Caldari, K. (2003), 'A list of the essays collected in bound volumes by Alfred Marshall: part 2', *Marshall Studies Bulletin*, **8**, http://www.cce.unifi.it/dse/marshall/welcome.htm.

Caldari, K. (2004), 'Alfred Marshall's idea of progress and sustainable development', *Journal of the History of Economic Thought*, **26** (4), 519–36.

Caldari, K. (2006), 'Progress', in T. Raffaelli, G. Becattini and M. Dardi (eds), *The Elgar Companion to Alfred Marshall*, Cheltenham, UK and Northampton, MA, USA: Edward Elgar, pp. 483–7.

Chadwick, E. (1865), 'Opening address of the President of the Department of Economy and Trade at the meeting of the National Association for the Promotion of Social Science', *Journal of the Statistical Society of London*, **28** (1), 1–33.

Checkland, S.G. (1959), 'Growth and progress: the nineteenth century view in Britain', *The Economic History Review*, new series, **12** (1), 49–62.

Clapham J. (1952), *An Economic History of Modern Britain. Free Trade and Steel. 1850–1886*, Cambridge: Cambridge University Press.

Collard, D. (1996), 'Pigou and future generations: a Cambridge tradition', *Cambridge Journal of Economics*, **20**, 585–97.

Court, W.H.B. (1967), *A Concise Economic History of Britain*, Cambridge: Cambridge University Press.

Faucheux, S. and M. O'Connor (1998), *Valuation for Sustainable Development. Methods and Policy Indicators*, Cheltenham, UK and Lyme, USA: Edward Elgar.

Fawcett, H. (1871), *Pauperism: Its Causes and Remedies*, London: Macmillan.

Forster Brown, T. (1891), 'The coal question', *The Economic Journal*, **1** (4), 663–74.

Fothergill, J.M. (1887), 'The effects of town life upon the human body', *National Review*, **X**, 166–72.

Garrison, R.W. (1998), 'The inter-temporal Adam Smith', *Quarterly Journal of Austrian Economics*, **1** (1), 51–60.

Grey, L.C. (1913), 'The economic possibilities of conservation', *The Quarterly Journal of Economics*, **27** (3), 497–519.

Groenewegen, P. (1995), *A Soaring Eagle: Alfred Marshall 1842–1924*, Aldershot, UK and Brookfield, US: Edward Elgar.

Groenewegen, P. (1999a), 'Perfect competition, equilibrium and economic progress: that wretched division of labour and increasing returns', in S.C. Dow and P.E. Earl (eds), *Economic Organization and Economic Knowledge. Essays in Honour of Brian Loasby*, vol. 1, Cheltenham, UK and Northampton, MA, USA: Edward Elgar, pp. 225–38.

Groenewegen, P. (1999b), 'Adam Smith and Alfred Marshall: some reflections', in D.S. Arestis, P. Arestis and J. Grahl (eds), *The History and Practice of Economics. Essays in Honour of Bernad Corry and Maurice Peston*, vol. 2, Cheltenham, UK and Northampton, MA, USA: Edward Elgar, pp. 81–95.

Guillebaud, C.W. (1961), *Alfred Marshall Principles of Economics, Ninth Variorum Edition, vol. II, Notes*, London: Macmillan.

Hamilton, R. (1883), 'Popular education in England and Wales before and after the Elementary Education Act of 1870', *Journal of Statistical Society of London*, **46** (2), 283–349.

Hobsbawm, E.J. (1968), *Industry and Empire. An Economic History of Britain since 1750*, London: History Book Club.

Hotelling, H. (1931), 'The economics of exhaustible resources', *The Journal of Political Economy*, **39** (2), 137–75.

Industrial Remuneration Conference (1885), *The Report of the Proceedings and Papers Read in Prince's Hall, Piccadilly*, London: Cassel & Co.

Jeans, J.S. (1884), 'On the comparative efficiency and earnings of labour at home and abroad', *Journal of the Statistical Society of London*, **47** (4), 614–65.

Jevons, W.S. (1865), *The Coal Question: An Inquiry Concerning the Progress of the Nation, and Probable Exhaustion of our Coal-Mines*, London: Macmillan.
Kurz, H.K. and N. Salvadori (2003), 'Theories of economic growth – old and new'; in N. Salvadori (ed.), *The Theory of Economic Growth: A 'Classical' Perspective*, Cheltenham, UK and Northampton, MA, USA: Edward Elgar, pp. 1–22.
Lowe, A. (1954), 'The classical theory of economic growth', *Social Research*, Summer, 127–58.
Malthus, T.R. (1798 [1926]), *An Essay on the Principle of Population, as it Affects the Future Improvement of Society, with Remarks on the Speculations of Mr Godwin, M. Condorcet, and other Writers*. London: Johnson, reprinted 1926, London: Macmillan.
Malthus, T.R. (1820), *Principles of Political Economy Considered with a View to their Practical Application*, London: John Murray.
Malthus T.R. (1829), *Letter to Senior*, 23rd March, in McCleary G.F. (1953), *The Malthusian Population Theory*, London, Faber & Faber, p. 116.
Marshall, A. (1873), 'Lectures to women', in T. Raffaelli, R. MacWilliams Tullberg and E. Biagini (eds), *Alfred Marshall's Lectures to Women*, Aldershot, UK and Brookfield, USA: Edward Elgar.
Marshall, A. (1884), 'Where to house the London poor', *The Contemporary Review*, in A.C. Pigou (ed.) (1925), *Memorials of Alfred Marshall*, London, Macmillan, pp. 142–51.
Marshall, A. (1885), 'How far do remediable causes influence prejudicially (a) the continuity of employment, (b) the rates of wages?', Industrial Remuneration Conference. *The Report of the Proceedings and Papers at the Prince's Hall, Piccadilly*, London: Cassell & Co., pp. 173–99.
Marshall, A. (1890), *Principles of Economics*, London: Macmillan.
Marshall, A. (1919), *Industry and Trade*, London: Macmillan.
Marshall, A. (1920), *Principles of Economics*, 8th edn, London: Macmillan.
Martin, R. (2006), 'The localization of industry', in T. Raffaelli, G. Becattini and M. Dardi (eds), *The Elgar Companion to Alfred Marshall*, Cheltenham, UK and Northampton, MA, USA: Edward Elgar, pp. 393–400.
Mill, J.S. (1848 [1900]), *Principles of Political Economy*, London and New York: Routledge.
Mouat, F.J. (1880), 'On the education and training of the children of the poor', *Journal of the Statistical Society of London*, **43** (2), 183–250.
Mundella, A.J. (1878), 'What are the conditions on which the commercial and manufacturing supremacy of Great Britain depends, and is there any reason to think they have been, or may be, endangered?', *Journal of the Statistical Society of London*, **41** (1), 87–134.
Nordhaus, W.D., Houthakker, H. and Solow R. (1973), 'The allocation of energy resources', *Brookings Papers on Economic Activity*, (3), 529–76.
Opocher, A. (2007), 'Does economic growth ultimately lead to a "nobler life"? A comparative analysis of the predictions of Mill, Marshall and Keynes', *Working Paper*, no. 013, http://growthgroup.ec.unipi.it/workingpapers.htm.
Perelman, M. (2002), 'Resources in the History of Economic Thought', HES Conference, University of California, Davis, 5–8 July; later published in *Idem* (2003), *The Perverse Economy: The Impact of Markets on People and Nature*, New York: Palgrave.
Romer, P.M. (1986), 'Increasing returns and long-run growth', *Journal of Political Economy*, **94**, 1002–37.

Roose, R. (1886a), 'The wear and tear of London life', *Fortnightly Review*, **45**, 200–208.

Roose, R. (1886b), 'Rest and repair in London life', *Fortnightly Review*, **45**, 500–508.

Royal Commission (1886), *First, Second* [two parts], *Third and Final Reports of the Royal Commission appointed to inquire into the Depression of Trade and Industry*, London, folios lxxvii, 229, 428, 429 and 496, 139pp.

Smith, A. (1776), *An Inquiry into the Nature and Causes of the Wealth of Nations*, in two volumes, London: printed for W. Strahan and T. Cadell in the Strand.

Smith, G.A. (1982), 'Natural resource economic theory of the first conservation movement (1895–1927)', *History of Political Economy*, **14** (4), 483–95.

Solow, R.M. (1974), 'The economics of resources or the resources of economics', *The American Economic Review*, **64** (2), 1–14.

Spengler, J.J. (1955), 'Marshall on the population question', *Population Studies*, **8**, 264–87.

Veblen, T.B. (1900), 'The preconceptions of economic science III', *Quarterly Journal of Economics*, **14**, 240–69.

Whitaker, J.K. (1975), *The Early Economic Writings of Alfred Marshall, 1867–1890*, 2 vols, London: Macmillan.

Whitaker, J.K. (1996), *The Correspondence of Alfred Marshall, Economist*, 3 vols, Cambridge: Cambridge University Press.

9. Rebuilding Schumpeter's theory of entrepreneurship

Richard Swedberg

For those who are interested in entrepreneurship, the last few decades have been both exhilarating and frustrating.[1] There has been a general realization, on the one hand, that entrepreneurship is at the centre of the type of high and stable economic growth that constitutes prosperity. On the other hand, and despite an avalanche of writings and courses on entrepreneurship, there has been little substantive theoretical progress when it comes to the theory of entrepreneurship itself. While there today exists a valuable and rapidly growing literature on ethnic entrepreneurship, emerging entrepreneurship, women and entrepreneurship, national innovation systems, and so on, there still does not exist one central theory of entrepreneurship, on which the various branches of entrepreneurship can build.

This is where Schumpeter comes into the picture. Of all the theories of entrepreneurship that exist, his theory is still, to my mind, the most fascinating as well as the most promising theory of entrepreneurship that we have. Let me clarify. I do not argue that Schumpeter's theory, as it is understood today, can supply the key to the mystery of entrepreneurship. What I suggest, however, and also devote this chapter to, is the argument that it may well constitute the point of departure for the development of *the* theory of entrepreneurship. Hence the title of my chapter: rebuilding Schumpeter's theory of entrepreneurship.

In order to use Schumpeter's ideas as one's point of departure for the construction of a new theory of entrepreneurship of Schumpeterian inspiration, at least two things are crucial. First, we need considerably better knowledge of Schumpeter's theory of entrepreneurship. Second, we need to start suggesting ways in which to complement and add to his theory of entrepreneurship.

Let me say something about both of these tasks. Our knowledge of Schumpeter's theory of entrepreneurship is, despite the giant secondary literature on Schumpeter, still somewhat limited. It is, for example, mainly centred around chapter 2 in his *The Theory of Economic Development*, the rest of Schumpeter's work on the entrepreneur is either not read or not available in English. *Business Cycles*, for example, is not read for what it may teach us about entrepreneurship, and neither is *The Theory of Economic Development* except for its chapter 2.

Still, Schumpeter saw *Business Cycles* as a study that worked out the results of entrepreneurial action, in historical time and in great empirical detail. *The Theory of Economic Development* (not just its famous chapter 2) is centred on the entrepreneur and gives expression to a vision of *a whole economy* (as well as a whole economic theory) that is influenced by entrepreneurship: the rate of interest, profit levels, the business cycle, and so on.

Finally, even if an attempt has recently been made to translate into English Schumpeter's most important works on entrepreneurship, several bits and pieces still remain. It is also my guess that one should be able to find items in Schumpeter's German production (that is, before 1932 when he moved to the USA) that do not primarily deal with entrepreneurship, but which nonetheless may contain some interesting ideas on this topic.

The second way of developing a new Schumpeterian theory of entrepreneurship – to complement and add to it – is ultimately more important. It is also harder to describe, except by example; later in this chapter I give two examples of what I have in mind. The way to proceed, I suggest, is the following: to select some ideas that are part of Schumpeter's theory of entrepreneurship and further develop these.

THE TASK OF FINDING OUT MORE ABOUT SCHUMPETER'S THEORY OF ENTREPRENEURSHIP

As just indicated there are a number of ways in which one can add to the current knowledge of Schumpeter's ideas on entrepreneurship. The one I have chosen in this chapter is to go back to the first edition of *Theorie der wirtschaftlichen Entwicklung* instead of relying on the translation of the second edition of this work, which is the edition that is typically used: *Theory of Economic Development* (1934, trans. Redvers Opie).

By drawing attention to the first and original version of Schumpeter's theory of entrepreneurship, it should be emphasized, I join a distinct and recent trend in Schumpeterian research that argues that we know much too little about the young Schumpeter. This trend began with the work of Yuishi Shionoya and has grown in strength during the last few years (see, for example, Backhaus, 2003; Becker and Knudsen, 2002; Koppl, 2003; Shionoya, 1990; 1997; Swedberg, 1991: ch. 2).

There exist a number of differences between the entrepreneur as he appears in the first edition of *Theorie* and in the translation into English from 1934. I have chosen to select two of these: Schumpeter's strong emphasis on the entrepreneur as someone who is first and foremost practical ('Man of Action') and that only a dynamic economic theory can do full justice to the notion of entrepreneurship.

Schumpeter repeatedly refers to the entrepreneur in the 1911 edition as 'Man of Action' (*Mann der Tat*), and he describes him as someone who does not accept reality as it is.[2] If there exists no demand for a good, for example, the Man of Action will create such a demand; he will *make* people want it. He (and the Man of Action as well as the entrepreneur is always a 'he' for Schumpeter) is full of energy and leaps at the obstacles. Schumpeter writes: 'The Man of Action acts in the same decisive manner inside as well as outside the usual tracks in the economy. He does not feel the restrictions that block the actions of the other economic actors' (Schumpeter, 1911: 132).

While the 1911 edition emphasizes the practical side of entrepreneurship, it downplays the role of ideas. Knowing that there exist different ways of doing things is not enough to turn someone into an entrepreneur, according to Schumpeter. 'Always and everywhere there is a richness of ideas and plans' (Schumpeter, 1911: 177). It is true, he says, that there is only a minority of people who have the capacity to envision that things can be done in a different way. But it is also true that only a minority of *this* minority has the force to transform one of these new combinations into reality.

Ideas are cheap, according to Schumpeter, and what is truly difficult to face is the risk and uncertainty that comes with doing something in reality, not just in your mind. Schumpeter makes this point with so much force in *Theorie* that one must conclude that he at this stage clearly prioritized the concrete tasks of the entrepreneur over the thinking. This is an interesting point and one that would recede in the 1934 edition.

The first edition of *Theorie* also has much more to say about the opposite of the entrepreneur or the static person. All populations consist of either leaders or followers, the reader is told. While the leader or the Man of Action is dynamic, breaks out of an equilibrium and does what is new, the Static Person is passive, seeks an equilibrium and repeats what has already been done (see Table 9.1).

Before leaving the 1911 edition, a few words should also be said about its last chapter, chapter 7, which was eliminated in later editions. This chapter is entitled 'The view of the economy as a whole', and is centred on Schumpeter's idea that the concept of the entrepreneur not only constitutes a key to the economic sphere, but to all other spheres in society, such as politics, art, and so on. While Schumpeter's argument on this point is interesting, I do not discuss it in this chapter, but only note that chapter 7 contains a very strong formulation of Schumpeter's important idea in 1911 that dynamic theory rejects the idea of equilibrium:

Table 9.1 Schumpeter in 1911: the Man of Action versus the Static Person

Man of Action	Static Person
Dynamic	Static
Breaks out of an equilibrium	Seeks an equilibrium
Does what is new	Repeats what has already been done
Active, energetic	Passive, low energy
Leader	Follower
Puts together new combinations	Accepts existing ways of doing things
Feels no inner resistance to change	Feels strong inner resistance to change
Battles resistance to his actions	Feels hostility to new actions of others
Makes an intuitive choice among a multitude of new alternatives	Makes a rational choice among existing alternatives
Motivated by power and joy in creation	Motivated exclusively by needs and stops when these are satisfied
Commands no resources but borrows from a bank	Commands no resources and has no use for new resources

Note: In *Theorie der wirtschaftlichen Entwicklung* (1911) Schumpeter contrasts the entrepreneurial to non-entrepreneurial person in a much more detailed fashion than in *The Theory of Economic Development* (1934). He refers to the former as the Man of Action (*Mann der Tat*) and the latter as static. All populations can be divided into a small number of Men of Action and a mass of static or non-entrepreneurial individuals. This is something that goes for the economy as well as other areas of society (chapter 7).

> There is no such thing as a dynamic equilibrium. Development, in its deepest character, constitutes a disturbance of the existing static equilibrium and shows no tendency at all to strive again for that or any other form of equilibrium . . . If the economy does reach a new state of equilibrium then this is achieved not by the motive forces of development, but rather by a reaction against it. Other forces bring development to an end, and by so doing create the first precondition regaining a new equilibrium. (Schumpeter, 1911 [2003]: 76)

To this should be added that just as Schumpeter removed chapter 7 from later editions of *Theorie*, he also eliminated much of this radical emphasis on dynamics and the idea that entrepreneurial change can *never* be at rest or reach an equilibrium. In the 1934 edition he chose instead to emphasize what he termed the discontinuous nature of economic reality and that it moved from one equilibrium to another – a formulation that is quite similar to the one that he in 1911 had used to characterize static theory (Schumpeter, 1934: 64). It should also be noted that the term 'dynamics' is not used in the 1934 edition, and the reason for this, according to the author, is that it has acquired too many meanings (Schumpeter, 1934: 64, n.1; cf. 82–3).

SCHUMPETERIAN IDEAS ON WHICH TO BUILD, PART 1

At the risk of leaving chapter 7 and the 1911 edition a bit too abruptly, I shall now proceed to the part of my chapter where I try to single out important Schumpeterian ideas about entrepreneurship that I think we can build on. This represents a way to use Schumpeter to, so to speak, surpass Schumpeter.

The first of the ideas that I discuss is his concept of *combination*. Schumpeter famously defines entrepreneurship as a new way of combining things, so it is indeed a central concept. It can be found, as already noted, in the 1911 edition, in essentially the same sense as it is used in the 1934 edition; and I now switch to the latter edition since it is better known, more accessible and represents a later formulation.

Let us first see how Schumpeter himself uses the concept of combination. As far as I can see he uses it in two different ways. First, he sees it as central to the economic process in general and, second, he sees it as central to the definition of entrepreneurship.

The very first use of 'combination' can be found in chapter 1 of *The Theory of Economic Development*, which is devoted to the topic of the circular flow of economic life. Schumpeter writes: 'An enterprise as such and even the productive combinations of the whole economic system we shall also regard as "combinations". This concept plays a considerable part in our analysis' (1934: 14). Schumpeter also argues that one should distinguish between 'economic combinations' and 'technological combinations'. Economic logic, he argues, typically prevails over technological logic. 'As a consequence', he writes, 'we see all around us in real life faulty ropes instead of steel hawsers, defective draught animals instead of show breeds', and so on (Schumpeter, 1934: 14–15).

In chapter 2 of *The Theory of Economic Development* Schumpeter uses the concept of combination in a different sense, namely, to define entrepreneurship. His famous definition of the entrepreneur is as follows: 'The carrying out of new combinations we call "enterprise"; the individuals whose function it is to carry them out we call "entrepreneurs" ' (Schumpeter, 1934: 74). To Schumpeter, for whom development equalled entrepreneurship, 'development in our sense is then defined by the carrying out of new combinations' (Schumpeter, 1934: 66).

When Schumpeter presents the two meanings of the term combination in this way, it is easy to see how they belong together and even seem to grow out of each other. This way of looking at things, however, does not give Schumpeter proper credit for the theoretical work he had put into this question in order to make the two meanings of combination become so close.

There is also the fact that the idea of *entrepreneurship* as a way of combining the different parts of production into some new way, actually has a history; and for this we have to turn elsewhere in Schumpeter's work than the editions of *Theorie*.

The first person to suggest that the core of entrepreneurship consisted in the idea of combination was, according to Schumpeter, Jean-Baptiste Say. Schumpeter's fullest description of Say's contribution in this regard can be found in *History of Economic Analysis*. We here read about Say:

> His contribution [to the theory of entrepreneurship] can be summed up in the pithy statement that the entrepreneur's function is to *combine* the factors of production into a producing organism. Such a statement may indeed mean much or little. He certainly failed to make full use of it and presumably did not see all its analytical possibilities. He did realize, to some extent, that a greatly improved theory of the economic process might be derived by making the entrepreneur in the analytic schema what he is in capitalist reality, the pivot on which everything hinges. (Schumpeter, 1954: 555; original emphasis).

In a long footnote that Schumpeter adds to this statement, he also fends off the objection that Cantillon and Adam Smith had developed the idea of entrepreneurship as combination well before Say. According to Schumpeter, Cantillon had said something quite different, namely, that the entrepreneur buys at certain prices with the intent to sell at uncertain but predicted prices. And Adam Smith's theory of entrepreneurship was, according to Schumpeter, contained in the notion that the entrepreneur is the capitalist who lends other people money.

Schumpeter concludes his discussion of the role of the concept of combination in Cantillon and Adam Smith in the following way: 'It might be said that the distinctive function that Say made explicit is implied both by Cantillon and Smith. But analytic progress – not only in economics – hinges in great part on making things explicit that have been implied or implicitly recognized for ages' (Schumpeter, 1954: 555).

Let us now leave Say and return to *The Theory of Economic Development* and the idea that entrepreneurship consists of making new combinations. The first thing that we want to know is what exactly does a new combination look like? Schumpeter tells us – just as in the 1911 edition – that a new combination is not the same as an invention. The reason for this is the following: 'as long as they are not carried into practice, inventions are economically irrelevant' (Schumpeter, 1934: 88).

A new combination – what Schumpeter also calls an innovation – is usually defined by him as a way of combining already existing 'resources', 'materials' or 'means of production' in some novel way (for example, Schumpeter, 1934: 65, 68). The terminology that Schumpeter uses –

'resources', 'materials' or 'means of production' – is interesting in itself, because it points to the fact that he was ready to accept a number of different items as building blocks in the economic process.

Does Schumpeter provide any examples of these new combinations? Yes, he does. In one of the book's most cited passages (which can also be found in the 1911 edition) Schumpeter enumerates five of these new combinations. The first is 'the introduction of a new good', the second 'the introduction of a new method of production', and so on (Schumpeter, 1934: 65).

Let us stop here for a moment. Would it be possible to develop a model for what novel combinations would look like? We know, for example, from modern genetics and DNA, how important the notion of combination is, and what huge numbers of possible combinations may result from just a few basic elements.

Schumpeter himself had briefly touched on this possibility, as we recall from the account of chapter 2 in the 1911 edition, where he says that one can combine things in an infinite number of ways. Schumpeter also thought that rational thought was of little use here; and that the only way that the entrepreneur could handle the nearly unlimited number of choices was through *intuition*. The entrepreneur, in other words, simply bypasses the difficult problem of calculated choice by relying on intuition. Is this a clue that we today want to pick up on, by developing a theory of entrepreneurship centred on a scientific theory of intuition? If so, what would such a theory look like? Can you argue, for example, that because of his or her background, an entrepreneur is likely to react in a certain way; and in this manner develop, say, an economic-sociological theory of entrepreneurship? Would not this way of arguing, however, be faulty since we would predict that just about everybody with this background would be entrepreneurial material – something that is not likely to be true.

Would it be better to use a psychological approach, say along the lines of behavioural economics, where experiments are used rather than surveys and history of the type that sociologists favour? There already exist experiments, for example, that show that some people are much better than others at figuring out if somebody is telling the truth or not. Would there also be some way of establishing which people have better economic intuitions than others; who is a Man of Action and who is a Static Person, so to speak?

Let me suggest another way of thinking about entrepreneurship and combinations. If you take the five types of innovations that Schumpeter mentions in his famous passage, you will find that they deal with the following areas: 'a new good', 'a new method of production', 'a new market', 'a new source of supply of raw material or half-manufactured goods' and 'a new organization of an industry' (Schumpeter, 1934: 66). Now, if we add all of these together, what do we get? The answer, I suggest, indicates that Schumpeter's seemingly innocuous list of innovations is quite systematic in nature; and the reason for this is that the five types of innovation cover the production of a good (for a firm or a whole economy) from the beginning to the end. Schumpeter starts with raw material, then proceeds to the process of production, the good itself, the market and the organization of the market.

What we have, in brief, is a number of steps that together make up the process that begins with the production of a good, all the way to its sale on the market. Entrepreneurship means to vary one of these factors from A to Z, so to speak. Or, to phrase it differently: we have now laid bare the real link between the term combination in its meaning as entrepreneurship and in its meaning as the process of production, as mentioned earlier in this chapter.

This way of reconceptualizing Schumpeter's notion of entrepreneurship as a form of continuous combination may be of use in developing a Schumpeterian theory of entrepreneurship. By conceiving the 'production' of a firm as a unitary process of sorts it may be easier to handle the idea of combination, in the sense that we know that there only exist five units so to speak. We realize also, for example, that very successful innovations may involve several innovations (a maximum of five to be precise, if we stick to Schumpeter's list).

Another way of going beyond Schumpeter would be to pick up on the idea of a unitary economic process (from production to sale), but to divide it in a different way than Schumpeter does. Instead of there being five elements, we may for example have a higher (or a lower) number; we may also choose other units/elements than those that Schumpeter selected. It is clear, for example, that Schumpeter pays too little attention to the organization of the firm, so we would perhaps like to change his scheme to make room for changes on this score. Other changes are conceivable as well.

My own view is that we may also want to complement Schumpeter's ideas on the economic process on one special point, and what I have in mind is actually a very Schumpeterian point. This is the notion that the economic process of entrepreneurship is not over once the goods are on the market; the entrepreneur also has to make a profit.

This point may seem trivial, but this is not how I see it. If we recall Schumpeter's argument in chapter 1, that it is important to distinguish between 'technological combinations' and 'economic combinations', and that the former always have to give way to the logic of the economy, we realize that all of Schumpeterian innovations – the new good, the new method of production, and so on – are only of interest (are only innovations!) if they make it possible for there to be a profit. The demand for profit weeds out many possible combinations, one could also say.

I feel that this last point is important because the fact that an entrepreneur always has to make a profit is a factor that tends to get lost in quite a few modern works on entrepreneurship. The entrepreneurial process, then, starts for Schumpeter with the production of a good, and it ends first when the profit is safely in the hands of the entrepreneur. Introducing a new good, a new method of production, and so on may well be commendable and 'entrepreneurial', as we use this word in everyday language, but unless there also is profit, there is no (Schumpeterian) entrepreneurship.

This way of adding to or clarifying Schumpeter's position may also be helpful in conceptualizing *failed entrepreneurship*. As an example of this I refer to a very interesting study by Swedish economic historian Torsten Gårdlund, entitled *Geniuses of Failure* (1993). The author discusses a handful of brilliant Swedish businessmen who went through all of the Schumpeterian steps – but failed to make a profit. These businessmen constitute, one could say, a special type of entrepreneur ('geniuses of failure'), just as the inventor differs from the innovator. But while they may be entrepreneurs, in the sense that this word is used in everyday language, they are not (in the Schumpeterian sense) *economic entrepreneurs*.[3]

Gårdlund also notes that once one of these failed geniuses had blazed the trail, so to speak, someone with a better sense of how to make money often came around, picked up the pieces and made a profit. What this tells us – and I will end the section on the concept of combination with this suggestion – is that the combinatorial process, if I may call it so, can be divided into different segments, each of which may be carried out by different people or organizations. From this perspective, the entrepreneur can be one person, several persons, one organization and perhaps even several organizations. Still, there has to be a profit.

SCHUMPETERIAN IDEAS ON WHICH TO BUILD, PART 2

My second candidate for a suggestive Schumpeterian idea, which we may want to build on and add to, is the notion that there exists a resistance to the entrepreneur that has to be overcome, if there is to be an innovation or a new combination. I refer to the central element here as *resistance (to innovation or entrepreneurship)*, but there does not exist one single concept or word that Schumpeter uses to denote this part of his theory. Again I first present Schumpeter's ideas and then suggest some additions.

The idea of resistance to entrepreneurship is present in chapter 1 of *The Theory of Economic Development* (1934) on the circular flow of economic life, but Schumpeter does not single it out, and the reader does not understand how central it is to his theory of entrepreneurship until chapter 2. In any case, Schumpeter mentions, for example, how the farmer, because of tradition, keeps repeating his production year in and year out; and that tradition has 'bequeathed him definite means and methods of production [and] all these hold him in iron fetters in his tracks' (Schumpeter, 1934: 6).

This way of phrasing things may give the impression that Schumpeter views tradition as working from the outside on the economic actor, but this is not the case. The traditional actor, he says, also wants *not* to change, even when the circumstances change. 'Everyone will cling as tightly as possible to habitual economic methods and only submit to the pressure of circumstances as it becomes necessary' (Schumpeter, 1934: 8).

In chapter 2 of the 1934 edition one can find a much fuller and more systematic discussion of resistance to innovation than in chapter 1, and how these may be overcome. The resistance, Schumpeter here says, can be divided into three types. First, there is the resistance that is associated with 'the task'; then there is the resistance associated with 'the psyche of the businessman'; and, finally, there is the resistance from 'the social environment' (Schumpeter, 1934: 86).

As to type number one – resistance to a new task – Schumpeter means by this that the economic actor will now have to do something that is not part of the circular flow and that he has never done before. As a result, the actor lacks 'data' for his decision as well as 'rules of conduct' that tell him what to do (Schumpeter, 1934: 84–5). The economic actor 'must [now] really to some extent do what tradition does for him in everyday life, viz. consciously plan his conduct in every particular' (ibid.).

The businessman has as a consequence to constantly think things through, which means that there will be 'much more conscious rationality in this than in customary action' (Schumpeter, 1934: 85). But since it is impossible to figure everything out (even in modern society, where life is becoming increasingly rational), the businessman has to somehow make a decision anyway. This brings us back to the element of intuition; and ultimately, Schumpeter says, 'the success of everything depends on intuition' (Schumpeter, 1934: 85).

The second type of resistance is to be found in the businessman himself and the way that he feels and thinks about doing something new. People have an inborn tendency to avoid what is new, Schumpeter says, as exemplified by the fact that people are reluctant to innovate even when there is no objective resistance. By objective resistance Schumpeter means the task to be carried out as well as resistance from the social environment.

Once you are settled in a routine, Schumpeter specifies, 'thought turns again and again into the accustomed tracks' (Schumpeter, 1934: 86). To break away from these routines is very difficult, and few people have that 'great surplus of force' or 'mental freedom' that is needed to do so (Schumpeter, 1934: 86).

The third type of resistance consists of 'the reaction of the social environment' and includes, first, 'legal or political impediments' (Schumpeter, 1934: 87). More importantly, however, there is also the hostility that any population of people tends to show to those who behave in a different way. Schumpeter notes, for example, that people are usually quick to spot and condemn differences in dress and manners. They are even more hostile, he adds, when it comes to behaviour that is different in areas that are more important to them, including the economy.

This is all the more the case, Schumpeter says, since certain groups have a material interest in the status quo. He sums up what an entrepreneur has to do in order to overcome the resistance in his environment in the following way:

> Surmounting this opposition is always a special kind of task which does not exist in the customary course of life, a task which also requires a special kind of conduct. In matters economic this resistance manifests itself first of all in the groups threatened by the innovation, then in the difficulty in finding the necessary cooperation, finally in the difficulty of winning over consumers. (Schumpeter, 1934: 87)

That the hostility in the social environment towards an entrepreneur can be extremely strong can be illustrated with an example that Schumpeter uses at one point in *Business Cycles*. In his discussion of early European economic history, Schumpeter says that 'entrepreneurs were not necessarily strangled but they were not infrequently in danger of their lives' (Schumpeter, 1939, vol. 1: 243). To this statement a footnote is added, in which Schumpeter cites a document that tells about an entrepreneur who was strangled to death in 1579 in Danzig. Since the accuracy of the source is unsure, Schumpeter adds in Italian '*se non è vero è ben trovato*' – 'if it is not true, it is well said'.

Before leaving Schumpeter's account of resistance to entrepreneurship in *The Theory of Economic Development*, a few words need to be said about what exactly he means by such resistance. As usual, Schumpeter presents us with some splendid metaphors. At one point, for example, he says that 'all knowledge and habit once acquired becomes as firmly rooted in ourselves as a railway embankment in the earth' (Schumpeter, 1934: 84). And at another point he says that 'carrying out a new plan and acting according to a customary one are things as different as making a road and walking along it' (Schumpeter, 1934: 85).

But even if these metaphors are suggestive, it has to be admitted that Schumpeter's terminology about resistance is somewhat imprecise. The idea of resistance covers a number of phenomena that are typically held apart in today's social science – such as 'habit', 'custom', 'tradition', and so on. To some extent, this may simply reflect the fact that Schumpeter discusses three different types of resistance. But when we try to pair off habit, custom and so on, with the three types of resistance (a new task, the psyche of the businessman and the social environment), there is no automatic fit. Resistance to a new task seems primarily to be associated with tradition and custom; resistance in one's mind, to habit and custom; and reactions of the social environment, to custom. But why does not tradition play a role in the latter type of resistance; why is habit not part of the resistance to a new task; and so on?

The confusion on this point gives me an opportunity to step in and suggest a way of complementing and adding to Schumpeter's thought. It needs to be complemented, first, with the concept of *norm* – that is, with the notion that there exist regular forms of behaviour that people want to see followed or they will react with some kind of sanction (positive or negative).

One reason for bringing up the concept of norm in this context is that the elements of tradition and custom are more important in pre-industrial society than in modern society. To include the concept of norm in the discussion would, from this perspective, represent a way of updating Schumpeter. Another reason is simply that the concept of norms is a concept that Schumpeter seems to have missed.

It is also possible to create a direct link between the idea of combination and that of resistance, and in this way add to Schumpeter's theory. A Schumpeterian combination, to recall, consists of six elements, five of which Schumpeter discusses in his typology of innovation, plus the demand that there has to be a profit. Now, one could argue that in an established industry the way that you have to behave in *all* of these six parts adds up to a norm, a custom, a habit, and so on for how things should be done – a model to follow, in short. If you want to produce, say, an electric fan, this is the raw material you should use, these methods of production are suitable, and so on. An existing combination, in brief, gets its power of resistance from the fact that it constitutes a norm, a custom and so on.

One could also argue, as a variation on this theme, that different norms, customs, habits and so on can be found at each of the six steps in the process of production.[4] An industry tends to be organized in some special way, its methods of production tend to be such and such, and so on. Resistance to innovation is perhaps also different in all of these cases. Each of the six steps in the economic process constitutes its own norm.

Up until now I have discussed Schumpeter's terms of habit, custom and tradition, and added the concept of norm; and I have done this in order to get closer to the kind of resistance that the entrepreneur is likely to encounter when something new is being tried out – be it in the way that the whole process of production is organized or just in one of its parts. Each of these resistances is presumably somewhat different in nature; and in this sense also teaches us something new about entrepreneurship.

A *habit* can be defined as repeated forms of the behaviour of an individual, and here the resistance consists of breaking with the way that things are regularly done.[5] A *custom* is more social in nature, in that many people are needed for there to be a custom. But it is otherwise similar to habit, in that there does not exist any force beyond the memory of the past behaviour that adds to the resistance to the new behaviour.

Such a force, however, exists when it comes to tradition and norms. In a *tradition*, behaviour is repeated, and not only because that is how things have always been done. To some extent the past also validates the repeated behaviour. It is seen as legitimate *because* it is traditional, and in this sense it is good to follow a tradition ('this is how things have always been done – and also how they should be done!').

In a *norm* this same element of approval (or disapproval) is also very much present, but it has nothing to do with age or the past. The normative element is much more varied and instead connected to something else, such as the strong element of shame that is attached to the norm against incest.

An entrepreneur, to summarize the argument so far, must face the existing habits–traditions–customs–norms that are attached to the current way of doing things, and somehow still be able to push through a new combination. My sense as a sociologist is, however, that we may want to develop this line of thought a bit further. What I especially have in mind is that the terms 'custom', 'habit' and 'tradition' – as well as 'norm' – may not capture all that well what is going on in modern industry.

By this statement I mean that even if we acknowledge that there do exist combinations for how things are done in various parts of economic life, Schumpeter's terms (plus the concept of norm) may not be so good in capturing what is actually going on. The main reason for this is that all of them were originally designed by social scientists to analyse social life in general, rather than economic life in advanced capitalism.

They are all also fairly old social science terms, and the world is changing quickly. The forces of say 'tradition' are not very strong in contemporary industry; and the idea of, say, 'economic norms' may not be so useful in a situation where many chief executive officers know that constant change has to be on the agenda or their corporations will go under.

What, then, to do? My suggestion is that we may want to keep the old terms and see how well they fit or not fit what happens in the economy. But we could also try to develop a new and better terminology that would be assigned the task of expressing, in as precise way as possible, the hold that we think combinations may have on businessmen today.

My own candidate on this score would be to use the term '*order*', a term that has a Weberian past but which is otherwise not too much burdened or associated with current social science notions. According to Weber, an order (*Ordnung*) can be defined as a prescription for how to act or a model to follow (for example, Weber, 1978: 31–3). The idea would be that a whole combination (or parts of such a combination), typically constitutes an *order* in the modern economy, and that this is what the modern entrepreneur is up against.

By using the term 'order', I also have in mind the simple fact that people like things to be in order, and that things need to be in order if anything is to be accomplished. Orders tend to look 'normal', but they are not necessarily infused with the type of strong and explicit sentiments that are linked to the concept of norm (except, perhaps, that *disorder* is usually frowned upon). The challenge for the modern entrepreneur, in brief, would be to replace an existing order with a new one.

CONCLUDING REMARKS

While the ideas I have presented in this chapter do not solve our central problem – to develop a new and powerful theory of entrepreneurship – they do point to some tasks that we may want to undertake, while waiting for the new theory of Schumpeterian entrepreneurship to be invented. In the first part of the chapter, where I presented a few of Schumpeter's ideas on entrepreneurship in the 1911 edition of *Theorie der wirtschaftlichen Entwicklung*, I tried to show that we need more information than we currently have on what Schumpeter has said about entrepreneurship.

This is especially the case if we seriously want to engage in the project of trying to complement and add to Schumpeter's theory of entrepreneurship. If this is the case, our interest in what Schumpeter has said about the entrepreneur and entrepreneurship at various points in his works, does not only have a historical interest to us, but also acquires a potentially analytical one.

The analytical task of reconstructing a Schumpeterian theory of entrepreneurship represents, of course, the most important as well as the most difficult and elusive part of the enterprise I have tried to outline. My own suggestions have been to single out and focus on Schumpeter's two concepts of combination and resistance to entrepreneurship. But one can imagine others as well; and, the general truth about all research is also applicable here: whatever works, works.

But, again, until the theoretical breakthrough occurs, there are some modest tasks that need to be carried out. When it comes to the idea of combination, I think that some kind of creative formalization may be possible; and I am currently involved in an enterprise of this type with my colleague Thorbjørn Knudsen at Odense University. We hope to have something to show along these lines in about a year.

As to the idea of *orders* as obstacles to the development of new entrepreneurial combinations, I think that this project invites some immediate tasks. One may, for example, draw up an empirical research programme for trying to investigate how strong these orders are and what their structure is like. This also goes for profit itself, since there may be definite opinions in an industry about what the profit should be and how it should be acquired.

Schumpeter should not be counted out. Not only must he be credited with having produced, nearly a century ago, what is still the most interesting theory of entrepreneurship, but add to this that Schumpeter's ideas are also very suggestive – and that they may be of help in developing that theory of entrepreneurship that economists have been looking for ever since Schumpeter.

NOTES

1. For comments and inspiration I thank Mabel Berezin, Thorbjørn Knudsen, Yuichi Shionoya, Tamotsu Nishizawa and the other participants at Conference on Marshall, Schumpeter and Social Science at Hitotsubashi University, 17–18 March.
2. While Schumpeter refers to the leader in the 1934 edition, he does not use the expression Man of Action.
3. The term 'economic entrepreneur' might seem redundant, but there has recently been such an inflation in the use of the term 'entrepreneur' – think of moral entrepreneur, political entrepreneur, institutional entrepreneur and, most recently, social entrepreneur! – that the expression 'economic entrepreneurs' has become necessary.
4. This idea is close to the idea in the French School of Conventions that the most important analytical fact about economic life is that it has to be co-ordinated through *conventions*. For an attempt to make a connection between this school of thought and Schumpeter's notion of the entrepreneur, see Swedberg (2006).
5. For helpful definitions of habit, custom and tradition, see, for example, paragraph 4 in Weber's *Economy and Society* (Weber, 1978: 29–31). Weber's term for norm is convention. For habit, see also Charles Camic (1986).

REFERENCES

Backhaus, Jürgen (ed.) (2003), *Joseph Alois Schumpeter: Entrepreneurship, Style and Vision*, Boston, MA: Kluwer.

Becker, Markus and Thorbjørn Knudsen (2002), 'Schumpeter 1911: farsighted visions on economic development', *American Journal of Economics and Sociology*, **61** (2), 387–403.

Camic, Charles (1986), 'The matter of habit', *American Journal of Sociology*, **91**, 1039–87.

Gårdlund, Torsten (1993), *Misslyckandets genier* (*Geniuses of Failure*), Stockholm: Norstedt.
Koppl. Roger (ed.) (2003), 'Austrian economics and entrepreneurial studies', *Advances in Austrian Economics*, **6**, 1–298. This volume includes a translation of Schumpeter's important article 'Entrepreneur' from 1928 as well as a symposium on this article with contributions by Markus Becker, Thorbjørn Knudsen and others.
Schumpeter, Joseph A. (1911), *Theorie der wirtschaftlichen Entwicklung*, Leipzig: Duncker & Humblot.
Schumpeter, Joseph A. (1911), 'The theory of economic development', in Jürgen Backhaus (ed.) (2003), *Joseph Alois Schumpeter*, Boston, MA: Kluwer, pp. 61–116. This text constitutes ch. 7 in *Theorie der wirtschaftlichen Entwicklung* (1911) and has been translated by Ursula Backhaus.
Schumpeter, Joseph A. (1934), *The Theory of Economic Development*, trans. R. Opie, Cambridge, MA: Harvard University Press.
Schumpeter, Joseph A. (1939), *Business Cycles: A Theoretical, Historical and Statistical Analysis of the Capitalist Process*, 2 vols, New York: McGraw-Hill.
Schumpeter, Joseph A. (1954), *History of Economic Analysis*, London: Allen & Unwin.
Schumpeter, Joseph A. (2002), 'New translations: *Theorie der wirtschaftlichen Entwicklung*', *American Journal of Economics and Sociology*, **61** (2), 405–37. Translations of parts of ch. 2 (pp. 103–07, 156–64) and ch. 7 (pp. 525–48) by Markus Becker and Thorbjørn Knudsen.
Shionoya, Yuichi (1990), 'The origin of the Schumpeterian research program: a chapter omitted from Schumpeter's *Theory of Economic Development*', *Journal of Institutional and Theoretical Economics* (*JITE*), **146** (2), 314–27.
Shionoya, Yuichi (1997), *Schumpeter and the Idea of Social Science: A Metatheoretical Study*, Cambridge: Cambridge University Press.
Swedberg, Richard (1991), *Schumpeter: A Biography*, Princeton, NJ: Princeton University Press.
Swedberg, Richard (2006), 'Quand la sociologie économique rencontre l'économie des conventions' in François Eymard-Duvernay (ed.), *L'économie des conventions. Méthodes et resultats*, Vol. 1, Paris: La Découverte, pp. 77–92.
Weber, Max (1978), *Economy and Society: An Outline of Interpretive Sociology*, Berkeley, CA: University of California Press.

10. Schumpeter in the Harvard Yard: inventions, innovations and growth

Kiichiro Yagi

10.1 SCHUMPETER'S TWO DISTINCTIONS

Joseph A. Schumpeter is generally considered one of the most influential originators of contemporary evolutionary economics. Although he competes with Thorstein Veblen, Friedrich Hayek, Alfred Marshall and others for this position, a group of evolutionary economists are proud to call themselves neo-Schumpeterians.[1] The main concern of this group is technological and institutional innovation as the driving forces of economic development. Their interests cover not only theoretical investigation but also a wide range of research, from historical analyses of innovations to science and research policy.

Indeed, Schumpeter reformulated his theory in a chapter of *Business Cycles* (Schumpeter, 1939), under the title, 'How the economic system generates evolution'. In this chapter, Schumpeter limits the source of 'economic evolution' exclusively to 'innovation' in the sense of 'the setting up of a new production function' (ibid.: 87). To reach this conclusion, he maintains two distinctions, upon which not all contemporary evolutionary economists agree. The first is the distinction between economic growth and economic evolution (development), and the second is that between invention and innovation. The first distinction is well known, since discerning qualitative change from quantitative change is a logically necessary step to grounding economic evolution (that is, development) in innovation. It is the theoretical position that Schumpeter manifests first in *Theorie der wirtschaftlichen Entwicklung* (1911), whose English edition, *Theory of Economic Development* (1934), was published several years prior to *Business Cycles*.

As Schumpeter considers that an economic system has the inherent tendency to move to a static state (equilibrium) as long as innovation does not hinder it, quantitative growth that maintains equilibrium is classified by him as being in a static state (circular flow/equilibrium) and not a dynamic state (evolution/development). However, the question remains as to whether Schumpeter would approve of a growth theory that would be constructed by integrating a Schumpeterian concept of innovation.

The second distinction between invention and innovation is more difficult to grasp, since it comes from Schumpeter's scheme of economic sociology, to which he could not give definite form within his lifetime. Although Schumpeter admitted that many innovations (changes of production function) were based on inventions, he still adheres to their distinction on the grounds that they need different means and personalities. It is true that successful inventors occupy leading positions for their respective followers, making them similar to successful entrepreneurs and their followers. However, an invention is a breakthrough in the world of knowledge (that is, science and technology), while innovation is that in the world of economy; in the latter world, it is not enquirers but entrepreneurs who are heroes, and the effective means is not knowledge but money or capital:

> even where innovation consists in giving effect, by business action, to a particular invention which has either emerged autonomously or has been specially made with a view to a given business purpose and in response to a given business situation*, the making of the invention and the carrying out of the corresponding innovation are, economically and sociologically, two entirely different things. They may, and often, have been, performed by the same person; but this is merely a chance coincidence which does not affect the validity of the distinction. Personal aptitudes – primarily intellectual in the case of inventor, primarily volitional in the case of businessman who turns the invention into an innovation – and the methods by which the one and the other work, belong to different spheres. The social process which produces inventions and the social process which produces innovations do not stand in any invariant relation to each other and such relations as they display is much more complex than appears at first sight. (Schumpeter, 1939: 85–6)

The motive that forced Schumpeter to make a strict distinction between invention and innovation was his wish to treat 'innovation' as 'a distinct internal factor of change'. Did Schumpeter regard 'invention' as an exogenous factor to economic evolution? The answer is not so clear, since Schumpeter acknowledges his indebtedness to three American invention researchers – A.P. Usher, S.C. Gilfillan and R.K. Merton – in a footnote placed at (*) in the previous citation; all three consider inventions socially conditioned phenomena. That footnote reads as follows:

> Meanwhile, it should be pointed out that we may accept a theory of invention as presented for example, by Mr. S.C. Gilfillan in his *Sociology of Invention* – the present writer, as a matter of fact, substantially does – and yet adopt another point of view for our purposes. We take the opportunity to refer to Professor

> A. P. Usher's *History of Mechanical Inventions*, 1929, from which work the present writer has derived much help, and R. K. Merton, Fluctuations in the Rate of Industrial Inventions, *Quarterly Journal of Economics* for May 1935. The writer wishes to acknowledge his obligation, in the matter of invention, to a report made for him by Mr. Gilfillan. (Schumpeter, 1939: 85 fn)

In this footnote, Schumpeter on the one hand admits an internalist view of invention, such as that proposed by Gilfillan, as being acceptable; on the other hand he declares that 'we may . . . yet adopt another point of view for our purposes'.

My interpretation of this apparently confusing footnote is in line with the general question of determinateness and indeterminateness in Schumpeter's economic sociology.[2]

First, he regards 'innovation' and 'invention' as belonging to different sectors of socio-economic activity: 'innovation' belongs to economy, whereas 'invention' belongs to science and technology. Economics deals with the former, and the sociologies of science and technology deal with the latter. To economics that deal with 'innovation' as an internal factor of economic change, 'invention' is an external factor that derives from the socio-cultural sector; to the sociologies of science and technology, economic factors are external factors. However, since the publication of the first German edition of his *Theory of Economic Development*, Schumpeter kept in mind the task of deriving a holistic view by which the interactions of entire sectors are grasped. In the last stage of his writing, he named it 'economic sociology' (Schumpeter, 1954: 21).

We then remember that Schumpeter divides the approaches of the social sciences into static ones (equilibrium approach) and dynamic ones (evolutionary or developmental approach). The former view internal factors as determinate relations, while the latter view them in indeterminate relations. The nature of equilibrium, as well as the qualification and activity of the breakthrough, is different (innovation and invention) in the economic sector and in the science and technology sectors. In economic sociology, the static approach is applied also to the interrelations among sectors that bring forth an affinity of economic life and cultural and social life in a nation; in its extension, a change in one sector may be explained by the given data of another. Most of the changes in one sector (whether it is an 'invention' or 'innovation') can be explained as an adaptation to the given data (unchanged or changed state) within its own sector or in other sectors. This is an internalist explanation for the change.

However, Schumpeter has another purpose that is not reduced to the rational explanation for the change. In both the economic and cultural (that is, science and technology) sectors, novelty that cannot be predicted by the existing data can emerge and trigger a process of evolutionary change. I presume that Schumpeter's last purpose is to attain a total view of 'social evolution' that comprises the interaction of such evolutionary changes of the sectors in their entireties.

10.2 ANOTHER INNOVATION THEORY: ABBOTT PAYSON USHER

One of the closest fellow scholars that Schumpeter had in his early years at Harvard was Abbott Payson Usher (1883–1965).[3] The topics of their discussion covered even their research plans, which were directed at the evolutionary development of economic societies. Born in Lynn, Massachusetts, Usher was a genuine Harvard scholar who acquired the degrees of BA (1904), MA (1906) and PhD (1910) at Harvard; after a decade of teaching in other universities, he returned to his Alma Mater in 1921. When he met Schumpeter, Usher was an associate professor of economic history, but he was promoted to full professor in 1936 and retired in 1949. His first book in 1913 was on the topic of the grain trade in France in the early modern age, but he turned to a study of the industrial revolution in England. From this study, he formed an interest in inventions that had changed the structure of industries. The outcome was *A History of Mechanical Inventions* (1929). In this book, he uses the term, 'innovation' as a key concept to understanding economic change, prior to the appearance of the English edition of Schumpeter's *Theory of Economic Development*. 'Changes in technique involve a series of individual innovations that are finally embodied in practical accomplishments. These series or sequences of relatively independent inventions are among the most intense manifestations of the dynamic process of history' (Usher, 1929: 4).

Like Schumpeter, Usher stresses that innovations are nothing other than the creative activities of individuals. However, he was against the 'great men' theory that hypostatized exceptionally heroic persons who could guide others. Rather, he would understand innovations together with the process of recognition and learning of individuals and their groups that lived with given resources and institutions:

> we are beginning to realize that these phenomena of innovation are neither more nor less mysterious than the most humble and commonplace phases of our mental life.
>
> Innovation is an integral part of the process of learning, an inescapable necessity for the individual as for the group as a whole. (Ibid.: 8)

According to Usher, subconscious elements that are formed by experiences and habits play an important role in the emergence of innovation. An 'inspiration' is, in reality, nothing other than a discovery based on a critical analysis of existing experiences. However, many inventions are necessary to bringing to its practical application a general concept behind this 'inspiration'. A synthetic effort to combine various knowledge and ideas, as well as their critical modifications, is needed to attain the full achievement of the potentialities that exist implicitly in the new general concept or principle. Thus, Usher constructs a sequential view of inventions that consists of critical analysis and constructive synthesis, and whose weights shift in the initial, intermediate and completion phases:[4]

> The individual act of invention is not an isolated item, nor does any one invention make possible the full achievement of the potentialities implicit in the general concept or principle. It is thus important to recognize that these inventions form part of an orderly sequence, which embraces in its entirety the full record of the steps by which we achieve the complete realization of our ends. (Ibid.: 19)

As an attentive historian, Usher notices also the transformation of the process of innovation by the emergence of organized science and research laboratories:

> This change in the character of the process of achievement involves ultimately the organization of research laboratories; and this increased deliberation of effort has given rise in the minds of many to an impression that the development of scientific knowledge makes some fundamental change in the character of the process of invention in the narrow sense. It is suggested that invention becomes more systematic and regular, and that the 'inspirational' or salutatory elements are less considerable. (Ibid.: 21)

> The application of organized science and the imaginative powers thus transforms the process of achievement much more than they transform the process of invention in its restricted sense. Under the guidance of conscious effort the process of technological improvements becomes more orderly; it proceeds towards a wider range of ends, and it undoubtedly achieves its ends more rapidly than would be possible under conditions of sheer empiricism. (Ibid.: 22)

This remark may have some influence on the Schumpeterian idea of the automatization of innovation in modern big business. However, in this respect, too, Usher was not the sole person to have such a view of the nature of inventions.

It is apparent that Usher used the term 'innovation' in a way different from Schumpeter's: indeed, it is not limited to the economic world. Rather, it signifies generally a psychological process that produces new recognition or a new behaviour pattern. It suggests that Usher explains this process by citing an intelligence experiment using apes, in which they used a stick to get food (Ibid.: 11 f.).

Usher contributed to the 1951 Schumpeter memorial publication initiated by his Harvard colleagues, with 'Historical implication of the theory of economic development'. In Usher's view, Schumpeter's theory of economic development provides 'a basis for the comprehensive analysis of events in terms of history, statistics, and theory' by forming a 'defensible and workable concept of process' in 'the process of cumulative innovation' (Usher, 1951: 125). However, Schumpeter was still constrained by an 'idealistic philosophy' that explains social change as 'the result of unconditional acts of great men, to whom underlying truths are directly revealed' (ibid.: 126). Although Schumpeter clears the way to refuting an idealistic view of the historical process, he does not liberate himself completely from it:

> The theory of economic development advances beyond the limits of idealistic position both in terms of the number of innovators and in terms of the explicit interest in the process of change as such. It moves into positions that subject the idealistic categories to severe strains, and really require a complete abandonment of the idealist position. Even in the first edition of *The Theory of Economic Development*, innovation is conceived as a massive social process closely related to the process of learning by an individual of techniques already significantly established in the traditions of the group. But the application of a concept of innovation to cyclical fluctuation involved a truly final break with earlier interpretations of social change. The romantic idealists and the various historical sociologies identified change with the transitions from one stage to another. The discontinuities of history were, thus, restricted to long-term movements dated in terms of centuries. In *The Theory of Economic Development*, change became a completely pervasive feature of social life. It was presented as a fundamental internal phenomenon in addition to the purely external factors which would in some measure account for many of the cyclical phenomena. (Ibid.: 126 f.)

This is a surprisingly penetrating interpretation of Schumpeterian contribution. A 'massive social process' of innovations based on a socially embedded learning process and its cyclical fluctuations is the very vision of social change that contemporary evolutionary economists are exploring. Usher considers this a criticism of an idealistic theory of stages; presumably, he supposes that theoreticians characterize the features of each stage idealistically, and he explains transitions in terms of extraordinary powers (for example, ideals, religions, wars and revolutions) or long-term intervals. This is the sort of idealism that appears typically in historical science.

Usher's criticism of idealism is not confined to the massive process. It is apparent also in the understanding of every individual innovation as a 'social process':

> Once innovation is conceived as a social process, differences and changes that seem to involve qualitative differences are actually resolved into quantitative differences. The theory of innovation is therefore inconsistent with a qualitative

> differentiation between routine and novel action. Even when action has been stylized and stabilized by habits and policies, much novelty still emerges. Some forms of novel action are ignored by Schumpeter, and the pervasiveness of novelty is certainly underestimated. (Ibid.: 127 f.)

Making use of gestalt psychology instead of an idealistic philosophy, Usher wishes to explain the emergence of novelty in every layer, from the unconscious formation of a skill to a deliberative action with clearly defined purposes. The cumulative process from which innovation emerges is described in greater detail in the revised edition of his *History* (1954).

In *Business Cycles*, Schumpeter classifies increases in population, technological knowledge and capital in the category of quantitative growth, and thus outside the realm of innovation. If we concur with Usher and conceive that microscopic novelties emerge at any place and at any time and form a massive process, we cannot maintain a clear distinction between quantitative growth and qualitative development.

10.3 SOCIOLOGY OF INVENTION: S.C. GILFILLAN AND R.K. MERTON

Seabury Colum Gilfillan (1889–1987) was a sociologist who made pioneering investigations into the social aspects of invention and patents, although he could not assume a stable academic position. Born in St Paul, Minnesota on 5 April 1889, he graduated from the University of Pennsylvania in 1910 and acquired an MA (1920) and PhD (1935) from Columbia University. In the late 1920s, he had begun to publish his research into inventions in several journals; in 1935, he simultaneously published the case study, *Inventing the Ship*, and the theoretical consideration, *The Sociology of Invention*, with the publisher Follett. We cite his self-introduction from the preface of *The Sociology*:

> The present writer cannot qualify as an inventor, engineer nor patent lawyer, despite some efforts in the first two fields; and he is very little of a mariner. He is a sociologist, interested especially in the history and prophecy of the developments of civilization, and in the social aspects of invention, on which he has done further work; but he claims also some knowledge of nautical and mechanical matters. (Gilfillan, 1935: xi)

In *The Sociology of Invention*, Gilfillan summarizes his research results in terms of 38 social principles: numbers 1–5 summarize the nature of invention; numbers 6–7, the changes evoking inventions; numbers 8–14, the rate of growth and the lifecycle of an invention; numbers 15–22, the factors that foster, retard and locate inventions; numbers 23–5, the principles of change; numbers 26–33, the inventors and other classes, and tendencies in the craft; and numbers 34–8, the effects of invention.

As we cannot reproduce here all of these somewhat clumsy albeit interesting principles, we cite a passage in which his direction is especially evident:

> the very essence of invention is commonly misunderstood, not alone by the laity, but often by inventors, engineers and sociologists. Above all its outstanding characteristic, its evolutionary nature, its being almost wholly an age-old, multitudinous accretion of little details, modifications, perfectings, minute additions, is not fully appreciated by even the best of authorities. As to inventions we are still in the antediluvian geologic age, holding a cataclysmic rather than evolutionary theory of the origin of things. The great inventions are supposed to have been made by certain great men, much as Adam was made and then leaned against a fence to dry, according to the song. (Ibid.: 3)

From such an evolutionary view of invention – which comprises a continuous series of incremental changes – Gilfillan maintains that not only an empirical generalization but also some degree of prediction is possible with respect to inventions. Although he opposes the 'great men' theory, he does not argue the creating role of inventors. However, he sees them as a function of surrounding, concomitant factors, including preceding inventions:

> [Principle 6:] (a) The achievements of the inventor himself, and of his compeers, are a major cause of changes in the milieu out of which is compounded the inventional complex described in Prin. 2. 'Invention is (one) mother of necessity.' (b) Some other chief changes causing invention are growths of wealth, education, population, industrialism, and commercial organization. (Ibid.: 6–7)

> [Principle 26:] There is no indication that any individual's genius has been necessary to any invention that has had any importance. To the historian and social scientist the progress of invention appears impersonal. (Ibid.: 10)

> [Principle 27:] Yet invention can only come at the hand of some sort of investors, and its directions, frequency and efficiency are determined wholly thru deliberate actions by these men, in some proportion to their absolute numbers, intelligence, moral traits, strength of motives for inventing, time free for it, and mental and mechanical equipment for it. (Ibid.: 10)

> [Principle 28:] Perception of the need and the way to meet it depends first upon any individuals of a numerous inventive class, but indirectly upon the suggestions tost [*sic*] up by a wider intelligent and technologically minded class, more indirectly upon the whole population's thoughts, and ultimately upon [the] physical environment and the general social and racial heritage, which determine the mental level and slant of each class and country. (Ibid.: 11)

In contrast to the unstable professional career of Gilfillan, Robert King Merton (1910–2003) became one of the most respected sociologists in twentieth-century America. Born in Philadelphia on 4 July 1910, he graduated from Temple University in 1931 and was a graduate student of Harvard University when he published the article mentioned in Schumpeter's *Business Cycles*. Given that he stayed a further three years at Harvard as a tutor and instructor of sociology after earning a PhD in 1936, he probably had a direct acquaintance with Schumpeter. After leaving the Harvard Yard and experiencing the teaching life in Tulane University in New Orleans, he joined the staff of the sociology department of Columbia University in 1941 and became Giddings Professor of Sociology in 1963. In 1994, he was awarded the National Medal of Science – the first sociologist to receive this prize. The sociology of science is one of the research fields of sociology that he established – of which Merton's 1935 article was one of the pioneering works in this area, despite an apparently general negligence.

On the origin of Merton's interest in the sociology of science, N.W. Storer says that

> In the early 1930s, however, Merton's interest was not primarily in the sociology of science. During his graduate studies at Harvard, he undertook, at the suggestion of the economic historian E. F. Gay, an analytical book review of A.P. Usher's *History of Mechanical Invention*. Gay liked it and suggested that George Sarton, also a Harvard [colleague], publish it in *Isis*, the prime journal in the history of science which he had founded and still edited. Sarton did so, and he encouraged Merton's interest in the history of science by having him work in the renowned workshop in Widener Library. Noting his growing expertise in this field, Pitirim A. Sorokin recruited Merton to assist him in the studies of the development of science that would make parts of his *Social and Cultural Dynamics*. (Storer, 1973: xiv)

Collaborating with Sorokin in the study of the cultural sociological analysis of science in Islam, Merton began his dissertation study 'Science, technology, and the society in seventeenth-century England' (Merton, 1938). Although Sorokin remained rather ambivalent about statistics, he recognized the necessity of a systematic statistical analysis, in order to grasp the secular changes in various sociocultural phenomena; Merton was more talented in this respect. Later, Merton developed the quantitative approach to cultural change in a collection of biographies of the persons involved in such change.[5] However, in the 1935 article, he uses the patent statistics directly.

Gilfillan also uses patent statistics in his analysis of the development of marine technology. While this work is limited to one sector in isolation,

Merton widens the statistical analysis of the patent to the whole industry and focuses on the shift of interest in inventions. This was because S. Kuznets's view of the retardation tendency of the technical progress and A.C. Pigou's suggestion of the shift of the inventive interest between different industry sectors of a country stimulated the young Merton.

After corroborating his two predecessors' views on invention by way of statistical analysis, he enquires into the factors that can account for such patterns of technical progress. He mentions three kinds of factors. First, there is the 'intrinsic' factor of inventive interest:

> The 'intrinsic' category refers to the progressive limitation to the possibilities of continued invention within a restricted field with an approach to the exhaustion of possibilities. Immediately upon the appearance of a successful pioneer invention, inventors are stimulated to activity in that particular field in an effort to arrive at the many important improvements which are usually possible . . . But in time – which is the more brief [and] the more limited the field under consideration – the major possibilities are realized and the sheer possibility of further economically feasible inventions is greatly diminished. (Merton, 1935: 464 f.)

The formation of the established interest of the prevailing technology may come into play as an 'economic' factor:

> The fact that in certain industries the probability of economic advantages to be gained from [the] utilization of new inventions decreases in time, due to the growth of the capital investment which must be sacrificed, may partially account for the relative decline in the rate of technologic change as the industry becomes more firmly established. (Ibid.: 466)

Following this stagnation view of a mature industry comes, finally, a Schumpeterian 'social' explanation:

> The psycho-social factors influencing the rate of technologic change act in the same direction as those already mentioned. At the outset, the individuals in control of a given industry generally are in Pareto's terminology *speculateurs*, in Professor Schumpeter's 'innovators'; that is, individuals who are daring, speculative, restless, imaginative and, more pertinently, eager to exploit new inventions. During this initial period invention is encouraged, new paths are tried, [and] the attitude of 'all to gain and nothing to lose' is prevalent. As the industry, if it is favored by fortunate speculation of this kind, grows, the capital investment increases and the rentier or routineer type of individual becomes involved. These individuals are systematic, accustomed to run[ning] things along familiar lines; the primary concern being safety of investment and assurance of certain profits, rather than speculative attempts at expansion and innovation. Disturbing, pioneering innovations tend to be discountenanced. (Ibid.: 467 f.)

In Merton's case, the innovator (that is, the Schumpeterian entrepreneur) is taken as a sociological actor, and economic factors are interpreted from the viewpoint of established capitalistic interest.

10.4 TOWARDS RECASTING GROWTH THEORY

Both Gilfillan and Merton cite the same article that Simon Kuznets (1901–85) published in the first volume of *Journal of Economic and Business History* (August 1929), namely, 'Retardation of industrial growth'. In *Secular Movements in Production and Prices*, which Kuznets published the following year, that article occupied a place in the first chapter, thus providing 'a definite hypothesis concerning characteristics of industrial growth' that was based on a 'tentative generalization' (Kuznets, 1930a: iv) of historical and statistical data; nonetheless, a few of its initial pages were rewritten when the 1929 article was included in the 1930 book. It is of some interest to the historians of economic theory to know that Kuznets had mentioned Schumpeter in the original journal version. The 1971 Nobel Prize winner in economics and father of both national income statistics and the concept of 'modern economic growth', he was encouraged in his early years by Schumpeter's development theory, in addition to W.C. Mitchell's empiricist-type institutionalism.[6]

Born in Pinsk, Russia (now in Belarus) and educated in Kharkov, Ukraine, Kuznets immigrated to the USA in 1922; there, he earned BSc (1923), MA (1924) and PhD (1926) degrees at Columbia University. After acquiring the PhD, he became a member of the research staff of the National Bureau of Economic Research in New York; he maintained that affiliation until 1961, although he held professorial appointments at the University of Pennsylvania (1930–54), Johns Hopkins University (1954–60) and Harvard University (1960–71).

In the introduction to the 1929 article, Kuznets wrote:

> While the question of long-time changes dropped out of sight in 'pure' economic theory, it began to come back through different channels; in the study of crises and cyclical fluctuations, in a separate series of studies to which they have given rise, such as Schumpeter's theory of development, and in the recent articles of H. L. Moore, in which we observe the introduction of the concept of moving equilibrium into the mathematical scheme. But in spite of these conceptual reapproaches to the problem, inductive knowledge of the type that can be formulated in general statement is still lacking. (Kuznets, 1929: 535)

Despite the elimination of the citation in the later version, he mentions Schumpeter's *Theory of Economic Development* again, in another article in the following year.

> From the point of view of business-cycle theory, a significant milestone in this formulation of its logical relation to static theory was Schumpeter's *Theory of Economic Development*. While in 1913 W.C. Mitchell unfolded the problem of business cycles to its full empirical extent, in 1914 Schumpeter presented a tentative theory of dynamic economics, in which business cycles became an integral part of the new theoretical system. (Kuznets, 1930b [1953]: 6)

As is easily seen from both citations, Kuznets at around 1930 was in a quest for a theoretical frame by which growth dynamics and fluctuations could be contained. In his view, the phenomena of economic growth consist of ceaseless change that accompanies cyclical fluctuations. The aim of his 1929 article was to acquire a working hypothesis that explains general empirical observations, as per the following:

> If we take the world from the end of the eighteenth century, we see a process of seemingly unslackened growth . . . But if we single out the various nations or separate industries, the picture becomes less uniform . . . As we observe the various industries within a given national system, we see that the lead in development shifts from one branch to another. For a rapidly developing industry does not retain its vigorous growth forever but slackens and is overtaken by industries whose period of rapid development is beginning. Within one country we can observe a succession of different branches of activity in the highlight of the country's general process of development, and within each industry we can notice a conspicuous slackening in the rate of increase. (Kuznets, 1929: 535 f.)

Kuznets mentions four reasons behind the decline in the speed of the growth of industries. The first is the slowing down of technical progress in each industry; he states that 'The introduction of the initial invention exercises a stimulus to bring about, as soon as possible, a corresponding change and improvement in the other processes within the industry', and that 'as the industry advances technically, the economic stimulus to further innovations becomes weaker and weaker' (ibid.: 548). The second is the negative effect of the interaction of both the complementary branches and competitive branches of industry. 'Slower growing industries exercise a retarding influence upon the faster growing complementary branches. [There are] Similar influence[s] of the rapidly growing industries upon their competitive branches' (Kuznets, 1930a: ix). The third is the relative decrease in the available funds for expansion with regard to industrial growth, and the fourth is competition within the same industries in countries that are 'catching up' economically. It is clear that Kuznets based his theory of economic growth on the ability of innovations and conditions to enable further innovations.

When Schumpeter's *Business Cycles* appeared, Kuznets was its reviewer in the *American Economic Review*. Despite his homage to Schumpeter's wide perspective and lofty theoretical conception, it is a rather devastating review that points to an insufficient linkage between the theoretical model involved and statistical analysis. Apart from an examination of the statistical analysis of cycles and economic fluctuations, Kuznets discusses the relationship between distributions of entrepreneurial ability and the cyclical character of economic change. He argues that in order to defend Schumpeter's view of the 'bunching' of innovation or the sporadic (dis)-appearance of innovation waves, one requires a limitation of innovations – a limitation to such significant ones, as to disturb existing economic relations – or an assumption of the cyclical fluctuations of the possible innovation stock (inventions and the like). Further, he suggests that Schumpeter's negligence of 'secondary factors' weakens the persuasiveness of his analysis (Kuznets, 1940 [1953]: 111–14).

10.5 SCHUMPETER'S SUPPORT OF ENTREPRENEURIAL HISTORY

Schumpeter seems to refrain from entering into the history of technology and limits himself to concentrating on a pure study of innovation. Schumpeter did not deny the empirical approach held by the American scholars he met at Harvard; according to R. Swedberg, a reformulation of 'entrepreneurship' hid in several of Schumpeter's writings in the 1940s. Swedberg argues that the reformulation is first less individualistic, second more theoretically indifferent, and third more empirically oriented.[7] It is controversial whether this is a new version or a necessary adaptation to empirical research; I am inclined to accept the latter.

Schumpeter's relationship with the researchers of invention seems not to have survived. Instead, he found another historian who would agree with him. Arthur Harrison Cole (1889–1975) was also a genuine Harvard scholar who acquired MA (1913) and PhD (1916) degrees and became an associate professor (1928) and full professor (1933) there. From 1932 to 1956, he worked also as a librarian and maintained the Research Center in Entrepreneurial History from 1948 to 1958. Together with other senior professors – namely, Fritz Redlich and Thomas C. Cochran – Schumpeter supported the Research Center actively. Cole's study approach was genuinely empirical, since he believed that research into entrepreneurship had to start with the collection of business documents:

> Innovation, management, and the imposed adjustments. The actions for these three purposes along any other six lines are the resultants of executive decisions; these decisions are the acts of a real person, or a real, but variantly composed,

group of persons at or near the top of individual business units; and these decisions are made in response to divers psychological imperatives and are conditioned by various and changing environmental forces. (Cole, 1946: 7)

Schumpeter's 1947 article, 'The creative response in economic history', was written originally to support Cole's proposal for the documentation of entrepreneurial history. This article begins with the hope of collaboration between historians and theorists in economics: 'Economic historians and economic theorists can make an interesting and socially valuable journey together, if they will. It would be an investigation into the sadly neglected area of economic change' (Schumpeter, 1947: 149).

He calls the reactions to the change in the data, along with existing practice, an 'adaptive response', and reactions that surpass it a 'creative response'. The function of the entrepreneur is to produce the latter. This response may be an inevitable result, but even in such a case, *ex ante*, it depends on creative action on the part of entrepreneurs.

In his article, Schumpeter rehearses his distinction of entrepreneurs from managers and inventors. The distinction of entrepreneurs and inventors is more precise than that in *Business Cycles*:

> Many inventors have become entrepreneurs and the relative frequency of this case is no doubt an interesting subject to investigate, but there is no necessary connection between two functions. The inventor produces ideas, the entrepreneur 'gets things done,' which may need not embody anything that is scientifically new. (Ibid.: 152)

Thus, entrepreneurs and inventors – or, innovation and invention – are separated into the two different worlds of actions and ideas. However, Schumpeter's discussion of entrepreneurship nonetheless follows a path similar to those of invention researchers, that is, the path towards the problem of 'automatization'. In the process, he asks himself, 'Does the importance of the entrepreneurial function decline as time goes on?' and answers with, 'There are serious reasons for believing that it does': 'it [the personal intuition of the entrepreneur] could be expected to yield its place to the teamwork of specialists; in other words, improvement could be expected to become more and more automatic' (ibid.: 157).

If we interpret 'specialists' to mean researchers and scientists in laboratories owned by private businesses, his definition coincides with the view of invention researchers; however, Schumpeter would extend his terminology not in this direction, but to military affairs:

> Our impression to this effect is reinforced by parallel phenomena in other fields of activity. For instance, a modern commander no doubt means less in the

> outcome of a war than commanders meant of old, and for the same reasons; campaigns have become more calculable than they used to be and there is less scope for personal leadership. (Ibid.: 158)

From this discussion, he suggests its impact on the 'class structure of capitalist society':

> Just as warrior classes have declined in importance ever since warfare – and especially the management of armies in the field – began to be increasingly 'mechanized,' so the business class may decline in importance, as its most vital figure, the entrepreneur, progressively loses his most essential function. This would mean a different social structure. (Ibid.: 158)

Such an interest in command and leadership characterizes the interest of Schumpeter. Ultimately, I have the impression that his final interest consists more of the hegemonic aspects of social structure than the effects of ideas.

In 1959, Cole could recollect Schumpeter in the final stage of the life as a patron theorist to entrepreneur-based history:

> Thanks to the extraordinary path-breaking contributions of Prof. Schumpeter, entrepreneurship has tended to be made synonymous with the introduction of technological innovations, especially innovations of a momentous character. I believe this identification to be an error, and that Schumpeter came in his latter years to take a broader view. (Cole, 1959: 180)

10.6 AFTER SCHUMPETER'S DEATH

Schumpeter died abruptly of a heart attack in the early morning of 8 January 1950. In the lecture series he had prepared until the day before he died, it was clear that he wished to talk about the broad issues of the interaction between both the economic factors and institutional change, and the social influence and personal element; it was the topic that Schumpeter discussed intensively with Usher in the Harvard Yard.[8]

In 1954, Usher published the revised edition of *A History of Mechanical Inventions*, with an additional four chapters in which he elaborates his view of innovation and his frame of social evolution.

The new research directions, which had their origin in the young American academism of the early 1930s' had established their existence around the year of Schumpeter's death. A group of young scholars began to examine Schumpeter's views, such as the entrepreneurial push theory of innovations and the advantage of big business in innovations. In their research into industrial dynamics, the strict distinction between invention and innovation had already disappeared.

One year before Schumpeter's death, Merton published *Social Theory and Social Structure* (1949), in whose fourth part he compiled his five articles on the sociology of science. His 1935 article on 'industrial invention' was not included; rather, Merton's main concern was directed to the cultural and social backgrounds of scientific inquiry, and it was estranged from economic research.

The activities of the Research Center in Entrepreneurial History since 1948 have enhanced research into business history, so that it is now a new academic branch of history. The Center has also contributed to business education at Harvard by supplying it with ample materials and historical reflections. Cole, whose involvement in the Center was pivotal, summarized his concept of entrepreneur study in *Business Enterprise in Its Social Setting*, in 1959.

In 1965, Kuznets published one of his major works, *Modern Economic Growth*, in which he based the continuous growing trend of Western (and Japanese) economy on the concept of 'epochal innovation'. He defined it as 'a major addition to the stock of human knowledge which provides a potential for sustained economic growth' (Kuznets, 1965: 2), and he regarded the extended application of science to economic production as 'the epochal innovation' that distinguishes the 'modern economic epoch'.

It appears that the academic seeds of 1930s evolutionary economics have grown into an established research field. All of them were (and are) the rich origins for contemporary evolutionary economics. Schumpeter was not always involved wholeheartedly in it, but he was nonetheless there. The fact that Schumpeter had been involved in those streams of thought justifies mentioning him as one of the most representative founders of this stream, despite his hesitations in founding his own school.[9]

NOTES

1. See Hanusch and Pyka (2007).
2. From the beginning of his academic career, Schumpeter maintained an interest in both economics and sociology, and he embraced the wish to explore the interrelation of economic factors and social (cultural) factors. On the one hand, the interrelationship between the economic sector and the social (cultural) sector enhances the determinateness of individual actions (and thus the historical process); however, a deterministic view of history fails, on the other hand, due to the possibility of a 'creative' response in either sector. See Yagi (2006).
3. See Allen (1991, vol. 2: 6 f). In the Schumpeter Papers housed in the Harvard University Archive, there are two typescript versions of the plan 'Social Evolution and Historical Process', dated 11 March and 9 April 1933, respectively (HUG(FP)-4.42/Joseph Schumpeter/Identified Notes Box I). In a conference paper (Yagi, 2003), I wrongly attributed their authorship to Schumpeter. Thanks to the suggestion of Professor Esben Sloth

Andersen (Alborg University), I now assume they came from Usher and were handed to Schumpeter, probably for discussion.
4. See the comparison of Schumpeter and Usher by Ruttan (1959).
5. See also Merton (1977).
6. According to Mark Perlman (2007), Kuznets had already taken up Schumpeter in his master's essay in 1924. It seems that Kuznets remained aligned with the empiricists, despite his expectations vis-à-vis progress in economic theory.
7. Swedberg (1991: 171–4). Swedberg further maintains that even those who knew Schumpeter closely misinterpreted his theory in his former, 'heroic' version of the definition of 'entrepreneur'.
8. See Yagi (2006).
9. With respect to the reappraisal of Schumpeter before the emergence of the neo-Schumpeterian economics, see Fageberg (2003) and Freeman (2007).

REFERENCES

Allen, R.L. (1991), *Opening Doors: The Life and Work of Joseph Schumpeter*, 2 vols, New Brunswick, NJ and London: Transaction Publishers.

Cole, A.H. (1946), 'An approach to the study of entrepreneurship: a tribute to Edwin F. Gay', *The Journal of Economic History*, **6**, Supplement: The Tasks of Economic History (May), 1–15.

Cole, A.H. (1959), *Business Enterprise in Its Social Setting*, Cambridge, MA: Harvard University Press.

Fageberg, J. (2003), 'Schumpeter and the revival of evolutionary economics: an appraisal of the literature', *Journal of Evolutionary Economics*, **13** (2), 125–59.

Freeman, C. (2007), 'A Schumpeterian renaissance?', in H. Hanusch and A. Pyka (eds), *Elgar Companion to Neo-Schumpeterian Economics*, Cheltenham, UK and Northampton, MA, USA: Edward Elgar.

Gilfillan, S.C. (1935), *The Sociology of Invention: an Essay in the Social Causes of Technic Invention and Some of Its Social Results Especially as Demonstrated in the History of the Ship*, Chicago: Follett.

Hanusch, H. and A. Pyka (eds) (2007), *Elgar Companion to Neo-Schumpeterian Economics*, Cheltenham, UK and Northampton, MA, USA: Edward Elgar.

Kuznets, S. (1929), 'Retardation of industrial growth', *Journal of Economic and Business History*, **1**, 534–60.

Kuznets, S. (1930a), *Secular Movements in Production and Prices: Their Nature and their Bearing upon Cyclical Fluctuations*, Boston, MA: Houghton Mifflin (Riverside Press).

Kuznets, S. (1930b), 'Equilibrium economics and business-cycle Theory', *The Quarterly Journal of Economics*, **44** (May), reprinted in S. Kuznets (1953), *Economic Change: Selected Essays in Business Cycles, National Income, and Economic Growth*, New York: W.W. Norton, pp. 3–31.

Kuznets, S. (1940), 'Schumpeter's business cycles', *American Economic Review*, **30** (2), 250–71, reprinted in S. Kuznets (1953), *Economic Change: Selected Essays in Business Cycles, National Income, and Economic Growth*, New York: W.W. Norton, pp. 105–24.

Kuznets, S. (1953), *Economic Change: Selected Essays in Business Cycles, National Income, and Economic Growth*, New York: W.W. Norton.

Kuznets, S. (1965), *Modern Economic Growth: Rate, Structure, and Spread*, New Haven, CT and London: Yale University Press.

Merton, R.K. (1935), 'Fluctuations in the rate of industrial invention', *The Quarterly Journal of Economics*, **49** (3), 454–74.

Merton, R.K. (1938), *Science, Technology and Society in Seventeenth-century England*, Bruges, Belgium: St Catherine Press.

Merton, R.K. (1949), *Social Theory and Social Structure: Toward the Codification of Theory and Research*, New York: Free Press.

Merton, R.K. (1977), 'The sociology of science: an epidemic memoir', in R.K. Merton and J. Gaston (eds), *The Sociology of Science in Europe*, Carbondale, IL: Southern Illinois University Press.

Perlman, M. (2007), 'Schumpeter's views on methodology: their source and their evolution', in H. Hanusch and A. Pyka (eds), *Elgar Companion to Neo-Schumpeterian Economics*, Cheltenham, UK and Northampton, MA, USA: Edward Elgar.

Ruttan, V.W. (1959), 'Usher and Schumpeter on invention, innovation, and technological change', *The Quarterly Journal of Economics*, **73** (4), 596–606.

Schumpeter, J.A. (1911), *Theorie der wirtschaftlichen Entwicklung*, Leipzig: Duncker & Humblot.

Schumpeter, J.A. (1934), *The Theory of Economic Development: An Inquiry into Profits, Capital, Interest, and the Business Cycle*, trans. Redvers Opie, Cambridge, MA: Harvard University Press.

Schumpeter, J.A. (1939), *Business Cycles: A Theoretical, Historical and Statistical Analysis of the Capitalist Process*, New York and London: McGraw-Hill Books.

Schumpeter, J.A. (1947), 'The creative response in economic history', *The Journal of Economic History*, **7** (2), 149–59.

Schumpeter, J.A. (1954), *History of Economic Analysis*, New York: Oxford University Press.

Storer, N.W. (1973), 'Introduction' to R.K. Merton, *The Sociology of Science: Theoretical and Empirical Investigations*, Chicago, IL and London: University of Chicago Press.

Swedberg, R. (1991), *Joseph A. Schumpeter: His Life and Work*, Cambridge: Polity Press.

Usher, A.P. (1929), *A History of Mechanical Inventions*, New York and London: McGraw-Hill.

Usher, A.P. (1951), 'Historical implications of the theory of economic development', in S.E. Harris (ed.), *Schumpeter, Social Scientist*, Cambridge, MA: Harvard University Press, pp. 125–9.

Usher, A.P. (1954), *A History of Mechanical Inventions*, revised edn, Cambridge, MA: Harvard University Press, reprinted 1982, New York: Dover Publications.

Yagi, K. (2003), 'Schumpeter's view on social evolution: the 1933 plan and his publications', *Economic Transformation and Evolutionary Theory of J. Schumpeter*, The fifth International Symposium on Evolutionary Economics, Pushino, Moscow Region, Russia, 25–27 September, Center for Evolutionary Economics, Moscow.

Yagi, K. (2006), 'Schumpeter and the concept of social evolution: determinateness and indeterminateness in economic sociology', paper presented to the Schumpeter Session of the First Joint Conference of the European Society of History of Economic Thought and the Japan Society of the History of Economic Thought, 16–20 December, Nice-Antipolis.

PART IV

Evolution and Capitalism

11. Schumpeter on development

Harald Hagemann

11.1 INTRODUCTION

In the Preface to the first German edition of *The Theory of Economic Development* Schumpeter (1911: VIII) points out that he had started his analysis with the concrete theoretical issues involved in the crisis problem in 1905. Furthermore, he makes clear that this book and his earlier one, *Das Wesen und der Hauptinhalt der theoretischen Nationalökonomie* (Schumpeter, 1908), form an entity, although the second book can be read independently of the first. The division of labour between the two books can be understood best with regard to the two masters: *Walras*, whose theory comprises the pure logic of an interdependent system in economic equilibrium, and *Marx*, whose views on the long-run development of the capitalist economy form a lifelong challenge for Schumpeter.

In Schumpeter's view not only chapter 6 but in fact any page of his *Theory of Economic Development* (*TED*) is dedicated to the problem of the business cycle[1] and '[a]nalyzing business cycles means neither more nor less than analyzing the economic process of the capitalist era' as he states in the opening sentence of his monumental study *Business Cycles* three decades later (Schumpeter, 1939: V). *Economic development* in the sense of Schumpeter is endogenous, spontaneous and discontinuous. It is the task of dynamic theory to explain the origin and effects of these transition processes, which essentially are a disturbance of equilibrium.

In chapter 2, 'The fundamental phenomenon of economic development', Schumpeter gives a definition of *development* which he understands as

> such changes in economic life as are not forced upon it from without but arise by its own initiative, from within. Should it turn out that there are no such changes arising in the economic sphere itself, and that the phenomenon that we call economic development is in practice simply founded upon the fact that the data change and that the economy continuously adapts itself to them, then we should say that there is *no* economic development. . . . Nor will the mere growth of the economy, as shown by the growth of population and wealth, be designated here as a process of development. For it calls forth no qualitatively

> new phenomena, but only processes of adaptation of the same kind as the changes in the natural data. Since we wish to direct our attention to other phenomena, we shall regard such increases as changes in data. (Schumpeter, 1934: 63)

Schumpeter thus excludes continuous endogenous changes. Without any speculation it is difficult to imagine him to have become an adherent of a Solovian-type neoclassical growth model after 1956, with an economy moving along a steady-state growth path. On the other hand, it is also clear that the endogenous changes Schumpeter has in mind are located on the supply side and not on the demand side of the economy. The five cases he repeatedly mentions as new combinations of productive means include the introductions of a new good and a new method of production, that is, product and process innovations, the opening of a new market, the making use of new raw materials and the carrying out of the new organization of sectors of the economy.[2]

In the following I first discuss in section 11.2 the influences the German historical school had on Schumpeter's analysis of the development problem. Section 11.3 deals with Schumpeter's use of the notion 'economic evolution' in contrast to the concept of 'economic development'. Section 11.4 focuses on the three main building blocks of Schumpeter's theory of economic development: innovations, the pioneering entrepreneur and the role of credit, and the original twist of Schumpeter's theory due to a new combination of these three components. Research on business cycles was a dominant theme in the inter-war period, and Schumpeter was an attentive observer of the new developments. Thus the Kitchin, the Kuznets and the Kondratieff cycle all were discovered in the 1920s, and Schumpeter struggled hard to integrate them in his theoretical system in the 1930s, particularly after his move in 1932 from Bonn to Harvard where he wrote his *Business Cycles* which was published in 1939. He was impressed by Kondratieff's idea of long waves which fit well into his original vision. Section 11.5 deals with Schumpeter's move from a simple-cycle hypothesis to the three-cycle scheme, in which Kondratieff's long waves constitute the basic framework in which they are superposed with the classical Juglar and the shorter Kitchin cycles. The chapter concludes with some reflections on Schumpeterian influences on development economics which evolved as a new subdiscipline after the Second World War, predominantly in the UK and at the United Nations and its ancillary organizations.

11.2 SCHUMPETER AND THE GERMAN HISTORICAL SCHOOL: THE 'LOST SEVENTH CHAPTER'

According to Shionoya, Schumpeter understood the *essence of the German historical school* as comprising

1. a belief in the unity of social life and the inseparable relationship among its components
2. a concern for development.

> The greatest significance of the *historical* method for Schumpeter was the recognition that historical materials reflect the *development* phenomenon and indicate the relationship between economic and non-economic facts, thus suggesting how the disciplines of the social sciences should interact. (Shionoya, 2000: 9; my italics)

In the 'lost seventh chapter' of the first German edition of *The Theory of Economic Development* (Schumpeter, 1911) '*Das Gesamtbild der Volkswirtschaft*' ('The economy as a whole'),[3] Schumpeter had analysed already the theoretical and historical development problem and emphasized the importance of statistical analysis. He recognized that economic development is essentially discontinuous since innovations arise unevenly over the various industries. Entrepreneurs are followed by many imitators so that innovations tend to cluster.

However, not only the much broader 'sociological' approach but also the style of the seventh chapter differed substantially from the other chapters, so Schumpeter omitted it from the later editions. In the very same year, 1926, when Schumpeter reflected and discussed intensively the research programme of the younger historical school in his essay 'Gustav v. Schmoller and the problems of today' (Schumpeter, 1926), he made the only substantial revision of *TED*, which was also seriously abridged. We find a certain tension in Schumpeter's work which is also highly relevant for modern economics. On the one hand, Schumpeter develops and characterizes *economic sociology* as an important subdiscipline in which theory and history cooperate in particular to deal with the dynamic aspects of an economic system, and recognizes the Schmollerian research programme as a contribution to this discipline.[4] On the other hand he apparently dissociates himself from his lifelong goal of a universal social science (Shionoya, 1997) by several changes, most importantly the elimination of the seventh chapter on 'The economy as a whole' for which he gave the following rationale:

> Thus this edition above all has been shortened. The *seventh chapter* of the first edition has been left out completely. Insofar as it had effected at all, it has done

> so in a thoroughly undesired way. In particular the *fragment of cultural sociology*, which it contained among other things, now and then has distracted the attention of the reader from the problems of dry economic theory whose solutions I want to see understood, and sometimes given to me a kind of consent which I find as annoying as the refusal of not being able to follow. (Schumpeter, Preface to the second German edition, 1911 [1926]: XI, my translation and emphases)

Despite this new emphasis on a pure economic analysis in his theory of economic development as a theory of business cycles, overall Schumpeter from the very beginning holds a certain way of looking at development which he basically kept over time. According to Schumpeter development is not only proceeding in waves and discontinuously but also refers 'to changes in the whole social system of which the economy [is] a part' (see Stolper, 1994: 110), as he argues in a lecture to the social-philosophical workshop at the University of Bonn on 28 April 1932, shortly before moving to Harvard and six years after the publication of the second edition of *TED*. The subtitle of *Business Cycles* as well as his later sociological studies, including his seminar on Pareto at Harvard in the late 1940s, and the economic sociology in his *Capitalism, Socialism and Democracy* (1942) clearly indicate that Schumpeter retained his ambitious research programme which comprises a genuine interest in dynamics, as is indicated by his early contributions on crises theory and business-cycle theory.

11.3 ECONOMIC EVOLUTION OR ECONOMIC DEVELOPMENT?

Without doubt the *evolutionary* perspective has been a key ingredient of the *Austrian school* in economics and in other social sciences.[5] However, in its specific combination with the Marxian research programme giving emphasis to the long-run development of the capitalist economy including capital accumulation and technical progress as central elements, the evolutionary perspective in Schumpeter's work takes a form which places him outside the mainstream of the Austrian school.

Schumpeter argued against the biological analogy which the use of the term 'evolution' can imply. This comes out most clearly in the first German edition of his opus magnum *Theorie der wirtschaftlichen Entwicklung* (1911), which has recently been republished with a new introduction (Schumpeter, 2006) by Duncker & Humblot in Berlin. Furthermore, in the article 'Development', written as a contribution to the 'Festschrift for Emil Lederer' in 1932 but only published in the *Journal of Economic Literature* in 2005, Schumpeter also makes it very clear in a Max Weberian manner that he wanted to protect himself against an unscientific connotation of the term *Entwicklung* (development) with value judgements of progress.

However, whereas he kept the cautious attitude against the biological analogy until his death and argued against the dilettante use of the term 'evolutionary' in economics, especially at the beginning of chapter 2 'The fundamental phenomenon of economic development' of the 1934 English version of his *Theory of Economic Development* (pp. 57 ff.), he seems to have modified his attitude towards the use of the term *evolution* shortly afterwards. In a letter to Stewart S. Morgan of 18 May 1934, two months after he wrote the preface to *TED*, Schumpeter refers to his book as *The Theory of Economic* ***Evolution***,[6] and in his subsequent *Business Cycles* main conceptual chapters such as chapter 3 ('How the economic system generates *evolution*') and chapter 4 ('The contours of economic *evolution*') take up the term *evolution* as a key ingredient. Schumpeter now fundamentally defines *economic evolution* as 'the changes in the economic process brought about by innovation, together with all their effects, and the response to them by the economic system' (Schumpeter, 1939, vol. 1: 86).

Thus changes caused by innovations are no longer regarded as economic development but as economic evolution. However, the central point remains that innovations of various sizes are the key endogenous factor causing cyclical fluctuations in the capitalist economy. In *Capitalism, Socialism and Democracy* Schumpeter continues to emphasize the *evolutionary character of the capitalist process* which 'is by nature a form or method of economic change and not only never is but never can be stationary', but gets its fundamental dynamic impulses which 'sets and keeps the capitalist engine in motion' from the introduction of new combinations (see Schumpeter, 1942: 82–3).

11.4 SCHUMPETER'S TRIAD: INNOVATIONS, THE PIONEERING ENTREPRENEUR AND THE ROLE OF CREDIT

As is well known and has often been discussed, *innovations* which give rise to wave-like movements, *pioneering entrepreneurs* as the agents of creative destruction, and *bank credit* as the prerequisite for the foundation of new enterprises and the financing of innovative investments are the three essential building blocks of Schumpeter's *theory* of economic development. Economic development requires new combinations of productive means brought about by entrepreneurs as the carriers and credit as the means of innovation. As Streissler (1982; 1994) has shown in his detailed analysis of the influence of German and Austrian economics on Schumpeter's work, all three elements were already in existence. However, it was the innovative combination of the three themes and the novel shift of emphasis he gave to them, such as the idea of creative destruction by entrepreneurial innovation and the creation of purchasing power in the form of credit as a necessary condition for the required reallocation of resources into innovation activities, that was original in Schumpeter. Thereby equilibrium is disturbed and a process of cyclical development begins.

Innovations which are of an endogenous nature and occur in bursts are at the root of cyclical fluctuations and give rise to great fluctuations in investment demand.[7] Schumpeter shares the view of Knut Wicksell that the disturbance of economic equilibrium is primarily caused by an enlargement of profitable investment opportunities owing to technical progress. However, there is no reason to expect that the rate of productivity growth is constant over time showing a uniform pattern which could be comprised in a kind of steady-state growth path. Instead, technical progress is discontinuous and comes up in different forms which produce different effects and dynamic adjustment processes. It is here in the dynamic setting of the development process that interest and profit emerge in Schumpeter's theory, which postulates zero profits for the circular flow.

Innovations are identified by Schumpeter as discrete changes of production functions. He clearly distinguishes inventions, which are of an exogenous nature and do not necessarily bring about innovations, and the decisive concept of innovations as an endogenous phenomenon guided by business behaviour and unavoidably leading to periods of prosperity and depression. From the beginning it was therefore central for Schumpeter that a theory of economic development had to be constructed as a theory of business cycles.[8] Profits in Schumpeter are of a transitory nature. The emergence of temporary monopoly profits are a main driving force for entrepreneurs to innovate, thereby generating technical progress in the economic system. The activities of imitators who are guided by the profit motive lead to a generalization of the new combinations of productive means and thereby to a gradual erosion of the (extra) profits of the innovators until a new static equilibrium or circular flow is reached. Imitators who otherwise would be driven out of the market are an important mediator for the diffusion process. Although Schumpeter's vision of the capitalist development process is very clear, his analysis lacks a modern theory of the time pattern of the diffusion process[9] for which new capital goods are an essential vehicle to implement new technologies or product innovations.

In the Preface to the Japanese edition of his *Theory of Economic Development* Schumpeter points out that in his book he 'was trying to construct a theoretic model of the process of economic change in time, or perhaps more clearly, to answer the question how the economic system generates the force which incesssantly transforms it' (Schumpeter, 1937, in Clemence 1951 [1989]: 165) and that Marx was most original in his 'vision of economic evolution as a distinct process generated by the economic system itself' (ibid.: 166). However, whereas in Marx there are systemic forces such as the pressure of competition which give the capitalist economy its innovative drive, Schumpeter makes the pioneering entrepreneurs, whose function it is to innovate, the prime movers of economic dynamics. In contrast to the great number of mere managers who are the static organizers of production locked in routine activities, the entrepreneur with his will, energy and role-taking becomes the *Demiurg* of economic change and development. With this emphasis on pioneering entrepreneurs, which he clearly distinguishes from inventing engineers and capitalists alike, and to whom he attributes central characteristics of the elite theories of his time, Schumpeter stands in the tradition of the Austrian school, where on this point it was Friedrich von Wieser who exerted the greatest influence.

The innovating entrepreneurs need financial means for their investment activities which are given to them in the form of credit by the banking system. In capitalist evolution credit becomes a characteristic phenomenon. Although in Schumpeter's view the banker is not the trader but the producer of purchasing power, and credit creation is a necessary condition for the financing of innovations and thus development in competitive capitalism, the banking system is not the decisive producer of business cycles but plays a rather passive role: 'It adapts itself to the demand which comes from entrepreneurs and submits to contraction by their repayment of loans' (Schumpeter, 1931: 17).

The supply of credit moves pro-cyclically with the demand by innovating entrepreneurs. Credit clearly serves for economic development. Schumpeter's assumption that available resources are fully utilized in the circular flow implies that the putting of new combinations into practice requires some reallocation of these resources. The effect of credit creation, that is, of new purchasing power not rooted in previous savings, is an increase of aggregate demand in monetary terms which implies temporary inflation which acts as a tax on the mere managers engaged in routine activities. Schumpeter thus makes forced savings an integral part of his theory. Although interest is a monetary phenomenon it is ultimately based on a real factor, namely, the productivity-enhancing effects of innovations. Interest thus becomes the product of economic development. Schumpeter's profits are 'extra profits' or 'quasi-rents' due to a temporary monopoly induced by innovations which in the process of diffusion by imitators are either reduced gradually or can be eroded quickly as a consequence of new and better follow-up innovations.

Schumpeter's views found the most innovative resonance in the contemporary German literature in Ludwig Albert Hahn's *Economic Theory of Bank Credit* (1920), a fact which is explicitly emphasized by Schumpeter in the second edition of *TED* when he refers the reader to Hahn's 'original and meritorious book, which has essentially advanced our knowledge of the problem' at the beginning of his discussion of the nature and function of credit (Schumpeter, 1934: 95, n. 1). Hahn emphasizes, as later Keynes, the deflationary effects of voluntary savings and the positive effects of an expansionary credit policy for innovations and employment. A key statement reads: '*Capital formation is not the result of saving but of credit*' (Hahn 1920: 120; original emphasis). Hahn takes up Schumpeter's distinction between '*normal*' and '*abnormal*' *credit* and elaborates the distinction between '*non-inflationary*' *credit* (in the amount of overall savings) and *inflationary credit* due to the money-creating ability of the banking sector.

However, in the second German edition of *TED*, Schumpeter (1911 [1926]), feels obliged to keep some distance from Hahn, whose much stronger emphasis on the directly production-enhancing effects of an inflationary credit creation caused accusations of Hahn to be an 'inflationist'. Thus Schumpeter points out: 'Against his formulation it appears to me correct to say: although not by *existing* goods, the quantity of new purchasing power that it is possible to create is supported and limited by *future* goods' (Schumpeter 1911 [1926]: 165; original emphasis). It is clear that for Schumpeter the *spending of credit for innovative investments* is decisive, not for increased consumption. This becomes particularly evident in his statements on *capital* which is regarded as a fund of purchasing power. '*Capital is nothing but the lever by which the entrepreneur subjects to his control the concrete goods which he needs, nothing but a means of diverting the factors of production to new uses, or of dictating a new direction for production*' (Schumpeter, 1934: 116; original emphasis).

11.5 FROM THE SIMPLE-CYCLE HYPOTHESIS TO THE THREE-CYCLE SCHEMA

In his *Business Cycles*, which was the late sequel to *TED*, Schumpeter (1939) distinguishes four phases of economic fluctuations: prosperity, recession, depression and recovery, and presents *a three-cycle schema*, in which *Kondratieff* long waves constitute the framework where they are combined with the classical *Juglar* and the shorter *Kitchin* cycles (Figure 11.1). In the preface to the English edition of *TED* we find the following statement:

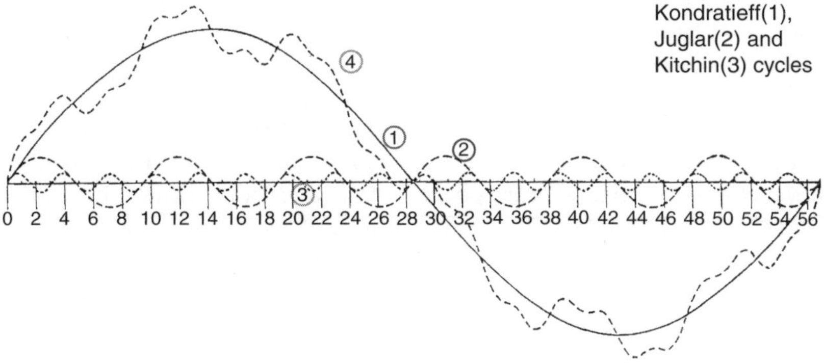

Source: Schumpeter (1939: 213).

Figure 11.1 Schumpeter's basic idea that cyclical fluctuations consist of many waves: a composite of three cycles of different length

> I took it for granted that there was a single wave-like movement, viz. that discovered by Juglar. I am convinced now that there are at least three such movements, probably more, and that the most important problem which at present faces theorists of the cycle consists precisely in isolating them and in describing the phenomena incident to their interaction. But this element has not been introduced into the later editions. (Schumpeter, 1934: IX)[10]

This statement is not surprising because the Kitchin and the Kondratieff cycle were born in the economic literature only in the 1920s. Schumpeter himself was the co-editor of the journal in which Kondratieff's famous article on 'The long waves in economic life' was published in German in 1926. However, it is quite interesting to notice that the idea of *superposition* of different complexes of causality was already there when Schumpeter presented the main ideas on the wave-like fluctuation in economic activity to the Harvard faculty shortly before the outbreak of the First World War (Schumpeter, 1914–15: 4–5).

As Schumpeter's outstanding and long-run student at Bonn and Harvard, Wolfgang Stolper, has documented, Schumpeter's 'idea of a multi-cycle scheme can be traced back at least to 1928' (Stolper, 1994: 63). In *Business Cycles* Schumpeter (1939) still emphasizes 'that there is a theoretically indefinite number of fluctuations present in our material at any time' (ibid.: 168) and that '[t]here are no particular virtues in the choice made of just three classes of cycles. Five would perhaps be better, although, after some experimenting, the writer came to the conclusion that the improvement in the picture would not warrant the increase in cumbersomeness' (ibid.: 169). For some time Schumpeter had tried hard to construct a five-cycle schema (see Stolper, 1982b), or at least a four-cycle schema including also the Kuznets cycle (Table 11.1). Schumpeter was one of the first business-cycle theorists who took notice of Kuznets's (1930) empirical observation for the US economy that there are long-rung fluctuations with intervals of 18–25 years associated with construction investment, with expansionary phases significantly longer than contraction phases. In a letter from California to his colleague Arthur Spiethoff, in Bonn, dated 8 January 1931, he reflected the possibility that besides the long waves, the Juglar and the shorter cycles there may also exist the Kuznets cycles, an idea he further elaborated in a lecture on 'The theory of the business cycle' given at the University of Tokyo at the end of the same month (Schumpeter, 1931).

Whereas there can be no doubt concerning the simultaneous presence of cyclical fluctuations of different order, it is more for pragmatic reasons that Schumpeter in his detailed discussion of the multiplicity of cycles focused on the three-cycle schema with the superposition of Kondratieff, Juglar and Kitchin cycles 'as a convenient descriptive device' (Schumpeter, 1939: 170). However, he also wanted to have 'the families of long, medium, and short cycles', or what Kondratieff already in 1925 had called 'major, middle, and minor cycles' (see Kondratieff, 1925: 581), represented. Thus the decision for a three-cycle schema is not an arbitrary one, although Schumpeter never held the view 'that there are just those three and no other cycles of this kind'.[11]

The jerky character of economic evolution can hardly be denied and it is one of Schumpeter's great merits to emphasize the importance of integrating the study of business cycles with an analysis of long-run economic development which does not follow a steady-state or balanced growth path. Innovations are not only the decisive impulse of cyclical fluctuations but the period of their implementation also determines the different length of the cycles. With some qualification with regard to the Kitchin cycle the simultaneous presence of cycles of different order for Schumpeter 'is a problem of interference only and not . . . *a problem of different causation*' (Schumpeter, 1939: 172, my italics).

Schumpeter's mono-causality argument is at odds with the later understanding of economic theory that the cycles of different duration are related to different types of investment goods as the causal factor, that is, that we have to distinguish between fluctuations in inventories (Kitchin), fluctuations in fixed capital investment (Juglar or Marx's echo effect), fluctuations in construction investment (Kuznets) and fluctuations in basic capital goods as the medium for basic innovations (Kondratieff).[12] Although Schumpeter was willing to consider and integrate the most

Table 11.1 Business and growth cycles

Name	Kitchin cycle	Juglar cycle	Kuznets cycle	Kondratieff cycle
Type	Business cycle	Business cycle		Growth cycle Long waves
Length	3–5 years	7–11 years	18–25 years	45–60 years
Causal factor	Fluctuations in inventories	Fluctuations in fixed capital investments	Fluctuations in construction investments	Fluctuations in basic innovations and/or basic capital goods

recent and important developments in economic theory, he clearly did not want to change his early vision laid down in his theory of economic development.

In contrast, 'Schumpeter does *not* associate each cycle with a specific reason' (Stolper, 1994: 65; original emphasis). For him the cyclical process of development or evolution gives rise to multiple wave-like movements, and it is innovations which are at the root of cyclical fluctuations. These innovations can be major or important ones causing Kondratieff's long waves, or of medium or minor size leading to, respectively, Juglar or Kitchin cycles. It is characteristic for Schumpeter that he aims for a reconciliation of historical specificity or uniqueness with theoretical regularity. Theory for him is a vehicle to organize the great masses and variety of statistical and historical facts. Whereas innovations of different size or time spans give rise to a multiplicity of cycles, economic history very often is characterized by a sequence of cycles which are not fully independent of each other. 'Major innovations hardly ever emerge in their final form or cover in one throw the whole field that will ultimately be their own' (Schumpeter, 1939: 167). Thus railroadization, electrification, motorization, or we may add computerization, are carried out in steps or sequences. Innovations also tend to cluster. The Industrial Revolution, according to Schumpeter 'consisted of a cluster of cycles of various span that were superimposed on each other' (ibid.: 168). Although Kondratieff's long waves cannot be linked to any particular type of innovations, there is a critical mass of important innovations or basic innovations giving rise to the creation of entirely new industries (Mensch, 1975) which constitute the hitherto five Kondratieff cycles (Table 11.2) of which Schumpeter (1939) discussed the first three in great details.[13]

Table 11.2 Long waves of economic cycles

Long waves	Important innovations	Prosperity	Recession	Depression	Recovery
1.	Industrial Revolution (division of labour, steam engine)	1782–1802	1802–25	1825–36	1836–45
2.	Railroads, steel mechanization	1845–66	1866–72	1872–83	1883–92
3.	Electricity, automobiles, chemical industry	1892–1913	1914–29	1929–37	1938–48
4.	Atomic energy, computer, robots, electronics	1948–66	1966–73	1973–82	1982–95
5.	Information and communication technologies, biotechnologies	1995–			

11.6 CONCLUDING REMARKS: SCHUMPETER'S INFLUENCE ON DEVELOPMENT ECONOMICS

Development economics, which evolved predominantly in Great Britain and in the USA at the United Nations and its ancillary organizations after the war, is among those areas where the contributions made by German-speaking émigré economists are most significant (see Hagemann, 2007: 340–48). It is no accident that among the pioneers in development economics we find leading students of Schumpeter, such as Wolfgang F. Stolper and Hans W. Singer who were already educated by the master on his *Theory of Economic Development* at the University of Bonn before Schumpeter's move to Harvard in 1932. Stolper (1912–2002) who wrote his PhD with Schumpeter at Harvard in 1938 later spent many years as an economic adviser in Africa as, for example, chief of the planning department of the ministry of economic development in Nigeria 1960–62, and became Director of the Center for Research on Economic Development at the University of Michigan at Ann Arbor from 1963 to 1970.

Hans Singer (1919–2006) who got his name as a development economist with his famous study on the long-run relative decline of the prices for primary products compared with the prices of manufacturing goods, thus discriminating against developing countries (Singer, 1950), which gave way to the Prebisch-Singer hypothesis, time and again emphasized the intellectual stimulus he had received by Schumpeter and Keynes in his formative years. Singer had started his doctoral thesis on Kondratieff cycles at the University of Bonn with Schumpeter as his supervisor in 1931 just after the latter had become fascinated with long waves and entered into the conceptualization of a scheme of long-run capitalist development superposing various cycles. After Schumpeter's move to Harvard, Singer became research assistant of Arthur Spiethoff in summer 1932 before, only some months later, he had to emigrate from Nazi Germany. After a short period in Turkey, Singer came to Cambridge in 1934 where he finally finished his PhD in 1936. With his two 'heroes', Schumpeter who influenced him in his German period, and Keynes who influenced him during his Cambridge period, Singer is unique. During the Cambridge period the unemployment problems of the depression years and Keynes's attack on classical economics were engraved on the young Singer. As Hirschman (1981) has emphasized, Keynes had a strong indirect influence on development economics in its formative period by overcoming orthodox mono-economics and by his analysis of unemployment, which provided the basis for Joan Robinson's conceptualization of 'disguised unemployment' (Robinson, 1936). The overcoming of neoclassical mono-economics paved the way for the incorporation of historical and institutional aspects or elements of

Schumpeter's 'economic sociology'.[14] Thus Singer time and again has emphasized that there can be no blueprint for development that is suitable and proper for all backward economies.

Emphasis on the mass phenomenon of hidden unemployment as a crucial characteristic of underdevelopment was a common theme in the pioneering contributions to the new subdiscipline of development economics by Rosenstein-Rodan, Mandelbaum and Nurkse up to the most elaborated version in Arthur Lewis's famous article 'Economic development with unlimited supplies of labour' (Lewis, 1954). As Shaw (2002) has shown 'Singer has remained a strong and persistent advocate of Keynesianism and its relevance for understanding the problems of developing countries' (Shaw, 2002: 270).[15]

On the other hand, Singer did not become tired to emphasize how much his work as a development economist has got stimulus from Schumpeter and his early opus magnum *The Theory of Economic Development* as probably comes out best in the following statement:

> I realise now more clearly than in earlier years how deeply relevant many of its [*TED*] themes are to the development of poor countries and the problems of underdeveloped countries. I would single out two key themes: first, the great importance of technology, innovation, access to innovation and ability and the means of linking innovation with the production process in the form of new products or new processes or the development of new markets. Secondly, there is the emphasis placed on the fact that development represents a disruption of familiar and traditional processes of stationary circulation, arousing resistances and hurting established interests. How modern and up-to-date does this approach to development sound: 'By development we shall understand only such changes in economic life as are not forced upon it from without but arise by its own initiative, from within.' Shades of self-reliance, self-sustaining growth, dependency, backwash effects and all that! It took me many years of work in development studies before I came back to the full implications of this definition. These two great themes of Schumpeter's *Theory of Economic Development* now seem to me the key to the problems of development in poor countries. (Singer, 1997: 131)

There can be no doubt that Schumpeter's *Theory of Economic Development* definitely was not intended to apply to underdeveloped countries but to the most advanced capitalist economies whose long-run development is characterized by wave-like movements. It may also be said that a development economist could find in Schumpeter's theory more inspiration in looking for obstacles to economic development which have been responsible for economic backwardness than for a blueprint for development. Thus underdeveloped countries are characterized by a lack of pioneering entrepreneurs as agents of economic development or by a framework not comprising the social capabilities necessary for a successful catching-up process, including institutional factors such as the rule of law or a modern infrastructure, which gave room to (non-Schumpeterian) economic or investment planning by the government in many countries. Underdeveloped countries can also reduce their economic backwardness by technology transfer, that is, the import of already existing techniques from the more advanced economies. Whereas in Schumpeter's theory of economic development there is more emphasis on the supply side including the development of new products, the growth process in developing countries very often has been more demand-driven in the desire for increased consumption. Finally, underdeveloped economies typically lack a financial system generating credit to finance innovative investment activities.

It can be stated that thanks to his two mentors, Schumpeter and Keynes, Singer was intellectually prepared for the insight that different rules of the game apply to developing countries. Schumpeter made him aware of the problems of long-run development and the role of innovations. In some sense Singer's analysis of the distribution of gains between investing and borrowing countries with its emphasis on the deterioration of the terms of trade for most developing countries can be interpreted as a negative analogy to the temporary monopoly profits reaped by pioneering entrepreneurs. Most important, however, would be a modern revival, elaboration and adaptation of basic ideas in the 'lost seventh chapter' of Schumpeter's *Theory of Economic Development* which gives room to non-economic factors such as politics, law, history or religion. There is a mutual interdependence. Economic development and technological progress cause societal changes of a non-economic nature, but these other factors also influence the innovation system and thereby economic development.

NOTES

1. See Schumpeter's Introduction to the fourth German edition published in 1934.
2. See, for example, Schumpeter (1934: 65).
3. For a full English text of the seventh chapter of the original 1911 edition see the translation by Ursula Backhaus in J. Backhaus (2003: 61–116).
4. On the importance of economic sociology and an assessment of its role in Schumpeter's analysis see the writings of Shionoya as, for example, the essays collected in Shionoya (2005).
5. See also Karl Popper (1961).
6. Schumpeter (2000: 267).
7. For insightful analyses of Schumpeter's theory of innovation see Stolper (1982a) and Tichy (1984).
8. See Schumpeter's early article 'On the nature of economic crises' (Schumpeter, 1910 [2005]), and the analysis in Hagemann (2003).
9. See, for example, Holwegler (2003).

10. Juglar was credited by Schumpeter as the founder of modern business-cycle theory and praised as one of 'the greatest economists of all times' (Schumpeter, 1954: 1123). For a comparison of Juglar's explanation of cyclical fluctuations with Schumpeter's analysis see Dal-Pont Legrand and Hagemann (2007).
11. Letter to Wesley C. Mitchell, 6 May 1937. See Schumpeter (2000: 303).
12. See, for example, van Duijn (1983: ch. 1).
13. For a modern analysis of the five long waves from the Industrial Revolutions to the Information Revolution in a Schumpeterian spirit see Freeman and Louçã (2001).
14. Nevertheless Schumpeter's response to Singer when the latter visited him at Harvard in 1947 and informed his former teacher about his work as a development economist at the United Nations which he had taken up shortly before was typical for Schumpeter as were his contradictory statements in 1926: 'But I thought you were an economist – isn't this more a matter for anthropologists, sociologists, geographers, etc.?' (see Shaw, 2002: 43).
15. For a qualification of Singer's own emphasis of his discipleship of both Schumpeter and Keynes see the recent paper by Toye (2006) who alternatively stresses Singer's personal debts to both Schumpeter and Keynes for rescuing him and his academic career from Nazi persecution.

REFERENCES

Backhaus, J. (ed.) (2003), *Joseph Alois Schumpeter. Entrepreneurship, Style and Vision*, Boston, MA/Dordrecht/London: Kluwer Academic.

Clemence, R.V. (1951), *Essays of Joseph A. Schumpeter on Entrepreneurs, Innovations, Business Cycles, and the Evolution of Capitalism*, Cambridge, MA: Addison-Wesley Press; with a new introduction by R. Swedberg, New Brunswick, NJ and Oxford, 1989.

Dal-Pont Legrand, M. and H. Hagemann (2007), 'Business cycles in Juglar and Schumpeter', *The History of Economic Thought*, **49** (1), 1–18.

Duijn, J. van (1983), *Long Waves in Economic Life*, London: George Allen & Unwin.

Freeman, C. and F. Louçã (2001), *As Time Goes By. From the Industrial Revolutions to the Information Revolution*, Oxford and New York: Oxford University Press.

Hagemann, H. (2003), 'Schumpeter's early contributions on crises theory and business-cycle theory', *History of Economic Ideas*, **11**, 47–67.

Hagemann, H. (2007), 'German-speaking economists in British exile 1933–1945', *Banca Nazionale del Lavoro Quarterly Review*, **60** (242), 323–63.

Hahn, A. (1920), *Volkswirtschaftliche Theorie des Bankkredits* (*Economic Theory of Bank Credit)*, Tübingen: J.C.B, Mohr, 2nd edn 1924, 3rd edn 1930.

Hirschman, A.O. (1981), 'The rise and decline of development economics', in A.O. Hirschman, *Essays in Trespassing. Economics to Politics and Beyond*, Cambridge: Cambridge University Press, pp. 1–24.

Holwegler, B. (2003), *Innovation, Diffusion und Beschäftigung*, Frankfurt am Main: Peter Lang.

Kondratieff, N. (1925), 'The static and the dynamic view of economics', *The Quarterly Journal of Economics*, **39**, 575–83.

Kondratieff, N. (1926), 'Die langen Wellen der Konjunktur', *Archiv für Sozialwissenschaft und Sozialpolitik*, **56**, 573–609; shortened English translation, N. Kondratieff (1935), 'The long waves in economic Life', *Review of Economics Statistics*, **17**, 105–15.

Kuznets, S. (1930), *Secular Movements in Production and Prices. Their Nature and Their Bearing upon Cyclical Fluctuations*, Boston, MA: Houghton Mifflin.

Lewis, W.A. (1954), 'Economic development with unlimited supplies of labour', *Manchester School of Economic and Social Studies*, **22** (2), 139–91.

Mensch, G. (1975), *Das technologische Patt, Innovationen überwinden die Depression*. Frankfurt am Main: Umschau Verlag.

Popper, K. (1961), 'Evolution and the tree of knowledge', Herbert Spencer Lecture, Oxford, 30 October.

Robinson, J. (1936), 'Disguised unemployment', *Economic Journal*, **46** (182), 225–37.

Schumpeter, J.A. (1908), *Das Wesen und der Hauptinhalt der theoretischen Nationalökonomie*, Leipzig: Duncker & Humblot.

Schumpeter, J.A. (1910), 'Über das Wesen der Wirtschaftskrisen', *Zeitschrift für Volkswirtschaft, Sozialpolitik und Verwaltung*, **19**, 271–325; English translation, 2005, 'On the nature of economic crises', in M. Boianovsky (ed.), *Business Cycle Theory. Selected Texts 1860–1939. Vol. V: Economic Growth, Technical Change and Business Cycles*, London: Pickering & Chatto, pp. 3–50.

Schumpeter, J.A. (1911), *Theorie der wirtschaftlichen Entwicklung*, Munich and Leipzig: Duncker & Humblot; reprint edited and introduced by J. Röpke and O. Stiller, Berlin 2006: Duncker & Humblot; 2nd edn 1926.

Schumpeter, J.A. (1914–15), 'Die Wellenbewegung des Wirtschaftslebens', *Archiv für Sozialwissenschaft und Sozialpolitik*, **39**, 1–32.

Schumpeter, J.A. (1926), 'Gustav v. Schmoller und die Probleme von heute', *Schmollers Jahrbuch für Gesetzgebung, Verwaltung und Volkswirtschaft*, **50**, 337–88.

Schumpeter, J.A. (1931), 'The theory of the business cycle', *Keizaigaku Ronshu – The Journal of Economics*, **4**, 1–18.

Schumpeter, J.A. (1932), 'Soziale und wirtschaftliche Entwicklung', lecture to the social-philosophical workshop, 28 April, University of Bonn, typewritten. Lecture notes by W.F. Stolper.

Schumpeter, J.A. (1934), *The Theory of Economic Development. An Inquiry into Profits, Capital, Credit, Interest, and the Business Cycle*, Cambridge, MA: Harvard University Press.

Schumpeter, J.A. (1939), *Business Cycles. A Theoretical, Historical and Statistical Analysis of the Capitalist Process*, 2 vols, New York: McGraw-Hill.

Schumpeter, J.A. (1942), *Capitalism, Socialism, and Democracy*, New York: Harper Brothers; 1943, London: Allen & Unwin.

Schumpeter, J.A. (1954), *History of Economic Analysis*, London: Allen & Unwin.

Schumpeter, J.A. (2000), *Briefe/Letters*, selected and edited by U. Hedtke and R. Swedberg, Tübingen: Mohr Siebeck.

Schumpeter, J.A. (1932 [2005]), 'Development', with an introduction by M.C. Becker, H.U. Esslinger, U. Hedtke and T. Knudsen, *Journal of Economic Literature*, **43** (1), 108–20.

Shaw, D.J. (2002), *Sir Hans Singer. The Life and Work of a Development Economist*, Houndmills and New York: Palgrave Macmillan.

Shionoya, Y. (1997), *Schumpeter and the Idea of Social Science: A Metatheoretical Study*, Cambridge: Cambridge University Press.

Shionoya, Y. (2000), 'Joseph Schumpeter and the German historical school', in P. Koslowski (ed.), *The Theory of Capitalism in the German Economic Tradition, Histrorism, Ordo-Liberalism, Critical Theory, Solidarism*, Berlin and Heidelberg: Springer, pp. 3–23.

Shionoya, Y. (2005), *The Soul of the German Historical School. Methodological Essays on Schmoller, Weber and Schumpeter*, New York: Springer.

Singer, H.W. (1950), 'The distribution of gains between investing and borrowing countries', *American Economic Review*, **40** (2), 473–85.
Singer, H.W. (1997), 'The influence of Schumpeter and Keynes on the development of a development economist', in H. Hagemann (ed.), *Zur deutschsprachigen wirtschaftswissenschaftlichen Emigration nach 1933*, Marburg: Metropolis, pp. 127–50.
Stolper, W.F. (1982a), 'Schumpeters Theorie der Innovation', *Ifo-Studien*, **28**, 239–70.
Stolper, W.F. (1982b), 'Aspects of Schumpeter's theory of evolution', in H. Frisch (ed.), *Schumpeterian Economics*, Eastbourne and New York: Praeger Special Studies, pp. 28–48.
Stolper, W.F. (1994), *Joseph Alois Schumpeter. The Public Life of a Private Man*, Princeton, NJ: Princeton University Press.
Streissler, E. (1982), 'Schumpeter's Vienna and the role of credit in innovation', in H. Frisch (ed.), *Schumpeterian Economics*, Eastbourne and New York: Praeger Special Studies, pp. 60–83.
Streissler, E. (1994), 'The influence of German and Austrian economics on Joseph A. Schumpeter', in Y. Shionoya and M. Perlman (eds.), *Schumpeter in the History of Ideas*, Ann Arbor, MI: University of Michigan Press, pp. 13–40.
Tichy, G. (1984), 'Schumpeter's business cycle theory. Its importance for our time', in C. Seidl (ed.), *Lectures on Schumpeterian Economics. Schumpeter Centenary Memorial Lectures Graz* 1983, Berlin: Springer, pp. 77–88.
Toye, J. (2006), 'Hans Singer's debts to Schumpeter and Keynes', *Cambridge Journal of Economics*, **30**, 819–33.

12. Frictions in Schumpeter's theory of unemployment

Mauro Boianovsky and Hans-Michael Trautwein

12.1 INTRODUCTION

Joseph Alois Schumpeter (1883–1950) is world renowned for various innovations that he introduced to economic thinking, such as the concept of innovation itself and the notion of economic development as an evolutionary process of creative destruction. He is less well known for his views on unemployment. This may largely be due to the fact that unemployment was not a prominent theme in his writings. Throughout his long career, Schumpeter dedicated only one article (1927) and one section in *Business Cycles* (1939) to a systematic discussion of unemployment. His other comments on the issue are brief and scattered over a wide range of publications from more than four decades.[1]

Furthermore, Schumpeter presented his views on unemployment in a fashion that seemed to downplay its relevance. In his *Theory of Economic Development* (1911; 1934) and elsewhere, he considered unemployment to be a *frictional* phenomenon that occurs *temporarily*, when production factors are reallocated from contracting to expanding units during the cyclical process of creative destruction. Expounding his 'liquidationist' conviction, according to which depressions should be understood as cures of previous maladjustments to technological and economic change, Schumpeter argued that cyclical unemployment and other 'recurrent troubles of the capitalist society . . . are the means to reconstruct each time the economic system on a more efficient plan' (1934 [1951]: 113). With regard to the debates about the employment effects of technical progress, which had started with Ricardo's (1821 [1951]) chapter 'On machinery', Schumpeter declared that '[t]he controversy that went on throughout the nineteenth century and beyond, mainly in the form of argument pro and con "compensation", is dead and buried' (1954: 684). Throughout his academic life, he argued nevertheless *pro* compensation and rejected any notion of an upward trend of technological unemployment.

All this does not seem to warrant any closer look at Schumpeter's writings on unemployment. However, a different picture emerges if those writings are seen in synopsis and in relation to his theory of economic development. In the following we argue that Schumpeter employed a wide notion of frictions which enabled him to explain both cyclical unemployment and persistent technological unemployment as different effects of the same cause. In Schumpeter's view, frictions are an integral part of the process of creative destruction, partly endogenous to the latter. This differs from the contemporaneous literature where frictions were seen as exogenous obstacles to instantaneous and smooth adjustments to changes in supply or demand. In the tradition of Beveridge (1909) and Hicks (1932 [1963]), frictional unemployment was generally associated with transitory spells of disequilibrium or regarded as a dysfunctional part of equilibrium unemployment, in the sense of a deviation from the hypothetical results of perfect competition. Schumpeter integrated both cases into his concepts of temporary and normal unemployment, connecting the latter through the subcategory of 'vicarious unemployment' with his theory of economic development.

Schumpeter's frictional explanation of technological unemployment contrasts, on the other hand, with the contemporaneous literature on the employment effects of technical progress, which was largely influenced by the Marxian prediction of a growing 'industrial reserve army'. As mentioned before, Schumpeter rejected that hypothesis, but his theory of economic development did not per se exclude negative long-term effects of technological change on wage income and employment. In his attempt to reach beyond the confines of the debate on Ricardo's machinery problem, Schumpeter actually made use of Hicks's marginalist analysis in the latter's *Theory of Wages* (1932 [1963]). By its Wicksellian origins Hicks's approach was open to the possibility that labour-saving technical progress under full competition makes wages fall to the extent that full employment would imply a marginal productivity of labour that depresses wage incomes permanently below the existence minimum. Wage earners would then either have to receive transfers from other sources of income or a part of them would remain permanently unemployed.

In our chapter we describe how the aspects of frictions, technical progress and creative destruction are internally connected in Schumpeter's views on cyclical and structural unemployment, and how they are related to other types of unemployment. In section 12.2 we outline Schumpeter's discussion of unemployment in the context of his theory of economic development. Section 12.3 summarizes his main writings on unemployment. In section 12.4 we compare Schumpeter's notion of frictions with those of Beveridge (1909) and Hicks (1932 [1963]). In section 12.5 we consider the parallels and differences between Schumpeter's view on technological unemployment with the contemporaneous contributions of Lederer (1931a; 1938) and Neisser (1932; 1936; 1942). In the conclusion, we argue that Schumpeter's frictional notion of unemployment, even though only sketchily developed in scattered writings, was fully consistent with his theory of economic development and rich in structure.

12.2 UNEMPLOYMENT IN THE *THEORY OF ECONOMIC DEVELOPMENT*

Schumpeter's most famous work is without doubt *The Theory of Economic Development*, which appeared in two German editions in 1911 and 1926, and in English translation in 1934. In both editions, unemployment was discussed only in the last parts of the final chapter. While chapter 7 of the 1911 version contained a discourse on displacement and compensation effects in terms of Ricardo's machinery problem, that chapter was eliminated in the 1926 edition. The discussion of unemployment was now relegated to the last sections in the sixth (and now final) chapter which contained Schumpeter's theory of the trade cycle. In the following, we summarize Schumpeter's 1926 discussion of cyclical and technological unemployment, and add relevant passages from chapter 7 of the 1911 edition, which has become known as 'the lost chapter' (Shionoya, 1997) in the literature and was translated only in 2002.

In chapter 6, section 5 of *The Theory of Economic Development* (1934: 241–51), Schumpeter continues the analysis of the 'phenomena of the process of normal depressions', which he had begun in the preceding section. The section is centred on two propositions. First, depressions are to be understood as processes of adjustment to the disturbances that were caused by the swarms of innovations in the upswing. They are phases of destruction of old and obsolete combinations of production factors, and of their reabsorption into new combinations. Schumpeter argues that (normal) depressions return the system to an equilibrium position that differs positively (in terms of output) from the original one. Second, 'apart from the digestion of innovations', the depression 'fulfils what the boom promised. And this effect is lasting, while the phenomena felt to be unpleasant are temporary' (ibid.: 245). While bankruptcies, unemployment and other reductions of economic activity tend to go over with the depression, the lasting effect of creative destruction[2] is that the 'stream of goods is enriched, production is partly reorganised, costs of production are diminished, and what at first appears as entrepreneurial profit finally increases the permanent real incomes of the other classes' (ibid.: 245).

At this point, Schumpeter begins to examine the changes in the real wage in the course of the business cycle (ibid.: 248–51). He states that money wages rise in the upswing, owing to increased demand for labour. However, real wages do not rise as much, since the additional demand for consumer goods induces a price rise, in particular as it is competing with the entrepreneurs' additional resource demand for the production of capital goods that is financed by an expansion of bank credit. The depression comes with a 'self-deflation' of the system which increases the purchasing power of the nominal wage rate. This tends to contribute to a rise in workers' real income in the long run. Contrary to that tendency, however, a number of circumstances of the depression will temporarily lower workers' income. This is where, finally, unemployment comes into the picture. Schumpeter points out that the depression leads to unemployment, whose essentially temporary character does not prevent it from being a disaster for those who are affected. Furthermore, it contributes to the depressive mood of this phase of the business cycle, owing to the existential uncertainty that a rise in unemployment brings even for those who still have a job. The sheer fear of unemployment may lead to a pressure on wages that is greater than one would actually think in view of the observed changes in unemployment.

In the following paragraphs Schumpeter shifts the attention from temporary unemployment to the possibility of permanent technological unemployment. He argues that the displacement effect of technical progress, which makes itself felt during the depression, will often be overcompensated by the demands for labour to operate the new plants. But this need not be the case, and the usual difficulties of adjustment can, at any rate, be aggravated by the imperfect functioning of the labour market. Furthermore, it must be taken into account that the additional labour demand for the construction of new machinery will cease when the process is completed. The increasing mechanization of the production process may, moreover, reduce the total demand for labour. Nevertheless, implicitly invoking Say's law Schumpeter argues that 'the expenditure of that part of entrepreneurial profit which is not annihilated by the fall in prices necessarily more than prevents any lasting shrinkage' (ibid.: 251). He points out that economic development leads to a permanent reduction in the 'real demand for labour' *only if* 'in the new combinations it shifts the relative marginal significance of labour and land which obtained in the old productive combinations sufficiently to the disadvantage of labour' (ibid.: 251).[3] Schumpeter does not draw the conclusion that the fall in labour's relative significance will lead to a permanent increase in unemployment. According to him, it may cause a fall in the wage share, or even the absolute amount of aggregate (real) labour income, but normally it will produce only a 'shift in the demand in favor of produced means of production already in existence' (ibid.: 251).

The very last section of Schumpeter's *Theory of Economic Development* (1934: ch. 6, s. 6) deals with the case of an *abnormal* depression, characterized by the outbreak of a crisis. Unemployment is not an issue, other than as an implicit part of the general policy conclusion. Schumpeter suggests that, while normal depressions should run their course in order to increase the efficiency of the economy, abnormal depressions should be prevented by selective credit policies that mitigate the 'useless and dysfunctional losses and destruction' which hit those hardest 'who have nothing to do with the causation and the function of the cycle, especially the workers' (ibid.: 253). He emphasizes that the distinction between normal and abnormal depressions is important, because abnormal depressions lead to abnormally low equilibria, with path dependence of the further development: 'What has been mistaken and annihilated, cannot in general be corrected and recovered, and creates situations that in their turn have further consequences, must be coped with, imply new disturbances and require particular, otherwise redundant activities of adjustment' (ibid.: 252). However, Schumpeter does not mention the possibility that cyclical unemployment becomes permanent in the wake of an abnormal depression.

How far does Schumpeter's original treatment of unemployment in the 1911 edition of the *Theory of Economic Development* differ from the 1926 edition? As mentioned above, Schumpeter (1911 [2002]: 117–20) approaches the issue of unemployment in the framework of the machinery problem. He stresses that the employment effects of the introduction of labour-saving methods are determined by the elasticities of supply and demand for the goods produced in the industry in question. If there is sufficient demand for the goods, labour-saving methods lead to an expansion in production, not to a reduction in demand for labour. If the demand for goods is not sufficiently elastic, there will be a price effect – and here Schumpeter implicitly invokes the law of free goods by remarking that

> workers who lose their position due to the introduction of machines could not remain permanently unemployed. After all, there is no market where it can happen that a part of the supply of a good does not find its relevant demand, while the rest is being sold for the usual price. The freed workers would push towards bringing the wage down, but would have to find employment at the lower wage. (Ibid.: 119–20)

Consistent with this argument, Schumpeter had pointed out a few lines earlier that the decline of wages would present a 'counterweight' to the pressures on labour and an 'effective break' in the decline of demand for labour.[4]

While Schumpeter in the 1926 edition starts with cyclical unemployment before turning to technological unemployment, the discussion in the original version follows the reversed order. After rejecting the view that technical progress leads to increasing and permanent unemployment, Schumpeter (1911 [2002]: 120) mentions cyclical unemployment, which occurs 'in the normal process of liquidation and reorganization' in the depression. 'It is often very serious. It is in practice much more important than' the cases discussed in the context of the machinery problem, '[y]et no one doubts the temporary character of this kind of unemployment.'

All this leads to the conclusion that technical progress causes business cycles through swarms of innovations and subsequent elimination of obsolete production processes, which results in unemployment, because the reabsorption of displaced labour does not occur without frictions:

> The cause which leads to practically very striking unemployment is, essentially and in principle, temporary. Therefore, we can only explain transitory unemployment – and mainly as frictional phenomenon – but not other kinds of unemployment. This result is not sufficient, but it is not without value. It doubtlessly explains a good deal of the phenomenon of unemployment, in my opinion its better half. (Ibid.: 120)

Two things are striking about Schumpeter's differing approaches in the 1911 and 1926 editions of the *Theory of Economic Development.* While Schumpeter (1911) frames his discussion of unemployment in terms of the machinery problem, he makes use of marginalist analysis (even though incomplete) to assess the arguments *pro* compensation. Much later, in his *History of Economic Analysis* (1954: 684), he comes to praise the marginalist analysis in Hicks's *Theory of Wages* (1932 [1963]), which was based on Wicksell (1901), as far superior to the classical arguments about compensation. In between, Schumpeter (1926) is less observant of the marginalist approach, making use of such traditional arguments as Say's law. The 1926 edition is, on the other hand, more advanced with regard to the connection between cyclical unemployment and technological change, which is described in terms of cyclical growth. In the 1911 edition, Schumpeter merely hints at that connection, stating that his theory of economic development explains only a part of the observable unemployment. After the 1926 edition he makes further attempts to connect other kinds of unemployment with his theory of economic development and his notion of frictions. We turn to these attempts in the following section.

12.3 UNEMPLOYMENT CLASSIFIED

Among Schumpeter's many writings, two stand out for their attempts to classify and explain different kinds of unemployment. The first is a short article on unemployment, published in the 1926/27 volume of *Der deutsche Volkswirt*, a journal edited by Schumpeter's friend Gustav Stolper. The second is section D of chapter 9 in the voluminous work on *Business Cycles* (Schumpeter, 1939: 511–17).

Schumpeter's German article was written in March 1927, in reaction to a controversy about Gustav Cassel's campaign for wage cuts as the sole therapy to reduce German unemployment.[5] Cassel (1926) had argued that mechanization and other technical progress generates unemployment only if there are frictions, and even so it would be just temporary. Permanent unemployment could not emerge unless there is a lack of 'economic mobility', which must be explained by the 'monopolistic policy of the trade unions' and/or by the existence of unemployment benefits. Cassel's argument was based on Say's law, the idea that – in a system of free competition – general overproduction is impossible. Schumpeter (1927 [1985]: 155) agrees with Cassel in so far as he deems Say's law, 'if understood properly' to be 'irrefutable'. Yet he criticizes Cassel for making the naive assumption that *goods markets* are generally characterized by free competition.

According to Schumpeter, the persistence of high unemployment in Germany in the mid-1920s follows from 'monopoloid price and sales policies' that transform the temporary effects of labour-saving 'rationalization' of production processes into permanent unemployment. This does not, however, warrant the conclusion that anti-trust legislation and regulation would solve the problem. Schumpeter (1927 [1985]: 159) points out that 'cartels, trusts and conglomerates have become indispensable for the diffusion of technical progress that reaches beyond the framework of the single enterprise. Their elimination would lead to technical and commercial setbacks in many aspects'. Even though technical progress as such would cause only temporary unemployment, the evolution of 'quasi-monopolistic' market structures that come along with it could turn technological unemployment, at least partly, into permanent unemployment. In strong contrast with Cassel, Schumpeter (1927 [1985]: 159–60) concludes that 'if the monopoloid price and sales policies are the true cause of persistent unemployment, while we cannot abstain from the monopoloid forms of organization, the support of the unemployed is just as indispensable an element of our economic order as unemployment itself'.

In his comprehensive examination of the theory, history and statistics of *Business Cycles*, Schumpeter (1939: 511–17) approaches the phenomenon of unemployment from an empirical angle. While his 1927 article may suggest an upward trend of unemployment, owing to the endogenous emergence and increasing dominance of 'cartels, trusts and conglomerates', his 1939 book (ch. 9, s. D) puts forward the proposition that long-term unemployment is stationary, that is, it is not following any upward trend (ibid.: 516). Schumpeter's single piece of evidence is the English trade union percentage of unemployed members in the 60 years prior to 1914 (ibid.: 512, chart XX). Yet he repeats the claim of stationarity in his famous book, *Capitalism, Socialism and Democracy* (1942 [1952]: 69), where he sets the focus on the 'trustification' of the capitalist economy after the First World War. In a later essay on 'Capitalism' he asserts that there is evidence for stationarity in the same series until 1929, the start of the Great Depression (1946 [1951]: 200). We return to this issue in section 12.5.

A noteworthy feature of the 1939 book is the taxonomy that Schumpeter develops in order to analyse the variety of factors that affect the unemployment time series. He classifies unemployment in terms of two groups. The first group comprises all 'normal unemployment', 'the unemployment that would at any point exist if the system had already reached the neighborhood of equilibrium toward which it is tending' (Schumpeter, 1939: 511). The second group consists of those types of unemployment that are characteristic of economic fluctuations in disequilibrium.

The phenomena that should be considered as part of *normal* unemployment are, according to Schumpeter, the following: seasonal unemployment, individual unemployability, changes of residence, occupation or job, 'imperfections of competition or of equilibrium' and exogenous disturbances. While the first three categories correspond to standard definitions of equilibrium unemployment, Schumpeter's characterization of the last two as normal unemployment may warrant some further explanation. 'Imperfections of competition or of equilibrium' lead in certain cases to 'vicarious unemployment', which is Schumpeter's term for the unemployment that 'takes the place of adaptation of wages' to normal unemployment under perfectly competitive conditions (ibid.: 513). Under imperfect competition, vicarious unemployment could result from the power of trade unions that, fully rationally, try to maximize the workers' share of income by resisting a decline in wage rates and choosing to compensate the unemployed by way of internal transfers instead (ibid.: 515). Vicarious unemployment could also arise under perfect competition, if the state intervenes to keep wage rates above their equilibrium levels, thereby producing an 'imperfection of equilibrium' (ibid.: 513). Another part of normal unemployment is 'disturbance unemployment', caused by disasters, such as big accidents, wars or other events that are taken to be exogenous to the economic system in question.

In Schumpeter's view, vicarious and disturbance unemployment are part of the structure of the economy even when it is in or near its equilibrium position. In other words, subsuming disturbance unemployment under normal unemployment, Schumpeter does *not* consider the disturbances as 'shocks' or impulses that would produce disequilibrium unemployment by their propagation through cyclical oscillations of the system. There is, however, one important exception: 'For the special case of unemployment that develops from a disturbance caused by innovations in the system itself we will form a separate group under the notion of technological unemployment' (ibid.: 514). In his 1926 *Theory of Economic Development* (1934: 250) and in the 1927 article, Schumpeter had used the concept to describe only the displacement of workers by machinery. In his *Business Cycles* (1939) he now shifts to a broader notion of technological unemployment. The term comes to comprise all employment effects of labour reallocation that innovations produce in the process of creative destruction.

> Few, if any, economists realize the one major point that the writer wishes to make. They have a habit of distinguishing between, and contrasting, cyclical and technological unemployment. But it follows from our model that, basically, cyclical unemployment *is* technological unemployment. For vicarious and disturbance unemployment are, in the main, but understandable incidents, though quantitatively important in practice, which we could abstract from without thereby blotting out any essential contours. Technological unemployment, however, is of the essence of our process and, linking up as it does with innovation, is cyclical by nature. (Ibid.: 515, emphasis in the original)

Schumpeter's understanding of structural unemployment as normal unemployment (1939: 511) and cyclical unemployment as technological unemployment (quotation above) sets him clearly apart from the contemporaneous literature. It implies two other distinctive features that we will discuss in the following sections. The first is his broad concept of frictional unemployment. The second is his insistence on technological unemployment being essentially a temporary phenomenon, even though it could become permanent under certain conditions.

12.4 FRICTIONAL UNEMPLOYMENT IN BEVERIDGE, HICKS AND SCHUMPETER

The concept of frictions as obstacles to the smooth and instantaneous convergence of market transactions to a state of general equilibrium was apparently first introduced by Vilfredo Pareto (1897 [1964]). Attempting to construct a formal model of the trade cycle, he compared frictions to inertia in mechanics (Boianovsky and Tarascio, 1998). The first economist to apply the notion of frictions to labour markets is William Beveridge, whose

Unemployment: A Problem of Industry (1909) is a standard reference in the early twentieth century, also occurring in Schumpeter's 'lost chapter' (1911 [2002]: 119, n. 20). Observing a 'standing contradiction' between the 'normal condition' of excess supplies of labour, time-consuming job search, on the one hand, and the standard assumptions of perfect information and factor mobility in economic theory, on the other, Beveridge (1909: 70–76, 103) argues that 'the reserve of labour' is explained by 'the degree of friction' in the movement of labour between industries. Yet, contrary to some modern interpretations (for example, Darity, 1982), Beveridge does not consider all unemployment as frictional. He confines the term to the unemployment that is caused by obstacles to the instantaneous and smooth matching of job-searching workers with jobs on offer. Such obstacles exist always, but play a greater role when sectoral fluctuations of output necessitate intersectoral mobility of workers. Even so, Beveridge does not consider them to be the source of cyclical unemployment. Frictions explain the 'irreducible minimum of unemployment' only, not the total figures of observable unemployment (Beveridge, 1907: 68, 72; 1909, chs 4–5). This is the view essentially also followed by Pigou (1913; 1933), Clay (1929) and other British writers on unemployment in the early twentieth century.

Similarly, Hicks in his *Theory of Wages* (1932 [1963]: ch. 3) associates frictions with his concept of 'normal unemployment'. He considers it to be a central task for labour market theory to explain the 'paradox' of the coexistence of unemployment and rising wages (Hicks, 1932 [1963]: 42). To this end he comes up with the concept of normal unemployment, probably as the first writer in the English language area.[6] Normal unemployment in the Hicksian definition comprises all forms that do not involve any effective excess supply in the labour market and, hence, do not create any pressure on wage rates. Apart from predictable seasonal fluctuations in the demand for labour (ibid.: 50), the definition includes the 'unemployables' (whose net product would fall short of subsistence), 'casual labour' and the unemployment created by 'the interval of time that elapses between dismissal and re-engagement', regarded as 'the unemployment which is consistent with constant supply and demand for labour' (ibid.: 45). The last category is frictional unemployment.

In his early writings, Schumpeter (1911: ch. 7) still follows Beveridge's understanding of frictional unemployment as a microeconomic mismatch phenomenon. Over time he moves to the position that most, if not all unemployment is to be considered as frictional. He does not only associate it with a part of normal unemployment, as Hicks (1932 [1963]) does, but applies it to cyclical 'technological unemployment' as well, because the latter results from the failure of the system to adapt to a new equilibrium instantaneously (1934: 238; 1939: 515–16). Schumpeter's use of the word 'frictions' does not refer only to the time required for job search or other phenomena of individual mismatch, but to a large variety of factors that cause lags in the system's convergence to equilibrium. According to Schumpeter (1939: 50), the causes of such lags are

1. the costs incident to change of occupation, or shift from the production of one sort or quality of commodity to another,
2. transaction costs,
3. resistance to price changes,
4. long-term contracts, and
5. the difficulty of 'persuading oneself or other people to act'.

Not only do these frictions slow down the convergence to equilibrium; their presence also implies that the equilibrium that will eventually be reached is not identical with the equilibrium achievable with the identical data-set in a frictionless world.

In Schumpeter's view, 'frictions' become the overarching notion that binds together the different categories of unemployment. He stresses that they are interrelated, and that the rate of normal unemployment is the total rate of unemployment in the neighbourhood of equilibrium, but not an independent component of the total rate to which cyclical unemployment or other components would be added. This contrasts with the segmentations of unemployment into frictional, structural and cyclical parts that are so typical for the literature of Schumpeter's time.

The view that frictions essentially explain all unemployment is also behind Schumpeter's firm rejection of Keynes's allegation that Pigou and the other 'classical economists' knew of no unemployment other than frictional (Keynes, 1936: ch. 2). As Schumpeter points out in his posthumous *History of Economic Analysis* (1954), the criticism is either wrong, given that the pre-Keynesian literature on unemployment did deal with much more than just frictional unemployment, or it is void, if frictional unemployment is defined in broad terms.

> We are free, of course, to define the concept of frictional unemployment so widely as to include technological unemployment and also the other types of unemployment that were recognised – mainly: unemployment from imperfections of competition; unemployment from monetary causes; and unemployment from business fluctuations, whatever their cause – but then the indictment loses its force for, thus defined, friction is no longer an obviously inadequate explanation of the observed facts of unemployment. (Schumpeter, 1954: 944, n. 57, italics in the original – see also pp. 1135 and 1177, n. 12)

Even though Schumpeter (1954) is perfectly right in pointing out that the pre-Keynesian literature on unemployment was rich in explanations, his own wide notion of 'frictional unemployment' clearly contrasts with the general use of that term to describe a short-term phenomenon. He includes technological unemployment, which at the time was predominantly discussed in connection with the long-term trends of economic development and often described as part of 'structural' or 'permanent' unemployment. In the following section we therefore compare his view on technological unemployment with some contemporaneous contributions that were made from similar backgrounds.

12.5 TECHNOLOGICAL UNEMPLOYMENT IN LEDERER, NEISSER AND SCHUMPETER

The links between technical change and unemployment became the subject of intense debates in the late 1920s and early 1930s, especially in the USA and in Germany where waves of industrial 'rationalization' and the Great Depression had contributed to particularly strong increases in the unemployment figures. Here we cannot go into the details of these debates and their backgrounds (see, for example, Gourvitch, 1966; Woirol, 1996: chs 3–5; 2006), but we will briefly compare Schumpeter's views with those of Emil Lederer (1882–1939) and Hans Neisser (1895–1975). The reason for this choice of authors is that they had much in common and yet differed significantly in their views on technological unemployment. Schumpeter and Lederer were fellow students in Vienna in the first years of the twentieth century, with Eugen von Böhm-Bawerk and Friedrich von Wieser among their teachers. Lederer and Neisser worked both for the Socialization Commission in Germany after the end of the First World War. In the 1920s and early 1930s, all three held academic posts at prominent German universities: Schumpeter in Bonn, Lederer in Berlin and Neisser in Kiel. They were all involved in debates about unemployment in the final years of the Weimar Republic. In the 1930s, all of them emigrated to the USA – Schumpeter by invitation from Harvard in 1932, Lederer and Neisser as a consequence of their expulsion by the Nazis in 1933 (see Hagemann, 2000; 2005; Hagemann and Krohn, 1999). Their views on the relationship between the development of capitalist economies and unemployment showed, to varying degrees, some Marxian influence. And they all refined their positions on technological unemployment in English-language publications that they wrote after their emigration to the USA.

Lederer is probably best known for his *Technical Progress and Unemployment* (1938), an International Labour Office (ILO) publication that came out in three languages, based on an earlier monograph in German that he had published in 1931 in order to explain the mass unemployment of the Great Depression. The punch line of both versions is that a considerable part of the observable permanent unemployment, which he calls 'structural', is caused by an overly rapid pace of labour-saving technical progress that, moreover, retards economic growth in comparison with the progress in the reference case of a 'harmoniously growing system' (1938: 9–16). In the first version, Lederer tries to show that unemployment becomes 'structural', whenever technical progress increases capital intensity so fast that the demand for labour declines despite capital accumulation (1931a: 72). In the later version he confines the definition of 'technological unemployment' to the medium-term *net* effects of fast progress, that is, to that part of unemployment which is caused by technical progress, but 'is not counterbalanced within a given period of time by the effects of technical progress or the changes it produces, or by the spontaneous automatic development of the economic system' (1938: 48).

In order to specify the conditions under which technological unemployment emerges, Lederer (1931a; 1938) combines elements of Marx's theory of capital accumulation with Schumpeter's theory of economic development (even though he hardly refers to these two sources in the later version). He uses a cost theory of value, despite having criticized the classical theory of labour value in his *Aufriß der ökonomischen Theorie* (1931b: 170–82) for failing to determine market prices in cases of changes in consumer demand, market segmentation and monopolistic price setting. He is equally critical of marginal productivity theory, because it rests on the implausible assumption that all factors of production are fully employed whenever technical progress sets in, and because he deems it incapable of dealing with rapid technical progress (1938: 6–7, 202). Lederer (1938: chs 4, 5) bases his analysis on a general concept of production costs in a 'harmonious dynamic system' that is reminiscent of Marx's scheme of reproduction on an expanded scale, that is, the steady-state growth path of a two-sectoral economy (cf. Dickler, 1981). However, Lederer's sectoral classification runs not in terms of the production of producer and consumer goods, but in terms of a Schumpeterian distinction between the innovative 'dynamic producers' and 'static producers' (1938: 142). Lederer's static sector consists of various industries with small firms that produce all sorts of goods and grow, on average, at the steady-state rate of the system (that is, in conformity with population growth). The dynamic sector is an industry with large firms that produce capital goods and that tend to have a higher capacity to introduce technical progress.

According to Lederer, the system is on its steady-state growth path, as long as the pace of technical progress in production is such that the displaced workers will be fully reabsorbed and the profit rates in the two sectors are equal. If the dynamic producers manage to introduce labour-saving technical progress at a higher pace, they will tend to earn higher profit rates that attract investment from the static parts of the economy and create a boom. This starts a disequilibrium process, because it leads to an intersectoral restructuring of investments (1931a: 40; 1938; 168–80). The intersectoral flow of capital has two effects on the labour market: while it leads directly to a stronger-than-normal displacement of workers in the dynamic industries, it reduces the absorptive capacities of the static industries, as their rate of capital accumulation is slowed down. The total rate of unemployment is higher and the total rate of growth is lower than in the steady state. According to the 'Lederer stagnation theorem' (Dickler, 1981: 280–86), supernormal technical progress leads to a relative decline of the wage sum that is greater than the relative in increase in profits. Since total income (by Lederer's definition) consists of wages and profits only, an *acceleration* of technical progress induces a stagnation of economic progress.

The stagnation theorem leads Lederer (1931a) to be quite pessimistic about the capacity of unregulated capitalist economies to avoid economic crises and the emergence of an industrial reserve army, measured in terms of a rise of structural unemployment. In the second edition, he is considerably less pessimistic, introducing a new chapter about 'various forms of technical progress' (1938: 21–53), in which it is emphasized that product innovations (in contrast with labour-saving process innovations) could help to mitigate or even overcome crises and technological unemployment. Many of the clarifications and new parts that Lederer added to the (strongly expanded) second edition of *Technological Progress and Unemployment* can be understood as an implicit reaction to the harsh critique that Kaldor (1932) had levelled against the first edition. Under the title 'A case against technical progress?', Kaldor (1932) had criticized Lederer on the basis of Hicks's (1932 [1963]) marginalist theory of income distribution, arguing that the downward inflexbility of wages (due to monopolistic structures in the labour market) rather than technical progress is the cause of unemployment. Lederer (1938: 198–213) mentions neither Kaldor nor Hicks, but takes direct issue with Wicksell's views on the links between technical progress and wages, arriving at the conclusion that 'Wicksell's analysis actually show how difficult, and often even impossible, it is for the principle of marginal productivity to operate in the case of rapid technical progress' (Lederer, 1938: 202, fn. 1). Implicitly he thereby also criticizes Schumpeter's reliance on Hicks's Wicksellian-style solution of Ricardo's machinery problem.

A critique of Wicksell's view on technological unemployment (or rather: its elimination by wage flexibility and reswitching) is also at the centre of Neisser's famous essay on 'The wage rate and employment in market equilibrium'. Neisser (1932 [1990]: 141) starts by taking up the marginalist proposition that

> [u]nder free competition, full employment can . . . always be achieved if wages are sufficiently low. We shall ask whether this view can be maintained if the *physical capital* on which the workers are employed is taken into consideration. The hypothesis of the present essay is that the employment of the workers can only be increased if the amount of physical capital is increased at the same time. [Italics in the original.]

Neisser (1932 [1990]: 150–61) shows that the employment effects of wage changes are narrowly limited by the economies of scale associated with the given stock of physical capital. The displacement of labour through technical progress is not automatically compensated by the absorption of labour through capital accumulation, not even in the long run. The use of new techniques normally requires an increase in capital intensity. Net of that increase, the rate of accumulation is likely to fall short of the rate of growth required for full compensation. The secular increase in capital intensity cannot simply be reversed by wage reductions or rises in the interest rate level. The return to labour-intensive techniques is most often made unprofitable by the economies of scale that come along with technical progress (see also Neisser, 1942: 62–7). This ratchet effect may keep the labour market out of full-employment equilibrium, even if wages are pressed down to the minimum level of subsistence. Even though Neisser (1932) carries out his rigorous analysis of Wicksell's argument in a static framework, he argues that even in a dynamic framework, in which rising profits will induce capital accumulation,

> we may not yet conclude that capital accumulation will sooner or later eliminate any unemployment. For example, at the same time, as accumulation takes place, the technological horizon will expand normally, raising the capital requirements per worker (at a given wage rate). Accumulation may then even lead to a reduction in employment. (1932 [1990]: 162)

In a further evolution of the argument of 1932, Neisser (1942) concludes that technological unemployment may persist because 'demand for commodities is not demand for labour' (John Stuart Mill, 1848 [1909], Book I, Chapter V, 9: 79). Even though this follow-up paper appears to play down the historical and future relevance of technological unemployment, Neisser rigorously dissects various propositions that would declare it an impossibility on theoretical grounds. He uses Mill's dictum as subtitle for a comprehensive critique of neoclassical fallacies in the extension of Say's Law to labour markets.[7] A few years earlier, in a paper on 'General overproduction'

(1934) and in a monograph, *Some International Aspects of the Business Cycle* (1936), Neisser even questions the validity of Say's Law in its original domain, the commodity markets. Considering the structural relationships between the production of capital goods and consumption goods, he argues that certain combinations of technical progress and increases in capital intensity lead to periodical contractions of credit that produce a general glut of markets. In fact, Neisser endogenizes technical progress by making it dependent on cyclical variations in the volume of credit money. So in his framework of discussion, too, there is a direct connection between technological and cyclical unemployment.[8]

How does Schumpeter's view on technological unemployment, which we have described in the earlier sections, compare to the views of Lederer and Neisser? The views of the latter two are well epitomized by Neisser's famous description of 'the capitalistic process as a race between displacement of labor through technological progress and reabsorption of labor through accumulation . . . displacement and accumulation are two largely *independent* factors, and it is impossible to predict the outcome of the race between the two on purely theoretical grounds' (Neisser, 1942: 70, emphasis in the original). While Lederer sees the main factor behind technological unemployment in a high pace of technical progress, Neisser puts the stress on the insufficient speed of capital accumulation. Even in other aspects, these two authors differ. However, the differences appear to be small in comparison with Schumpeter's position. He comes across as an optimist who uses both traditional compensation arguments and marginal analysis to rule out permanent technological unemployment. Subsuming technological unemployment under frictional unemployment seems to indicate per se that Schumpeter considers it to be but a temporary phenomenon. The word 'frictions' itself suggest that technical progress and capital accumulation are not independent factors, but two parts of the same mechanism that may not work smoothly in reabsorbing displaced workers, but that works in general. This, at least, is the general interpretation in the literature, and there is some textual evidence for it – as shown in the earlier sections.

However, it should not be overlooked that some of Schumpeter's arguments complement those of Lederer and Neisser rather than standing in contrast with them. As pointed out in section 12.3, Schumpeter (1927) argues that rationalization (in the sense of a combination of substitution of machinery for labour and 'Taylorization' of the production process) could cause not just temporary, but permanent unemployment, because economic development leads to 'quasi-monopolistic' market structures. According to Schumpeter (1927), technological unemployment in imperfectly competitive markets was the main cause of persistent German unemployment in the 1920s. In terms of his 1939 taxonomy this is no longer expressed as disequilibrium unemployment (as which technological unemployment is then classified), but as an increase in the normal rate of unemployment. Schumpeter (1939: 511) actually suggests that his concept of normal unemployment should replace the notion of structural unemployment as it was used by Lederer, Neisser and other German economists at the time.

As pointed out by Schumpeter (1939: 516–17), 'institutional changes, insertion into the system of additional permanent rigidities, emergence at any time of imperfections that had been absent before, for instance, of the oligopolistic type' are able to shift the long-run (normal) rate of unemployment upwards. Yet this does not mean that these institutional changes are exogenous and dysfunctional. In Schumpeter's theory of development, oligopolistic structures tend to be the outcome of the evolutionary process, intimately connected with technical progress. Schumpeter would therefore not necessarily have agreed with Kaldor's 'static' objection to Lederer that unemployment is not caused by technical progress, but by monopolistic market structures – as if these were totally independent of the former. Likewise, it could be observed that Schumpeter is not under all circumstances in favour of wage and price flexibility. Discussing the dynamic process typical of depressions associated with widespread falling demand, he considers the observed short-run price rigidity in the cyclical downswing to be stabilizing, because it has positive effects on the financial position of the firms and hence prevents 'chaos in their markets'. As Schumpeter (1942 [1952]: 95) puts it,

> total output and employment may well keep on a higher level with the restrictions incident to [short-run price rigidity] policy, than they would if depression were allowed to play havoc with the price structure. In other words . . . perfect and universal flexibility of prices might in depression further unstabilize the system, instead of stabilizing it.

12.6 CONCLUSION

Schumpeter's views on unemployment may not have been a prominent part of his theory of economic development, and they may – at first sight – seem rather conventional and unspectacular. Yet, a closer look at Schumpeter's writings on unemployment reveals that his wide notion of frictions allowed him to come up with a rather unconventional taxonomy of unemployment that does not only include technological unemployment as a consequence of creative destruction in the process of economic development. It also includes forms of unemployment associated with imperfect competition and short-run reductions of the demand for labour in cyclical downswings and deep depressions, which can, to some extent, be seen as connected with creative destruction.

Schumpeter insisted, on the other hand, that there is no upward trend in unemployment, even though his own pattern prediction of increasingly 'quasi-monopoloid structures' seemed to suggest otherwise. With reference to Neisser (1942: 70, quoted above), one could argue that an upward trend of technological unemployment cannot be excluded on purely theoretical grounds. Yet, the absence of an upward trend can, in fact, be defended with reference to the older Schumpeter's theory of creative destruction. In his *Capitalism, Socialism and Democracy* (1942 [1952]: chs 5–8), Schumpeter argued that monopolistic competition generates a higher pace of innovation than atomistic competition and hence also a higher rate of growth. Contrary to his earlier writings, he thus suggested that the levels of output and employment are higher under monopolistic competition than under 'perfect competition' (1942 [1952]: 80–82). However, the dynamics of displacement and reabsorption of workers through technical progress under monopolistic competition have not ceased to give rise to much debate (see, for example, Aghion and Howitt, 1994; Caballero, 2007). One of Schumpeter's weaker moments was probably his declaration that '[t]he controversy that went on throughout the nineteenth century and beyond, mainly in the form of argument pro and con "compensation", is dead and buried' (1954: 684). He himself contributed to keeping that controversy alive.

NOTES

1. Boianovsky and Trautwein (2007) provide a systematic overview over Schumpeter's writings on unemployment and show that many of those writings have been neglected in earlier rounds of discussion about Schumpeter's views, including the recent neo-Schumpeterian literature.
2. Schumpeter did not use the term 'creative destruction' prior to 1942, but various metaphors in earlier writings suggest that he had been long aware of the notion as developed by Friedrich Nietzsche and Mikhail Bakunin, introduced to economics by Werner Sombart in 1913; see Reinert and Reinert (2006).
3. Regarding the concept of 'relative marginal significance' of labour and land, Schumpeter (1934: 251) refers to Schumpeter (1916/17), a long essay on the principles of income distribution.
4. Schumpeter (1911) did not make it explicit, though, that the decline in wages might increase the profitability of old, labour-intensive 'combinations' and lead to some 'reswitching', that is, substitution of labour for capital – an argument that had been put forward by Wicksell (1901) in volume 1 of his *Lectures on Political Economy.* That volume was translated into German in 1913 and into English in only 1934, so Schumpeter is not likely to have been aware of Wicksell's argument by 1911.
5. In September 1926, after German unemployment figures had risen from 1 to over 2.3 million within a short time, Cassel had published an identical article in several German newspapers and journals, in which he argued against public works and unemployment

benefits as measures that distort the price system and increase unemployment. In his view, wage cuts provided the only therapy for reducing unemployment. Cassel's article provoked an intensive and polemical debate, in which Lujo Brentano, Ferdinand Tönnies, Emil Lederer and numerous other German economists participated. Schumpeter's article was an attempt to evaluate the core arguments in that debate; for a survey see Janssen (2000: 394–404); see also Cassel (1926; 1927; 1932: 341–3).

6. For earlier uses of the concept by Wicksell and Cassel see Boianovsky and Trautwein (2003).
7. However, he also criticizes some of the standard beliefs of marginal productivity theory, as discussed in Neisser (1932).
8. For further discussion of the rich structures in Neisser's explanations of unemployment, which also include a complex monetary theory see Hagemann (1990) and Trautwein (2003).

REFERENCES

Aghion, P. and P. Howitt (1994), 'Growth and unemployment', *Review of Economic Studies*, **61**, 477–94.

Beveridge, W. (1907), 'Labour exchanges and the unemployed', *Economic Journal*, **17**, 66–81.

Beveridge, W. (1909), *Unemployment: A Problem of Industry*, London: Longmans, Green.

Boianovsky, M. and V. Tarascio (1998), 'Mechanical inertia and economic dynamics: Pareto on business cycles', *Journal of the History of Economic Thought*, **20**, 5–23.

Boianovsky, M. and H.-M. Trautwein (2003), 'Wicksell, Cassel and the idea of involuntary unemployment', *History of Political Economy*, **35**, 385–436.

Boianovsky, M. and H.-M. Trautwein (2007), 'Schumpeter on unemployment', mimeo, Departments of Economics, Universidade de Brasilia/University of Oldenburg.

Caballero, R. (2007), *Specificity and the Macroeconomics of Restructuring*, Cambridge, MA: MIT Press.

Cassel, G. (1926), 'Verringerung der Arbeitslosigkeit und Notstandsarbeiten', *Soziale Praxis*, **35**, 1057–80.

Cassel, G. (1927), *Recent Monopolistic Tendencies in Industry and Trade*, Publications of the League of Nations. II. Economic and Financial.

Cassel, G. (1932), *The Theory of Social Economy*, trans. S. Barron from the German 1932 5th edition, New York: Harcourt, Brace.

Clay, H. (1929), *The Post-war Unemployment Problem*, London: Macmillan.

Darity, W. (1982), 'Beveridge and the new search unemployment', *Journal of Post Keynesian Economics*, **4**, 171–80.

Dickler, R. (1981), Nachwort zur Neuausgabe, in E. Lederer, *Technischer Fortschritt und Arbeitslosigkeit. Eine Untersuchung der Hindernisse des ökonomischen Wachstums* (reprint of the German version of Lederer 1938), Köln: Europäische Verlagsanstalt, pp. 263–327.

Gourvitch, A. (1966), *Survey of Economic Theory on Technical Change & Employment*, New York: Kelley, first published 1940.

Hagemann, H. (1990), 'Neisser's "The Wage Rate and Employment in Market Equilibrium": an introduction', *Structural Change and Economic Dynamics*, **1**, 133–9.

Hagemann, H. (2000), 'Emil Lederer (1882–1939): economical and sociological analyst and critic of capitalist development', in P. Koslowski (ed.), *The Theory of Capitalism in the German Economic Tradition*, Berlin, Heidelberg and New York: Springer, pp. 26–51.
Hagemann, H. (2005), 'Dismissal, expulsion, and emigration of German-speaking economists after 1933', *Journal of the History of Economic Thought*, **27**, 405–20.
Hagemann, H. and C.-D. Krohn (eds) (1999), *Biographisches Handbuch der deutschsprachigen wirtschaftswissenschaftlichen Emigration nach 1933*, 2 vols, München: K.G. Saur.
Hicks, J. (1932 [1963]), *The Theory of Wages*, London: Macmillan.
Janssen, H. (2000), *Nationalökonomie und Nationalsozialismus. Die deutsche Volkswirtschaftslehre in den dreißiger Jahren*, 2nd edn, Marburg: Metropolis.
Kaldor, N. (1932), 'A case against technical progress?', *Economica*, **12**, 180–96.
Keynes, J.M. (1936), *The General Theory of Employment, Interest and Money*, London: Macmillan.
Lederer, E. (1931a), *Technischer Fortschritt und Arbeitslosigkeit*, Tübingen: J.C.B. Mohr.
Lederer, E. (1931b), *Aufriß der ökonomischen Theorie*, 3rd edn of *Grundzüge der ökonomischen Theorie. Eine Einführung*, 1922, Tübingen: J.C.B. Mohr.
Lederer, E. (1938), *Technical Progress and Unemployment. An Enquiry into the Obstacles to Economic Expansion*, Geneva: International Labour Office.
Mill, J.S. (1848 [1909]), *Principles of Political Economy, with some of their Applications to Social Philosophy*, 7th edn, edited by William J. Ashley, London: Longmans, Green and Co.
Neisser, H. (1932), 'Lohnhöhe und Beschäftigungsgrad im Marktgleichgewicht', *Weltwirtschaftliches Archiv*, **36**, 414–55 (trans. 1990, 'The wage rate and employment in market equilibrium', *Structural Change and Economic Dynamics*, **1**, 141–63).
Neisser, H. (1934), 'General overproduction. A study of Say's law of markets', *Journal of Political Economy*, **42**, 433–65.
Neisser, H. (1936), *Some International Aspects of the Business Cycle*, Philadelphia, PA: University of Pennsylvania Press.
Neisser, H. (1942), '"Permanent" technological unemployment', *American Economic Review*, **32**, 50–71.
Pareto, V. (1897 [1964]), *Cours d'Economie Politique*, vol. 2, Geneva: Droz.
Pigou, A.C. (1913), *Unemployment*, London: Williams & Norgate.
Pigou, A.C. (1933), *Theory of Unemployment*, London: Macmillan.
Reinert, H. and E. Reinert (2006), 'Creative destruction in economics: Nietzsche, Sombart, Schumpeter', in J. Backhaus and W. Drechsler (eds), *Friedrich Nietzsche 1844–2000*, New York: Springer, pp. 55–85.
Ricardo, D. (1821), *On the Principles of Political Economy and Taxation*, 3rd edn, 1951, ed. P. Sraffa, Cambridge: University Press.
Schumpeter, J.A. (1911), *Theorie der wirschaftlichen Entwicklung*, Leipzig: Duncker & Humblot.
Schumpeter, J.A. (1911), 'The Economy as a Whole', translation of ch. 7 of Schumpeter (1911) by Ursula Backhaus (2002), *Industry and Innovation*, **9**, 93–145.
Schumpeter, J.A. (1916/17), 'Das Grundprinzip der Verteilungstheorie', *Archiv für Sozialwissenschaft*, **42**, 1–88.
Schumpeter, J.A. (1926), *Theorie der wirtschaftlichen Entwicklung*, 2nd edn, Leipzig: Duncker & Humblot.

Schumpeter, J.A. (1927), 'Die Arbeitslosigkeit', in C. Seidl and W. Stolper (eds) (1985), *Aufsätze zur Wirtschaftspolitik*, Tübingen: Mohr.

Schumpeter, J.A. (1934), *The Theory of Economic Development*, trans. R. Opie from the 2nd German edition (1926), Cambridge, MA: Harvard University Press.

Schumpeter, J.A. (1934), 'Depressions – can we learn from past experience?', in R. Clemence (ed.) (1951), *Essays of J.A. Schumpeter*, Cambridge, MA: Addison-Wesley.

Schumpeter, J.A. (1939), *Business Cycles*, New York: McGraw-Hill.

Schumpeter, J.A. (1942), *Capitalism, Socialism and Democracy*, 5th edn, 1952, London: Unwin.

Schumpeter, J.A. (1946), 'Capitalism', in R. Clemence (ed.) (1951), *Essays of J.A. Schumpeter*, Cambridge, MA: Addison-Wesley.

Schumpeter, J.A. (1954), *History of Economic Analysis*, New York: Oxford University Press.

Shionoya, Y. (1997), *Schumpeter and the Idea of Social Science*, Cambridge: Cambridge University Press.

Trautwein, H.-M. (2003), 'Neisser's unorthodox quantity theory of money', in E. Nell and M. Forstater (eds), *Reinventing Functional Finance: Transformational Growth and Full Employment*, Cheltenham, UK and Northampton, MA, USA: Edward Elgar, pp. 66–82.

Wicksell, K. (1901), *Lectures on Political Economy*, vol. 1, trans. E. Classen, London: Routledge.

Woirol, G. (1996), *The Technological Unemployment and Structural Unemployment Debates*, Westport, CT: Greenwood Press.

Woirol, G. (2006), 'New data, new issues: the origins of the technological unemployment debates', *History of Political Economy*, **38**, 473–96.

13. Marshall on economic chivalry and business ethics

Kenji Fujii

13.1 INTRODUCTION

Marshall's advocacy of economic chivalry has been conventionally evaluated as trivial decorations which have no relation to his theoretical work. Many writers have ascribed it to his predilection for 'pious asides and prim moralisings' typical of late Victorians.[1] This chapter is an attempt to argue that the prevalent evaluation is erroneous because too naive an image is imposed on Marshall. We show a theoretical connection between economic chivalry and his theory of the firm.

We start from an identification of Marshall's view of a firm in the next section. Utilizing the concept of context-dependent recognition, we propose to identify a firm as one of social contexts which consist of shared knowledge and values. Then, in the third section, we discuss the role of an entrepreneur in Marshall; he required an entrepreneur to lead in morality as well as in knowledge. In the fourth section, the role of economic chivalry is discussed. Although economic chivalry is often misunderstood as mere preaching, we argue that it is to be understood as a latent mechanism which helps the chivalrous firms to develop the faculties of human beings.

13.2 CONTEXT-DEPENDENCY OF A FIRM

13.2.1 Context-Dependent Recognition

Economists have been accustomed to regard perfect competition as a reference point because 'perfect rationality' is considered one of the indispensable conditions for economics. But, instead of assuming perfect rationality, many economists nowadays are inclined to assume 'bounded rationality'. Although there are different meanings in 'bounded rationality', it has been recognized as a plausible analytical assumption to start with. As a consequence, routine behaviour once regarded as irrational has attracted much attention. The notion of bounded rationality has produced not only fruitful theoretical contributions, but also revaluation of past theoretical contributions related to that notion. It is hoped that revaluation of Marshall's economics can also benefit from this standpoint.[2]

One of the tasks for the revaluation of Marshall's economics is to resurrect his peculiar concepts. One of these is his concept of normal equilibrium. Although the concept was regarded as convenient but not wholly tenable, a negative interpretation needs a revaluation because it is based on the assumption that perfect rationality will prevail, at least in a theoretical world, if enough time is allowed. I proposed to interpret Marshall's normal equilibrium on the basis of context-dependent recognition.[3] Context-dependent recognition by my definition means that what and how agents recognize differ according to the contexts they belong to. Recognition of an agent in a context differs from that of others in other contexts even if they look at the same situation or the same fact. The reason lies simply in that one has much knowledge of a certain field if he values that field higher than others. A similar set of recognition tends to be shared among the members situated in the same context. For this reason, a context which produces common knowledge and values functions as a ground for common recognition. People are embedded in a context as a common cognitive framework.

There is seemingly some resemblance between context-dependent recognition and bounded rationality in the sense that both view our recognition to be imperfect. But, when we look at them closely, an important difference comes to a surface. Bounded rationality says that our recognition is not perfect because our ability to handle knowledge is limited. But, in the case of context-dependent recognition, recognition is not only imperfect but also socially conditioned by the context, the emphasis being on the latter.[4] The notion of 'context-dependent recognition is useful here because normal in Marshall's usage means that decisions conform to the conditions of a particular context. 'We may say that the course of action which may be expected *under certain conditions* from the members of an industrial group is the *normal action* of the members of that group relatively to those conditions' (Marshall, 1920: 34, emphasis in original).

13.2.2 The Firm as a Context

Although a context can be used to mean a variety of spheres such as a nation, a local community, an industry, or even an academic society, we restrict it to mean the organization of a firm until section 13.4 of this chapter. The role of the organization of the firm in Marshall's economics has been revaluated and resurrected to its due status by the post-Marshallians. The shared understanding of the role of an organization in Marshall's economics is that an organization helps to integrate production knowledge for production activities.[5] The need for integration arises because, contrary to exchange activities, a variety of production knowledge needs to be gathered and co-ordinated for production activities. The more production activities become specialized, the more production knowledge becomes diversified and fragmented. Therefore, the necessity to integrate production knowledge becomes greater as more specialized production develops. The organization of a firm is best regarded as a knowledge community.

Since the context has two dimensions, knowledge and values, the context of a firm comprises shared knowledge and values. Shared knowledge refers to how production activities are performed. Shared values refer to how rewards are distributed among the members in order to co-ordinate their diversified values. Shared knowledge and shared values contribute to the integration of the organization of a firm. Without them, the organization of a firm cannot perform well-concerted production activities. Whereas the organization of a firm is just one of many kinds of contexts, its influence on the members is greater than other kinds of contexts because its influence is both direct and constant. It is direct because more attention and energy motivated by the incentive for rewards are given to work than any other activities. It is constant because time spent on work is much more than on any other activities.

The context of a firm must be designed in order to realize concerted production activities because how a firm performs depends on how well it co-ordinates its members. If production activities of a firm are relatively simple, the necessary amount of common knowledge and values is small, and the task of the design is fairly simple. But, as a firm becomes larger and runs more complicated production activities, the design of common knowledge and values becomes more difficult.[6] Because both the variety and the extent of specialization of production activities tend to be large, it becomes difficult to provide appropriate subsets of the context according to the types of activities. In addition, much of management activities must be entrusted to salaried managers and officials. Then, a new seed of co-ordination failure gradually grows.

> And indeed this tendency to an increase in the size of businesses introduces an ever-growing discord into industry. The owner of a business, when contemplating any change, is led by his own interest to weigh the whole gain that it would probably bring to the business against the whole loss; but the private interest of the salaried manager or official draws him in quite another direction. For the trouble of a new experiment will come largely on him. If it fails, he will have to bear much of the blame; and, if it succeeds, only a small part of the consequent

> gain will accrue to him. So, the path of least resistance, of greatest comfort and least risk to himself is generally that of not striving for improvement himself, and of finding plausible excuses for not trying an improvement suggested by others, until its success is established beyond question. (Pigou, 1925: 307)

It is clear from the above that Marshall was fully aware of management problems which are nowadays known as the principal–agency problems. 'An ever-growing discord' is understood as a case of moral hazards in modern terminology. Furthermore, the discord is the product of division of the context into several sub-contexts, which means entrusting management activities to 'the salaried manager or official'. How can this discord in a firm be resolved? We are led to examining the personality who is responsible for co-ordination, an entrepreneur.

13.3 ENTREPRENEUR IN MARSHALL

13.3.1 Two Faculties of an Entrepreneur

An entrepreneur designs the context of a firm by designing and/or transforming intra-firm contexts. How should he execute this task? Marshall says that there is no universal formula for this question, because it is difficult to generalize the conditions for an ideal entrepreneur. He thinks that necessary faculties are different according to industrial specificities and/or sizes of firms.

> The abilities required to make an ideal employer are so great and so numerous that very few persons can exhibit them all in a very high degree. Their relative importance however varies with the nature of the industry and the size of the business; and while one excels in one set of qualities, another excels in another; scarcely any two owe their success to exactly the same combination of advantages. (Marshall, 1920: 298)

In this respect, Marshall wholeheartedly supported the view of Francis Walker, as shown below.

> For indeed the stock of capital has grown so much faster than the scope for its use in industry, that capital is always at the command of *those who have the mental faculty and the moral character for turning it to good account*. The keynote of this change was struck by the American Francis Walker, who said as early as 1876 that the man who has the faculties required 'to shape and direct production, and to organize and control the industrial machinery . . . rises to be master of the situation. It is no longer true that a man becomes an employer because he is a capitalist. Men command capital because they have the qualifications to profitably employ labor. To these captains of industry . . . capital and

> labor resort for opportunity to perform their several functions." (Marshall, 1919: 168–9, emphasis added)

Entrepreneurs are qualified for such a task because they 'have the mental faculty and the moral character for turning it to good account'. It is natural to interpret this passage in the sense that mental faculty refers to production knowledge and moral character to morality. In fact, Marshall lists up two requirements for an entrepreneur. One is leadership in production knowledge. 'The manufacture who makes goods not to meet special orders but for the general markets, must, in his first role as merchant and organizer of production, have a thorough knowledge of *things* in his own trade' (Marshall, 1920: 297, emphasis in original). The other is leadership in morality.

> But secondly in his role of employer he must be a natural leader of *men*. He must have a power of first choosing his assistants rightly and then trusting them fully; of interesting them in the business and getting them to trust him, so as to bring out whatever enterprise and power of origination there is in them. (Marshall, 1920: 297, emphasis in original)

As we have already shown, the context consists of two factors, that is, knowledge and values. It follows that the role of an entrepreneur resides in constructing an appropriate context for a firm. But, a question arises. Why did Marshall require an entrepreneur to have leadership in both production knowledge and value judgements? With regard to the leadership in production knowledge, we can easily find the answer. As production becomes more and more complicated, it gets more difficult to operate production activities because relevant knowledge for production swells in terms of both width and depth. It gets more difficult to discern the values of relevant faculties of men rather than the values of machines.

> The value of a machine to a business cannot be calculated on the basis of its efficiency for its immediate work. But the value of an employee must be estimated, partly by instinct, with a view to the probable development of his capacities: and the difficulty of his task is increased by the conditions of modern business. (Marshall, 1919: 350)

The requirements for an entrepreneur far exceed the abilities of ordinary persons, who rather choose to be employed. The person who has more relevant knowledge of a field than ordinary people is entrusted the task of integrating diversified production knowledge and becomes an entrepreneur.[7] It is very probable that Marshall observed the fact that more and more people moved from self-employed status to employed status and that more and more firms became bigger.

13.3.2 Sympathy and Loyalty to a Firm

As we have observed, an entrepreneur is a leader with respect to production knowledge. Another question still remains as to why he is required to be a leader with respect to values. The first thing to be noted is the very fact that we have just observed, that is, an entrepreneur is a leader with respect to production knowledge. Those who choose to be employees do so because they judged that becoming employed is a better alternative than becoming self-employed. If an employment contract is short term, it is easy for both an employer and employees to find a fair contract. The agreement will be found on the principle that each employee should be rewarded according to his contribution to profit. But, this principle is applicable only if measurement of the contribution of each employee is made easily and at low cost. When a task of work is simple, this condition is roughly satisfied. But, as a task becomes higher in quality, it becomes difficult for the condition to be satisfied. As the previous quotation shows, Marshall thought that estimating the value of an employee was not an easy task even in his times. The difficulty increases further in the case of core staff whose task does not follow a fixed pattern and often requires tacit knowledge. Marshall noted as follows.

> Thus the head clerk in a business has an acquaintance with men and things, the use of which he could in some cases sell at a high price to rival firms. But in other cases it is of a kind to be of no value save to the business in which he already is; and then his departure would perhaps injure it by several times the value of his salary, while probably he could not get half that salary elsewhere. (Marshall, 1920: 626)

Employees entrust the residual right to an entrepreneur and follow the direction in which they are expected to work. In modern terminology, the head clerk is at the risk of opportunistic behaviour of the entrepreneur. The same applies to skilled workers, whose skill is firm-specific. If they are thrown out of work, their income will be diminished even if they managed to find jobs elsewhere. Then, a question arises why they will ever agree to accumulate firm-specific knowledge or skills in spite of the fact such accumulation might jeopardize themselves. If they estimate a high probability of opportunistic behaviour by the entrepreneur, it is too risky for them to build firm-specific knowledge or skills. Hence, Marshall noted that loyalty to the firm was necessary.

> sympathy is the one solid and strong force which has in it nothing sordid, and permeates the whole of human nature. This is more important with regard to joint stock companies than to private businesses. For, when once the ownership

> of a business has left the hands of an individual, who might attach his chief employees to him by bonds of personal friendship; when once faithfulness to the business has ceased to be enforced by the warm instincts of loyalty, and has been left to the colder support of impersonal duty; from that time forward the moral coherence and strength of the business depend largely on the growth of an esprit de corps, of a spirit of loyalty to the business itself. (Marshall, 1919: 326)

Marshall thought that sympathy to an individual entrepreneur would diminish in power as a firm got bigger. More precisely, as a firm changes from personally owned to corporate, the mere fact that an entrepreneur as a leader is reliable does not suffice to warrant that his firm will continue to be reliable. A decrease in the power of sympathy to an entrepreneur must be compensated by loyalty to a firm. Then, how can he get loyalty to a firm from employees? An obvious condition is that employees should be convinced that their firm does not behave opportunistically even when it finds itself in a position to do so. But, since it is impossible to make a perfect contract under the condition of bounded rationality, opportunistic behaviour by a firm cannot be eliminated. So, a contract is not sufficient to make employees trust a firm. Here is the complementary role of moral context. The moral context of a firm is an accumulated outcome of past management. There is no direct and quick way for an entrepreneur to change the moral context quickly.[8] All he can do is to work on it and to make it more reliable. It cannot be asserted that Marshall provided a systematic explanation of moral context of a firm. But it is certain that he recognized the importance of moral context which would contribute to the formation of loyalty to a firm by promoting the expectation of employees that the firm would not behave opportunistically.

13.4 ECONOMIC CHIVALRY RECONSIDERED

13.4.1 The Need for Economic Chivalry

We have concentrated exclusively on a firm as a context working as a kind of common platform for the members. Marshall identified an entrepreneur as a holder of both production knowledge and value judgements within a firm. Particularly, the leadership for moral faculty is needed to check opportunistic behaviour of an entrepreneur and to solicit loyalty from employees. In this section, we ask what is required for an entrepreneur to be a chivalrous entrepreneur, and why Marshall advocated economic chivalry.

In the essay titled 'Social possibilities of economic chivalry', Marshall described it as follows:

> Chivalry in business includes public spirit, as chivalry in war includes unselfish loyalty to the cause of prince, or of country, or of crusade. But, it includes also a delight in doing noble and difficult things because they are noble and difficult . . . It includes a scorn for cheap victories, and a delight in succouring those who need a helping hand. (Pigou, 1925: 330)

The key phrase in the above passage is 'public spirit', which can be paraphrased as a sense of duty to a society. This is the appropriate place to add another context, a society. Like any other context, a society as a context consists of common knowledge and common values, both of which serve as a platform for the members of a society. However, there is a difference because there is no leader in society who is comparable to an entrepreneur. Without a leader, contexts in a society are moulded gradually through interactions among the members. Two questions arise. First, 'what is good for society?', to which Marshall offered his answer.

> There are some doubts as to what social good is; but they do not reach far enough to impair the foundations of our fundamental principles. For there has always been a substratum of agreement that social good lies mainly in that healthful exercise and development of faculties which yields happiness without pall, because it sustains self-respect and is sustained by hope. (Pigou, 1925: 310)

It is very reasonable to speculate that Marshall considered the development of human faculties to be 'noble and difficult'.

The second question is whether there is any natural tendency for the contexts to approach to a good society. It should be recalled that Marshall did not favour the idealistic interpretation of evolutionism by Spencer, which equated the fittest with the best.

> The law requires to be interpreted carefully: for the fact that a thing is beneficial to its environment will not by itself secure its survival either in the physical or in the moral world. The law of 'survival of the fittest' states that those organisms tend to survive which are best fitted to utilize the environment for their own purposes. Those that utilize the environment most, often turn out to be those that benefit around them most; but sometimes they are injurious. (Marshall, 1920: 242)

The answer to the second question is definitely no. Putting the two answers together, it is possible to conclude that those firms that try to contribute 'the healthful exercise and development of faculties' do not necessarily survive. Believing that happiness consisted in acquiring and exercising abilities rather than acquiring wealth itself, Marshall emphasized the necessity to enquire into a way to modify a social context in favour of such firms.

> It is needful then diligently to inquire whether the present industrial organization might not with advantage be so modified as to increase the opportunities, which the lower grades of industry have for using latent faculties, for deriving pleasure from their use, and for strengthening them by use; since the argument that if such a change had been beneficial, it would have been already brought about by the struggle for survival, must be rejected as invalid. Man's prerogative extends to a limited but effective control over natural development by forecasting the future and preparing the way for the next step. (Marshall, 1920: 248)

13.4.2 Public Opinion and Economic Chivalry

What is the means to support chivalrous firms? It is obvious that preaching chivalry is too feeble a way to support those firms because it often happens that non-chivalrous firms never pay attention to it. If an entrepreneur restricts his scope strictly within his firm, his behaviour is likely to contradict social duty. They would change their minds only if they realize economic chivalry counts. The means Marshall resorted to was public opinion, which he referred to as 'informal Court of Honour'. He said as follows:

> An endeavour should be made so as to guide public opinion that it becomes an informal Court of Honour. Then wealth, however large, would be no passport to social success if got by chicanery, by manufactured news, by fraudulent dealing, or by malignant destruction of rivals: and that business enterprise which was noble in its aims and in its methods, even if it did not bring with it a large fortune, would receive its due of public admiration and gratitude; as the work of the progressive student of science, or literature, or art does now. (Pigou, 1925: 343)

One might wonder whether 'informal Court of Honour' is substantially different from preaching economic chivalry. Although these two might seem very similar at first sight, they are certainly different. Whereas preaching is purely individualistic behaviour, 'informal Court of Honour' is social assessment behaviour. Although Marshall was criticized for moralizing statements, he himself denied the effectiveness of preaching. In his letter to Bishop Westcott, he wrote: 'I think that, when the academic student takes on himself the role of a preacher, he is less effective than when he treats the problems of life objectively; that is when he assumes no major premises based on his own views of duty, his own ideals of social life' (Pigou, 1925: 397).

What Marshall thought necessary was not an appeal to individual conscience but transformation of the contexts; transformation of the social contexts. Of course, establishing 'informal Court of Honour' is much more difficult than mere preaching. Some might say that direct regulations by legislative measures are much easier and more effective than recourse to 'informal Court of Honour'.[9] While acknowledging an indispensable minimal function of legislative measures, Marshall never accepted these measures because their effectiveness was easily impaired by bureaucratic rigidities and corruptions. However long it might take for 'informal Court of Honour' to become dominant, there is no other way than transforming the social contexts to promote chivalrous firms. Surprising as it might seem, he was optimistic about the possibility of economic chivalry. Probably one of the reasons for his optimism can be found in his view that reputations of firms were intangible assets.

> The marketing reputation and connection of a business may be a larger (or 'capita') in proportion to its earnings, than is the fixed plant of a manufacturer in some industries. Reputation for fairness and generosity in doing, is property seldom acquired without special effort and sacrifice, and is a powerful factor of success in all the undertakings of a business. The reputation acquired by a large general advertising is easy of attainment, though expensive. It is indeed seldom of much value, unless accompanied by capable and honourable dealing. (Marshall, 1919: 270)

In the previous section, we observed that an entrepreneurial leadership in morality within a firm is expected to promote developing faculties of employees and to evoke loyalty from them by restraining entrepreneur's opportunistic behaviour. We can understand economic chivalry in a similar way. Building up and maintaining a good reputation prevents firms from committing opportunistic behaviour so that they will be credited with brand loyalty from customers and good trade connections with suppliers. We should recall that Marshall distinguished a special market from a general market. Brand loyalty contributes to enlarging a special market which is guarded to some extent from the pressure of harsh price competition. Similarly, good trade connections with suppliers will contribute to reducing costs. In this way, economic chivalry is expected to promote survival of chivalrous firms by providing them with intangible assets such as brand loyalty and good trade connections.

The second source of his optimism may be found in his observation that diffusion of knowledge reinforces public opinion. 'The strength of public opinion is steadily increasing with the increase and the diffusion of knowledge, and with the constant tendency of what had been regarded as private and personal issues to become public and national' (Pigou, 1925: 285). One might doubt this possibility. But, it is very probable that the more knowledgeable and the less naive people become, the more critical power they come to have. Thus, public opinion is strengthened in order to support chivalrous firms by means of credit and loyalty to them. Since employees working in chivalrous firms have more chance to develop their faculties, the prosperity of chivalrous firms brings about an increase of people with more developed faculties, strengthening public opinion further. We find a virtuous circle consisting of public opinion, economic chivalry and development of faculties.[10] As the following passage shows, Marshall observed that this virtuous circle was not an imaginary idea but was operating in fact at the time of writing:

> This loyalty is being fostered by a multitude of movements, designed to give the employees a direct interest in the property of the business for which they work; while others aim at developing their intelligence and ability in ways, some of which are likely to promote their efficiency as employees; and some, which are desired only as contributing to their higher well-being, are among the best fruits of the larger sense of *social duty which is characteristic of the present age*. (Marshall, 1919: 327, emphasis added)

It is no exaggeration to say that Marshall was one of the early advocators of corporate social responsibility.[11]

13.5 SOCIAL CHOICE OF SOCIAL CONTEXTS?

Individual rationality has been almost the sole criterion for checking the legitimacy of economic theory. But, owing to the resurgence of bounded rationality, those social elements such as customs, norms, commitments, and so on have come to attract much attention. Stimulated by these recent changes, this chapter tried to reevaluate the implications of Marshall's economic chivalry. Economic chivalry is not a mere plasterwork of Victorian *Zeitgeist*, but an integral part of his economics, in which a state of morality and a state of production knowledge matters. The fundamental logic underlying our analysis is that bounded-rational agents never live in a general context, but in a set of particular contexts in which we recognize and decide in a context-dependent way. There are several states of an economy corresponding to social contexts.

Even if admitting the above, one might raise the question whether economic chivalry can indicate an ideal state of an economy. More concretely, can it provide an answer to such a question as what social responsibility firms should owe? If one insists that firms should owe as much responsibility as possible, an economy will approach towards the verge of socialism. Contrarily, if firms are allowed maximum liberty, an economy will approach a libertarian state. In the former case, requirements of morality will suffocate an economy. In the latter, economic chivalry will have no role, and it is probable that strong but non-chivalrous firms will sweep away chivalrous firms. All we can say is that Marshall denied both extremes and favoured a position in the middle. If asked further, he would say that the answer depended on a social choice of a society, which economics has to leave to her master, the science of ethics: 'economics was a handmaid to ethics, not an end in itself, but a means to a further end: an instrument, by the perfecting of which it might be possible to better the conditions of human life. Things, organization, technique were incidents: what mattered was the quality of man' (Pigou, 1925: 82).

NOTES

1. This phrase is Shove's (1942: 316). Similarly, Schumpeter (1941: 245), in his semi-centennial appraisal of Marshall, wrote: 'I confess that few things are so irritating to me as is the preaching of mid-Victorian morality, seasoned by Benthamism, the preaching from a schema of middle-class values that knows no glamour and no passion.' Viner (1941: 228) also emphasized Marshall's moralizing tendency as typical of Victorians: 'The moral earnestness with which Marshall regarded the role of economics and his own role as an economist was thoroughly Victorian, was altogether in keeping with the spirit of his times in liberal educated circles.'
2. Raffaelli (2003: ch. 6) succinctly depicts how the Marshallian research programme collapsed and then has gradually been rehabilitated. He points out that the recently flourishing 'capability approach to the firm' has much in common with post-Marshallians. Raffaelli et al. (2006) is strong evidence for the revival of post-Marshallian research programme.
3. In the paper which I presented at the first ESHET-JSHET meeting held at Nice in December 2006, I proposed to interpret Marshall's Normal Equilibrium on the basis of context-dependent recognition.
4. The significance of contexts is emphasized in the 'knowledge-based approach to the firm'. Amin and Cohendet (2004: 86) wrote, 'All our arguments in the previous chapter on innovation and learning as a situated practice embedded in distinctive communities and actor networks suggests that the powers of contexts – spatial and temporal – should be placed at the center of any theorization of knowledge formation.'
5. It is the contribution of Brian Loasby to reevaluate the significance of Marshall's view of the firm on the basis of 'an organization aiding knowledge'. Although there are a lot of his writings worth reading, I refer to just three of them: Loasby (1998; 1999a; 1999b).
6. In modern terms of management science, the design of common knowledge in a firm is knowledge management and that of common values as corporate culture. Both are regarded as central themes for a modern so-called 'knowledge-based approach' to the firm. For more information about this field, consult Amin and Cohendet (2004).
7. When we talk about entrepreneur, J. Schumpeter cannot be passed without a word. We think that one must be careful enough to distinguish Schumpeter's entrepreneur and Marshall's. The difference between the two lies in the function an entrepreneur is expected to perform. Schumpeter's entrepreneur is exclusively characterized by his ability to innovate, whereas Marshall's is by his leadership within a firm. In Schumpeter's case, a firm can be operated without an entrepreneur, who is free from the task of running a business. In Marshall's case, an entrepreneur plays an integral and pivotal role of co-ordinating production activities of a firm. The difference between these two views probably reflects the underlying different understandings of a firm as an organization.
8. An original source of a moral context of a firm is corporate philosophy and corporate culture which a founder intended to embed in a firm. But, after the foundation, a moral context takes more stable forms such as corporate customs and intra-firm institutions. This is why a moral context can only be changed gradually.

9. The reason Marshall objected, though was sympathetic about, the socialistic scheme was that 'it is an irresponsible imagination, in that it proceeds on the suppressed assumption that human nature will, under new institutions, quickly undergo changes such as cannot reasonably be expected in the course of a century, even under favourable conditions' (Marshall, 1920: 721).
10. The importance of each of the three factors in Marshall's economics has been pointed out by a few, but noted, scholars such as Talcott Parsons (1931) and J.K. Whitaker (1977). The contribution of this chapter lies in pointing out a virtuous circle comprising these three factors as a mechanism supporting chivalry.
11. Whitaker (1977: 197) concluded his insightful article on Marshall as follows: 'The broadness of Marshall's concerns illustrates by contrast the narrowness of ours, and the questions he grappled with could well return to the economists' agenda. If so, a final assessment of his contribution will have to await future developments.' Surprisingly, he correctly identified and referred to Arrow (1974) and Laffont (1975) as the early signs of reevaluation by theoreticians of the role of trust and moral codes.

REFERENCES

Amin A. and P. Cohendet (2004), *Architecture of Knowledge: Firms, Capabilities, and Communities*, Oxford: Oxford University Press.

Arrow, K.J. (1974), *The Limits of Organization*, New York: W.W. Norton.

Fujii, K. (2006), 'Marshall's normal equilibrium and state of production knowledge', 1st ESHET-JSHET Meeting, Nice-Sophia-Autipolis, France, 17–20 December.

Loasby, B.J. (1998), 'The organization of capabilities', *Journal of Economic Behavior and Organization*, **35**, 139–60.

Loasby, B.J. (1999a), 'Marshall's theory of the firm', in R.E. Backhouse and J. Creedy (eds), *From Classical Economics to the Theory of the Firm*, Cheltenham, UK and Northampton, MA, USA: Edward Elgar.

Loasby, B.J. (1999b), *Knowledge, Institutions and Evolution in Economics*, London and New York: Routledge.

Laffont, J.J. (1975), 'Macroeconomic constraints, economic efficiency and ethics: an introduction to Kantian economics', *Economica*, **42**, 430–37.

Marshall, A. (1919), *Industry and Trade*, London: Macmillan.

Marshall, A. (1920), *Principles of Economics*, 8th edn, London: Macmillan.

Parsons, T. (1931), 'Wants and activities in Marshall', *The Quarterly Journal of Economics*, **46** (1), 101–40.

Pigou, A.C. (ed.) (1925), *Memorials of Alfred Marshall*, London: Macmillan.

Raffaelli, T. (2003), *Marshall's Evolutionary Economics*, London and New York: Routledge.

Raffaelli, T., G. Becattini and M. Dardi (eds) (2006), *The Elgar Companion to Alfred Marshall*, Cheltenham, UK and Northampton, MA, USA: Edward Elgar.

Schumpeter, J.A. (1941), 'Alfred Marshall's principles: a semi-centennial appraisal', *The American Economic Review*, **31** (2), 236–48.

Shove, G.F. (1942), 'The Place of Marshall's *Principles* in the development of economic theory', *Economic Journal*, **52**, 316.

Viner, J. (1941), 'Marshall's economics, in relation to the man and to his times', *The American Economic Review*, **31** (2), 223–35.

Whitaker, J.K. (1977), 'Some Neglected aspects of Alfred Marshall's economic and social thought', *History of Political Economy*, **9** (1), 161–97.

Index